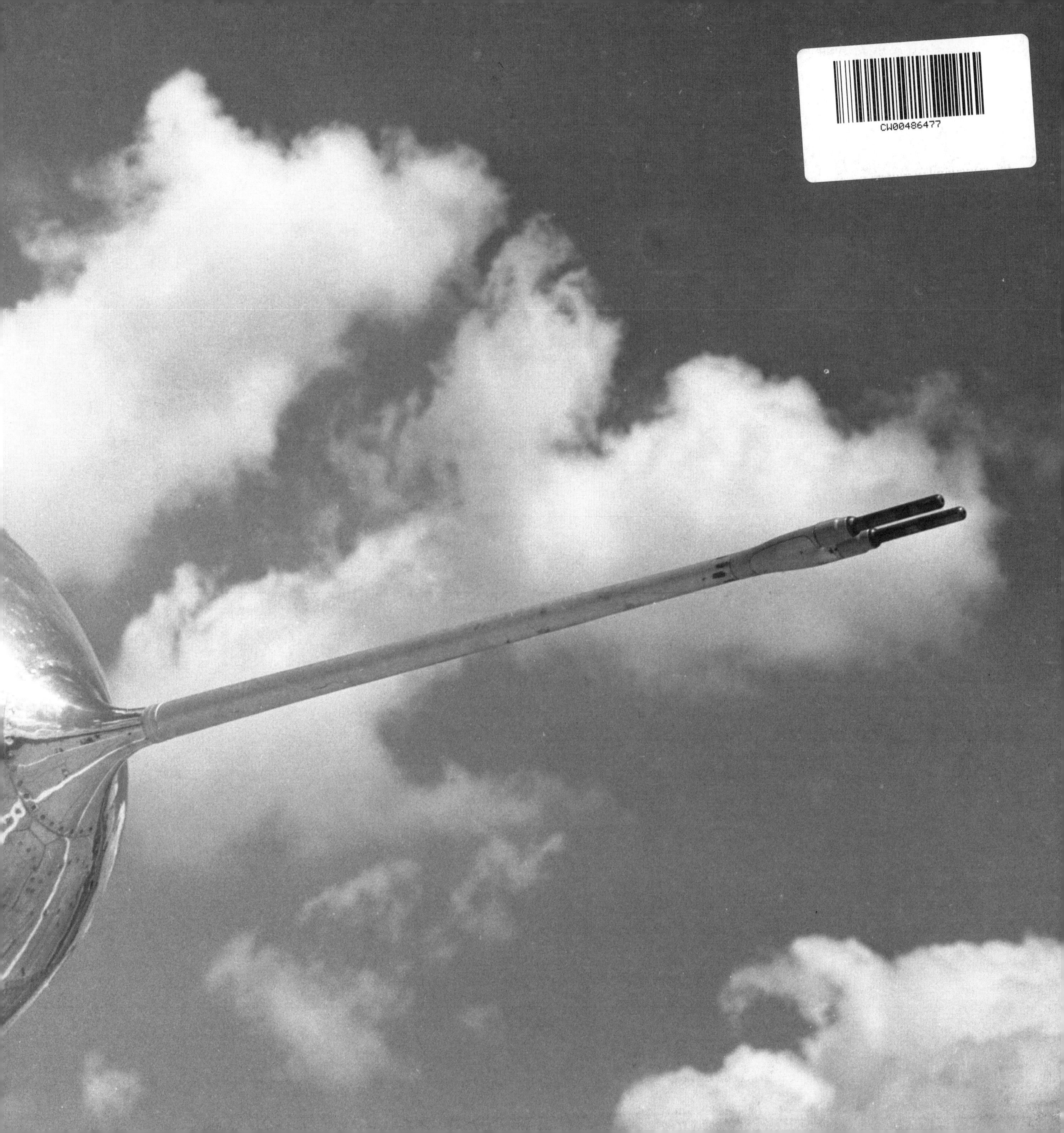

COMET

Unseen Images from the Archives

BRUCE HALES-DUTTON

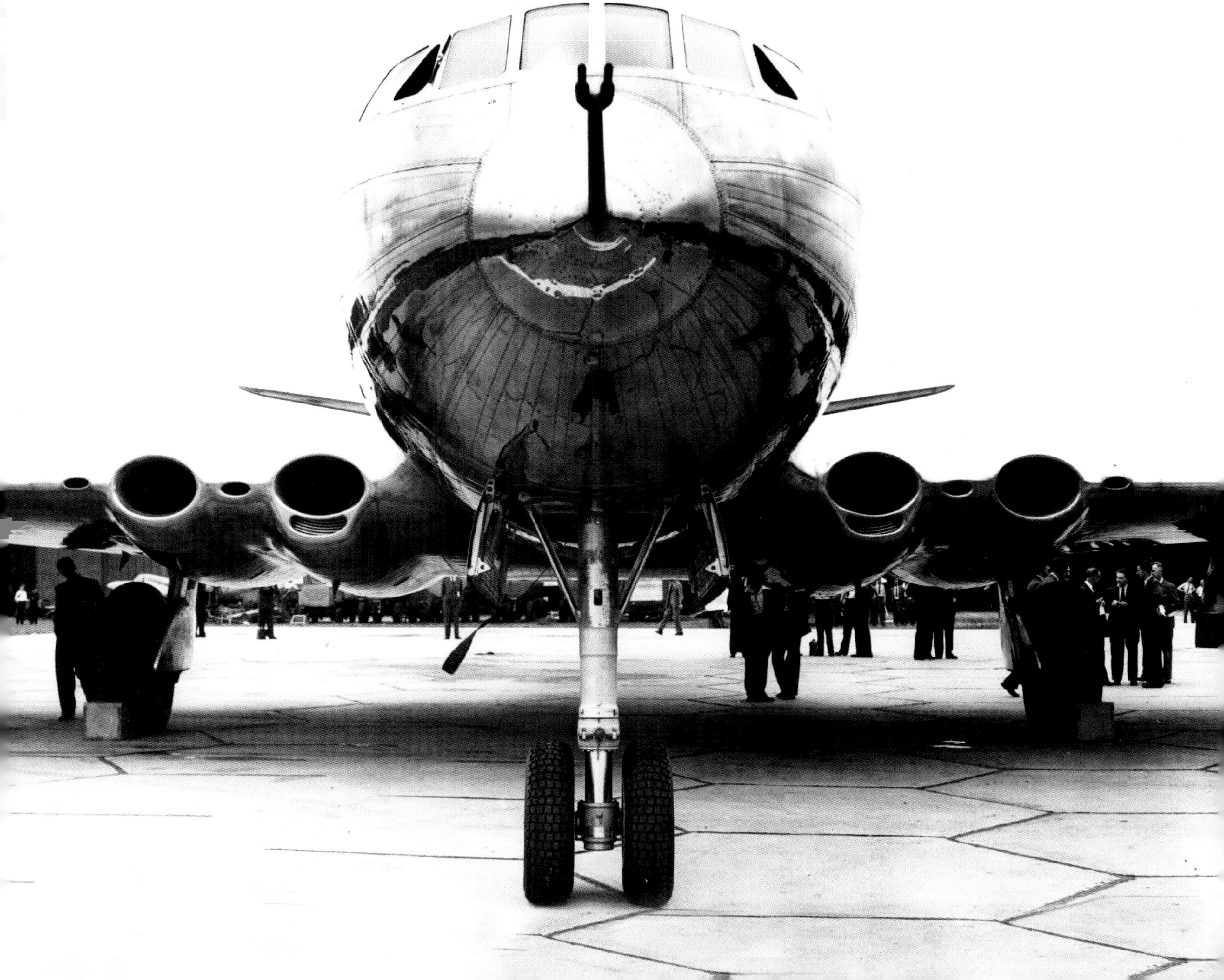

Danann BOOKS

First published 2015 Danann Publishing Ltd / A Flying History Ltd

The publishers would like to thank all the archives for their help in compiling the images for this unique book.
All images in this book are copyright and cannot be used or reproduced without the permission of the copyright holders.

Photography courtesy of

GETTY/CENTRAL PRESS front cover,

BAE SYSTEMS HERITAGE endpapers, pages 6, 7, 8 (top), 14-25, 27-29, 32-39, 40 & 41 (all except middle and bottom righ), 42-43, 46, 48-55, 58, 59 (middle & bottom), 61 (all but bottom right), 62-65, 68-72, 74-78 (except 76 middle left), 79 (left), 80-99 (except 96 bottom right), 101 (top), 102, 104 (middle and right), 105 (main image), 104 (middle & right), 108-115 (except 112 top right), 116 (left top and bottom), 118, 119, 120 (bottom), 121, 126 (bottom row), 128-133, 136-137, 145 row 2 (m&r), row 3 (m&r), row 4 (m), row 5 (l), row 6 (r), 147, 148, back cover

VIA BAE SYSTEMS pages 8 (top left), 13, 14 (top left), 26, 30-31, 44, 56-57, 67, 73, 76 (middle left)

THE PETER KEATING COLLECTION (C) A FLYING HISTORY pages 6-7, 8 (bottom), 9, 10-12, 45, 100, 101 (bottom), 104 (left), 105 (bottom row), 106, 107, 117, 122 ,140, 141-144, 145 (with exceptions above)

TATA STEEL page 39 (bottom left)

ROLLS ROYCE PLC page 59 (top)

RCAF pages 60, 116 (top)

GETTY / KEYSTONE page 125

PETER BERRY pages 134 & 135

PRIVATE COLLECTIONS pages 36 (bottom right), 66, 96, 112 (top right) 120 (bottom)

BRITISH AIRWAYS page 3, 79 (right)

AIR FRANCE pages 1,5, 47, 124, 126 (top), 127

BRUCE HALES-DUTTON page 148 (top)

Prints of all images from the Peter Keating Collection
are available to buy. For more information please go to
www.aflyinghistory.com

Book layout & design Darren Grice at **Ctrl-d**

Made in EU.
978-0-9930169-2-9

CAT NO: DAN0268

FLYING
HISTORY BOOKS

CONTENTS

INTRODUCTION

By Bruce Hales-Dutton

It is hard to overstate the breadth of achievement that produced the de Havilland Comet.

The design team began detailed work little more than five years after Britain's first jet engine had flown for the first time. Even by late 1946 jet fighters carrying at most two crew members and very little else were still a novelty. Yet de Havilland's engineers were visualising luxurious travel for 36 fare-paying passengers sitting in living room comfort and wearing their normal clothes, not specially-trained combat airmen in "G" suits and oxygen masks.

For a start this meant providing a comfortable cabin environment at altitudes of 40,000ft and above where the air was thin and the outside temperature unimaginably low. To take full advantage of the new form of propulsion the Comet's airframe had to be light and offer minimal drag.

Meeting these challenges meant new construction methods and a new approach to aerodynamics as well as many other innovations. Inevitably a Comet cost far more than a Constellation or a DC-6 and burned twice as much fuel. But the world's first jet airline, British Overseas Airways Corporation soon discovered that jets required less maintenance. They were more productive too: five Comets could do the work of eight conventional airliners.

The British aviation industry appeared to have achieved its long-cherished aim of pegging back the American lead in airliner design with a brilliant technological coup. For two glorious years the Comet was the unrivalled standard-bearer of aeronautical progress. But it turned out to be, as one observer noted, a magnificent false start.

Hopes so triumphantly raised were to be tragically dashed only two years later by a series of catastrophic accidents. The fact that the investigation into these crashes spotlighted a previously little-known phenomenon and so ensured the safety of future air journeys was scant consolation, particularly to the team of visionary engineers who had conceived and built the Comet.

But they were determined to use the investigation's findings to restore its reputation and the resulting Comet 4 emerged phoenix-like from the ashes of its past, bigger, stronger, with longer range and generally more capable.

Yet although BOAC was now able to operate the first scheduled trans-Atlantic jet service the delay had allowed America to catch up. Soon the bigger, faster Boeing 707 and Douglas DC-8 would dominate long-haul air travel and maintain the US lead in commercial aviation technology.

The Comet, though, was to enjoy a long service life. At first it was used only by wealthy travellers but ended its career carrying charter passengers to holiday destinations in the sun.

Public perceptions of air travel were changed for ever. But the Comet did more even than that. Crediting it with changing the world is surely not too big a claim to make for the world's first jet airliner.

September 2014

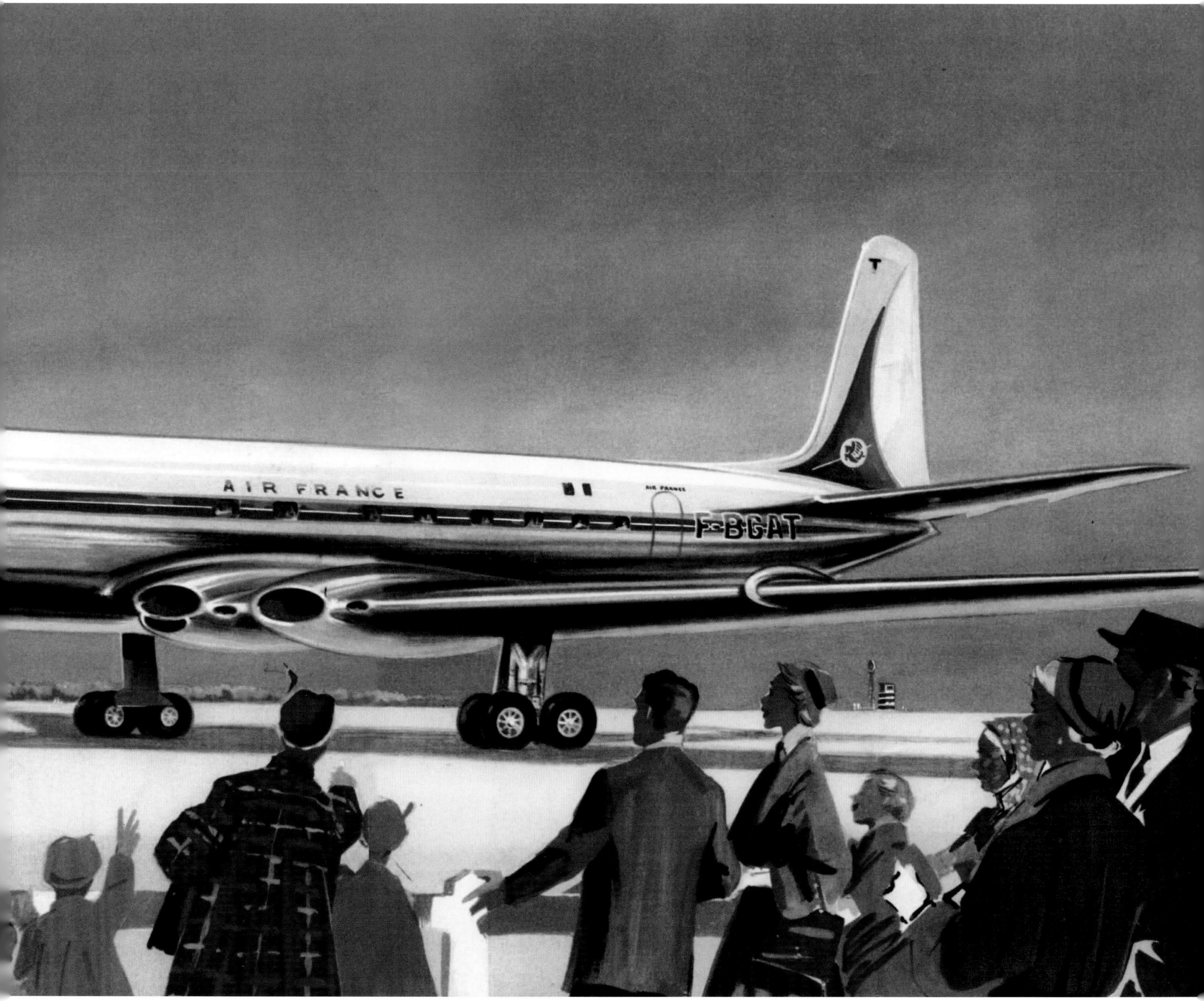
AIR FRANCE
F-BGAT

Taken from AF brochure

BACKGROUND

The Race for Efficiency

It was billed as the world's greatest air race, an idea dreamed up to celebrate the centenary of the Australian city of Melbourne.

Financial support for the England to Australia race came from confectionary manufacturer Sir Macpherson Robertson who agreed to donate the prize on condition that the race be named after his company.

Accordingly, on 20 October 1934 20 aircraft set off at intervals from Mildenhall airfield in Suffolk and headed for Melbourne. First away was Black Magic, the black painted de Havilland 88 Comet flown by Jim Mollison and his wife Amy. Better known as Amy Johnson, she had earlier won undying fame by becoming the first woman to fly solo from England to Australia.

But the Johnsons were forced to drop out with engine trouble leaving C W A Scott and Tom Campbell Black to win in their scarlet DH 88 called Grosvenor House. Their elapsed time was 71 hours.

It was a feat that captured public imagination and the pair was duly feted. Yet to many observers more significant was the Douglas DC-2 called Uiver (Stork) entered by the Dutch airline KLM which won the handicap section even though it finished nearly a day behind Grosvenor House.

And the impression it created was huge. The journal Flight noted wryly: *"From the panic in the press one would almost think that Great Britain had lost instead of won the great race to Australia."*

Yet the industry's reaction to the new Douglas airliner was hardly surprising. The aircraft had entered regular service barely six months before the race to Melbourne by which time Trans World Airlines was using it for US trans-continental operations. So while the Comet was a purpose-built racer with extremely cramped accommodation for two, the DC-2 was a commercial airliner able to carry up to 14 passengers.

In the days before the race, according to Flight, the DC-2 proved to be a *"magnet to everyone present including some of our most capable aircraft designers."*

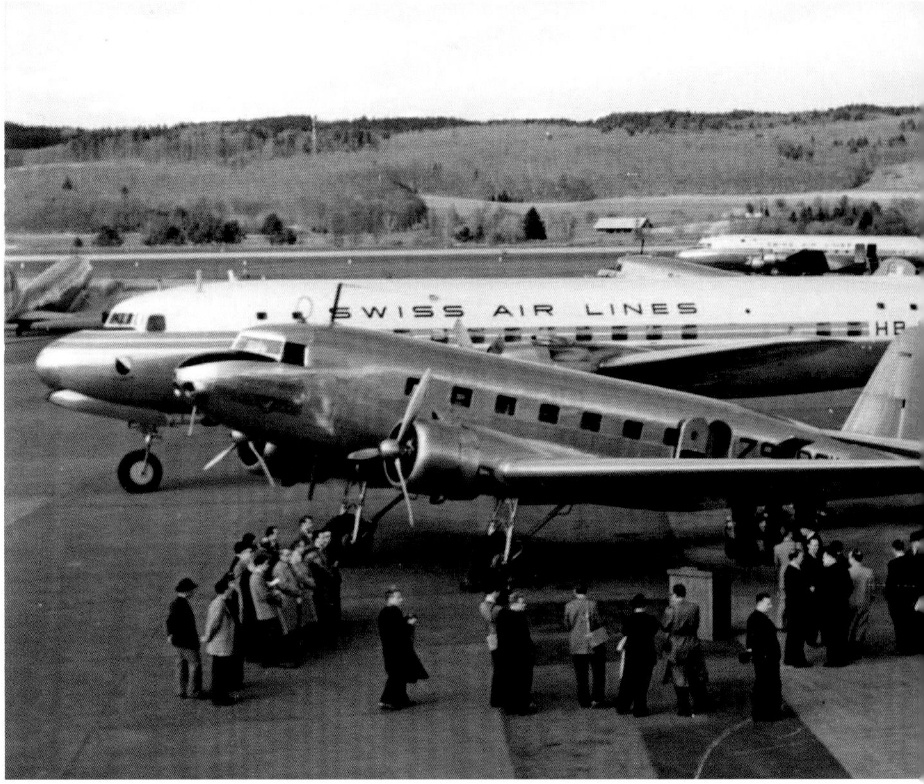
SWISS AIR LINES

These observers particularly admired its aerodynamic design, clean all-metal structure, semi-monocoque fuselage and powerful supercharged engines. The way that comfort had clearly not been sacrificed to performance also impressed them.

But Flight also pointed out that *"what has undoubtedly helped to make this very fine piece of aircraft engineering possible is the fact that initially an order was placed for 60 machines."* In Britain, the journal lamented, manufacturers could count themselves extremely fortunate if they secured orders for eight aircraft. More likely, Flight reported, *"British aircraft constructors have mostly had to be satisfied with orders for twos and threes. This inevitably means that there is no income out of which experiment can be paid."*

Apart from its performance de Havilland's first Comet had little in common with the pioneering jet airliner with which it was later to share its name. But for all its swooping, sexy lines the DH 88 did not represent the future. It was made of wood and therefore pointed the way towards the elegant if fragile DH 91 Albatross airliner and the wartime Mosquito rather than to the all-metal designs which followed the DC-2.

Mildenhall to Melbourne also signalled the start of another contest, that between two US manufacturers for supremacy in the commercial airliner market. Boeing's 247 preceded the DC-2 and one did well in the race to Australia but the DC-2 led to the immortal DC-3. It went into service with American Airlines as the Douglas Sleeper Transport in 1936 and by 1942 represented 80 per cent of the US domestic airliner fleet with 260 in service. The DC-3 also made an important contribution to the Allied victory in the Second World War.

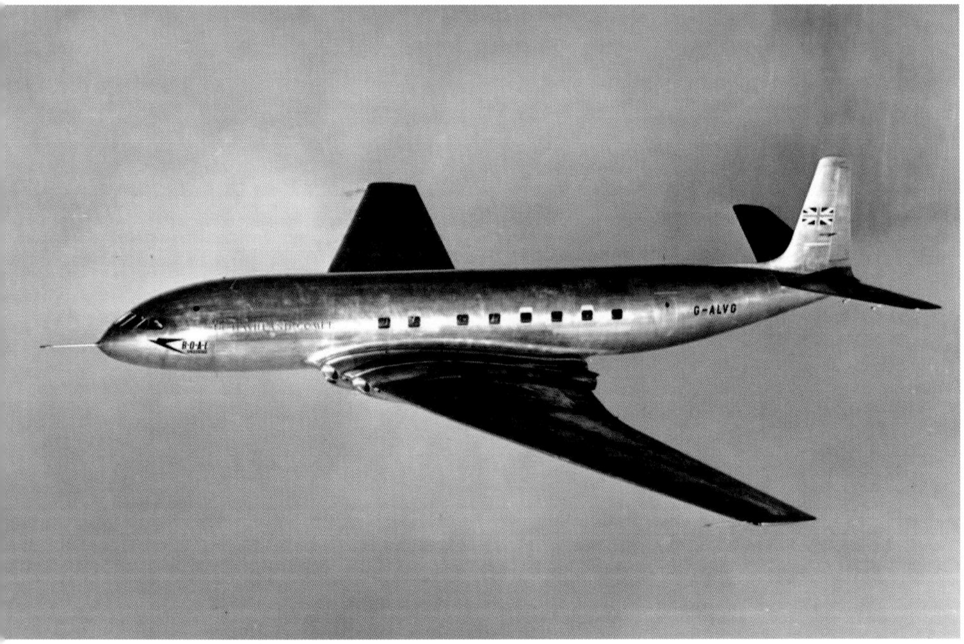
G-ALVG

ABOVE: Dramatic view of Comet prototype G-ALVG
TOP MIDDLE: When the Douglas DC-2 first appeared in Britain it made a huge impression because of the clear indication of the great strides being made by US airliner designers. Here a pair of South African DC-2s are pictured with a more recent stable made, a DC-4.

Meanwhile KLM began the trend for European airlines to buy American equipment when it ordered 14 DC-2s in 1934. Uiver's success had acted as a clear demonstration of the type's reliability. By 1939 it had been followed by orders for the Douglas twins from half a dozen European carriers.

On the eve of war Germany was Europe's leading air transport nation with Britain third after the USSR. This worried the Chamberlain government sufficiently for it to appoint a committee of inquiry under Lord Cadman to review the nation's aviation policy.

The committee could hardly fail to see that US manufacturers were dominating the European market and also gaining a "*firm footing in the Dominions.*" This, it said, created "*a position which, for national and imperial reasons alike, make it important to retrieve.*"

But although the government accepted Cadman's findings time was running out. The report was delivered in March 1938 and within the next 18 months the nation would be at war. Work on new civil projects, which had already taken second place to re-armament, was finally halted.

That meant the end of several promising designs including the four-engined Short S.32, which would have been fully pressurised and cruised at 275mph at 25,000ft, and the elegant Fairey FC-1. There were also offerings from the ambitious F G Miles, the most advanced of which would have had eight engines and cruised at 350mph.

But these designs represented paper aeroplanes at a time when such machines were moving towards reality in the USA. Spurred on by the competition between US airlines Boeing was building its 307 Stratoliner, the world's first

pressurised airliner. Douglas was producing the DC-4 for American and United while TWA's Howard Hughes was hoping to trump them all with the elegant Lockheed Constellation.

Although these aircraft were designed for the airlines the timing of their appearance meant they served initially with the military. But it was clear that when hostilities ended US airlines would have ready access to plenty of modern equipment: by December 1941 Douglas had turned out 800 DC-3s, a figure which rose to around 11,000 by the end of the war. At its peak production it averaged an astonishing five aircraft a day.

It was indeed evident that the British aircraft industry would have difficulty in re-establishing a civil capability against competition from the technically far superior US-built airliners so the British government put in hand preparations to help the industry overcome this disadvantage.

Even Winston Churchill himself had gained first-hand experience of Britain's lack of modern transport aircraft. He found himself obliged to travel to Moscow for a meeting with Soviet dictator Joseph Stalin wrapped in blankets and wearing an oxygen mask huddled in the freezing converted bomb bay of a (US-built) Liberator bomber. At this time the British Overseas Airways Corporation was also using converted bombers on many of its routes.

The Second World War was far from won in 1942 when the British government turned its attention to the post-war shape of civil aviation. That autumn it appointed the Transport Aircraft Committee to "*advise on the design and production of transport aircraft*" and to "*prepare outline specifications of several aircraft types needed for post-war air transport.*" A key consideration was ensuring the industry's post-war capacity was productively used during the transition from war to peace-time work.

Inevitably this group came to be known as the Brabazon Committee after its

TOP RIGHT: Posed view inside a Comet 1 mock-up

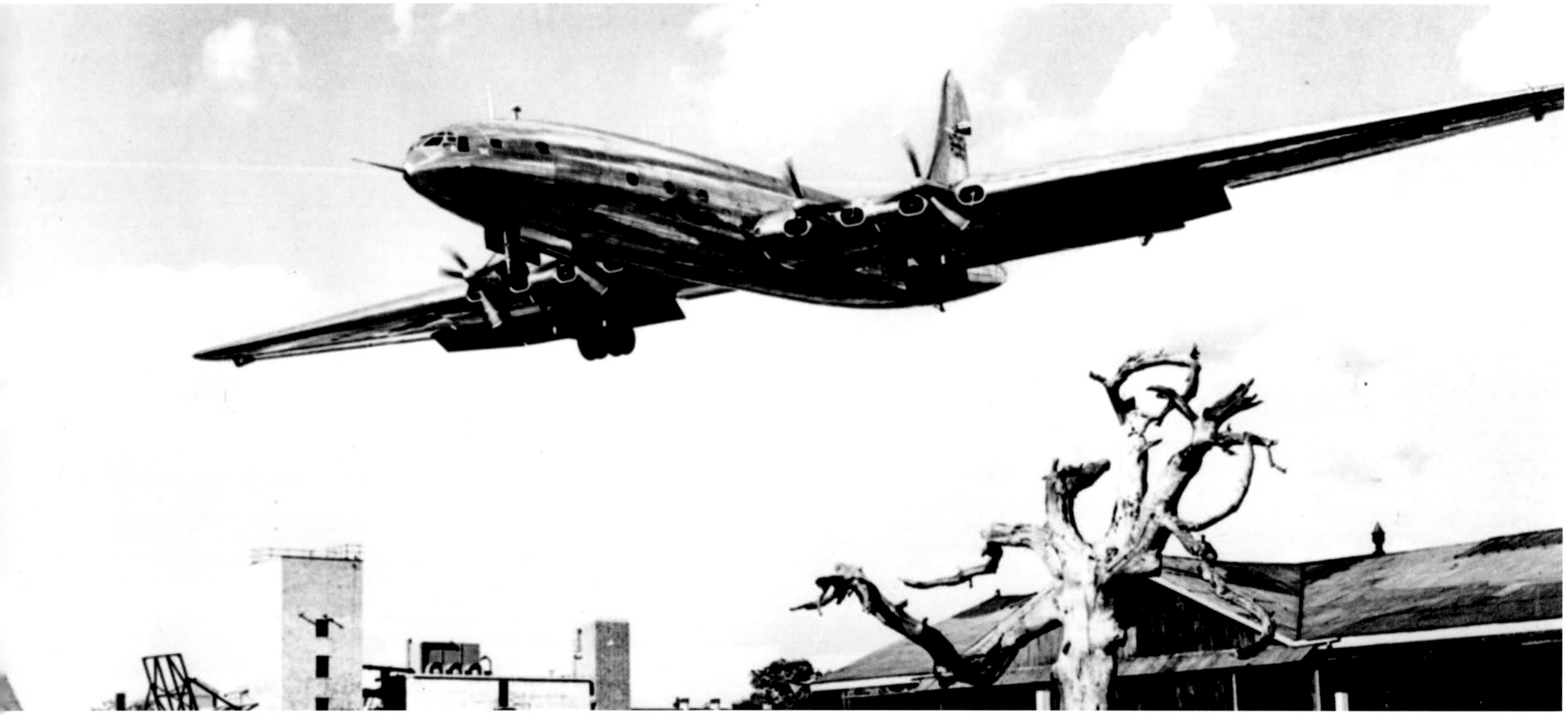

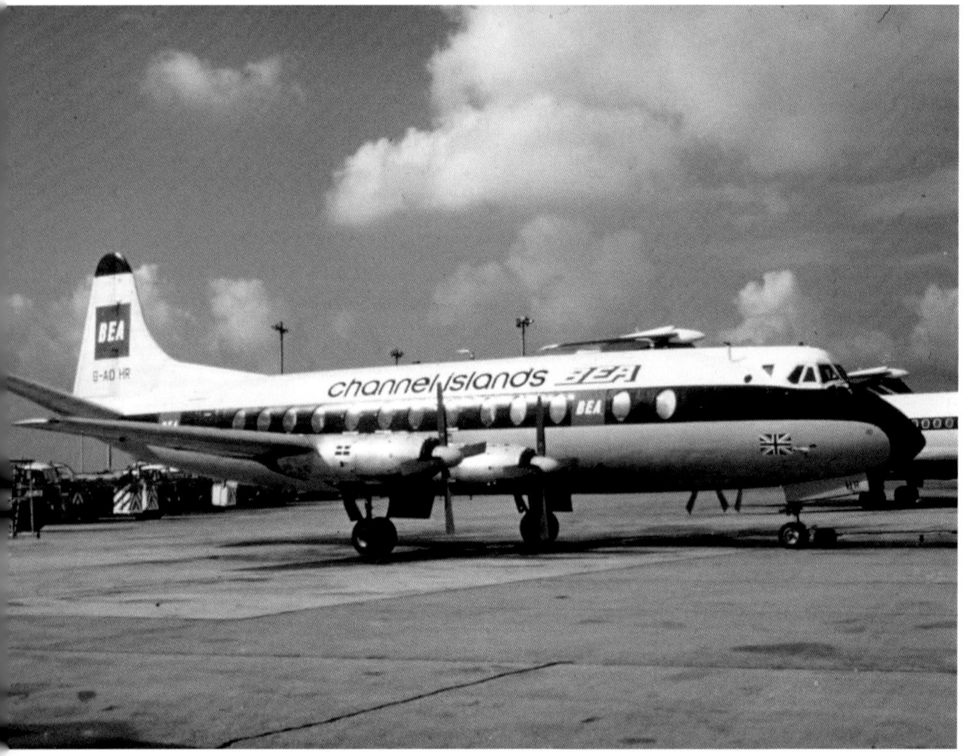
BEA
channel islands BEA

chairman Lord Brabazon of Tara (see p13). There was no public announcement but the committee, which included among its members Sir Francis Shelmerdine, a former director general of civil aviation, and William (later Sir William) Hildred, director general of the International Air Transport Association, started work in earnest in December.

It wasted little time. Its report, delivered to the War Cabinet in February 1943, contained a list of five aircraft types on which it believed preparatory work should begin at once, although no specific manufacturers were linked to the concepts at that stage.

To build on the committee's work a decision was taken to form another, also led by Lord Brabazon. Between 1943 and 1945 it issued a number of interim reports before producing a final report which refined its previous conclusions.

The Brabazon Committee has been described as *"visionary"* but it was not unqualified praise. By 1945, according to the late Sir Peter Masefield, a former aviation journalist who became secretary to the war cabinet committee on post-war civil air transport, *"this committee occupied a substantial slice of the attention of several cabinet ministers, including Churchill, and senior civil servants in five government departments."*

The resulting aircraft enjoyed distinctly mixed fortunes. Masefield said: *"Sadly, the implementation of the resulting recommendations fell far short of the committee's hopes and ambitions. More than half the proposals fell by the wayside."*

That was true but some of the types which emerged from the committee's

TOP: Bristol Brabazon G-AOHR approaches to land at Farnborough over Cody's famous tree.
ABOVE LEFT: Another type foreshadowed by the wartime Brabazon Committee was the turboprop Vickers Viscount. This BEA example is pictured at Jersey in the early 1970s.

deliberations - the initial list of five basic projects had risen to seven by 1944 - could certainly be considered successful. In addition to the Comet, the list included the Vickers Viscount, the world's first turbine-powered airliner, the Bristol Britannia long-range turbo-prop and the more conventionally powered Airspeed Ambassador. And, with 542 built, the Ronald Bishop-designed de Havilland Dove feeder liner was Britain's best-selling post-war civil aircraft.

Professor Keith Hayward, research director of the Royal Aeronautical Society, has pointed out that Brabazon and his colleagues had to work under difficult conditions. Inevitably many of their assumptions and much of their evidence *"were derived from pre-war notions about air travel."*

Hayward noted: *"Accurate information about future trends, especially developments in the United States, was hard to obtain and the exigencies of war ruled out elaborate surveys and design studies."*

He saw the committee's work as *"a credible, if not always accurate, prediction of future civil requirements."* In spite of its limitations, *"it formed the backbone of government policy towards post-war civil aircraft production."* What elevated the committee's deliberations was its appreciation of the opportunity offered by Britain's substantial lead in the field of jet engine design to leap frog American superiority in conventional piston engine airliners. Hayward added: *"Four of the Brabazon types called for either prop- or turbo-jet engines."*

The most visionary proposal was Brabazon IV. Made less than two years after Britain's first jet aircraft had flown, it called for a jet-propelled mail carrier with North Atlantic capability.

In mid-1944 the committee issued an interim report which recognised that trans-Atlantic range was probably expecting too much at that stage. Accordingly, it recommended a jet airliner that could be used on European and Empire routes with seating for 14 passengers and the ability to cruise at 450 mph. It might, though, be followed by one using turboprop or ducted fan power for Atlantic operations.

A year later the war time coalition government had been replaced by Clement Attlee's Labour administration which inherited the work done so far by the Ministry of Aircraft Production to implement the Brabazon programme. The new government could hardly fail to be aware that aircraft manufacture had become one of the nation's most important industries and apart from any other benefits the production of airliners would help to maintain employment in a strategically and economically important sector. And if it turned in a profit then so much the better.

There was also pressure from the Ministry of Supply, which had absorbed MAP's functions, to advance the programme. According to Prof Hayward, *"officials were acutely conscious of the lead built up by the Americans and in their opinion unless the programme was rapidly and comprehensively implemented the gap would grow even wider."*

To Peter Masefield, Brabazon IV was the only really *"far out"* challenge posed by Brabazon and his colleagues. He also criticised the second Brabazon Committee for becoming "bogged down" in the details of its proposals.

Yet it had done enough to facilitate the biggest leap forward in airliner development made so far.

Many aviation historians see the decision of the Second World War coalition government to consider post-war airliner development at a time when the conflict's outcome was still in doubt as a visionary and highly significant act. Yet its chairman seems not to have viewed his appointment as a particularly important event in his life.

In his autobiography, published in 1956, Lord Brabazon of Tara has little more to say about his committee other than that its members were *"a talented group of people."*

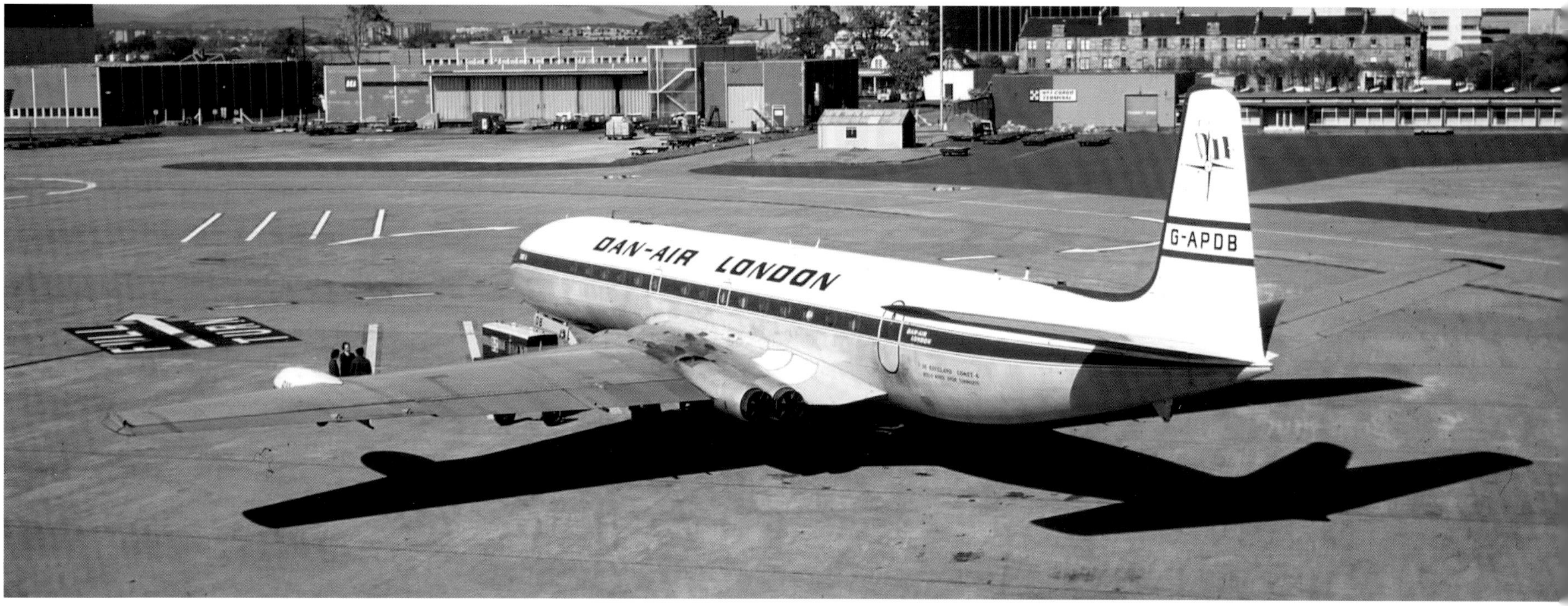
DAN-AIR LONDON
G-APDB

ABOVE: Dan-Air operated the biggest fleet of Comet 4s. This is G-APDB, originally delivered to BOAC in September 1958, pictured at Glasgow airport in the early 1970s, shortly before its withdrawal from service in 1974.

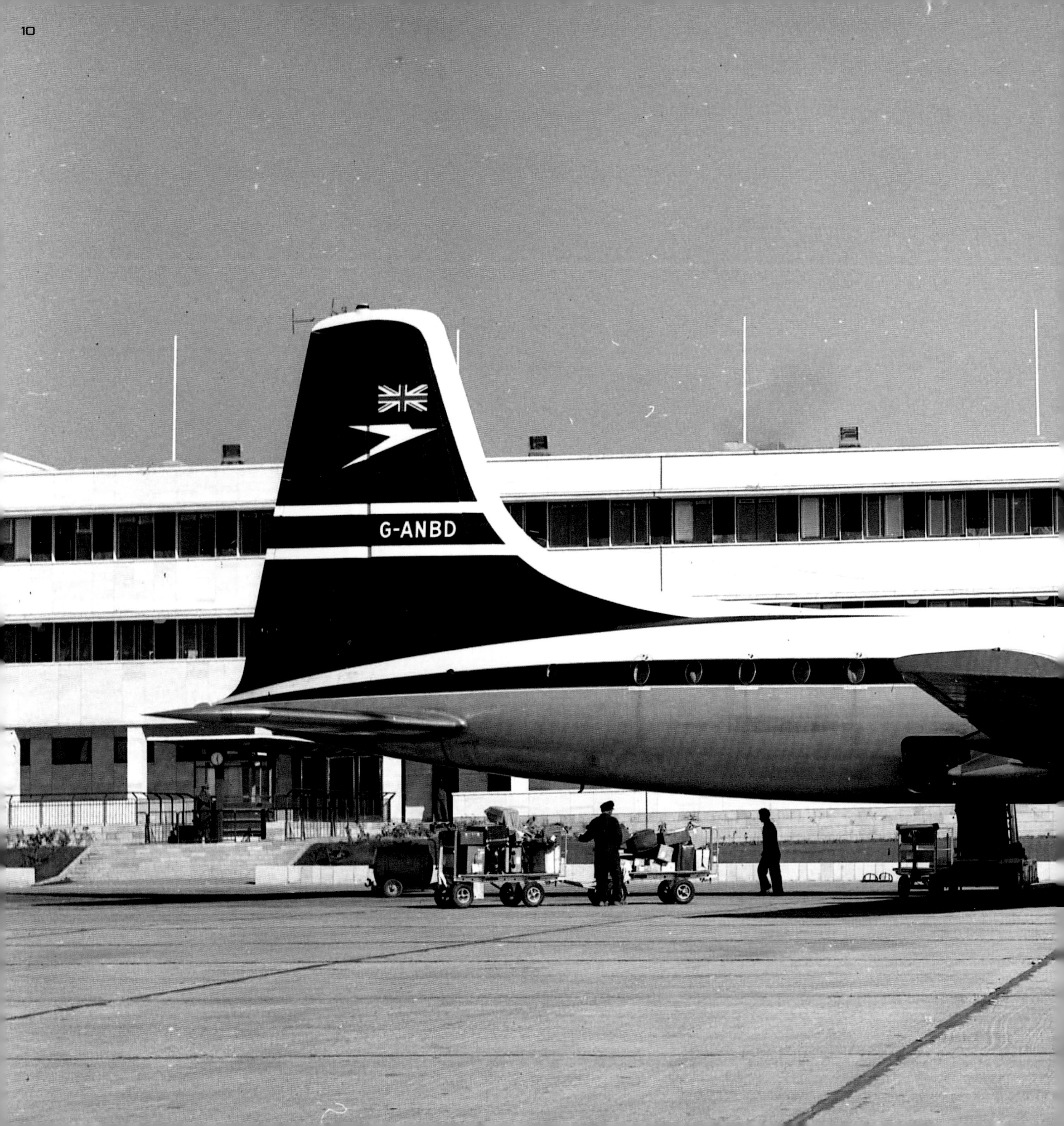
G-ANBD

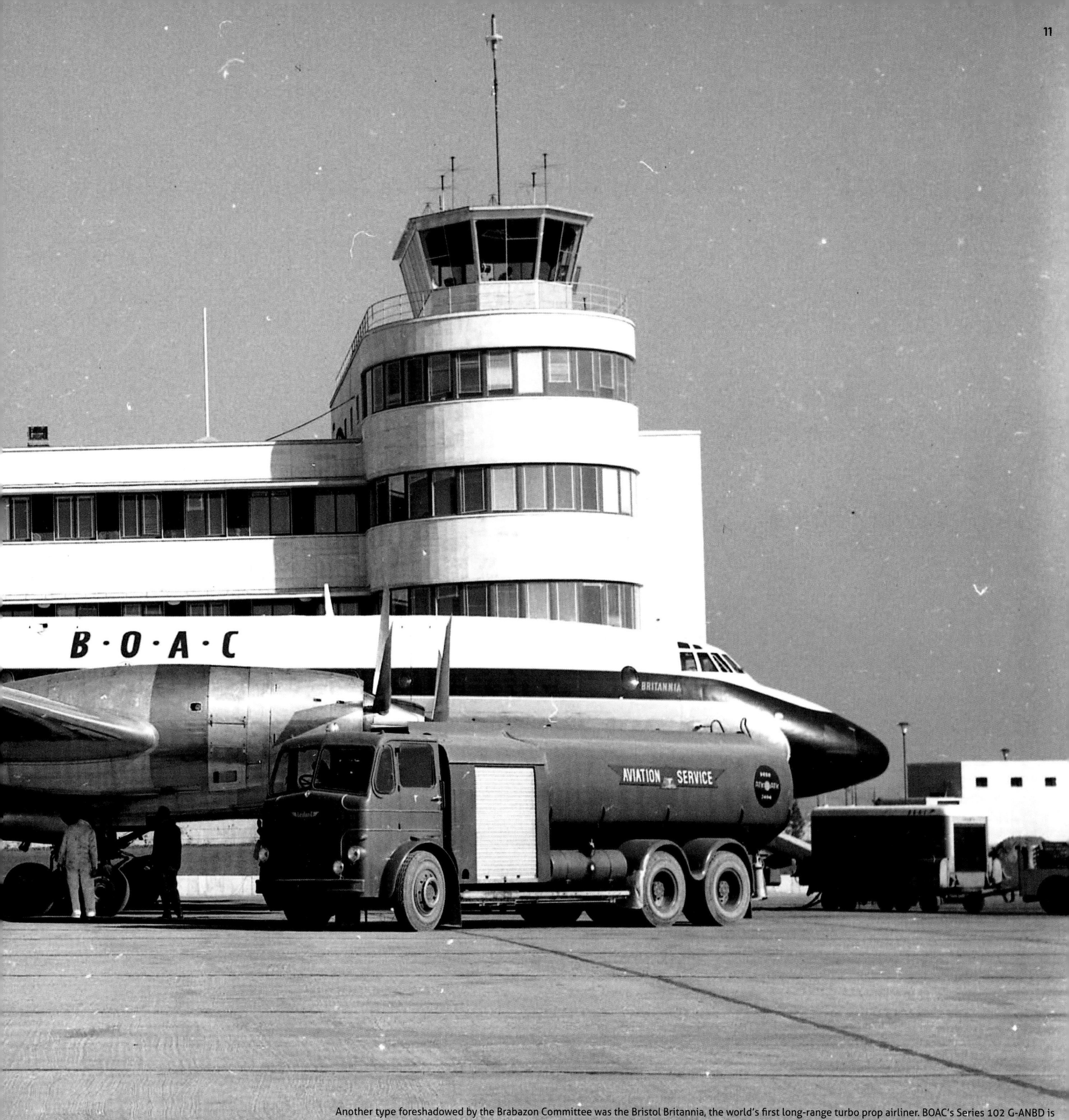
B·O·A·C
BRITANNIA
AVIATION SERVICE

Another type foreshadowed by the Brabazon Committee was the Bristol Britannia, the world's first long-range turbo prop airliner. BOAC's Series 102 G-ANBD is pictured here at Nairobi in 1956 during a proving flight.

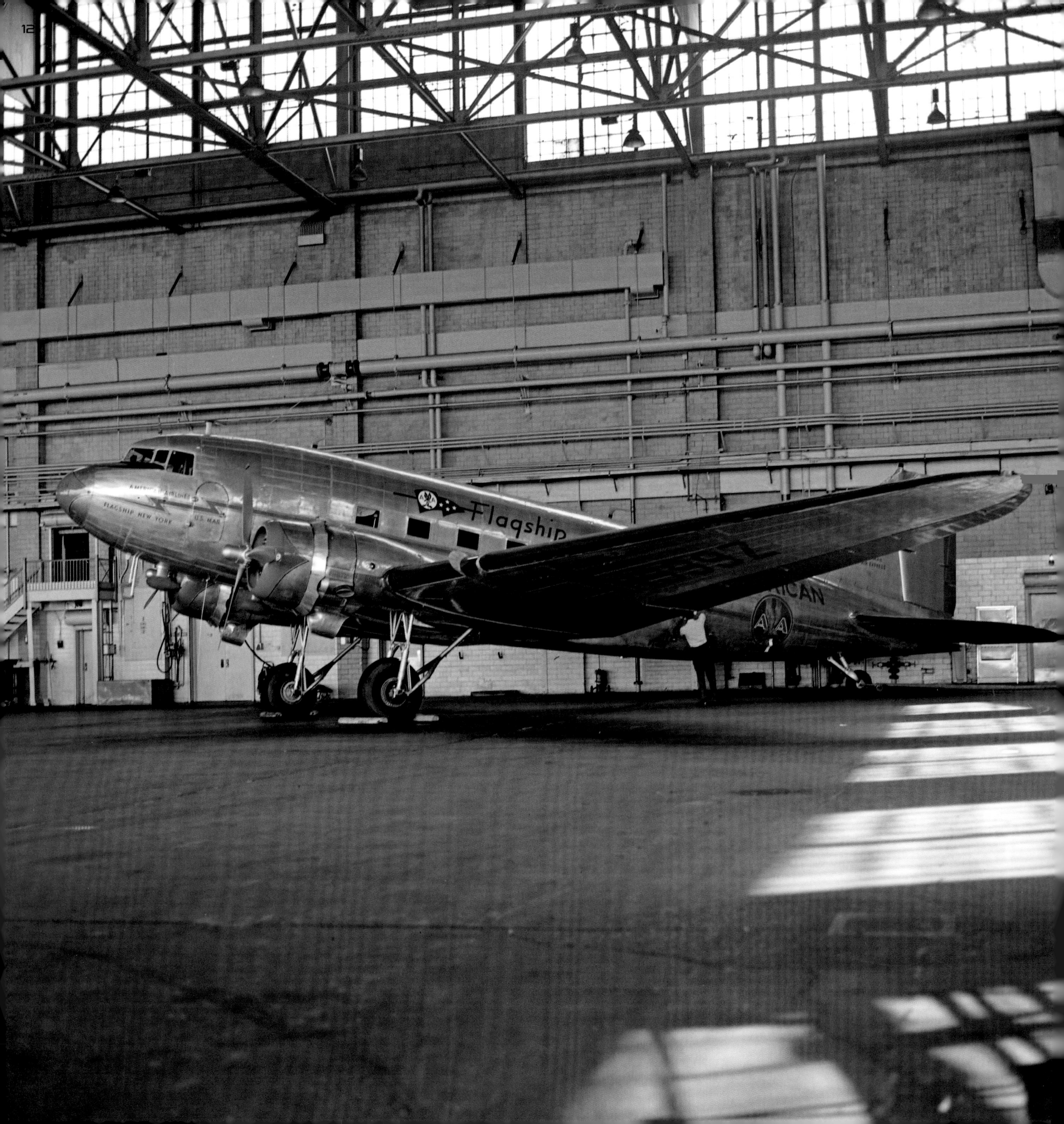
Flagship
FLAGSHIP NEW YORK
U.S. MAIL

Lord Brabazon of Tara

John Theodore Cuthbert Moore-Brabazon was born in 1884 to a wealthy and aristocratic family. Cars were his first love and an early ambition was to race them. He became friends with Charles Rolls who later introduced him to ballooning. That led to an interest in heavier-than-air machines and in 1908 Moore-Brabazon became the first Englishman to fly and be granted a pilot's licence then called an aviator's certificate.

He achieved this distinction in France but the following year Brabazon won a £1,000 prize awarded by the Daily Mail for making the first circular mile-long flight in Britain using a British-built aircraft, although his machine was actually inspired by a design produced by the Wright Brothers.

During the First World War Brabazon served with the Royal Flying Corps and played a leading role in the development of photographic reconnaissance. In 1915 he pioneered the corps' use of cameras during a mission over the German trenches.

After the war Brabazon entered politics and was elected Conservative MP for Chatham. He soon made his mark and was appointed parliamentary private secretary to the Air Minister, Winston Churchill. Later, Prime Minister Stanley Baldwin appointed Brabazon to the first of his ministerial posts as junior transport minister.

After a spell outside politics, Brabazon found himself back in the House of Commons in time for the outbreak of the Second World War. When Churchill became Prime Minister he appointed Brabazon to the job of transport minister and later minister of aircraft production.

A somewhat injudicious remark in which he expressed the hope that Germany and the Soviet Union, then engaged in the Battle of Stalingrad, would destroy each other made at what he assumed was a private function cost Brabazon his job. After his fall from grace he was offered a peerage and chairmanship of the committee that took his name.

In his previous job Brabazon had taken such a keen interest in the progress of the W. 1X jet engine that he'd taken to bombarding its creator, Frank Whittle, with daily inquiries, which, the jet pioneer noted in his autobiography, made him feel like *"a hunted man."*

Brabazon attempted to explain his action by saying: *"I believed so much in his invention that I wanted to help in every way."* This suggests that the committee's call for a jet-powered airliner may have been at least partly due to Brabazon's inside knowledge.

Rightly or wrongly history has credited him with being a visionary and his committee with providing the spark which ultimately ignited the jet-propulsion revolution in air transport. Yet it is also clear that it would probably have happened anyway and that the de Havilland company, with its interest in the new form of propulsion, would have been most likely to have pioneered its application to civil aviation.

What Brabazon did was to provide official encouragement and a focus for this work at a time when most of the effort was, quite naturally, being concentrated on winning the war.

Lord Brabazon of Tara died in 1964. He was 80.

LEFT: American Airlines' Douglas DC-3 N999Z is pictured at New York's La Guardia airport.
ABOVE: Because of his enthusiasm for jet propulsion and his encouragement of Sir Geoffrey de Havilland (second from left) to build an airliner using it Lord Brabazon (second from right) is one of the key people in the Comet story.

DESIGNING THE COMET
A well-founded step forwards

At this time Geoffrey de Havilland was holding regular discussions with technical colleagues about the possibility of applying jet propulsion to civil transport aircraft. Particularly prominent in these discussions were the company's veteran chief engineer C C Walker, chief designer Ronald Bishop, chief aerodynamicist Richard Clarkson, company treasurer Wilfred Nixon and Halford. During a discussion on the Vampire Walker was reported to have said that a similar performance could be available from a jet airliner.

Using his company's experience, de Havilland used his influence with the Brabazon Committee to refine its ideas so that jet propulsion was now seen as a less risky option.

In February 1945 de Havilland was given authority to proceed with its DH106. By this time a number of different ideas had been considered under this designation. It was perhaps inevitable that among them was a twin-boom mail carrier capable of accommodating passengers and powered by a trio of Goblins. A further unconventional suggestion involved a canard design with a rear-mounted straight wing and three engines mounted in the rear fuselage. More conventional, though, was the DH 95 Flamingo with jet engines replacing its reciprocating units.

But the end of the war opened up fresh possibilities. Within a few weeks of the surrender in 1945 technical personnel from the victorious Allied powers toured Germany's aircraft factories and research establishments. They were amazed by what they found. De Havilland's Bishop and Clarkson were among the visitors. *"We in the civil aviation field,"* Clarkson noted, *"will indeed be lucky in the post-war era in not having to meet German as well as American competition in civil air transport evolution."*

He returned from Germany convinced that future jet aircraft would have to feature the swept-back wings on which the defeated nation's aerodynamicists had been working. As a result, de Havilland considered the possibility of combining swept wings with a tail-less design similar to that of Messerschmitt's

Given the revolutionary nature of the technology it seems incredible that only six years elapsed between the first Brabazon Committee's call for a jet-powered trans-Atlantic mail carrier and the maiden flight of the world's first jet airliner.

Even allowing for the inescapable truth that the *"august body was less responsible for the Comet than for its stable companions the Dove and Ambassador,"* as noted by Flight in 1952, *"its foresight must nevertheless be acknowledged."*

Probably due to wartime secrecy and the way information about the Brabazon deliberations was released the precise sequence of events is not entirely clear. But one thing does stand out: the influence from an early stage of Geoffrey de Havilland. Although other firms were involved as required in the committees' deliberations, de Havilland was, in fact, the only permanent representative of UK aircraft manufacturers on the second Brabazon Committee.

It was not long, however, before the proposals were linked with the manufacturers assigned to take them from concept to reality. In the case of the committee's fourth proposal the chosen manufacturer was de Havilland's company, which comprised both an airframe and an engine manufacturer.

Indeed, the company was among the pioneers of jet propulsion through the work of Major Frank Halford who was not too far behind Frank Whittle in his approach to the new technology. By 1943 de Havilland was working on its Spider Crab, later renamed Vampire. The twin-boom fighter, which flew for the first time in September 1943, used a Halford-designed Goblin engine. When Whittle development stalled briefly a pair of Goblins had powered the fifth prototype of the rival Gloster Meteor on its maiden flight that March.

TOP: Veteran chief engineer, C C Walker, chief aerodynamicist Richard Clarkson and chief designer Ron Bishop, pictured here with Sir Geoffrey de Havilland (second from left), were three of the key figures behind the concept and design of the Comet.
BOTTOM RIGHT: John Cunningham was de Havilland's chief test pilot when the Comet made its maiden flight. Here he examines the Comet nose wheel test rig constructed from a lorry chassis

Me 163 rocket fighter.

At one stage the de Havilland team was visualising a tail-less airliner with 40 degrees of wing sweep-back and powered by four developed versions of the Goblin, later known as the Ghost. That this was, for a time, a serious proposition can be judged by de Havilland's decision to build a research aircraft to test the idea. Three DH 108 Swallows were constructed and all were lost in fatal accidents, de Havilland's son Geoffrey junior being killed in the first in September 1946.

The Royal Aircraft Establishment became involved with the DH 108 and the man who subsequently became recognised as Britain's most experienced test pilot, Eric "Winkle" Brown, made a series of flights in an improved Swallow. He soon discovered that it was *"a tricky aeroplane that had to be handled very carefully."* He added: *"It was one 'plane in which I found I could not relax for a second."*

De Havilland test pilot John Derry dived the Swallow beyond Mach 1.0, the first time this had been achieved by a British aircraft, but two of Brown's Farnborough colleagues were to fall victim to characteristics he had described as *"vicious."*

Many years later Brown recalled a conversation with Alexander Lippisch, the German aerodynamicist responsible for the Me 163's design. Brown said: *"He told me they (de Havilland) had gone at it like a bull at a gate and had got the centre of gravity wrong."*

Even though it had been widely assumed that the DH106 would have a more pronounced wing sweep back and feature a tail less lay-out, de Havilland eventually decided on a much more conventional concept. It rejected the idea of a 40-degree sweep-back, opting instead for a more modest 20 degrees.

In an analysis of the Comet's design published in July 1949 following the prototype's roll-out and first flight, Flight noted approvingly: *"It is, in our opinion, a great advantage that the de Havilland company has been able to meet the high speed, high altitude performance figures without resorting to unconventional layout or abnormal wing loading."* The Comet, the journal added, *"represents a logical, well-founded step forward, not a leap in the twilight, but it is no less enterprising for that."*

In September 1946 the aircraft's configuration was settled and the Ministry of Supply ordered two prototypes. At the same time the specification was agreed with the customer, BOAC, which had been closely involved in the design. Indeed, it had accepted de Havilland's basic belief that a jet-powered airliner was technically feasible and had initially thought it would need 25 aircraft.

This was scaled back when, in January 1947, de Havilland received its first production order for eight from BOAC. The order was made against specific performance guarantees, all of which were to be met. Further orders came from the short-lived British South American Airways, the third of Britain's post-war nationalised airlines, which wanted six. BSAA was later merged into BOAC which cancelled the order while increasing its own to nine aircraft.

In 1952 Flight reported: *"Clearly it was desirable to reduce the time normally taken to build and develop a prototype before delivery of the first aircraft from the assembly line so it was decided to go into full production immediately and to risk modifications 'on the line' rather than await prototype development."*

TOP: The first Comet is seen here under construction at de Havilland's Hatfield factory.

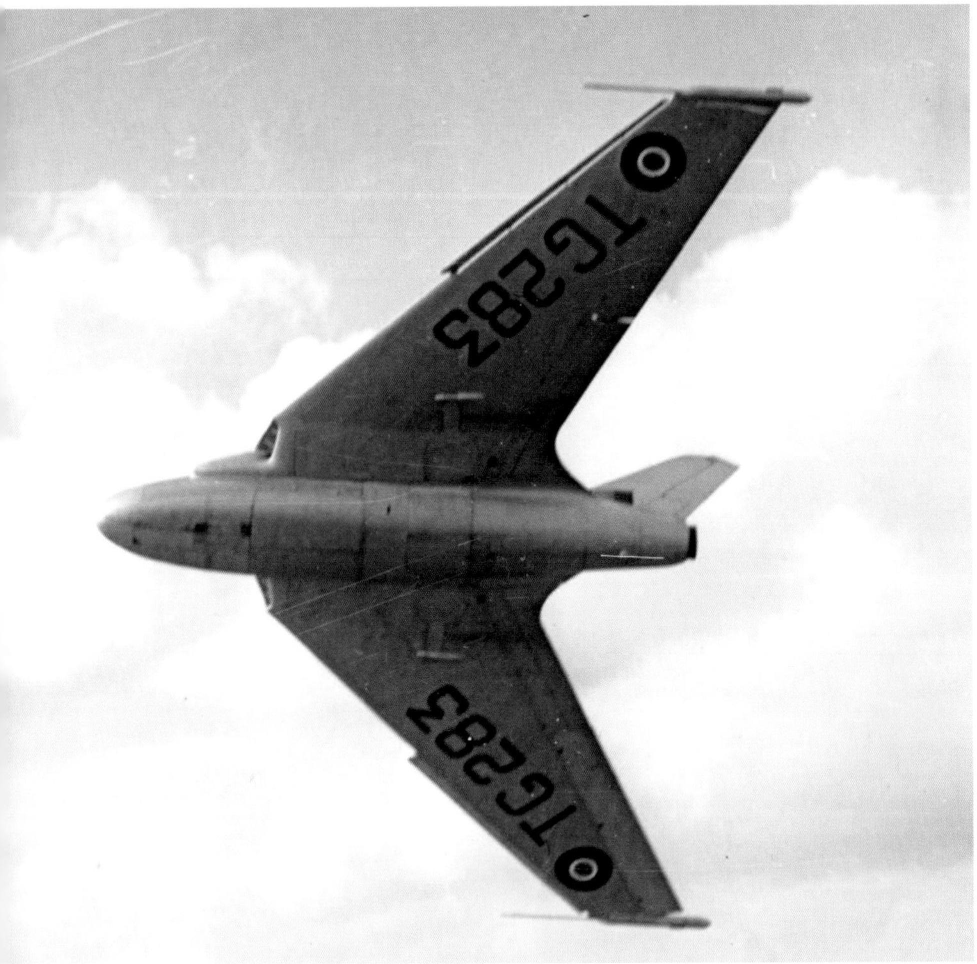
TG283
TG283

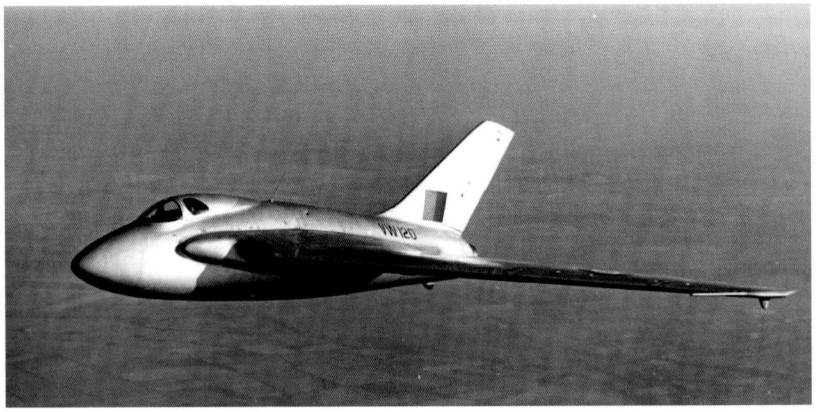
VW120

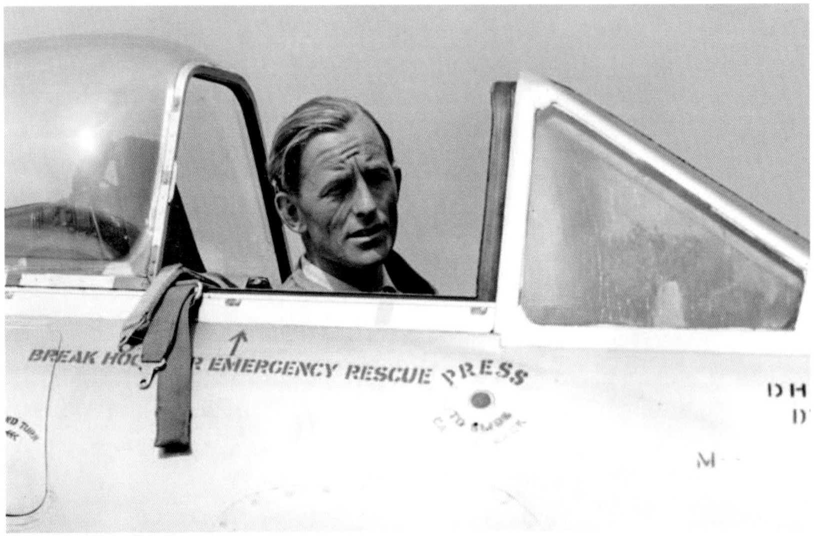
EMERGENCY RESCUE PRESS

The journal added: *"This, it will be realised, was a matter of the weightiest consequence but the decision has been fully vindicated by the performance of the production Comets."*

Even though such novelties as the tail-less configuration and even rocket-assisted take-off and in-flight refuelling had been considered and rejected, there were still plenty of novel features, apart, that is, from the power plant. Mike Ramsden, who later became editor of Flight, noted in a 1989 presentation to mark the 40th anniversary of the first fight that as a de Havilland apprentice he had felt *"conscious of watching the frontiers of technology being pushed back."*

Ramsden pointed out that the company took the biggest step forward ever taken in airliner design. He felt that subsequent events had obscured the full extent of the achievement made by the team of innovators involved in producing the Comet. The many world "firsts" included a wing that was an integral fuel tank, multiple wheel landing gear, full pressure refuelling and full power controls featuring simulated "feel."

In fact few large British aircraft featured a nose-wheel undercarriage. To test the nose gear and its steering de Havilland constructed a special rig involving a Dodge 3-ton lorry chassis. Mosquito main wheels were mounted outboard to prevent the rig overturning. Contemporary reports, which speak of Sir Geoffrey de Havilland himself being on board the rig, indicate that this safety feature had been a wise precaution.

Similarly, a Horsa glider was modified with a DH106 nose section to check if the windscreen would continue to provide pilots with clear vision when the aircraft was passing through rain. It was noted that the wartime glider featured a fuselage diameter of identical size to that of the rear frame of the airliner's nose. During the winter of 1946/47 the company's chief test pilot, John Cunningham, was airborne in the Horsa searching for rainfall of a suitable intensity.

For all its difficult handling characteristics the DH108 had contributed to the Comet's design in ways other than confirming that the unsuitability of the tail-less configuration. Components from the Lockheed Servodyne powered flight control system were tested on one of the Swallows as well as on a modified Hornet piston-engined fighter. A full-size control rig was built at Hatfield and operated continuously around the clock for over three years. The company was to claim that the only modification required to the airliner's control system was a slight increase in rudder area to improve cross-wind take-off characteristics.

Structural testing began with an investigation of skin-joint sealing. From then

ABOVE: The DH 108 Swallow was initially designed to test a possible Comet configuration. Clockwise from the **top left:** TG283 was the first of three examples; VW120 was the first British aircraft to fly faster than sound; John Derry was the pilot who achieved this distinction in September 1948. He was killed when the prototype DH110 broke up in mid-air during the 1952 Farnborough air show.

on there were to be hundreds of other tests ranging from routine destruction testing of small components to proof-load tests on wings and fuselage. The wings were subjected to deflection of up to 3 degrees at the tips, while the main undercarriage units underwent static load tests involving over 2,000 "hard landings." Both trials used the same rig so it was possible to observe the effects of the load on the undercarriage itself as well as on the surrounding structure and integral fuel tanks.

A decompression chamber large enough to accommodate a full-size fuselage section was constructed at Hatfield to simulate conditions at altitudes of 70,000ft (21,500m) and temperatures of minus 70-degrees Centigrade. Cabin windows were pressurised to over 8lb/sq every day for more than three years. At regular intervals they were removed, cleaned and treated with scratch remover to simulate actual conditions in airline service.

Meanwhile, the Ghost engine had been subjected to a similarly robust testing regime. The unit ran for the first time on 2 September 1945 but it was to be more than two years before the engine was airborne for the first time. On 24 July 1947 two of the new engines replaced the outer Merlins on Avro Lancastrian VM703. This first flying test bed was joined by VM749 and between them they

HIGH ENERGY IGNITION UNIT
DIFFUSER BOLT (TOP ENGINE MOUNTING)
FUEL TANK PRESSURISATION PIPE
FIRE EXTINGUISHER PIPE
CENTRE CASING
IGNITER PLUG
COMBUSTION CHAMBER
STARTER CONNECTION
GENERATOR
L.P. FUEL FILTER
GENERATOR COOLING DUCT
DIFFUSER CASING
CENTRE SHAFT
REAR LIFTING EYE
OIL FILLER CAP
BULKHEAD ELECTRICAL CONNECTION
AIR COMPRESSOR
STARTER MOUNTING
TACHO GENERATOR
TOP MOUNTING BRACKET
TOP WHEELCASE
IMPELLER
CENTRE HOUSING
FRONT BEARING
AIR INTAKE
STARTING AIR BLEED APERTURE
BOTTOM MOUNTING BRACKET
OIL SUMP
FUEL PUMP
HYDRAULIC PUMPS
OIL PUMP
OIL PRESSURE FILTER
OIL SUCTION FILTER
DRAIN BOX
AIR FUEL RATIO CONTROL
TURBINE ENTRY DUCT
DISCHARGE NOZZLE
REAR BEARING
COOLING MUFF
SUPPORT CYLINDER
INSULATING PLATE
FIREGUARD
OUTER EXHAUST CONE
PROPELLING NOZZLE
INNER EXHAUST CONE
FAIRING
FIREGUARD AND PROPELLING NOZZLE DRAIN
DIFFUSER BOLT (BOTTOM ENGINE MOUNTING)
BAROMETRIC PRESSURE CONTROL
DEFLECTOR ASSEMBLY
COMBUSTION CHAMBER DRAIN
BURNER
REAR COVER
FIREGUARD DRAIN
SEALING PLATE
OUTER EXHAUST CONE DRAIN
COMBUSTION CHAMBER INTERCONNECTOR
TURBINE BLADES
AIR-COOLED NOZZLE BLADES
DIAPHRAGM AND ANNULUS RING

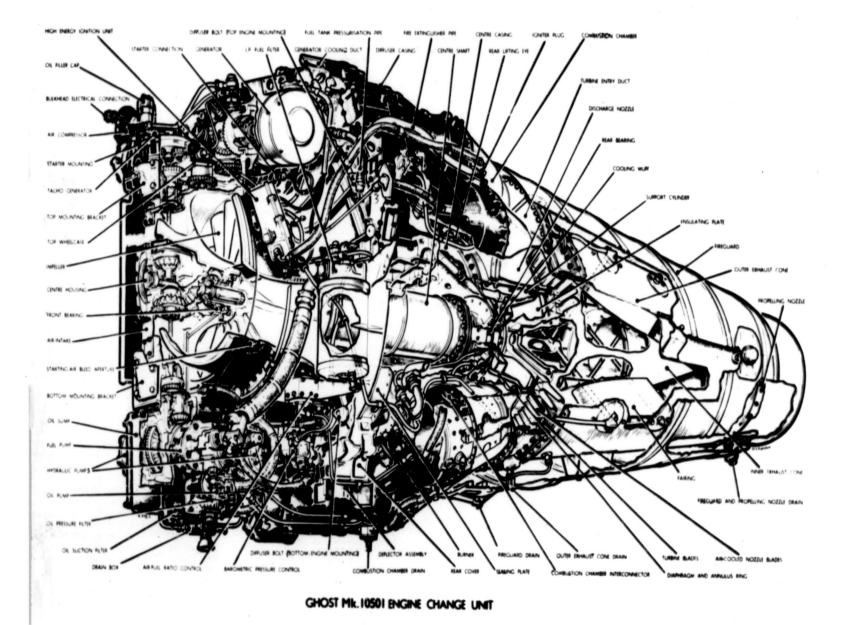

GHOST Mk.10501 ENGINE CHANGE UNIT

Ghosted Ghost: this cut-way drawing reveals the internal lay-out of the engine which powered the Comet 1 in fascinating detail.

much of the work was carried out in secrecy. Former de Havilland apprentice Mike Ramsden recalled how attempts to enter the experimental shop resulted in an order for him to "clear off."

As it happened, most of the company's 10,000 employees had some knowledge of what was going on but there were no leaks. Ramsden also recalled that Ron Bishop kept a model of a tail-less aircraft on his desk, apparently to confuse visitors. It was not until December 1948 that the name Comet was announced.

The aircraft emerged on July 25 1949 for its engines to be run. That evening several taxy runs were made up and down the runway. The following day a couple of "minor snags" prevented anything more ambitious and the day was devoted to engine runs.

Early on the 27th Cunningham made several more taxy runs. "*Then,*" reported Flight, "*at 0950hr with the tail almost in the hedge, Cunningham opened up all four Ghosts and, after a run of only about 200 yards 'nodded' the Comet off for a 500-yard (460m) hop at around 15 ft (5.75m). A repeat performance was made immediately afterwards and the aircraft then returned to the apron for later inspection by the considerable gathering of onlookers – ourselves included – who had been invited to Hatfield to make an external inspection of the Comet.*"

In fact the journalists were getting their first glimpse of the new aircraft. Eagerly, they listened to the briefing from de Havilland's key people but in answer to the question most insistently asked they were told that unsuitable weather meant the first flight would be made when the aircraft was ready and not before.

After the visitors had admired the jet's "graceful yet unmistakably workmanlike appearance," Cunningham took the aircraft out again using only the two outboard Ghosts to demonstrate the aircraft's tractable ground handling qualities. Then, he opened up all four engines to take-off power, holding it on the brakes.

The guests were duly impressed by the high pitched shriek emitted by the engines and the 200-yard (185m) plumes of dust their exhausts kicked up. But they were not too pleased to learn that the aircraft had actually made its maiden

accumulated over 425 flying hours, equivalent to about 1,700 engine hours, by July 1949.

On the Lancastrian the engines were limited to an altitude of 25,000ft (7,700m), although a Ghost-powered Vampire with extended wing tips joined the programme. Indeed, it was with this aircraft that on 23 March 1948 Cunningham set a new altitude record of over 59,000ft (18,100m).

The winter of 1946/47 is remembered as particularly severe but despite the intense cold the build-up of ice on the Ghosts' air intakes was never large enough to have a measurable effect on performance. The ice usually broke away in small pieces, which were ingested by the engines without noticeable effect. On one occasion, however, a block estimated as weighing 7lbs (3.2kg) was drawn straight into the impeller. Apart from a brief cough the Ghost carried on running but one of the impeller blades was later discovered to be slightly bent.

De Havilland's chief test pilot Cunningham was to play a key role in the development of the world's first jet airliner. An early task was to ensure it would incorporate the requirements of the pilots who would fly it in service. Accordingly, Cunningham, who was new to large transport types, attended BOAC's training facility at Dorval, Montreal to learn about the airline's major aircraft type, the Lockheed L049 Constellation.

"*I flew several scheduled north Atlantic flights during the winter of 1946 and `47 as a crew member, usually second pilot,*" he recalled later. "*I spent a month being checked out and also flew the Australia route.*"

Altogether Cunningham made five return trans-Atlantic trips and two to Australia. He also spent much time studying the airline's aircraft and engine overhaul organisation. As a result, the Comet layout and its cockpit in particular followed that of the Constellation.

Although a public announcement that Britain was developing a jet airliner was made in 1947 little information about design's details were revealed. Indeed,

TOP: A Comet nose was grafted on to Horsa glider TL348 to test its behaviour in rain.
BOTTOM RIGHT: View of the rear fuselage of the Comet prototype under construction.

flight after they had left. At least one of the air correspondents vowed never to mention the name de Havilland again.

Years later Cunningham recalled that he had insisted on making three preliminary "hops" to check the flying controls for satisfactory response. That accomplished the aircraft was jacked up so that the main undercarriage with its single 66in (1.7m) diameter wheel could be checked to ensure it had withstood the loads placed upon it.

At about 1700hr the experimental shop's chief inspector handed the aircraft over to the chief test pilot. "*I said: `Yes, let's do the flight now,'*" Cunningham recalled. "The weather was fine and at 1800hr we took off. I had made the first Comet take-off." He later reported that all the major features had performed as expected: "*Ghost engine performance, speed characteristics and full power controls.*"

Cunningham was accompanied on that historic 31-minute flight by Harold "Tubby" Waters (co-pilot), engineers John Wilson (electrics) and Frank Reynolds (hydraulics) and flight test observer Tony Fairbrother.

Cunningham took the prototype up to 10,000ft (3,000m) to check its handling at low and medium speeds. Before landing he made a pass over the airfield at a height of 100ft (30m) for the benefit of company staff who had turned out to watch. By this time, of course, the journalists had gone so it was left to Fairbrother to find the words to suit the occasion. He noted: "The world changed as our wheels left the ground."

Flight's man, however, appeared to have forgiven the company when he wrote his report of the flight. "Only three years since the decisions regarding the design were taken the first aircraft has been pushed out in readiness for taxying trials and the first flight," the journal reported. "This is a very creditable achievement and will come as a surprise to many who did not expect to see the Comet until the end of the year."

Over the next 18 working days the aircraft flew for a total of 32.5hr during which it reached the speeds and altitudes that would be expected during normal operations. General handling with medium loading was tested. On some days there were as many as five flights. Apart from refuelling the aircraft was found to need only a modest amount of attention.

Handling was found to be satisfactory both in the air and on the ground. And by trading fuel load for payload the aircraft seemed readily adaptable to operations on short and medium-length routes. Flights of up to 5.5hr duration were made during this time and an altitude of 43,000ft (13,200m) was attained. A speed of Mach 0.8 was reached in a shallow dive. The tests revealed that in service the aircraft could be expected to cruise at 490mph (780kph) at around 40,000ft (12,300m). Comfortable sector length was expected to be 2,140 miles (3,400km).

The prototype made its first public appearance at the SBAC Farnborough show in September 1949, followed by its first overseas trip, to Tripoli, Libya. This took just 3hr 23min at an average speed of 434mph (695kph). Among the many records broken during this period was London-Rome-London accomplished in under four hours. London-Cairo took 5hr 7min on the way to Khartoum where tropical trials were to be undertaken. In July 1950 the first prototype, now registered G-ALVG, was joined in the test programme by a second aircraft, G-ALZK which made its first flight in the hands of Cunningham and Peter Bugge.

In April 1951 this aircraft was delivered to BOAC for route-proving and for crews to learn about the new handling techniques required. On 19 October it returned to Heathrow at the end of the Comet's 12th overseas tour. It had flown 460hr, covered over 91,000 miles (145,500km) and made 91 landings at 31 overseas airports.

TOP: This shot of the Comet prototype in the factory at Hatfield clearly shows the engine mountings.

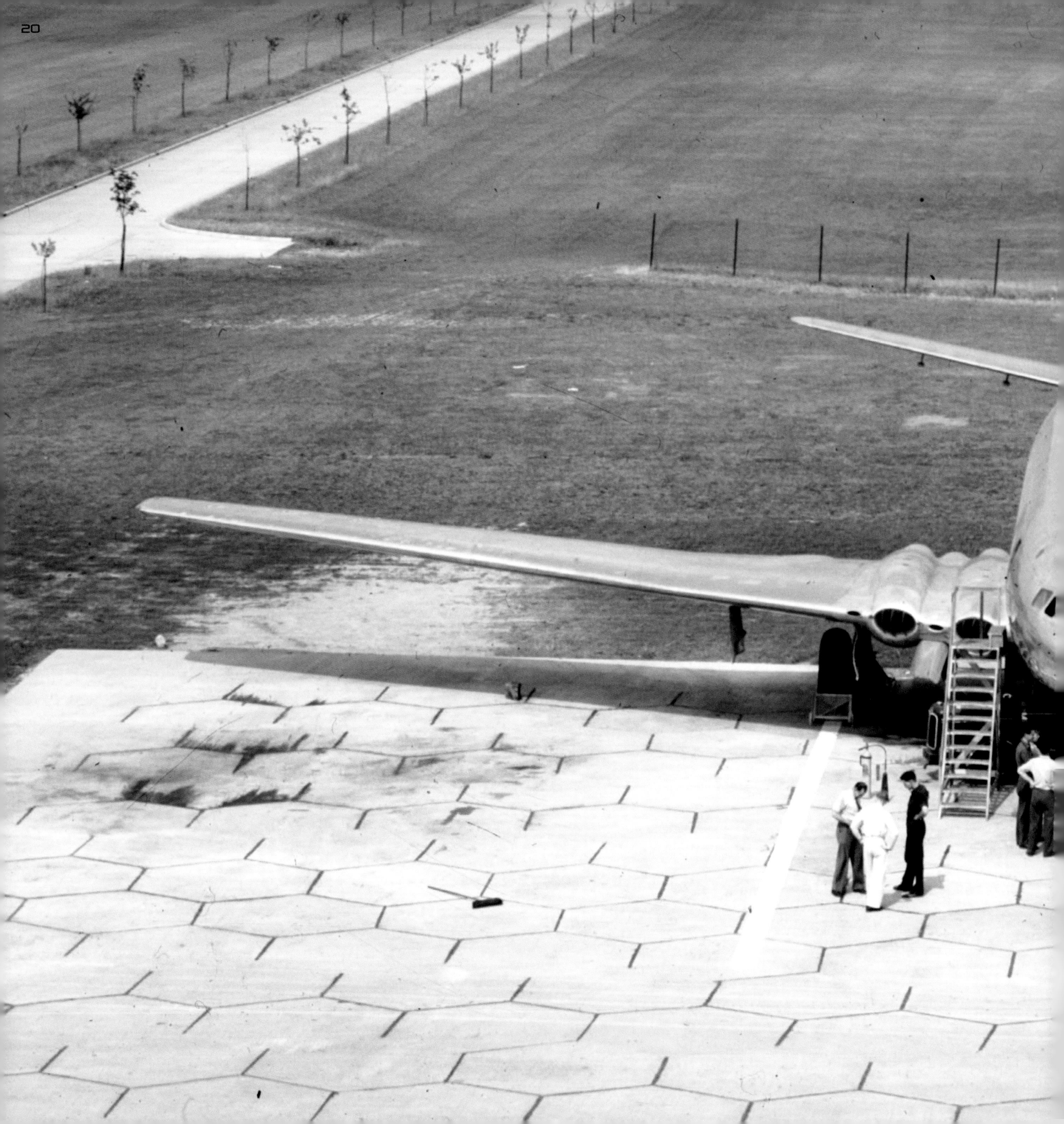

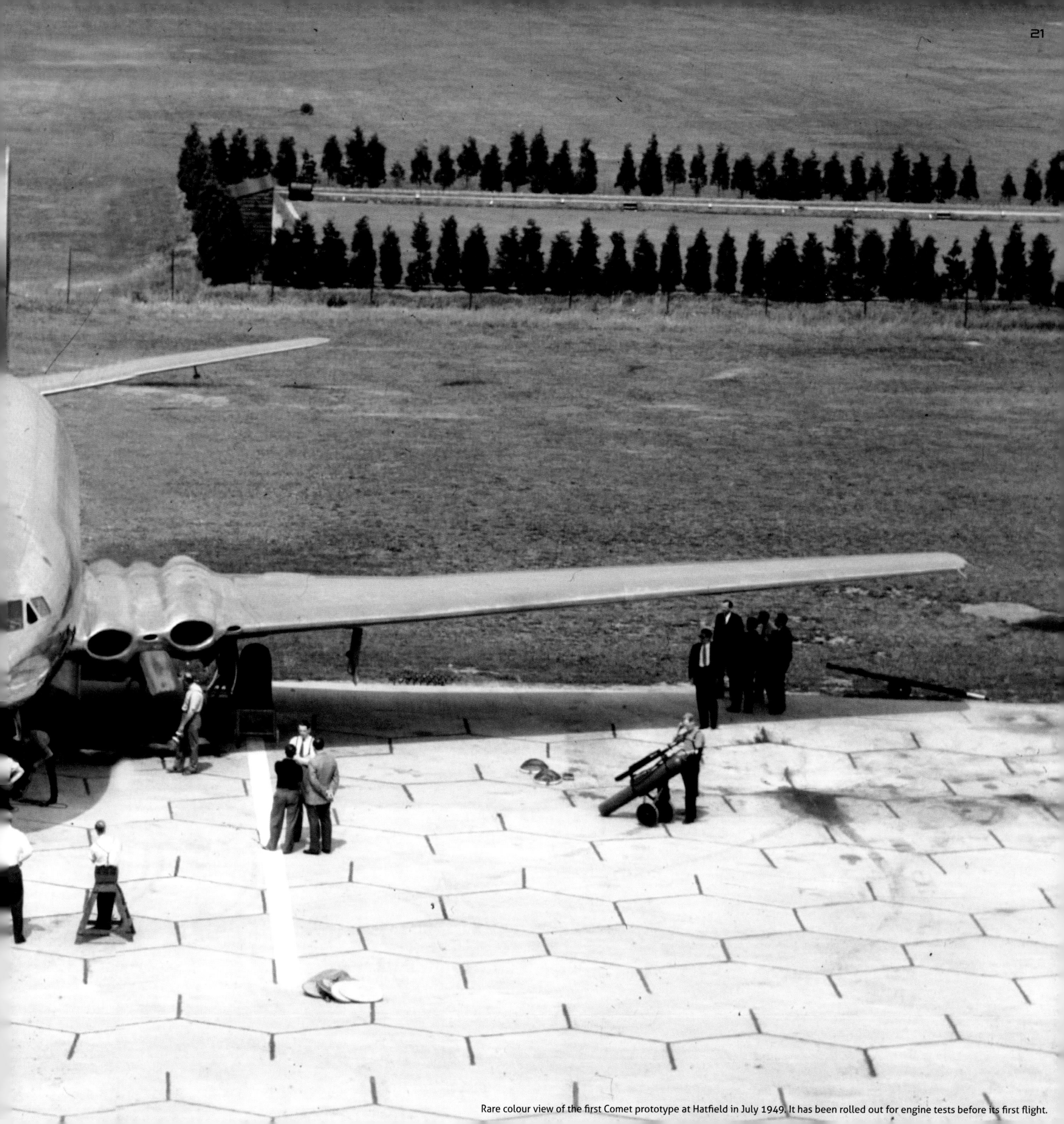

Rare colour view of the first Comet prototype at Hatfield in July 1949. It has been rolled out for engine tests before its first flight.

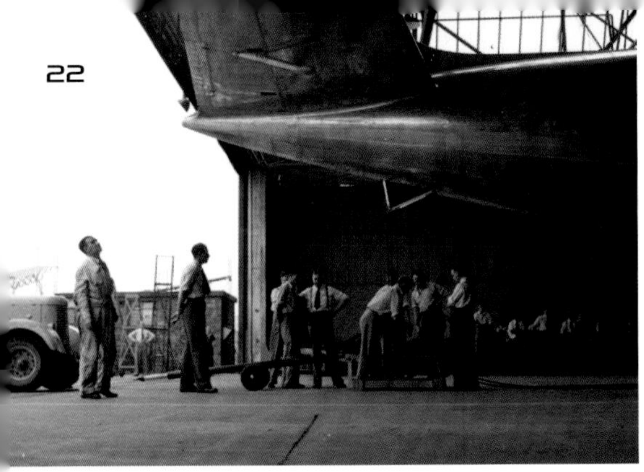

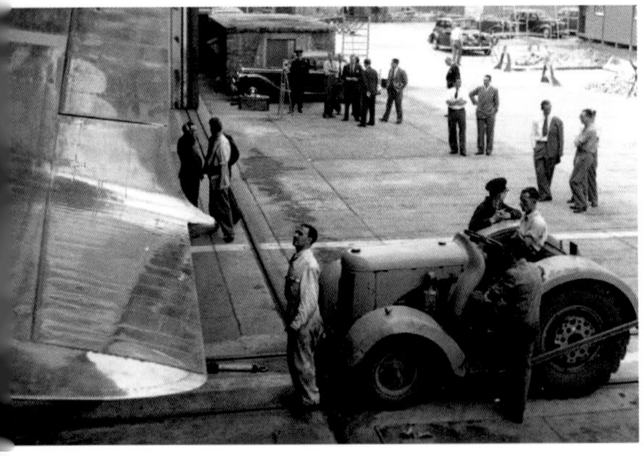

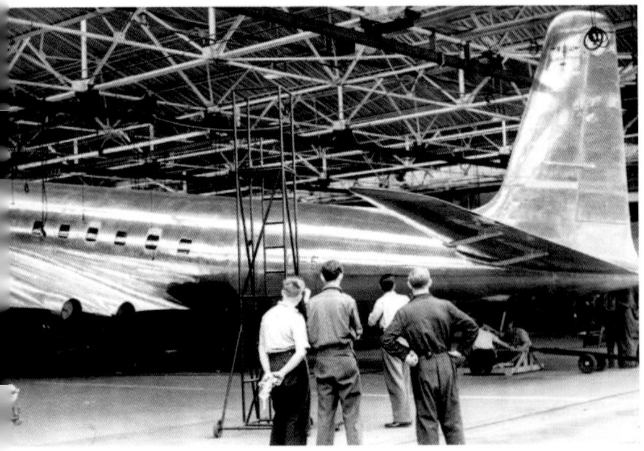

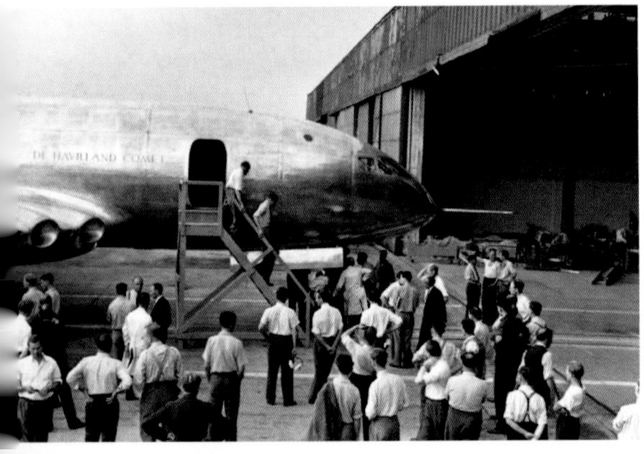
DE HAVILLAND COMET

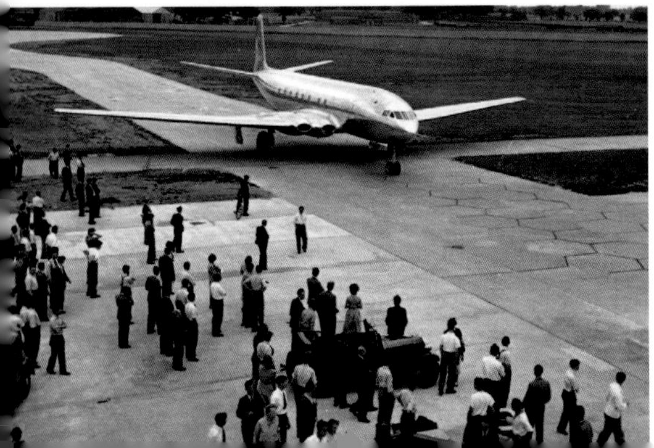

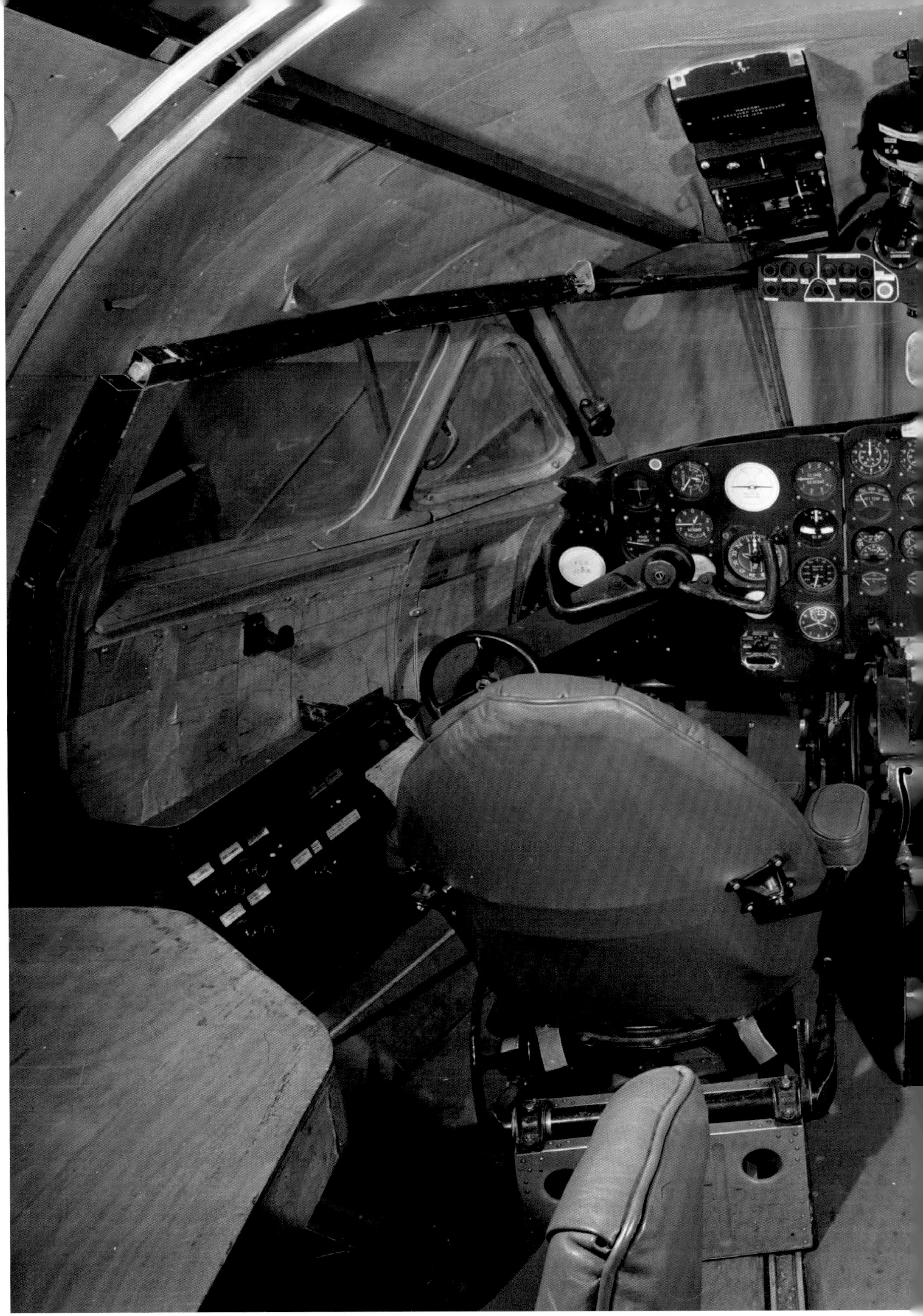

ABOVE: The spacious but still incomplete flight deck of the Comet prototype owned by the Ministry of Supply and displaying the Class B marking G-5-1. It later carried the registration G-ALVG. The navigator's seat and table are just visible, bottom left.
LEFT TOP TO BOTTOM: preparing the prototype Comet for its first flight, Hatfield, July 1949.

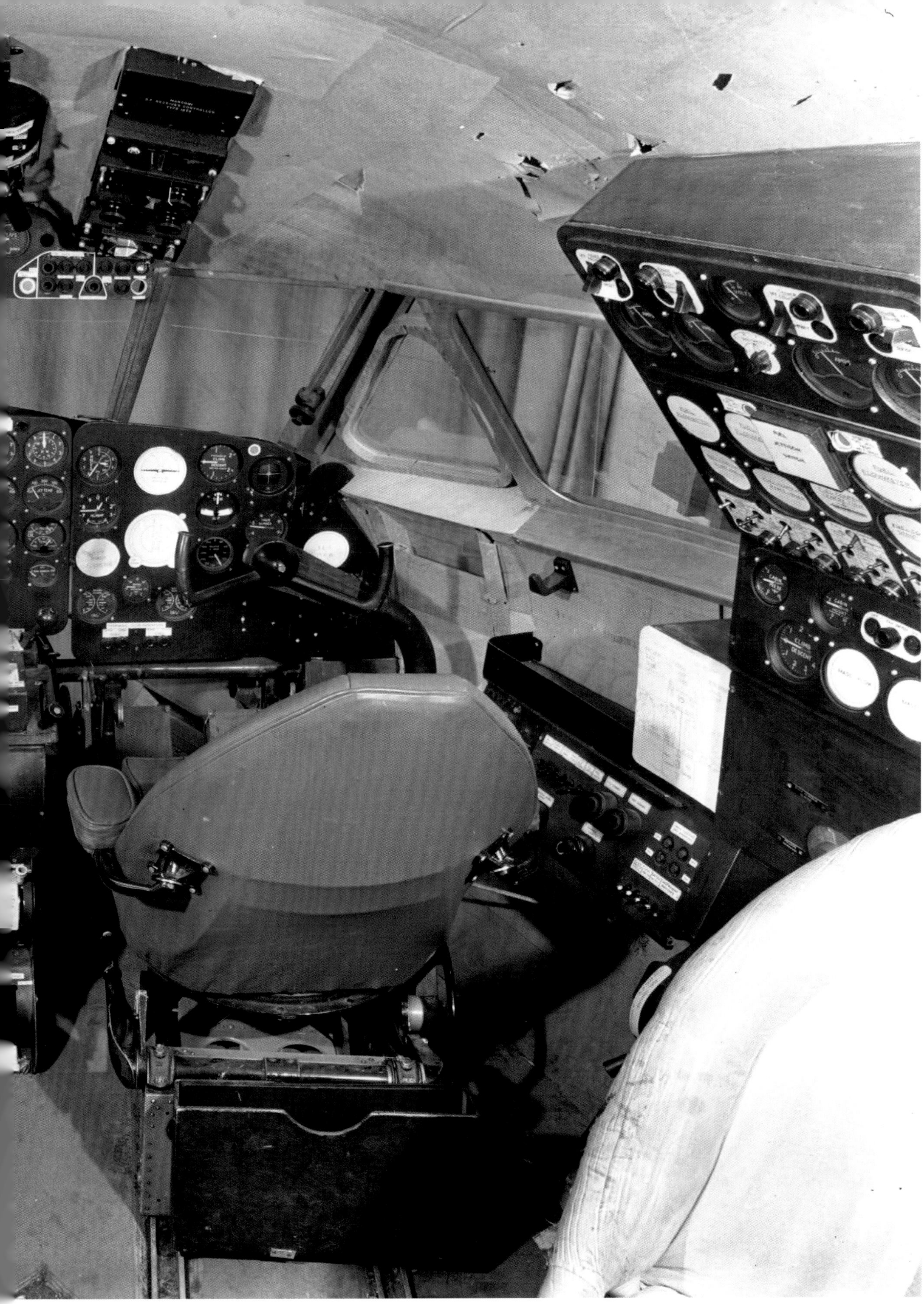

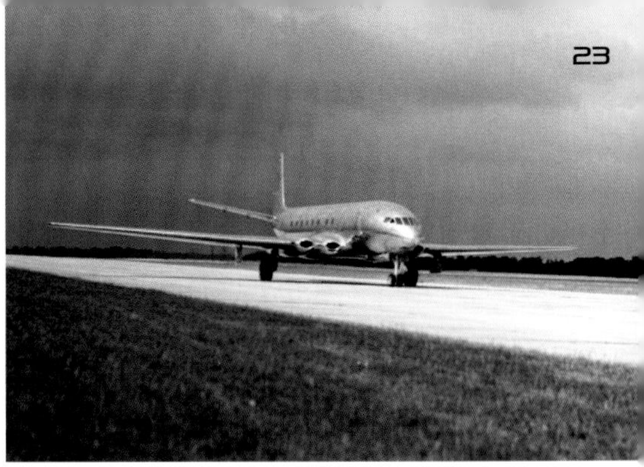

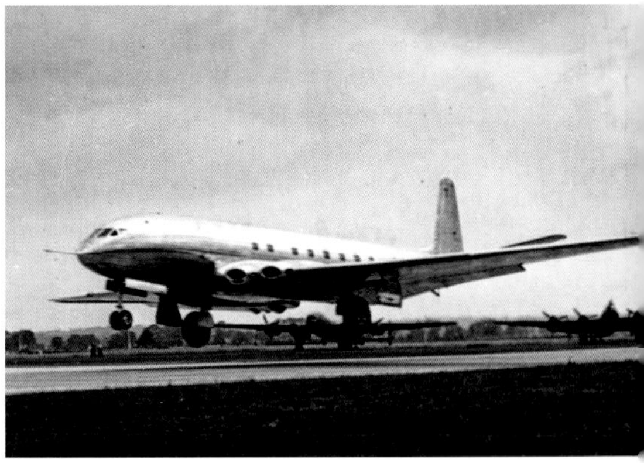

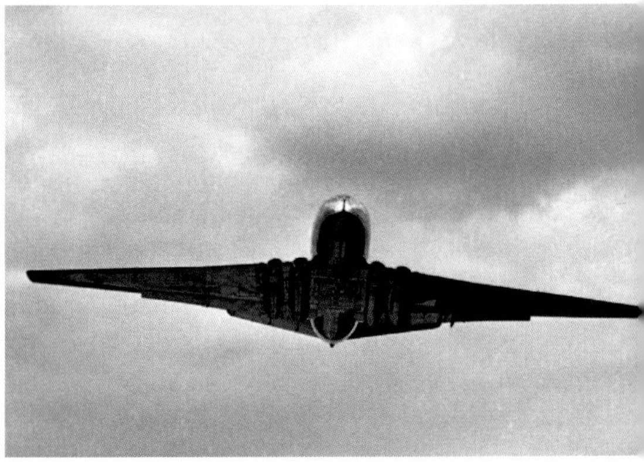

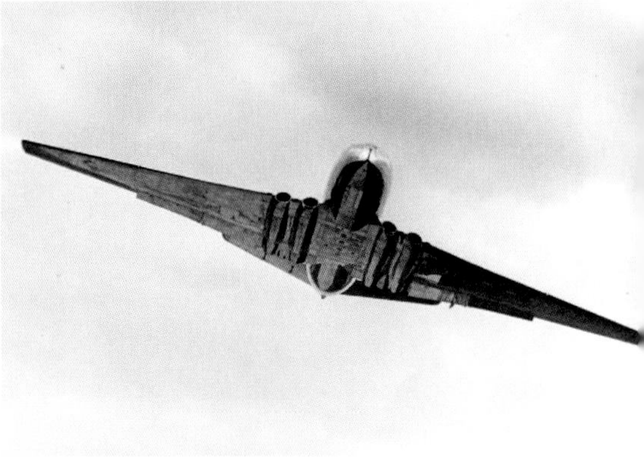

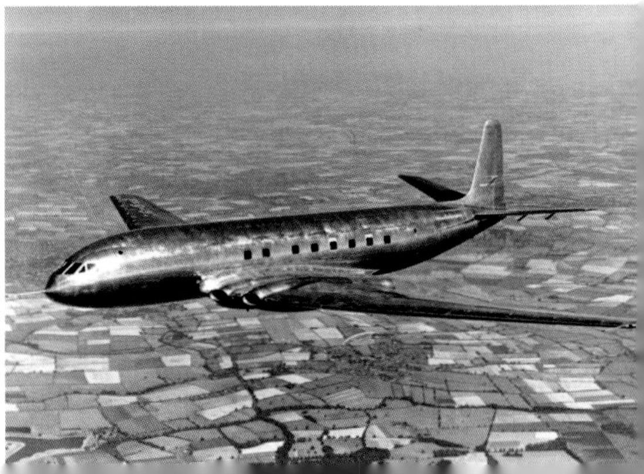

TOP TO BOTTOM: On 27 July 1949 the Comet made a high speed run and a short hop before its first flight with chief test pilot John Cunningham in command.

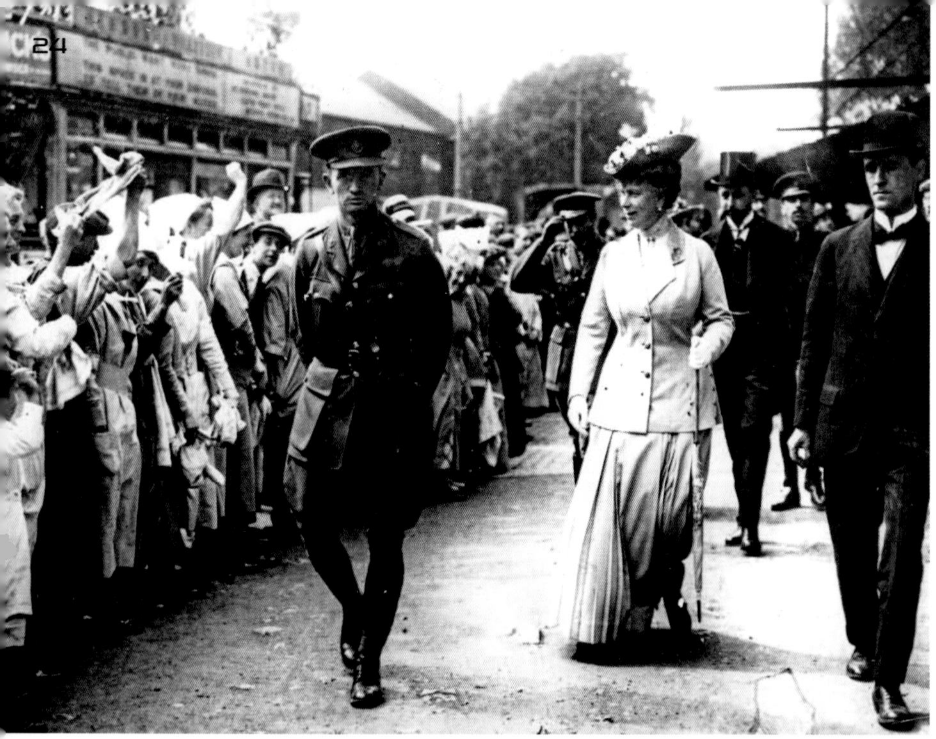

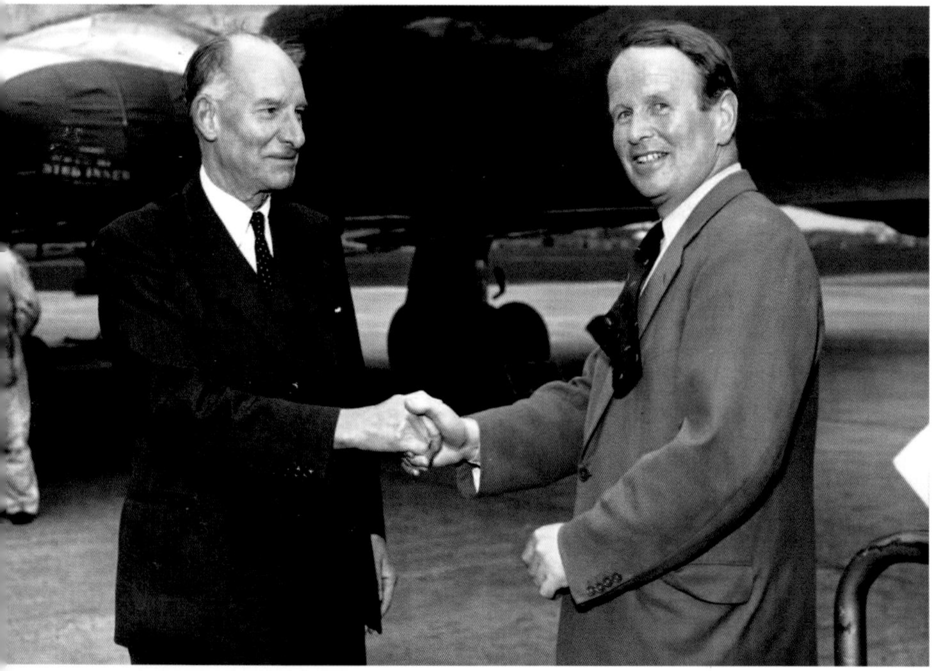

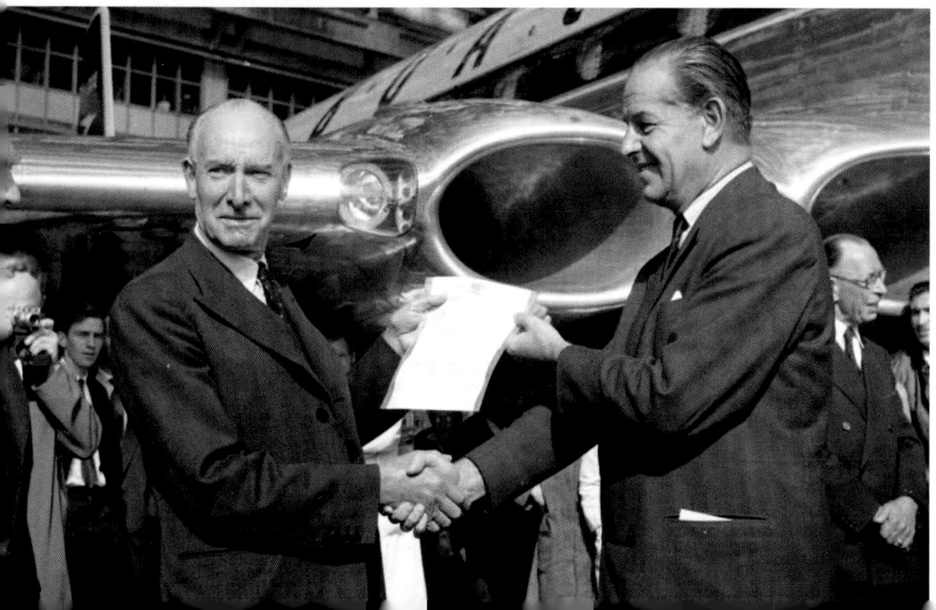

Geoffrey De Havilland and his company

The man who built the world's first jet airliner was the son of a curate who wrecked his first aircraft before it had even taken off.

Half a century later Geoffrey de Havilland was head of a well-known and highly -respected aircraft company which had built 46,000 aircraft, 9,000 jet engines and 115,000 propellers. Among its best-known creations were the Mosquito, considered to be the most versatile combat aircraft ever built, the Vampire, one of the world's first jet fighters, and, of course, the epoch-making Comet.

De Havilland was born in 1882 the second son of the Rev Charles de Havilland and his first wife. Although destined to follow his father into the church he opted instead to study engineering and between 1900 and 1903 attended Crystal Palace engineering school. One of his first engineering accomplishments was the design and construction of a motor cycle on which he commuted between the school and his home in Hampshire.

He started work in the motor industry but, bored with work as a draughtsman for the Wolseley company he left after six months and joined the Motor Omnibus Construction company. He was, however, inspired by the achievements of the Wright Brothers and by Louis Bleriot and borrowed money from his grandmother to build his first aircraft.

Despite its lack of success de Havilland sold his second machine to the government balloon factory at Farnborough for £400. The establishment, which was later to become the Royal Aircraft Factory, also hired him as a designer and test pilot and re-named his aircraft the FE1. For the next three years de Havilland designed several other types but he was unhappy with his next appointment, as an inspector of aircraft in the Aeronautical Inspection Department, because it took him away from his drawing board.

In May 1914 he left to become chief designer at Airco for which he designed a number of aircraft which used his initials in their designation. Large numbers of DH machines such as the DH4 and DH9 bombers were used by the Royal Flying Corps and later the Royal Air Force. The DH4 was also built in the USA. When Airco was bought out its new owner was more interested in its factories than its products.

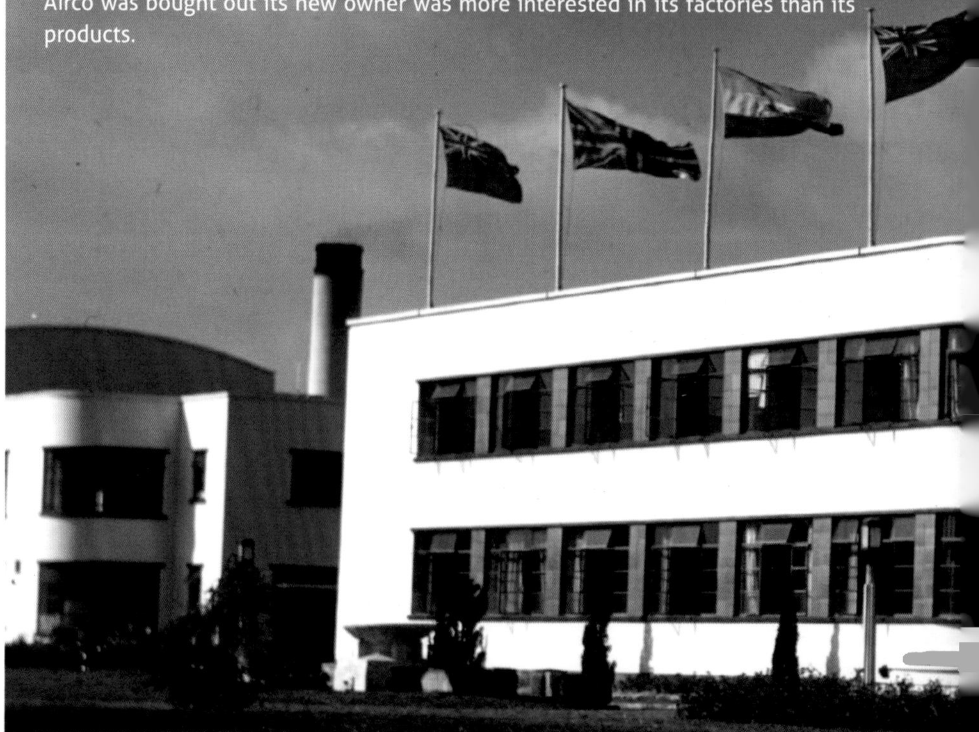

LEFT TOP TO BOTTOM: Three images from the life and career of Geoffrey de Havilland. Top: during a Royal visit to the Aircraft Manufacturing Company, Hendon, 1917, with Queen Mary and the company's founder, George Holt Thomas (right). King George V is behind the Queen and to her right; (middle) with de Havilland's chief test pilot, John Cunningham and (bottom) Officially handing over the first Comet 4, G-APDC, to BOAC Chairman, Sir Gerard D'Erlanger, on 30 September 1958.

Accordingly, de Havilland raised £20,000 to buy the assets he needed to start his own company and in 1920 the de Havilland Aircraft Company was established at Stag Lane aerodrome, Edgware. It was there that de Havilland assembled a talented team which included engine designer Frank Halford and Ronald Bishop who later became chief designer.

The new company's products included the ten-strong Moth family of light aircraft as well as airliners like the DH34 and the three-engined DH66 Hercules used by Imperial Airways. Other highly successful designs were the Dragon, Rapide and Dragonfly light transports.

In 1933 the company moved to Hatfield aerodrome and the following year its DH88 Comet twin-engined long-distance racing aircraft won the prestigious Mildenhall to Melbourne air race. Its wooden construction foreshadowed the elegant Albatross four-engined airliner which was noted for its purity of line and aerodynamic efficiency. The company also built the all-metal DH95 Flamingo.

On the outbreak of the Second World War de Havilland pledged to concentrate on supporting Britain's war effort which was notably achieved with the astonishing Mosquito, 8,000 of which were built as bomber, fighter and reconnaissance variants.

De Havilland was an early convert to the advantages of jet propulsion and the company's twin-boom Vampire, powered by the Halford-designed Goblin, was Britain's second operational jet fighter. It sold in large numbers and many were exported. A developed version, the Venom, used the more powerful Ghost engine which also powered the first Comets.

De Havilland had three sons two of whom died in test flying crashes. He was also affected by the loss of two BOAC Comets in 1954. *"There is no denying that we had been through a period of what might be called 'technical depression' during which difficulties loomed greater than they really were,"* he declared in his autobiography Sky Fever. *"Uncertainty and waiting can be mentally devastating."*

Knighted in 1944 de Havilland retired from active involvement in his company's affairs in 1955 although he remained its president. He continued flying up to the age of 70 and died of a cerebral haemorrhage in 1965.

He had, however, lived long enough to see the rationalisation of the British aircraft industry in 1960 during which de Havilland's company was merged into Hawker Siddeley. In 1977 there was a further merger, with the rival British Aircraft Corporation to form the nationalised British Aerospace.

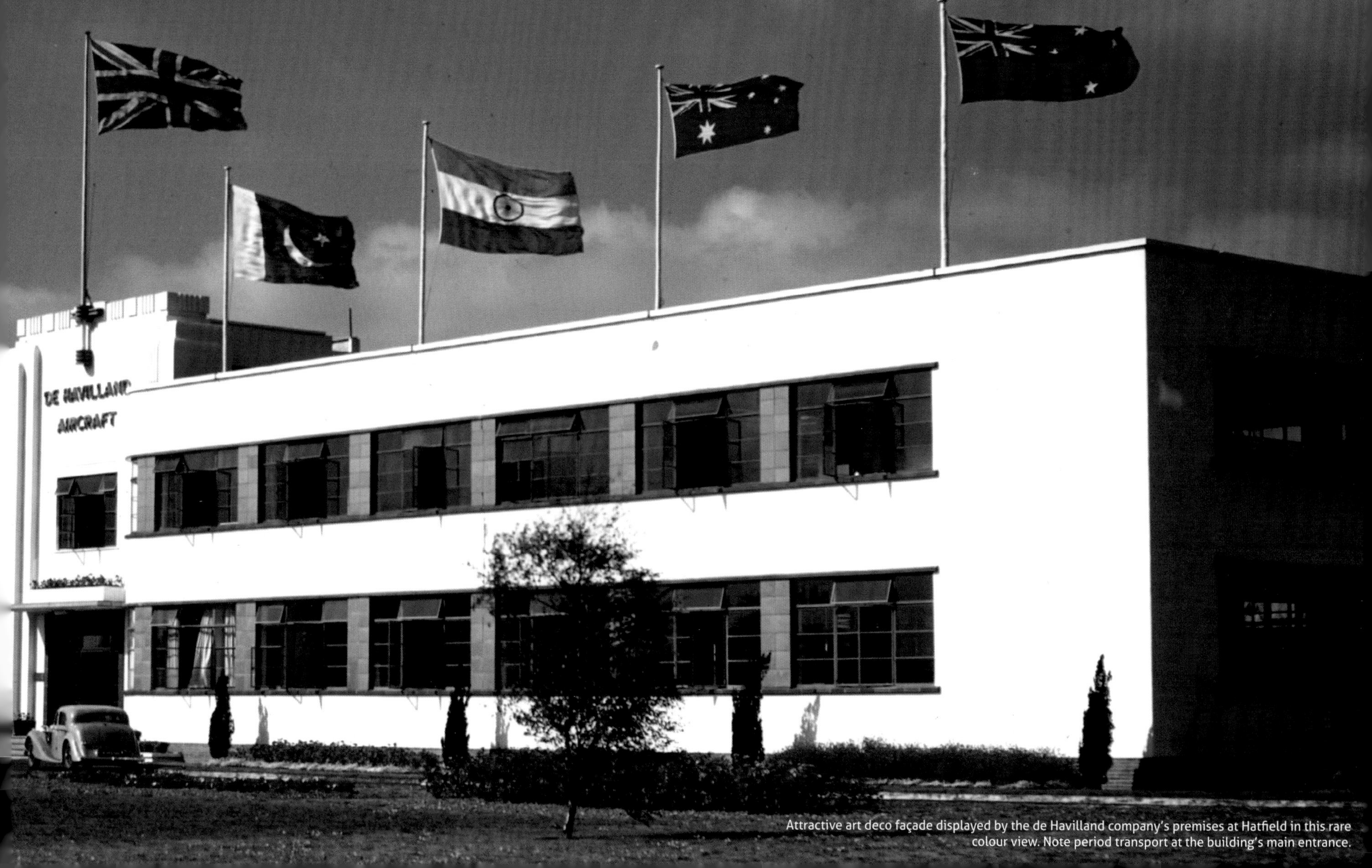
AIRCRAFT

Attractive art deco façade displayed by the de Havilland company's premises at Hatfield in this rare colour view. Note period transport at the building's main entrance.

THE COMET'S CONSTRUCTION

A Beautiful Beast

32'-1" OVERALL CABIN LENGTH
TOTAL CABIN CAPACITY 1800 CU. FT.
7'-6"
HAT RACK
WARDROBE
CAPACITY: 61 CU. FT.
9'-9" INTERNAL DIA
6'-6"5 HEADROOM
17"0 GANGWAY
8'-11"75 FLOOR WIDTH
SPACE FOR PRESSURIZING EQUIPMENT BATTERIES ETC.
LUGGAGE COMPARTMENT
CAPACITY: 140 CU. FT.
ACCESS DOOR
3'-9"
CHAIR SPACING
LUGGAGE COMPARTMENT
ACCESS DOOR
SMOKE ROOM FOR 8 PASSENGERS
CHAIRS WITH ADJUSTABLE BACKS
ONLY. CAPACITY: 420 CU. FT.
MAIN CABIN FOR 24 PASSENGERS
FULLY ADJUSTABLE CHAIRS
CAPACITY: 1380 CU. FT.
CURTAIN
GENTLEMENS WASH ROOM
CAPACITY: 109 CU. FT.
GENTLEMENS TOILET
CAPACITY: 68 CU. FT.
RADIO OPERATOR
CREW ENTRY DOOR
BAR STOWAGE
FIRST OFFICER AND ENGINEER
CREW'S TOILET
GALLEY
LADIES' TOILET
CAPACITY: 58 CU. FT.
LUGGAGE & FREIGHT HOLD
CAPACITY: 400 CU. FT.
LADIES' POWDER ROOM
CAPACITY: 113 CU. FT.
CAPTAIN
TOTAL CAPACITY OF CONTROL CABIN: 383 CU. FT.
NAVIGATOR
DISPENSING COUNTER ON DOOR
SEAT AND TABLE FOR STEWARDESS
PASSENGER ENTRY DOOR
STEWARDESS'S LOCKER
ALTERNATIVE ACCOMMODATION
8 ROWS OF 4 CHAIRS AT 45" SPACING FACING FORWARD
9 ROWS OF 4 CHAIRS AT 39" SPACING FACING FORWARD
D.H. 106
INTERIOR LAY-OUT
32 SEATER
[redacted]

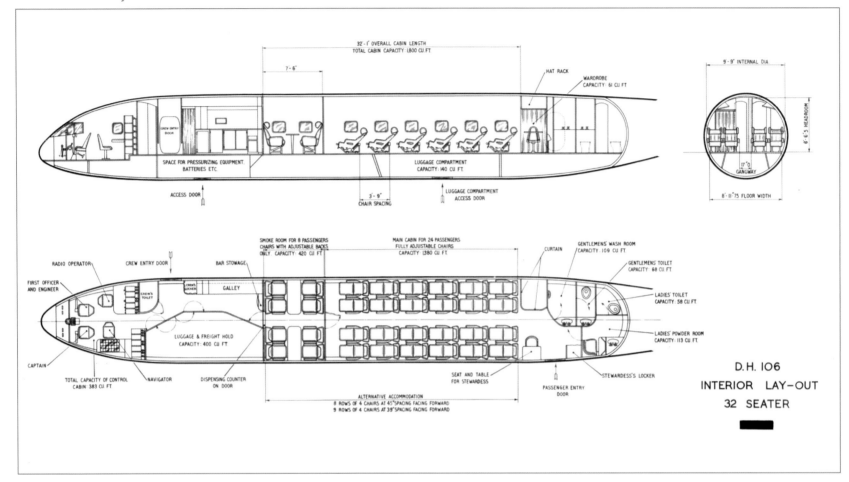

When it appeared in public for the first time the design of the Comet was revealed as less radical than it might have been and certainly as some observers had been led to expect.

Yet, appropriately enough for an aircraft whose introduction into passenger service would change air travel forever, the Comet bristled with innovative features in virtually every part of its aerodynamics, structure, propulsion and systems.

Further novel ideas were incorporated in the way it was built. Examples included extensive use of metal-to-metal bonding, which avoided conventional rivets, and advanced tooling.

Overall the Comet was an all-metal aircraft with a low-mounted wing whose 20- degree sweep resulted mainly from its taper. The tail was un-swept and its horizontal surfaces incorporated 10-degrees of dihedral. The major novelty was, of course, the pair of turbojet engines buried in each wing root.

The wings were built in a new plant built on the site of a Vickers factory at Hawarden airfield near Chester where Wellington bombers had been built during the war. Today Airbus wings are made there. The Comet wing itself incorporated three widely separated spars which passed through the fuselage under the floor. The inboard section of the wing on each side was bulged to house the 5,050lb (2291kg) thrust de Havilland Ghost engines. Plain oval intakes in the leading edges, one for each engine, admitted air while long jet pipes protruded just behind the trailing edge.

Each engine was carried on two simple trunnion bearings incorporating Metalastik bushes to prevent the transmission of high-frequency vibration to the rest of the airframe. The main engine air intake ducts were attached to the engine by a single toggle fastener. The lengthy jet pipes were secured by four clamps which, when released, permitted the pipe to slide rearwards on runners.

Engine bays were divided into three compartments by steel fire walls. The bays incorporated fire extinguishing nozzles or spray rings. Beneath the main intake duct of each inner engine was a further small intake intended to supply the cabin air heat exchanger. Access panels were provided above and below the engines. The wing sections outboard of the engines were used to accommodate integral fuel tanks.

Large plain flaps were fitted with split flaps under the jet pipes. The leading edge was fixed with a small wing fence mounted on each wing well outboard and ahead of the inner end of the powered aileron. Narrow perforated air brakes could be raised ahead of the outer flap sections. Thickness ratio was 11 percent.

William Tamblin was in charge of wing design. His main challenge was to produce a strong structure around the buried engines despite the potential source of weakness they offered. The first Comet had a lower stalling speed and was said to be easier to fly in some respects than contemporary piston engined airliners. The fact that the wing was later adopted for the Nimrod maritime patrol aircraft indicates that Tamblin's design stood the test of time.

The circular tube fuselage had a diameter of 10ft (3.05m). It was intended to retain a cabin environment representing 8,000ft (2,440m) while travelling at 40,000ft (12,190m). This was double the pressure of any previous airliner. The structure also had to withstand low outside temperatures, which also had a profound effect on materials throughout the airframe.

The pressurisation system broke new ground. Fresh air was bled at high pressure from the engine compressor and mixed with hot air from the turbine. It was then passed through a system of heat exchangers, humidifiers, regulators and silencers, which eliminated the need for cabin blowers, heaters and associated drives. It also featured extensive redundancy; if required any of the engines could be taken out of the circuit without affecting system performance.

Inevitably, the design of the pressure cabin was the subject of some controversy. In a detailed analysis of the Comet's engineering published in May 1953 Flight noted: *"Much has been made in the United States of the dire consequences of windows blowing out at 40,000ft."*

As Flight pointed out, *"The de Havilland company have approached the undisputed problem by treating windows as though they were part of the basic airframe and stressing them accordingly. In fact, not only have Comet windows been tested to 100lb per sq in but another has been pressurised to 8.25lb per sq in daily for several years and cleaned regularly with scratch-remover as are windows in service. The Air Registration Board is quoted as saying that explosive decompression at 40,000ft shouldn't happen 'any oftener than a wing falling off.'"* This seems an unfortunate remark in view of later developments.

A key innovation was the use of Redux metal bonding throughout the aircraft's structure to reduce weight, simplify manufacture, result in a smoother exterior skin and ease pressurisation and tank sealing issues. In effect a process of gluing under pressure, Redux had never before been used on such a scale or on such highly stressed parts. Also novel was its use for large double curvature areas of the structure.

De Havilland already had sufficient experience of Redux from its use on the Dove to be confident that it could safely be applied to the Comet. Even so the company was widely considered to be extremely bold in its adoption on the first jet airliner. Not only was it employed to attach minor stringers and stiffeners but also for primary airframe joints such as those between spar booms and webs, between large fuselage stringers and between window frames and the skin.

The Redux process had been invented in 1943 by Aero Research Limited of Duxford, Cambridgeshire, a company which had been involved with de Havilland since pre-war days and produced adhesive used in the Mosquito. As a bonding system it essentially involved mixing two chemicals, phenol formaldehyde resin and polyvinyl formal, which was used as a toughening agent.

The resin was applied to the surface to be bonded and the hardening agent applied to the wet resin. The two surfaces were mated under heat and pressure using a special heated press. Rivets were used to ensure that the mating surfaces bonded correctly during the curing process. Far fewer were used than in a purely riveted structure.

Despite its comparative novelty Redux proved to be one of the most durable adhesive bonding systems. Many years later this was confirmed by forensic analysis of bonded airframe stringers from a 30-year-old Comet. The Nimrod maritime patrol aircraft developed from the Comet used the Redux technique in essentially the same form as on the original airliner.

Also controversial was the provision of doors. The Comet featured two main doors, one aft on the port side for passengers and one on the starboard side of the forward fuselage for the crew. The passenger door opened inwards as did the crew door although it had a more complex mechanism. Neither found favour with the US Civil Aeronautics Administration which preferred outward opening doors on the grounds that they facilitated quicker passenger evacuation in an emergency.

The Comet made extensive use of hydraulic power for a variety of applications including primary and secondary flying controls, landing gear retraction, nose wheel steering, flaps, wheel and air brakes. To cope with the demand and provide back-up the airliner featured five separate hydraulic systems each colour coded to aid maintenance.

These de Havilland-designed systems were driven by separate pumps on each engine. Back-up was provided by electric pumps. Normal working pressure was 2,500lb/sq in. It was considered that as long as the aircraft could muster enough power to keep it airborne at least one hydraulic circuit would be available with

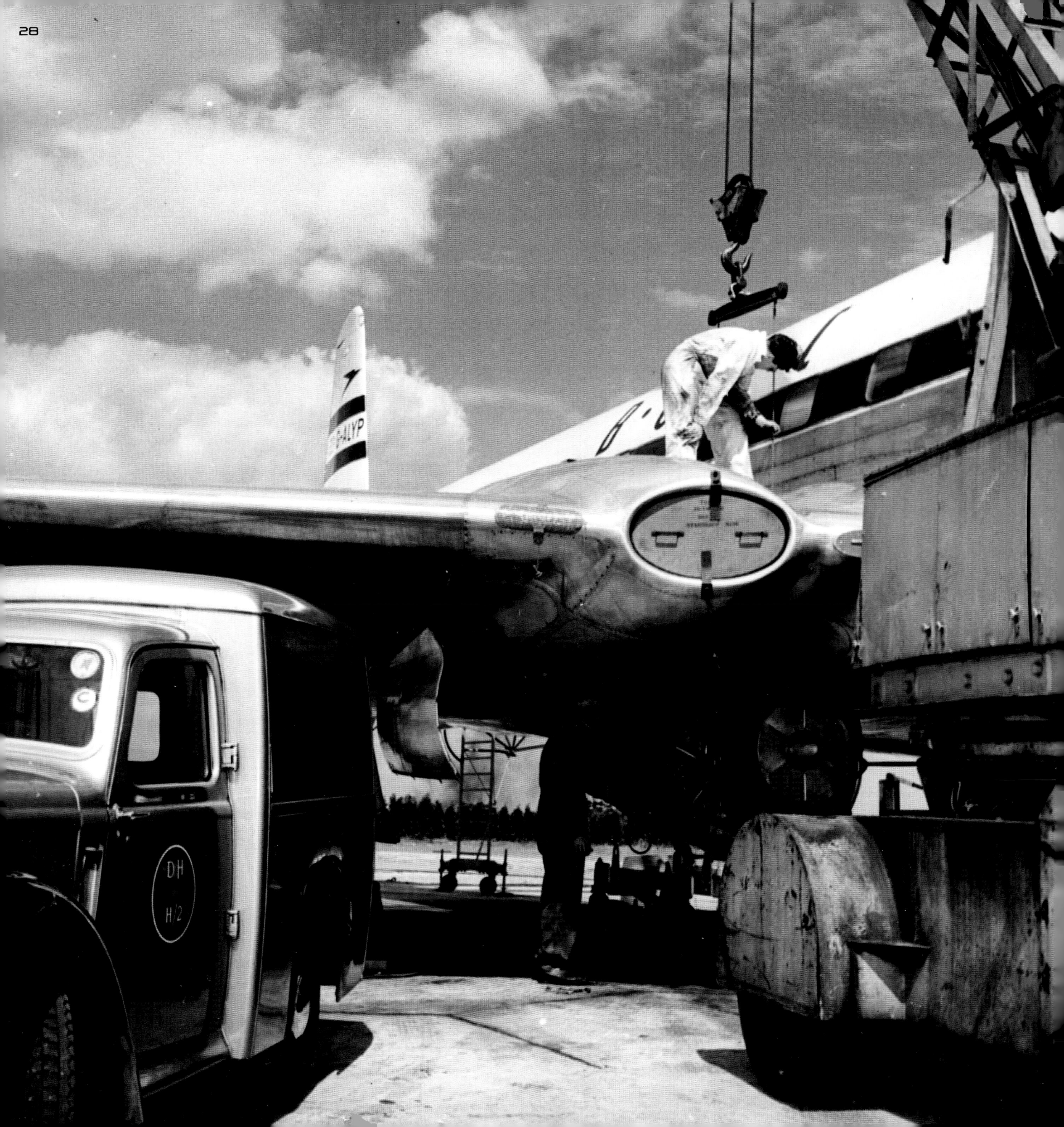
G-ALYP
DH
H/2

battery-powered circuits in reserve.

The Servodyne flying controls had been extensively tested before their application to the Comet. The intention had been to provide sufficient feel, although in practice pilots were to find that they needed time to become accustomed to the system. Trimming was provided by screw-actuated spring-loaded tabs.

The Comet 1 carried all its 5,976 gallons of fuel in the wings. This posed a challenge to the designers to find enough space for the required tankage in the thin structures. Although there was a bag tank in the centre-section under the cabin floor most of the fuel was contained in integral tanks formed by the outer wing structure. There were two immersed pumps in each tank and they could be removed through the access doors under the wing without the tanks having to be drained first.

Alternators were mounted on each engine to provide power for the aircraft's extensive electrical needs. Like the selenium rectifiers, which controlled the 28V delivery and were mounted in leading edge bays, the large three-phase alternators were blast-cooled. Much of the Comet's electrical equipment was contained in a pressurised bay under the forward fuselage floor. The bay was big enough for up to three men to work in it simultaneously. It also housed much of the aircraft's air conditioning and hydraulic components and was accessible both from the ground and in flight.

De-icing was accomplished by piping heated air from the main engine compressors along the leading edges of the wings and tail surfaces. Oil used to cool the rear bearing of each engine was then piped to keep the front of the unit, particularly the front bearing, clear of ice.

Apart from the two prototypes the Comet was the first airliner to feature a

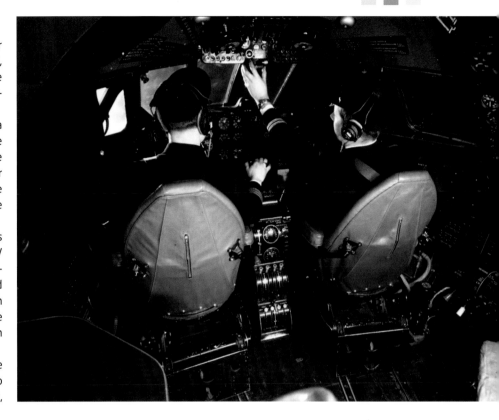

bogie main undercarriage. The units were built around large light-alloy forgings and each featured eight wheels. Ribbed Dunlop 35.00 X 17 tyres were fitted and operated at a pressure of 115 lb/sq in. Tyres lasted for around 100 landings. But the ribbed pattern were soon replaced by another featuring dimples rather than ribs.

The two-wheel nose gear units utilised power steering but were unbraked. The main gears featured duplicated Dunlop disc brakes – 16 for each unit. In 1952 the original type of discs were replaced by others with increased thickness designed to cope better with what were considered to be the worst-case accelerate-stop requirements without overheating. Being thicker also meant they could be machined to compensate for wear and grooving.

The Comet 1 featured a Sperry Zero Reader which presented the crew with a unified picture derived from the gyro-compass, altimeter, artificial horizon and ILS indicator. This equipment was found to be reliable in service. Early production aircraft had two Mach meters, one of which featured an audible warning horn which sounded at Mach 0.76.

Comet crews included a radio officer and considering the complex range of communications and navigation equipment carried it is likely he was kept busy. Duplicate ADF, HF and VHF equipment was featured together with an ILS receiver as well as other navigation equipment such as the ex-RAF Rebecca and ex-USAF Loran. The installation was similar to that found on contemporary BOAC aircraft like the Argonaut and Hermes and so was considered to be well-proved in service. Yet the need for smaller, more modern equipment for the Comet was acknowledged even then.

LEFT AND ABOVE: BOAC's first Comet 1 G-ALYP pictured during an engine change with a de Havilland Engines support vehicle in attendance.
TOP RIGHT: Navigator's view of the Comet 1 flight deck.

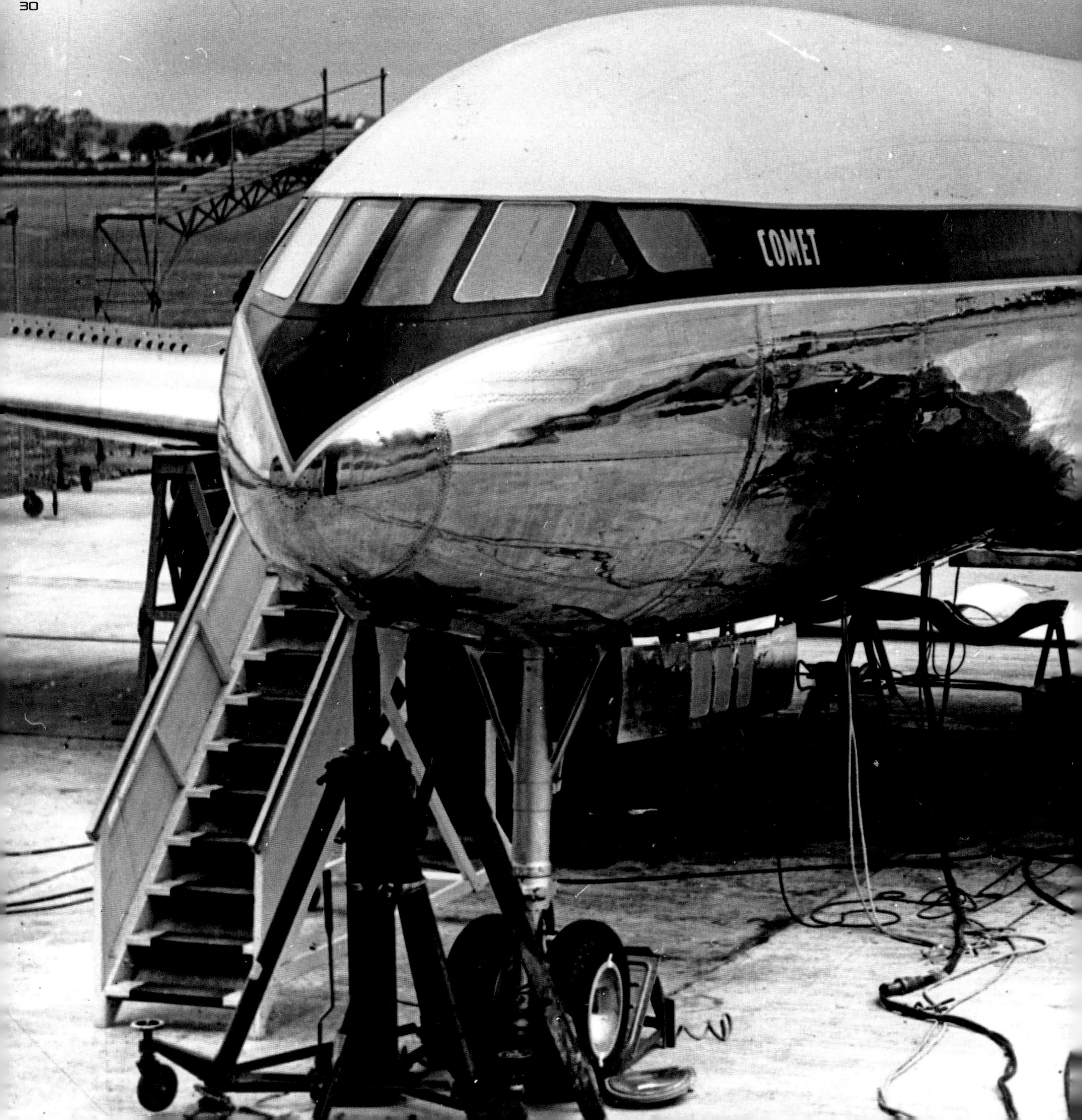
COMET

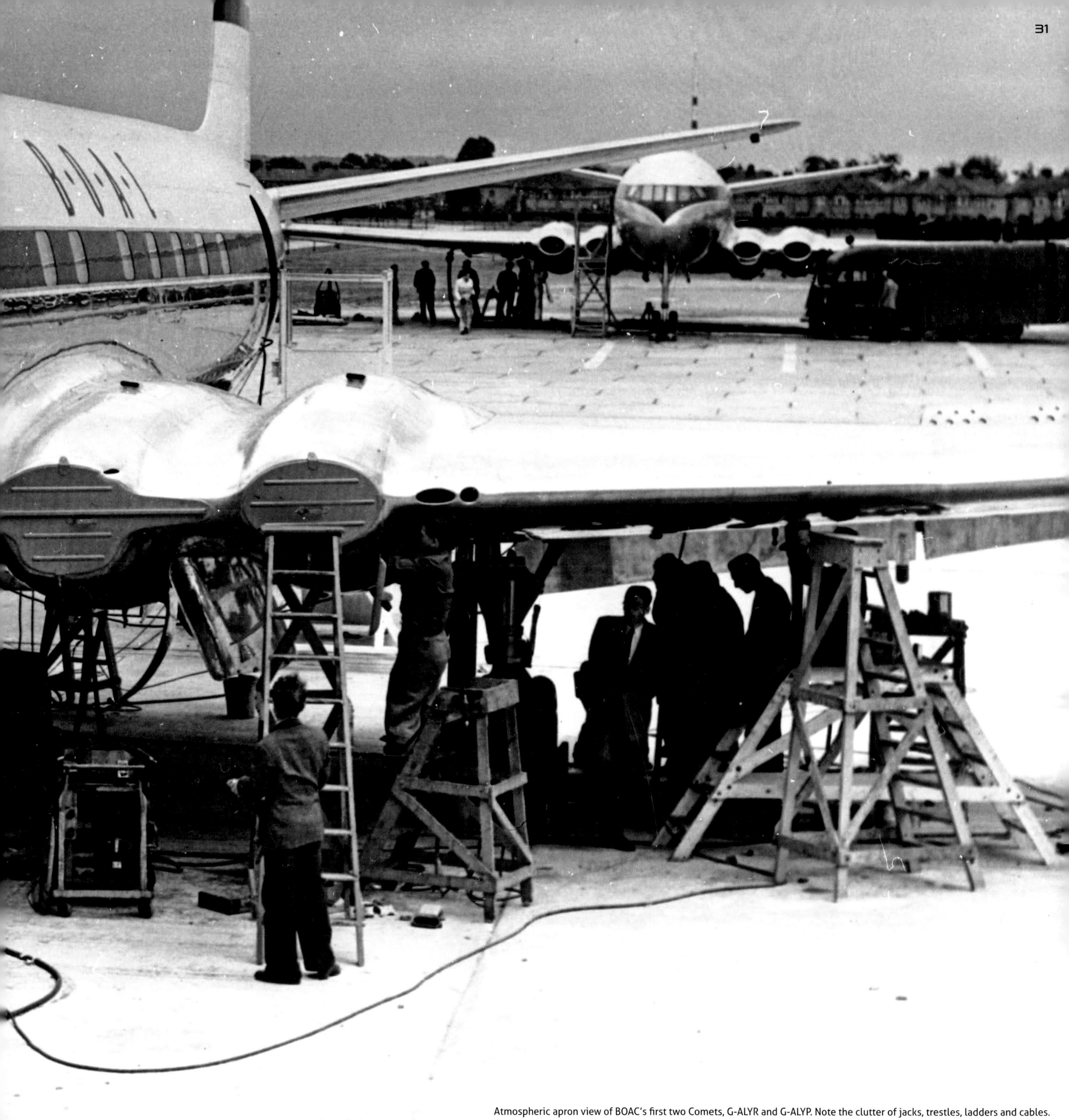
B·O·A·C

Atmospheric apron view of BOAC's first two Comets, G-ALYR and G-ALYP. Note the clutter of jacks, trestles, ladders and cables.

If the external shape of the Comet still looks reasonably modern even after six decades its interior lay-out definitely marks the aircraft as something from an earlier age. For a start the flight deck provided stations for four crew members: behind the co-pilot was the radio officer's rearward-facing seat with that of the navigator, plus table, facing to starboard.

BOAC's Comet 1s had 36 passenger seats in two cabins. Behind the forward crew stations and pantry was the first class cabin with eight seats, the forward one facing aft.

In terms of décor and furnishings much was expected from de Havilland and BOAC. According to Flight, which in September 1951 featured a detailed description of the aircraft's interior, they did not disappoint. *"It is perhaps quite enough to say that the interior of the Comet is a perfect complement to the beauty of the aircraft as a machine,"* the journal trilled.

It went on to wax lyrical about the *"remarkably beautiful weathered syca-more veneer beneath a plastic surface"* used for doors and walls, complemented by dark blue wool pile carpeting. In the passenger cabin the carpet extended up the base of the walls. The *"spacious"* rear entry foyer led to the main passenger cabin with seven rows of what were referred to as *"armchairs."* They were, however, standard BOAC "Overseas" Mk 4 units upholstered in foam rubber and covered in a herringbone weave blue wool-faced tapestry.

They were also described as being *"sumptuous receivers of the human body."* Seat pitch at a generous 46in (117cm) would indeed certainly be considered sumptuous by 21st century travellers. The windows were surrounded by beige-grey plastic material and there were red and white striped curtains. Walls and ceilings were finished in pale grey leather cloth. Open overhead racks running the length of the cabin were provided to carry small items of carry-on baggage.

Aft of the main passenger cabin and the entry foyer were two dressing rooms, port for ladies, starboard for gentlemen. In the ladies' compartment there was

Rare period colour shots of the BOAC Comet 1 cabin mock-up. Note the comfortable-looking chairs and soft furnishings from the days long before the lidded overhead luggage locker.

smoke grey nylon carpeting and grey leather cloth covered walls to provide a contrast with the delicate pink furnishings. Above the pink wash basin was a larger mirror with a ring tray and compartments for face tissues. Facing aft was a fixed seat for the fitted dressing table with bottles of lotions and creams.

Male passengers were clearly not offered "a boudoir" but the gentlemen's' dressing room was described as striking "a nice balance between masculinity and the sybaritic." PVC covered the floor and the wash-basin was of silver anodised light alloy. At the rear of each dressing room was a self-flushing toilet.

Other items not found on 21st century airliners included a drinking fountain and library at the rear of the main cabin. There was also a full-length wardrobe between the cabin and the entry foyer.

Tooling for production aircraft had to be achieved in a relatively short period despite the use of new processes and techniques. A key element was close liaison between the design team and production department. In a lecture to the Royal Aeronautical Society in April 1951 de Havilland's production director Harry Povey described the importance the company attached to this contact.

Povey, a veteran de Havilland man who had spent three years in Canada during the Second World War organising Mosquito production, said that he and his chief production engineer attended all design progress conferences. This enabled the production team to gain advance knowledge of design requirements and adopt a flexible approach to production needs so that timely decisions could be taken.

The Comet was widely regarded as an elegant machine whose beauty was its key recognition feature. In its Recognition Manual published in 1952 the Air League described the Comet as "perhaps the most aesthetically satisfying aircraft in the world today, quite apart from its quality as a flying machine." The world's first jet airliner was, it added, "a beautiful beast, sleek and unmistakable from any angle and any distance."

The Ghost in the Machine

The de Havilland Ghost engine was a development of the earlier Goblin which made its maiden flight in a Gloster Meteor, Britain's first operational jet fighter, in March 1943. This was just 11 months after its first test-bed run. The Goblin-powered de Havilland Vampire flew that September and soon exceeded 500 mph.

Both were centrifugal turbo-jets and the more powerful Ghost was originally developed to power the Venom, a developed version of the Vampire. But to suit its use in the Comet the engine had to be 80 per cent re-designed. The most obvious difference was that the civil engine featured a single round air intake rather than the split intakes on the military variant. The Ghost received type approval in June 1948 to become the world's first commercial jet engine. It developed up to 5,500 lb of thrust.

Although consideration was given to installing the Rolls-Royce Avon axial-flow engine in the Comet 1 the decision was taken to adopt the Ghost rather than delay the project by waiting on the civilian version of the Avon, which was later used to power the Comet 4.

The man behind the Goblin and Ghost, as well as several other notable aero engines, was Major Frank Halford. A Royal Flying Corps pilot and talented engineer, he was removed from front-line duties to develop engines for the government. After the war he turned his attention to motor cycles and cars, finishing 13th in the 1922 Isle of Man Senior TT. He also competed in the 1926 British Grand Prix at Brooklands in a car of his own design.

Halford set up a design consultancy and numbered de Havilland among his more influential clients. He designed the de Havilland Gipsy series of air-cooled engines and also worked for Napier on its Sabre which became recognised as among the most powerful piston engines ever built.

Halford constructed his own jet engine based on Frank Whittle's designs but simplified. He called it the Halford H.1 but the project was taken up by de Havilland which produced it as the Goblin. Halford's company was bought by de Havilland to form its engine division and then a separate subsidiary in 1944. Halford was its chairman and technical director.

He died suddenly in 1955 at the age of 61.

ABOVE RIGHT: Maj Frank Halford (middle), creator of most of de Havilland's engines, is pictured with two of his colleagues, J Brodie (left) and Dr E Moult. The engine is a Goblin from which was developed the Ghost which powered the Comet 1.

INTO SERVICE

The Jet Age Arrives

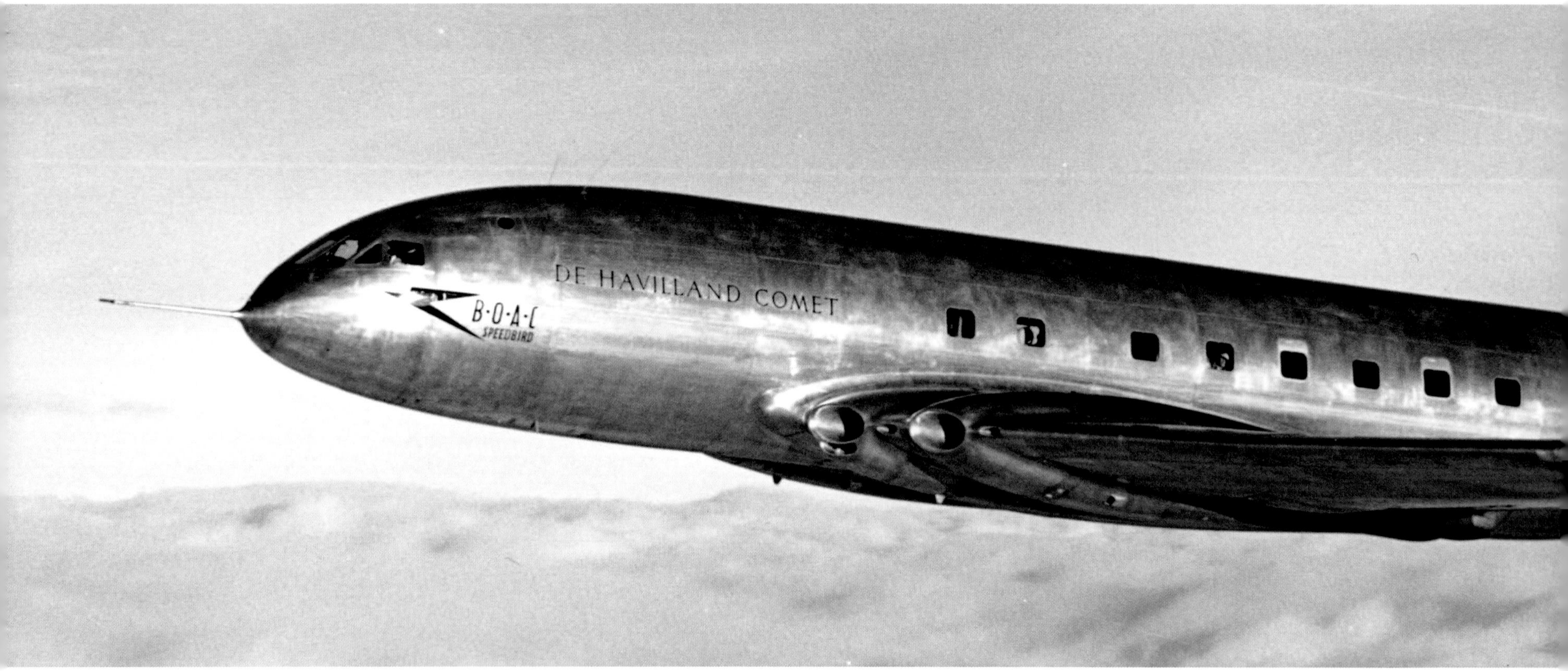
DE HAVILLAND COMET
B·O·A·C
SPEEDBIRD

In the early 1950s people got most of their news from newspapers or the radio. If they wanted to see it enlivened by moving pictures they usually had to go to the cinema. Consequently, the news reels were always a popular part of the programme on offer.

In May 1952 when most cinemas in Britain were showing movies like smash hit musical Singing' in the Rain or Battle of Britain epic Angels One-Five they were also able to see the Pathe News report of one of the biggest news stories.

The newsreel had sent Ced Baynes to show audiences what it was like to fly in the world's first jet airliner. In the event it turned out to be more of a travelogue than news story with much footage of the Alps and Victoria Falls but Baynes, an experienced traveller, also remarked on the jet's lack of vibration and noise.

"Like all newsreel cameramen flying is no novelty to me," Baynes observed, *"but this was something new."*

Of the climax to the flight, the landing at Johannesburg, Baynes had this to say: *"Britain had made air history again: the world now had its first passenger jet air service. Nearly 7,000 miles by jet. I landed at Jo'burg full of smiles."* He added: *"Any time I have to record history in the making again I'll travel Comet, please, every time."*

The tone was perhaps typical of the age. But Baynes' observations about the absence of vibration and noise compared to contemporary piston-engined types echoed those made by other Comet passengers.

For commercial aviation the jet age arrived at 1512 hr on Friday 2 May 1952 when Capt A M Majendie, flight captain of the British Overseas Airways Corporation's Comet fleet, lifted G-ALYP off Heathrow's runway for the flight to Johannesburg. The weather had been overcast but a sudden burst of sunshine illuminated the historic moment of departure. There were comments on the thunderous noise that trailed the Comet.

And a large crowd had turned out to watch. Among them were some of the people who had made the event possible including Sir Geoffrey de Havilland, Ronald Bishop, Richard Clarkson, Frank Halford and John Cunningham. One whose absence had been noticed was Sir Frank Whittle.

Twenty-first century travellers would probably be highly unimpressed by the time taken by the world's first commercial jet service to cover the 7,000 miles to South Africa but the Comet's 23 hr 38 min flying time was viewed as amazing by 1952 standards. It was, though, dictated by the number of en-route replenishment halts required by the thirsty engines: Yoke Peter stopped at Rome, Beirut, Khartoum, Entebbe and Livingstone.

BOAC's contemporary Handley-Page Hermes aircraft took just short of 28 hours for the trip but their longer range meant they followed a route 1,000 miles shorter than that of Comet Yoke Peter. Because of the journey's length the jet had to take on fresh crews at Beirut and then Khartoum.

The single fare cost £175 and the return trip £315, the same as BOAC charged for the journey by Hermes. That was at a time when the average wage in Britain for a 42-hr week was £8.68. An average house cost around £1,800.

Capt Majendie had expected headwinds on the first leg and, indeed, the Comet was 9 min late when it landed at Rome at 1646hr GMT. Time was made up on the

TOP: This view of the prototype Comet 1 in flight in December 1949 accentuates the grace of the world's first jet airliner. Note the BOAC Speedbird logo beneath the flight deck windows, the nose probe and the fact that the aircraft is now displaying on the registration G-ALVG.

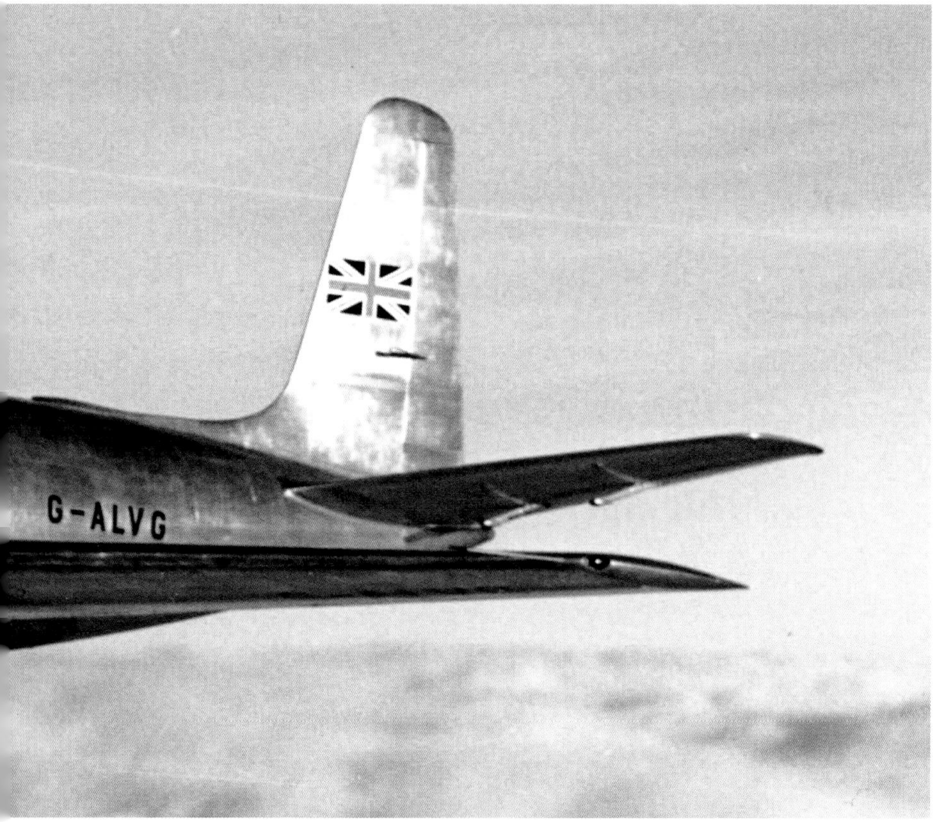
G-ALVG

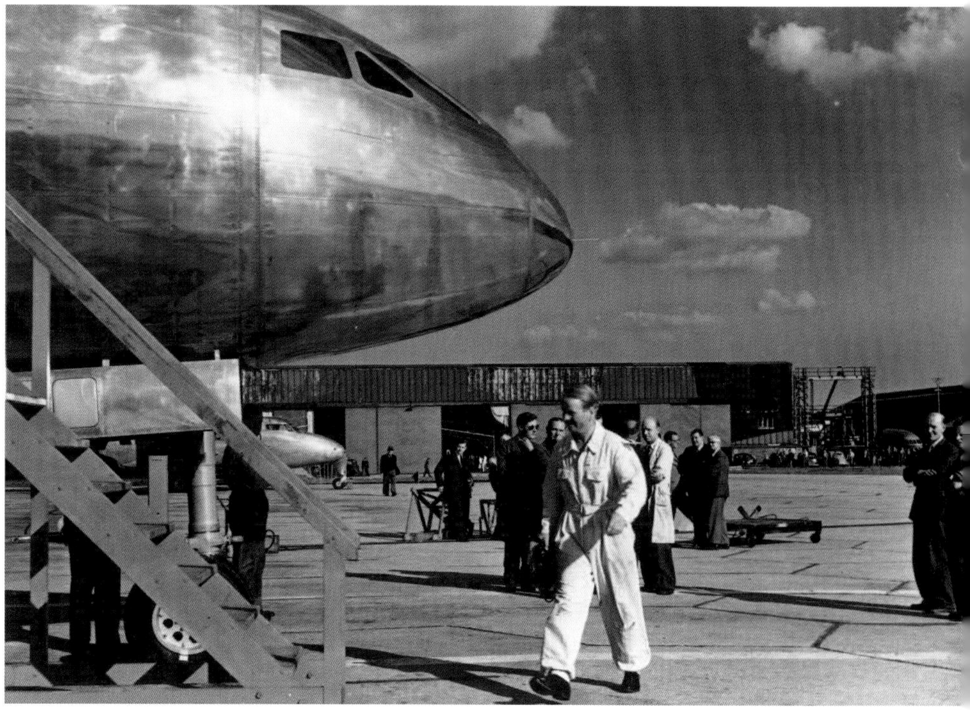

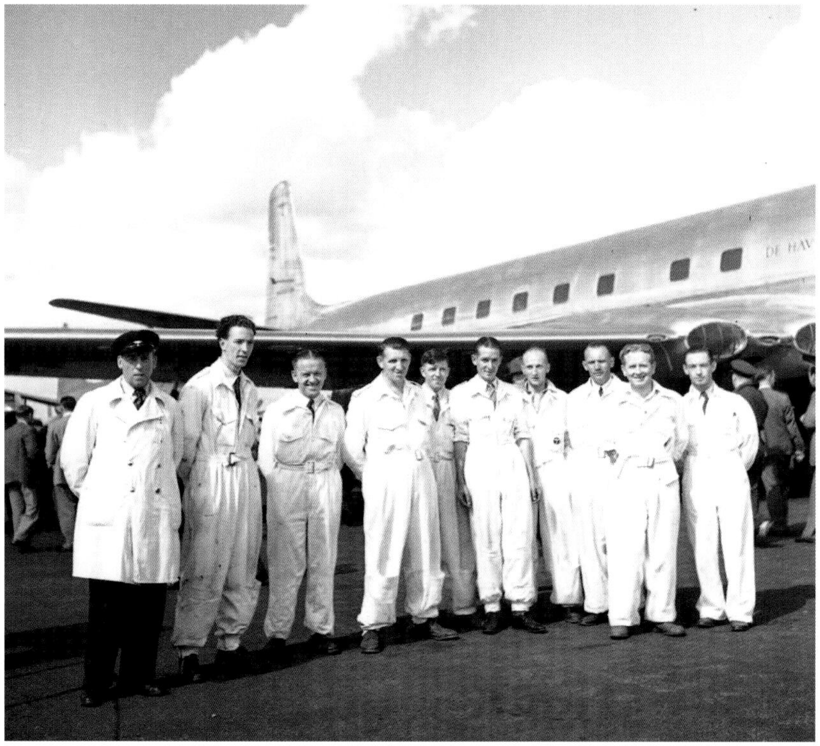

TOP: John Cunningham strides towards the second Comet G-5-2/G-ALZK before taking in to the air for the first time on 27 July 1950, exactly a year after the first prototype had made its first flight.
BOTTOM: de Havilland engineers at Farnborough for the first public appearance of the Comet prototype in September 1949

stage to Beirut and a tailwind helped the aircraft average 525 mph (840 kmh). Later in the flight Capt R C Alabaster actually had time to spare. Because the airline considered it essential to adhere to the published schedules he had to leave Livingstone late and make wide turns.

When the aircraft arrived at Johannesburg's Palmietfontein airport there were reported to be 20,000 spectators waiting to catch their first sight of this harbinger of the future. It arrived two minutes ahead of schedule. The passengers were said to be *"without the slightest sign of fatigue."* Each one later received a special certificate. The following Monday the aircraft left for home and arrived just under 24 hr later at 0740hr BST.

"It went without a hitch," declared BOAC chairman Sir Miles Thomas, who had joined the aircraft at Livingstone. The flight, he added, had *"put British aviation – jet-propelled – on the map of the world."* Before leaving Heathrow Capt Majendie had said simply: *"We are very glad to have the honour of launching this service. We are also very proud to be using this British aeroplane."*

It was indeed a heady time for British aviation. For BOAC it represented the start of a new phase in its relationship with the Comet which would be no less busy than the earlier ones which had been occupied by preparing the aircraft for its entry into commercial service.

In June the corporation increased the frequency of round-trip Comet flights between London and Johannesburg to three a week. On 11 August it launched a weekly return service to Colombo, Ceylon (now Sri Lanka) and then, two months later, a weekly service to Singapore soon increased to two. The following year Tokyo was added to the schedules (see box).

This increase in activity was made possible by the delivery to BOAC of the last of the nine Comet I's it had ordered. The final one, G-ALYZ, was handed over to the airline in September but less than a month later was damaged beyond economic repair in a take-off accident at Rome.

One result of the launch of jet services was that Johannesburg and Colombo flights were booked solid to mid-November. Even after that BOAC reported that *"only a few odd seats"* were available to Johannesburg up to July 1953. The airline said that load factors had averaged 79 per cent, which enabled it to operate the service profitably despite the requirement to carry generous fuel reserves.

The journal Flight noted: *"The novelty of jet travel is, of course, largely responsible for the high load factors: many passengers are willing to postpone a journey by weeks simply because the prospect of flying by Comet appeals to the imagination."*

And not just to the imagination. Word had been getting around about the comfort offered by the jets. One passenger, who sampled the Comet – it was always the Comet in the early days just as later it was to be the Concorde - said the same. A journalist who obviously possessed a sophisticated taste in cars described the sound audible in the first two rows of seats in the main cabin – its noisiest area – as "a medium-pitched hum which I can best liken to that wonderful sound one hears from an Alfa cruising at about 80mph."

But, he pointed out, "the whole thing is relative and even at its loudest the noise is appreciably less than one experiences in other aircraft." The same applied to the levels of vibration, causing the passenger to add: "I have never flown so quietly or so smoothly in anything."

On a pre-service trip to Rome, Flight's editor Maurice Smith reported on a journey that had taken 2hr 15min. On arrival, he told his readers: *"We all stepped out, exhilarated and unfatigued, into the warm Roman sunshine. The smooth fast ride and absence of exhaust and airscrew noise had eliminated that battered feeling often experienced after a 1,000 mile (four hour) journey in the older types of* airliner."

Less than a month after the first commercial Comet flight the Queen Mother and Princess Margaret became the first members of the Royal Family to sample the new aircraft. Although an occasion organised by the manufacturer, G-ALYR had been loaned to de Havilland by BOAC. John Cunningham piloted the aircraft on its 1,850-mile (2,960 km) flight with Peter Bugge in the right-hand seat.

The aircraft took off from Hatfield at 1225 hr and, after a flying a route which took it as far south as Turin, the aircraft touched down at 1625 hr. It cruised at 40,000 ft (12,300m) and recorded an average speed of 462 mph (740 kmh). After landing the Queen Mother, who had for some time, apparently, been keen to fly in the Comet, declared that it *"was a lot faster than the aircraft of the King's Flight."* At that time the King's Flight was equipped with the Vickers Viking whose cruising speed was about half that of the jet's.

Overseas trips had been part of the Comet's schedule since just after the prototype's first flight. On 25 October Cunningham and Bugge flew the aircraft to Castel Benito, Libya in 3 hr 23 min to average 440 mph (704 kmh). Two hours later the aircraft had been refuelled and took off for home, reaching London after averaging 458 mph (733 kmh).

The following March the aircraft flew to Rome and back setting two records in the process: Hatfield-Ciampino in just over 2hr at a 447 mph (715 kmh) average and the return leg, in a similar time, at 442 mph (707 kmh). Cunningham was again the commander but also on board were senior Ministry of Supply officials and de Havilland representatives. Flight's Maurice Smith was there too to record his observations.

"Truly," he reported, *"it might have been a routine passenger service to and from Ciampino Airport at Rome."* Looking ahead to the start of commercial services, Smith mused: *"Above all else, airlines must be able to offer safe, reliable and uneventful journeys. The Comet has demonstrated once more that it can fulfil this requirement and offer as well as speed, better-than-average comfort*

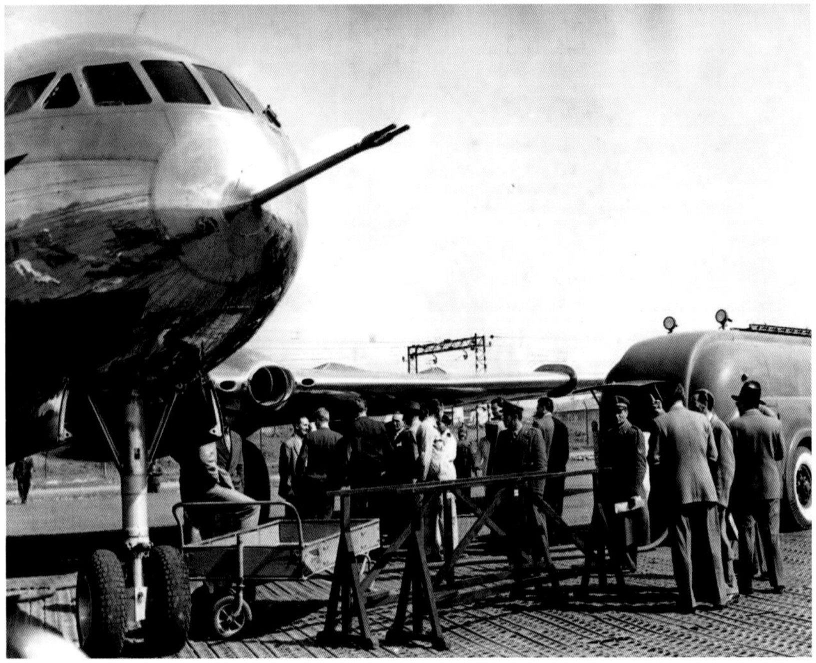

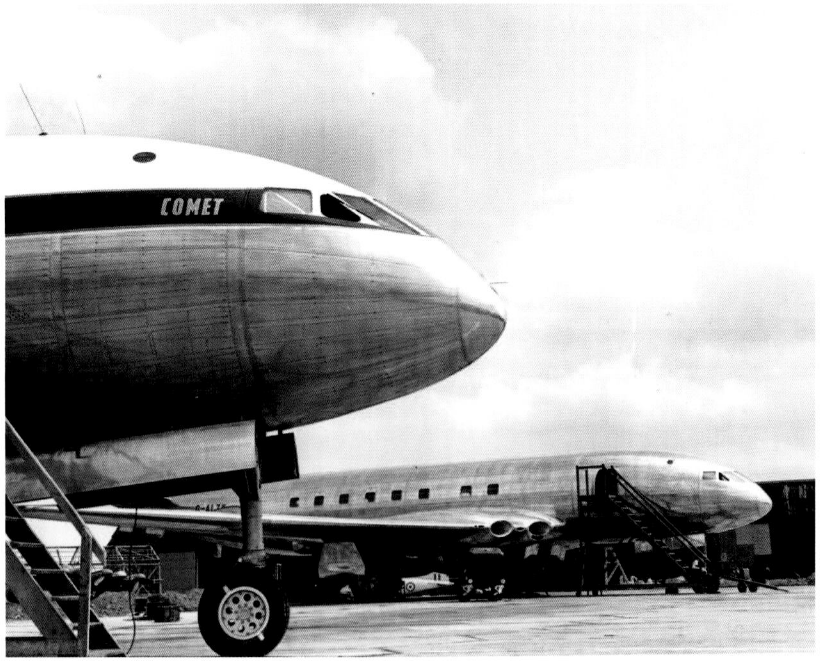
COMET

BOTTOM LEFT: G-ALVG pictured at Ciampino airport during its record-breaking flight to Rome on 16 March 1950.
BOTTOM RIGHT: The two Comet prototypes, G-ALVG and `ZK, side by sided at Hatfield in July 1950.

and economy for the operator."

In July 1950 British cinema audiences saw a particularly stirring Pathe News account of a Comet trip to Rome. The newsreel reported: *"On Rome's Ciampino airfield, 970 miles (1,550 km) from London, diplomats and air attaches saw the Comet fly in at 490mph (784 kmh) to lower the record to 2hr 2min. A proud day for John 'Cat's Eyes' Cunningham, de Havilland's chief test pilot. His achievement proves that jets will enable Britain's future airliners, now in mass production for 1953, to do twice the work in almost half the time at four-fifths the cost. Tails up for Britain!"*

Within eight months of the Comet prototype's first outing the aircraft had made three overseas trips as part of its first 200hr testing. It was reported that all performance expectations had been realised and no unforeseen difficulties had been encountered in an aircraft that was breaking fresh ground.

The next stage of the programme involved operations from *"hot and high"* airports. Accordingly, Cairo was visited in April 1950, the aircraft taking little more than five hours for the 2,200 mile (3520 km) trip. It averaged 425 mph (680 kmh) and set another inter-city record. The next day the aircraft landed at Nairobi's airport, 5,370 ft (1,650m) above sea level. A defective undercarriage delayed the schedule but as soon as a replacement part had been fitted the aircraft was able to get on with a programme of take-offs and landings in temperatures of 44 degrees Centigrade.

The maiden flight of the second prototype, G-ALZK, in May 1950, signalled a change of tempo in the test programme. Pending the arrival of the first production aircraft the Ministry of Supply loaned `ZK to BOAC in March 1951. After some preliminary flights the aircraft was flown from Hatfield to Heathrow in early April and, on 24 May, set off for a 6,000 mile (9,600 km) round trip which would see it visit Nicosia via Rome and Cairo.

There were three more overseas flights over the next three weeks during which the aircraft covered 16,000 miles (25,600 km). At the end of June an African tour took it as far south as Entebbe, Uganda. This time the aircraft had covered over 9,000 miles (5,600 km) by the time it returned to Heathrow. A month later the Comet arrived at Johannesburg via Cairo and Entebbe. It took 17hr 34 min.

Between then and the end of 1951 the aircraft was to have little rest, making several trips to Asia. The eleventh tour, in September and October, involved visits to Karachi and Bombay. The longest of these trips took the aircraft as far as Bangkok. It covered over 16,000 miles. The journey to Singapore took just over 24hr and included 5hr spent on the ground. The total distance covered in these overseas tours was around 93,000 miles (149,000 km).

The primary purpose had been route proving and also to establish the best way of operating the aircraft under a wide variety of conditions. To see how the

TOP RIGHT: Brabazons both: the first prototype Comet 1, a design inspired by the deliberations of the wartime committee chaired by Lord Brabazon, overflies the Bristol Brabazon airliner prototype at the 1950 Farnborough Air Show.
TOP LEFT: The second Comet, G-ALZK, pictured in flight on 4 September 1950.

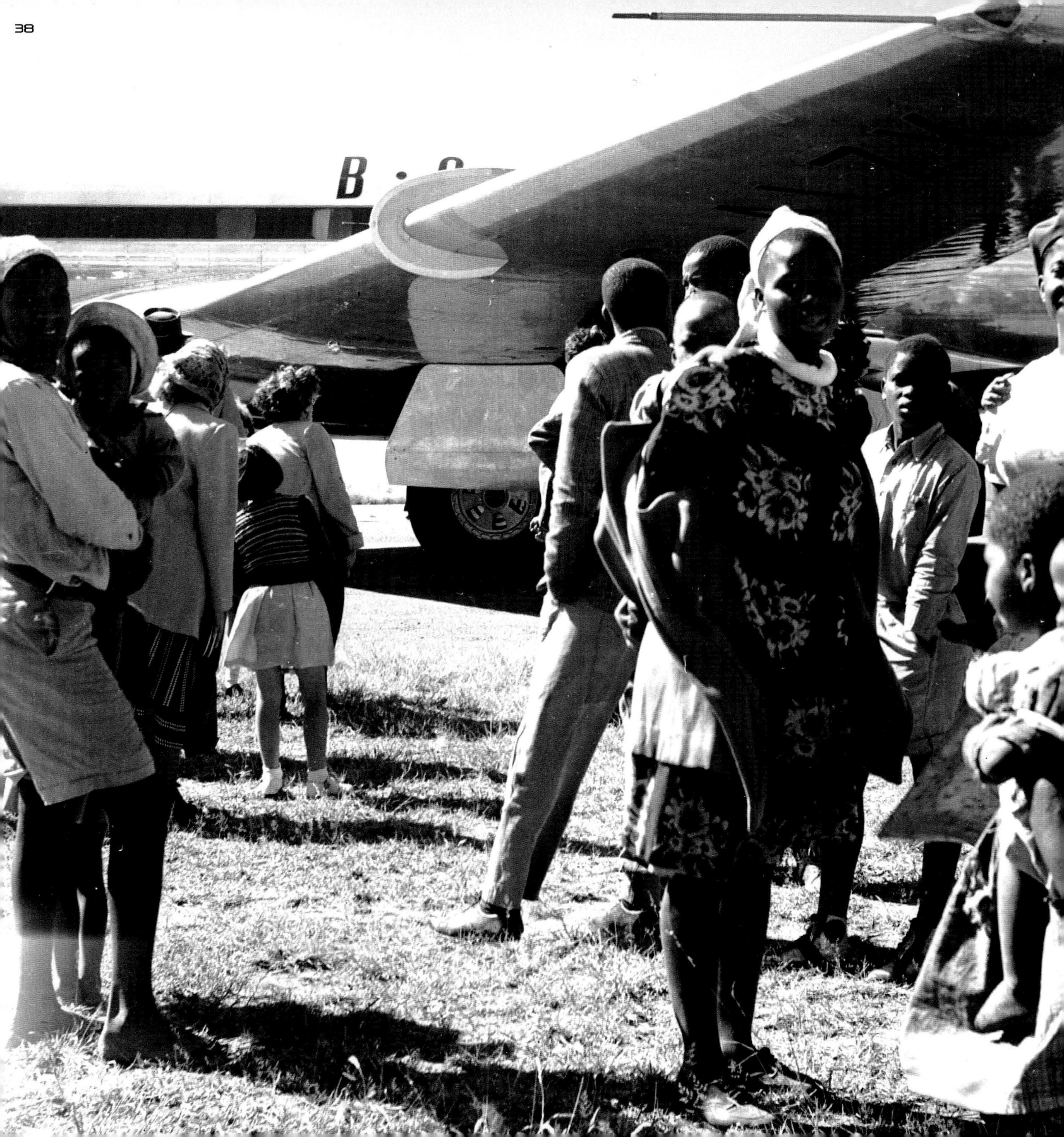

Comet fitted in with existing traffic patterns 91 landings were made at 31 different overseas airports. Maintenance work was undertaken by BOAC engineers assisted by manufacturer's representatives when required. In fact, a de Havilland flight engineer accompanied the BOAC crew as a supernumerary member on every flight.

The tempo of route proving trials undertaken by BOAC's Comet Unit increased as the date of the Comet's service introduction approached and deliveries of production aircraft increased. That meant `ZK could be returned to its manufacturers.

The crews also had to become familiar with the new aircraft. The first stage in the conversion to the Comet was a seven-week course at BOAC's central training unit at Cranford near Heathrow. Initial courses had been run by de Havilland at its own servicing school. For some crews there was much to learn. While most ex-service pilots were familiar with power-boosted controls, bogie undercarriages and air brakes, many would-be Comet flight crews were not, especially when these features were combined in the same aircraft.

Included in the course, therefore, were periods of instruction on the engines, airframe and other aspects. One student remarked that he thought visits to the Comet assembly line particularly valuable: *"I found that the invaluable help of actually seeing in the afternoon what had been discussed in the morning was a major contribution to a keen knowledge of the aircraft as a whole."*

At the end of the course pilots and engineers had to undergo the Air Registration Board (forerunner of today's Civil Aviation Authority) examination to gain the necessary endorsement to operate as a crew member on passenger-carrying Comet flights. The exam took a day to complete and involved answering about 100 questions.

After that came the airline's own training programme which involved four 90-minute sessions of circuits and landings, two at night and two during the day, as well an instrument-flying period. Familiarisation with the approach of compressibility, emergency descents using air brakes and how to start an engine after an in-flight flame-out were also part of the syllabus.

Successful completion of this part of the training was marked by the various instructors signing off the pilot. That enabled an approach to be made to the Ministry for a Comet licence endorsement at a cost of two guineas (£2.10p). Even that did not end the training required to fly a Comet on revenue flights.

Route familiarisation represented the final stage of Comet conversion training. Captains were required to complete two full trips on any particular route before they could be authorised to fly in command. First officers also made two trips under supervision. The same was true for navigators, who also had to demonstrate an ability to work fast and accurately.

At the completion of the Comet's first year of service it was apparent that apart from the aircraft's popularity with its passengers the accountants liked it too. Load factors had averaged around 79 per cent, with 80 per cent being recorded on the Johannesburg route, 81 on the Singapore service and 72 to Colombo.

BOAC's Comet fleet was now covering a combined daily average of 17,000 miles (27,000 km) on eight long-haul return services a week on four routes. Including training and route-proving the equivalent annual utilization per aircraft was approaching 2,000hr. A total of 9,450 revenue hours had been flown over 104,600,000 revenue miles (170,560,000 km) and 27,700 passengers carried.

Another way of viewing the first year of Comet operations was that a revolutionary aircraft type had coped well with operating conditions. On the Johannesburg route, the aircraft and its crews had encountered temperatures of up to 50 degrees Centigrade and airports up to 6,000 ft (1,846m) above sea level. And they had done it at speeds the operators of piston engine airliners could only dream about: by the time the best of them had reached Johannesburg from London the Comet was half way home.

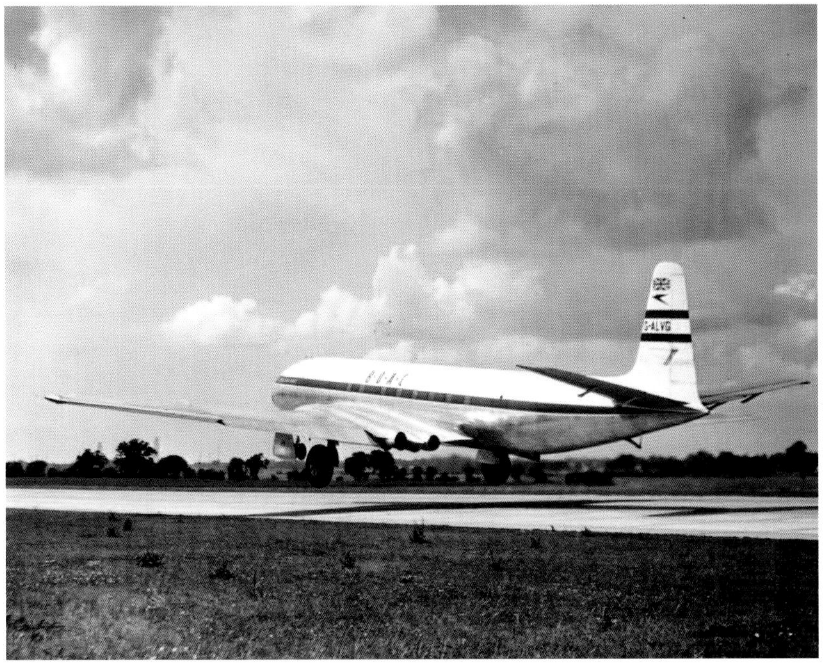
G-ALVG
B.O.A.C

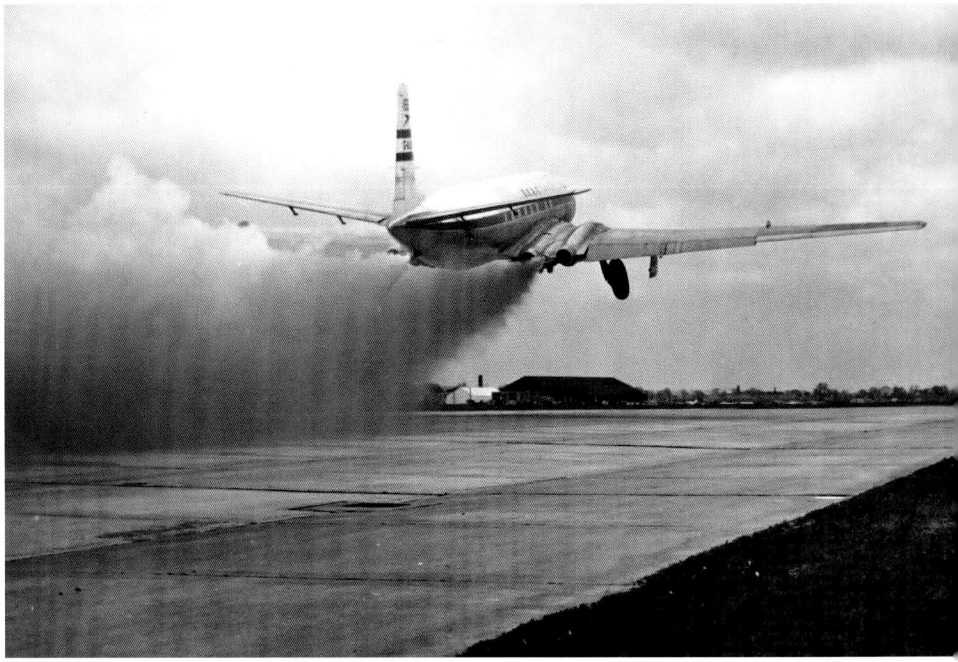

LEFT: G-ALZK, now in BOAC livery, pictured at Nairobi during a proving flight on 3 August 1951.
BOTTOM LEFT: G-ALVG in flight on 1 July 1951 during a BOAC proving flight.
BOTTOM RIGHT: During the flight development programme G-ALVG was fitted with a pair of de Havilland Sprite rocket motors between the Ghost jet pipes to boost take-off performance at hot and high airfields. As shown here, it was tested but not used operationally.

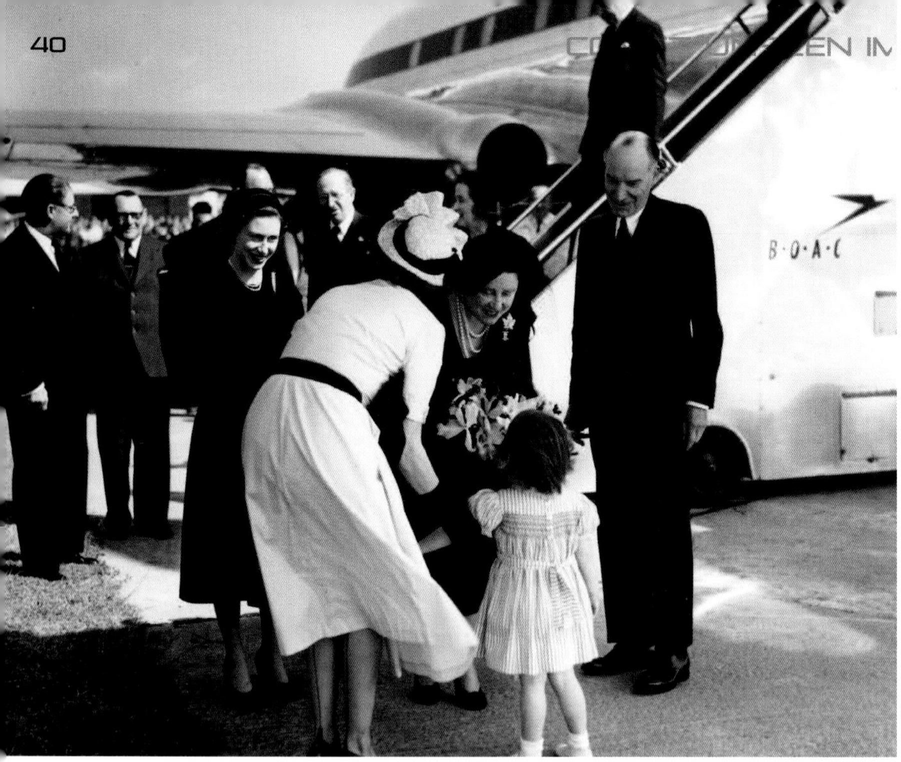
B·O·A·C

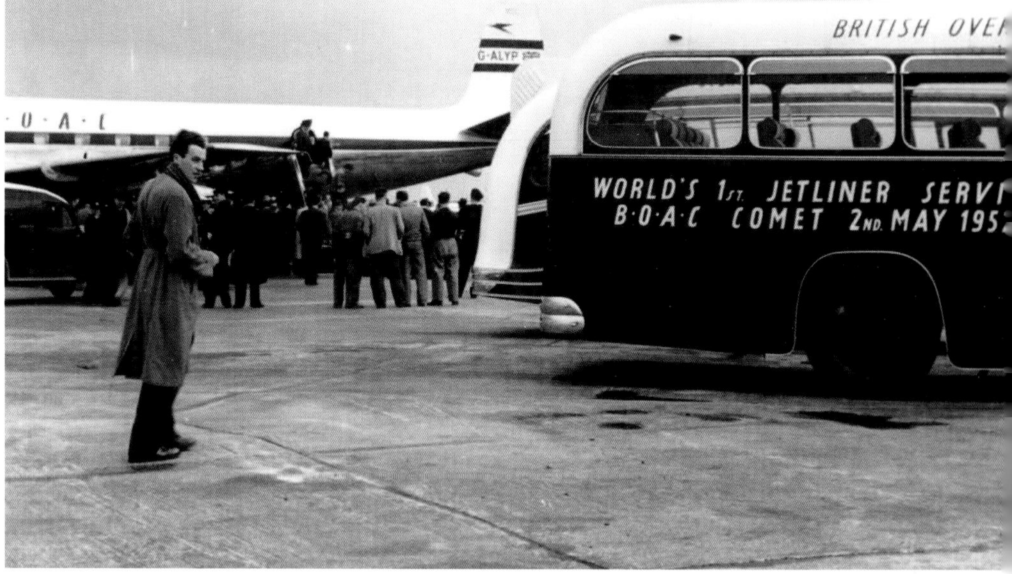
BRITISH OVE
G-ALYP
WORLD'S 1st JETLINER SERVI
B·O·A·C COMET 2nd MAY 195

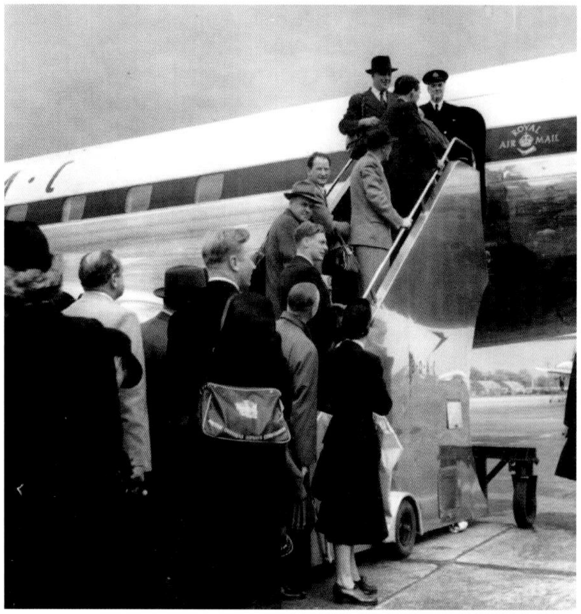
ROYAL AIR MAIL

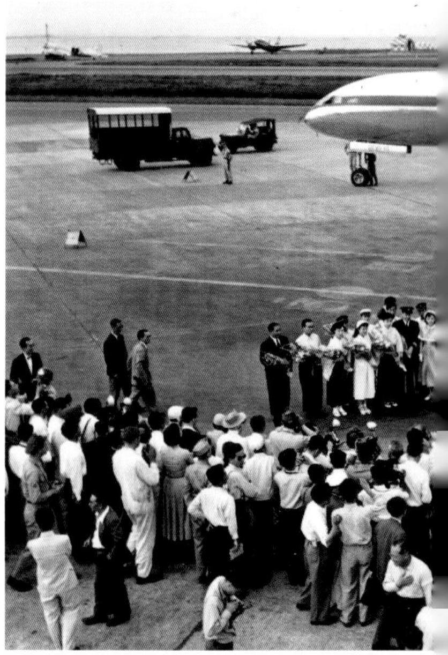

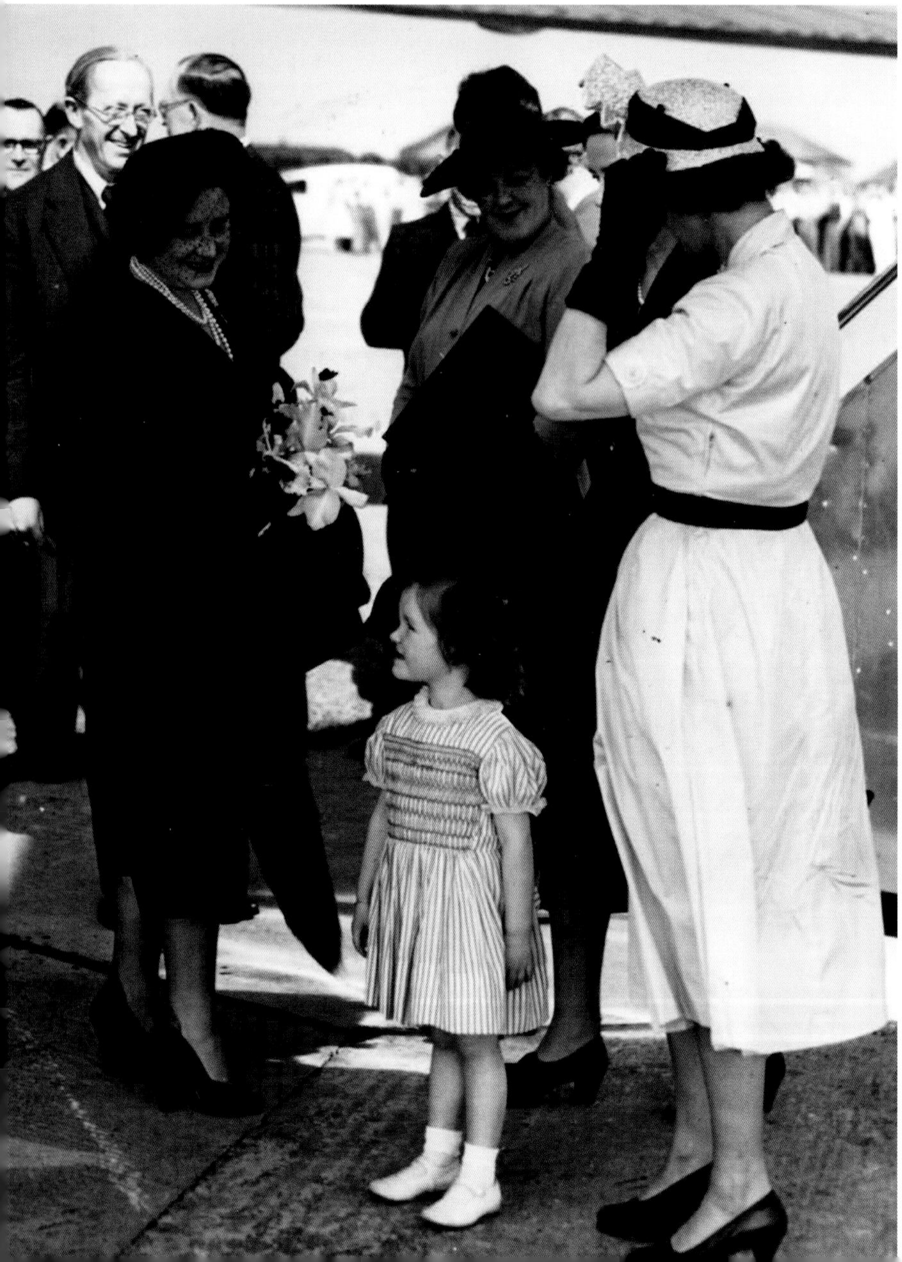

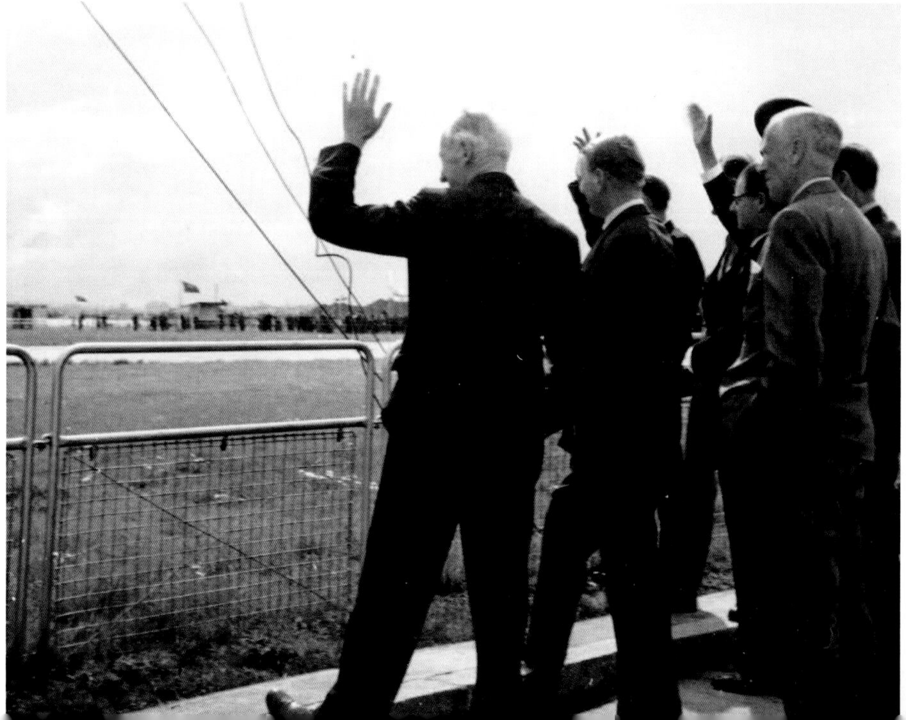

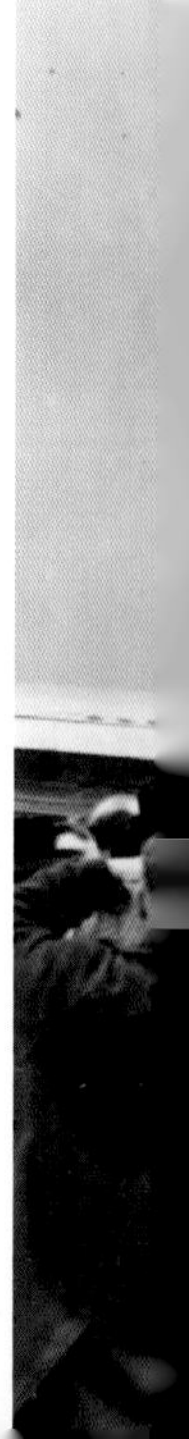

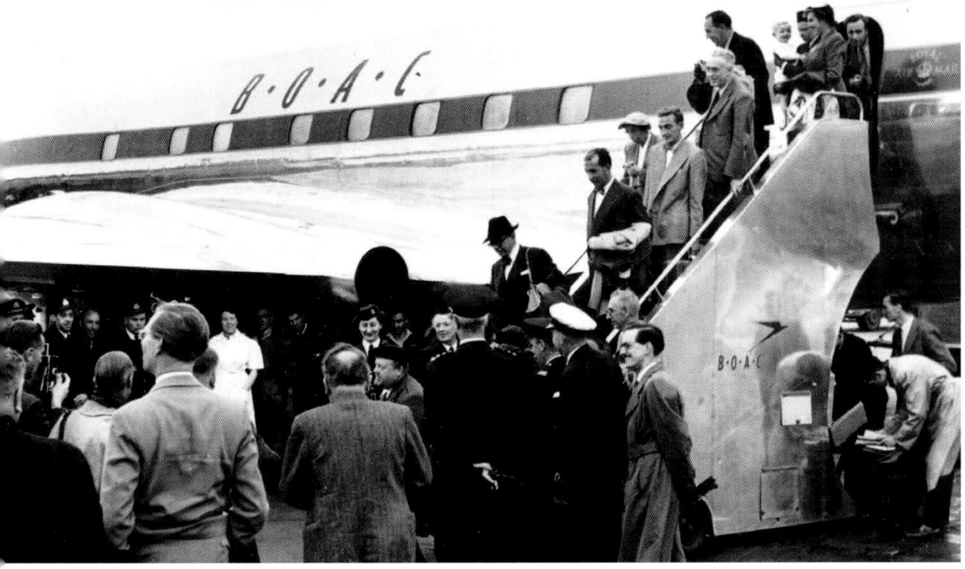
B·O·A·C
B·O·A·C

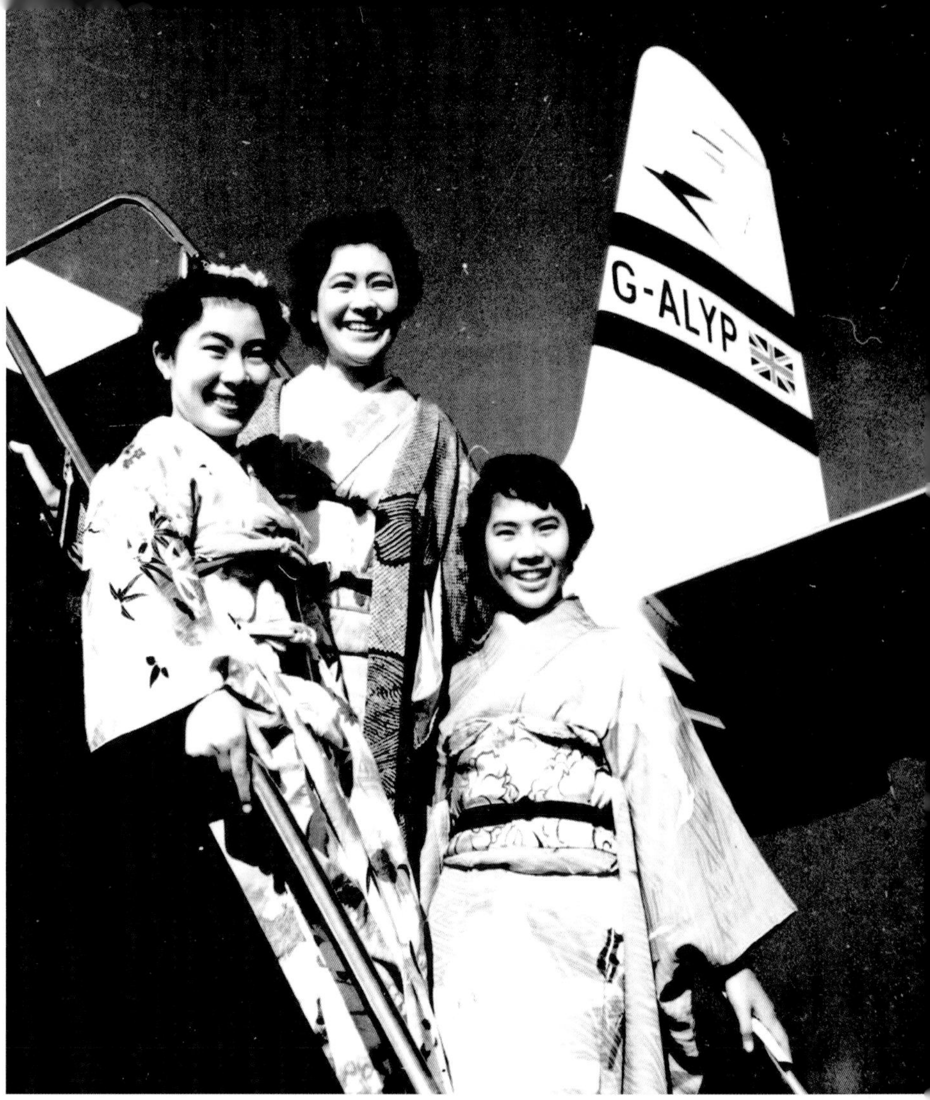
G-ALYP

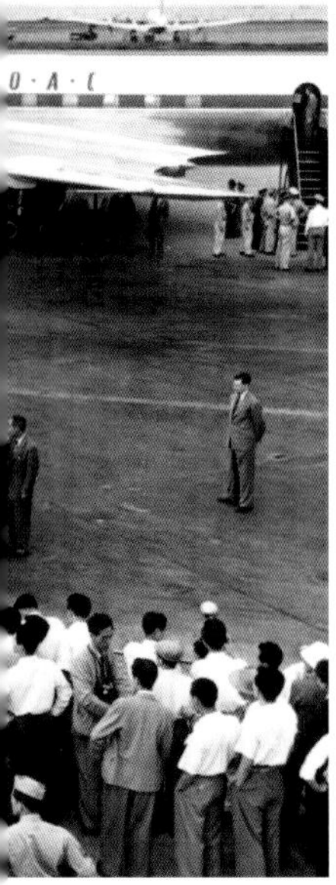

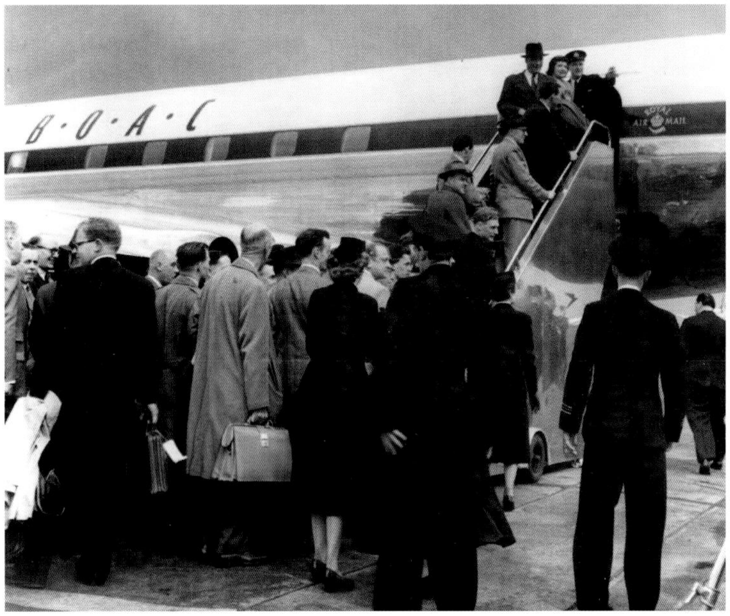
B·O·A·C

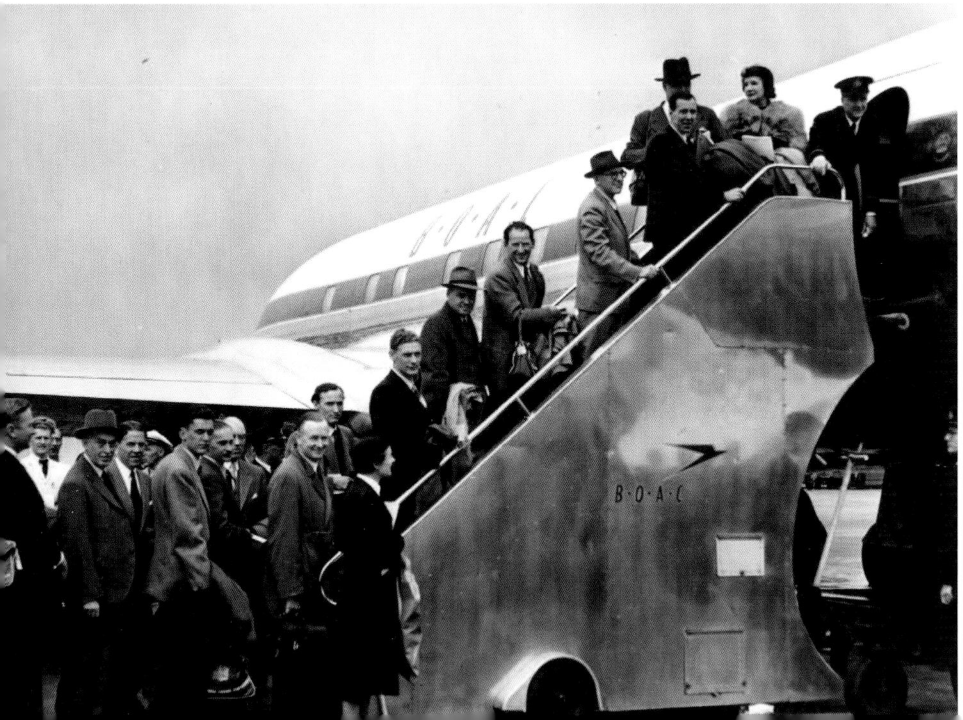
B·O·A·C
B·O·A·C

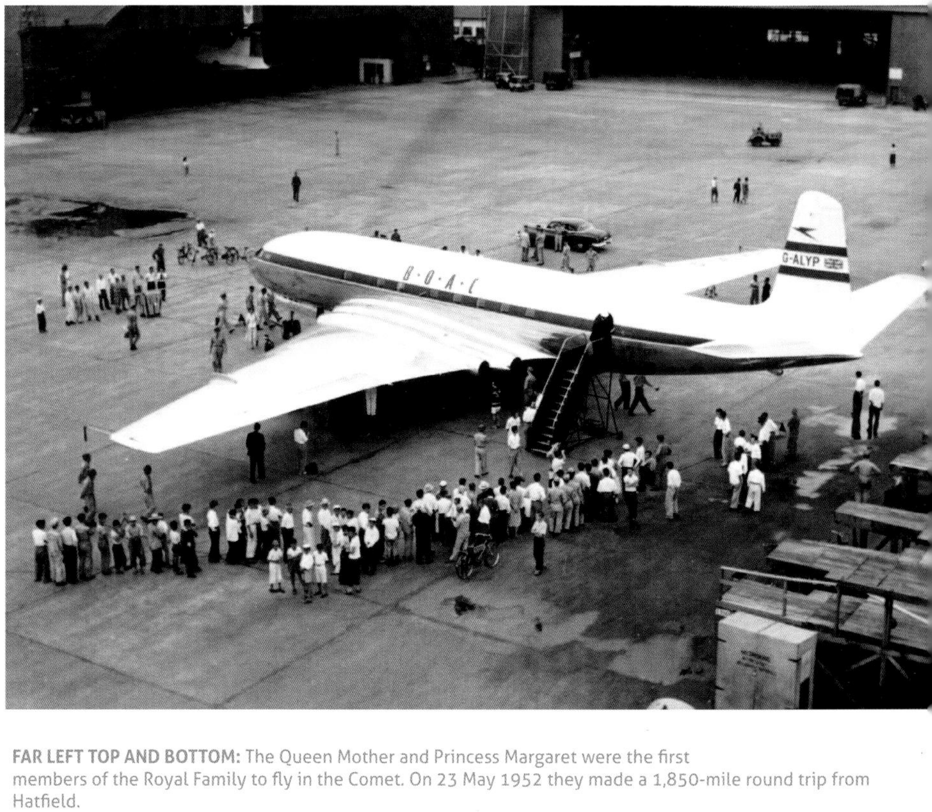
B·O·A·C
G-ALYP

FAR LEFT TOP AND BOTTOM: The Queen Mother and Princess Margaret were the first members of the Royal Family to fly in the Comet. On 23 May 1952 they made a 1,850-mile round trip from Hatfield.

MIDDLE SECTION: images of air transport entering the commercial jet age on 2 May 1952; top right: passengers disembark from `YP on its return to Heathrow on 6 May.

ABOVE AND TOP: BOAC Comet 'YP arrives at Tokyo's Haneda Airport on 8 July 1952.

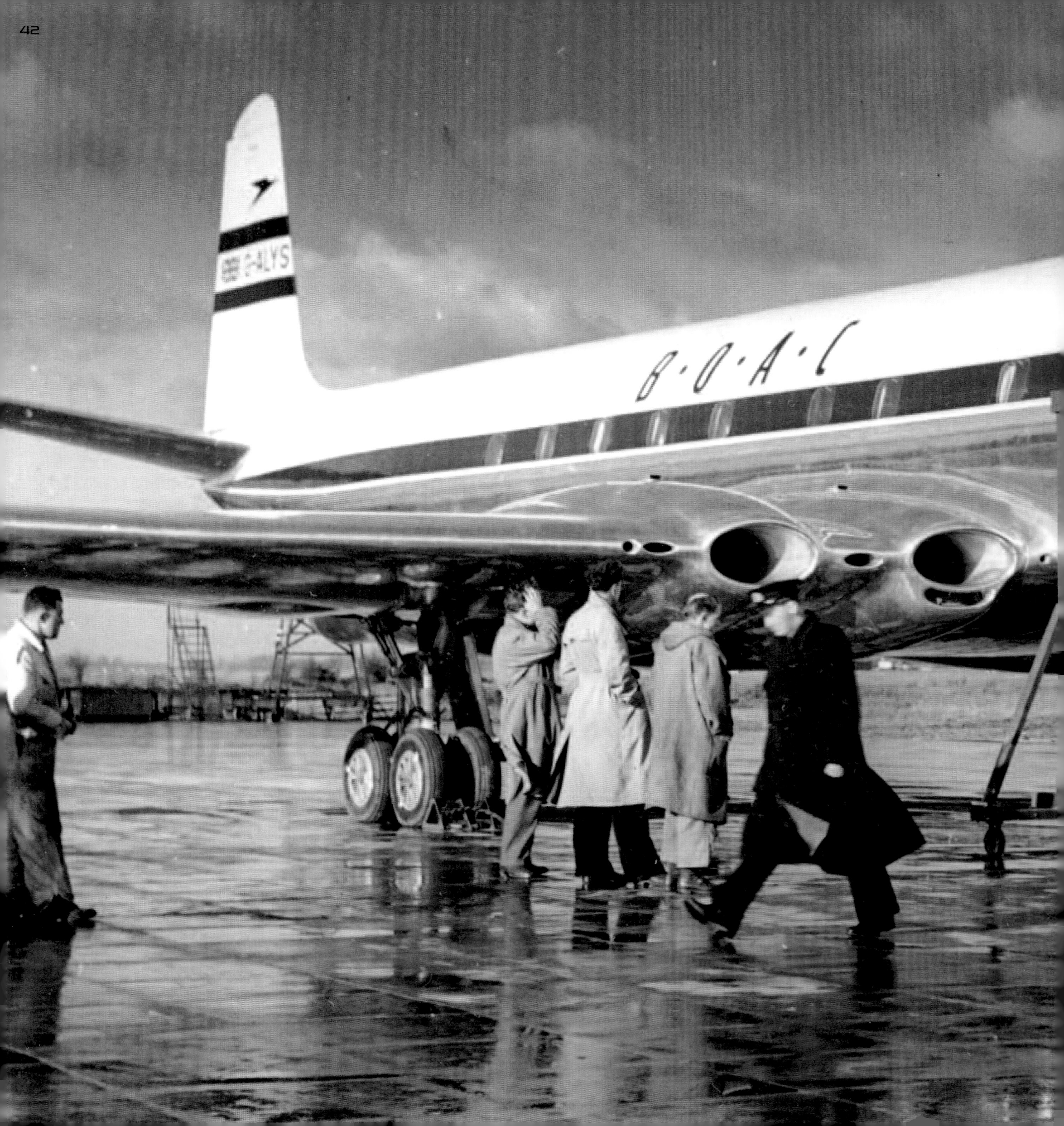
G-ALYS
B·O·A·C

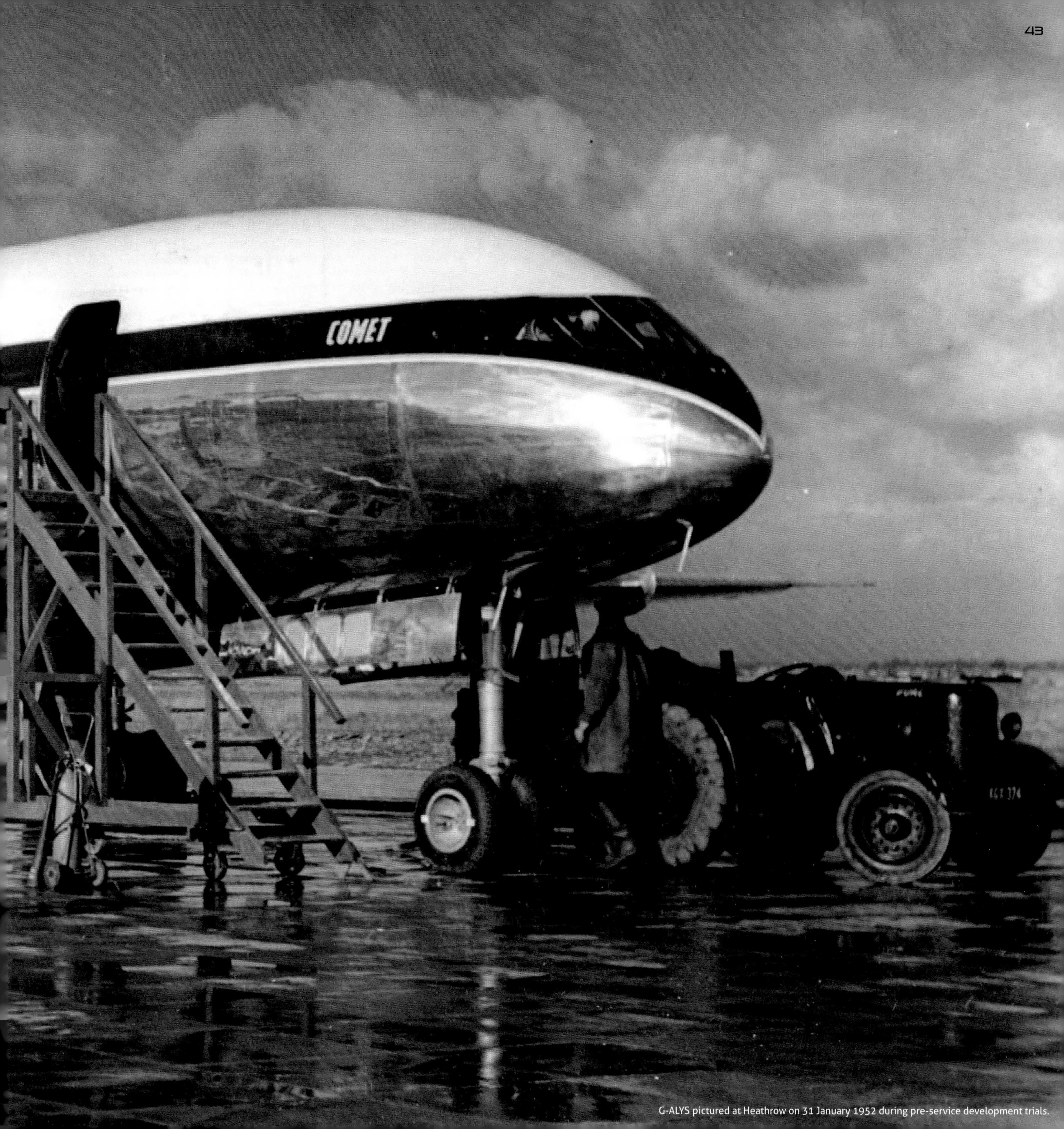
COMET

G-ALYS pictured at Heathrow on 31 January 1952 during pre-service development trials.

Kerosene was cheaper than the high-octane fuel used by the Constellations and DC-6Bs. Maintenance costs were lower too. Airframes not subjected to the constant vibration of piston engines had longer lives; with the Comets popped rivets were virtually a thing of the past. On the prototypes time between major engine overhauls was set at 250 hr. When BOAC started operations it moved to 375 hr and then, for much of the first year, approval was gained for a 450 hr cycle.

Although the established piston-engines were working to a 1,000 hr cycle, major overhauls took considerably longer. So too did engine changes. BOAC's engineers took 12 man-hours (three men working four hours) to change a Comet's Ghost engine; the same job on a Boeing Stratocruiser took 40 man-hours.

It was also clear that five Comets could be as productive in a year as eight piston-engined types despite having only 36 first-class seats. But the jets were also showing that there could be problems to come resulting from the introduction of faster airliners.

Even before the aircraft entered commercial service it was clear that, in Maurice Smith's words, *"The Comet is ahead of its passenger organisation."* In a perceptive comment he noted: *"It will take almost everyone longer to get from home to airport and through the various formalities...than it will take them to cover a 1,000 miles [1,600 km] of their journey in the Comet."* He called for *"some sort of time and motion study"* to be made of Comet passengers from arrival at city terminal to chocks away.

One of BOAC's Comet pilots reflected that while the introduction of the gas turbine engine might well open a new era of cheap long-distance travel there would no doubt be new problems to be overcome along the way.

"The Comet," Smith wrote, *"is a stimulant. It throws out a grand challenge to each man and machine engaged in the intricate business of international air travel to try to match its new and remarkable standards."*

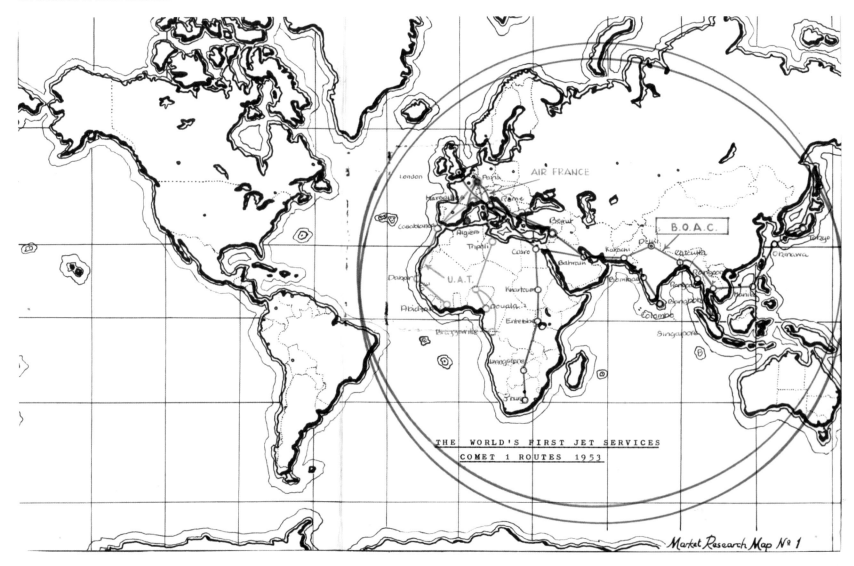

AIR FRANCE
B.O.A.C.
U.A.T.
London
Paris
Rome
Casablanca
Algiers
Tripoli
Cairo
Beirut
Bahrain
Karachi
Delhi
Calcutta
Bombay
Colombo
Singapore
Tokyo
Okinawa
Dakar
Khartoum
Entebbe
THE WORLD'S FIRST JET SERVICES
COMET 1 ROUTES 1953
Market Research Map № 1

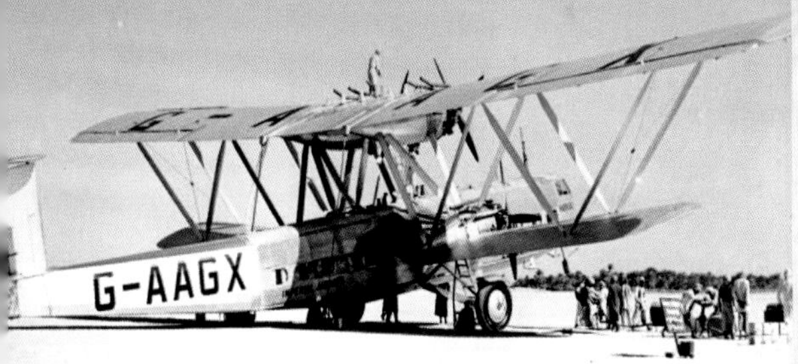
G-AAGX

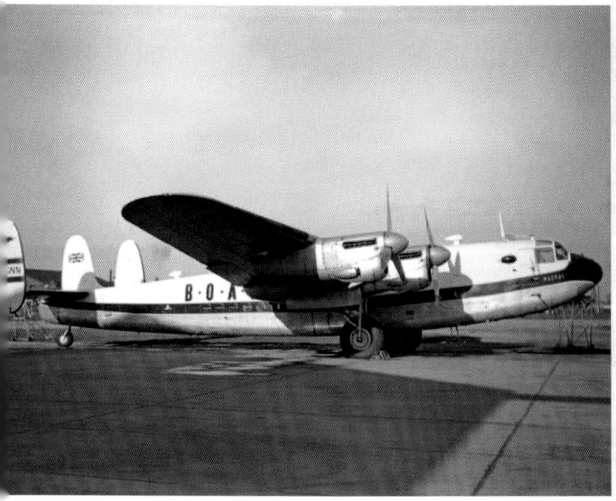

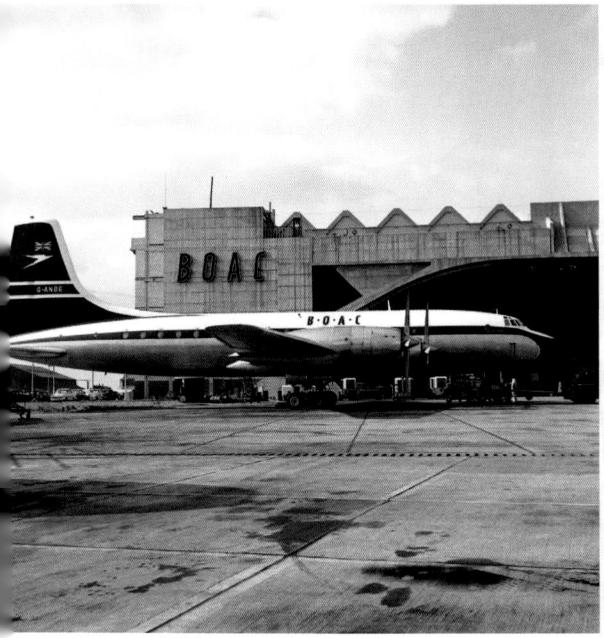
BOAC
B·O·A·C

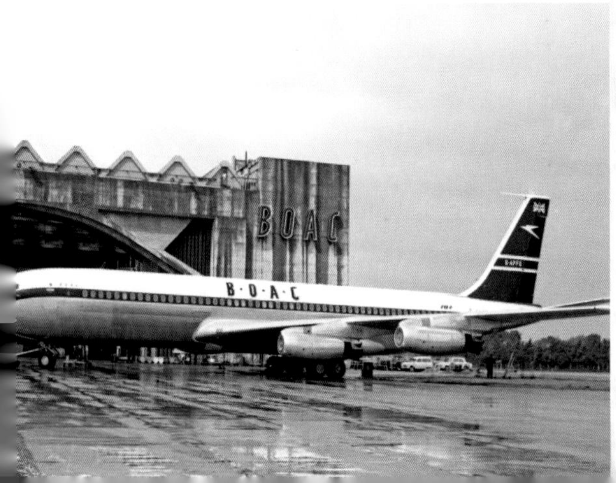
BOAC
B·O·A·C

The British Overseas Airways Corporation

For BOAC the start of commercial jet operations in May 1952 represented one chapter in a story which opened at the dawn of air transport and would end just short of the launch of supersonic operations nearly a quarter of a century later.

In 1924 a group of four struggling independent airlines, one of which had operated the first British air service from London to Paris in August 1919, were brought together and nationalised under the name of Imperial Airways. The new airline's main task was the development of air routes linking the UK with British territories overseas. Accordingly, regular services were operated to East and South Africa and to India and Australia. Experimental flights across the North Atlantic did not begin until 1937.

On 1 April 1940 Imperial Airways was merged with the independent British Airways, which had been operating short-haul services to form BOAC. The corporation continued flying during the Second World War and emerged from the conflict with a fleet that mainly comprised converted warplanes. In 1946 the government created two further state-owned airlines, British European Airways, to operate domestic and European services, and British South American Airways to fly between the UK and South America. The latter was subsequently incorporated into BOAC.

By the time it became the first airline in the world to operate jet aircraft BOAC operated a 70,000-mile (112,000 km) world-wide route network. Its fleet comprised Stratocruisers, Constellations, Hermes and Argonaut passenger aircraft with Yorks used for cargo operations. Turboprop Britannias were on order. In the year 1951-52 BOAC posted a £1 million profit, the first to be recorded by a British state-owned airline.

In 1958 BOAC became the first carrier to offer trans-Atlantic jet services following the introduction of the enlarged and improved Comet 4. But it was also seeking to acquire a substantial fleet of Boeing 707s as well as Vickers VC-10s. In the 1970s BOAC became one of the first operators of the wide-bodied Boeing 747 and had the supersonic Anglo-French Concorde on order when it was merged with BEA.

On 1 April 1974 the BOAC name disappeared from the schedules to be replaced by that of its successor, British Airways.

BOAC had played a major role in the development of the Comet. It was well aware that the jet represented a gamble. But, the airline noted in an official report, "The aircraft represents a great improvement over any existing or proposed aircraft." Prototype development was funded by the government but the manufacturer bore much of the development risk on the basis of BOAC's order placed in January 1947.

The government saw it as a partnership between private industry, a nationalised airline and the state and one which it hoped would benefit civil aircraft development and bring wider economic benefits. At this stage BOAC was happy to go along with the buy British principle but this would change as time passed. The airline's lack of interest was at least partly blamed for the failure of the Vickers V.1000 and for hobbling the promising VC10.

The first year of BOAC Comet operations

1952

02 May opening of first service between London and Johannesburg
15 May start of development and training flights to Singapore
01 June weekly frequency of London-Johannesburg service increased to three
11 August launch of weekly return London-Colombo service
30 September last Comet 1 delivered
14 October launch of weekly return London-Singapore service
31 October weekly return frequency to Singapore raised to two

1953

08 February first 10,000hr of Comet flying completed
03 April launch of weekly return London-Tokyo service
13 April weekly frequency to Tokyo increased to two.

LEFT: Imperial Airways and BOAC aircraft, top to bottom: Handley-Page HP 42 G-AAGX; Avro York G-AGNN; Bristol Britannia G-ANBE; Boeing 707-436 G-APFG

DEVELOPING THE COMET

Building on Success

It was inevitable that BOAC should regard the launch of the first commercial jet service in May 1952 as the start of a glorious era in British air transport.

Sir Miles Thomas, the airline's chairman, said a few weeks afterwards that the aviation world was poised on the threshold of historic and momentous new developments. He was convinced that jet aircraft would not only generate profits for their operators but also stimulate the steady expansion of airline traffic. He felt the jets' arrival, combined with the effects of the recent introduction of tourist class travel on the north Atlantic route, would produce a demand which airlines might find it hard to meet.

The plan was that the Comet 1 would be followed into BOAC service by the more capable Comet 2 and also the long-range Britannia turboprop. *"With these two types we plan to cater not only for first-class express services but for tourist services which will girdle the earth,"* Thomas declared. He added: *"It is an aim that excites the imagination and inspires all our efforts."*

The British government certainly saw the Comet's development in distinctly nationalistic terms. The minister of supply declared: *"During the next few years the UK has an opportunity, which may not recur, of developing aircraft manufacture as one of our main export industries. On whether we grasp this opportunity and so establish firmly an industry of the utmost strategic and economic importance, our future as a great nation may depend."*

The minister was Duncan Sandys. As defence minister in 1957, he published a controversial Defence White Paper which envisaged the virtual end of manned combat aircraft for the RAF and foreshadowed the rapid consolidation of the nation's aircraft industry.

The first Comet customers other than BOAC ordered an improved variant with 44-seats and Ghost engines up-rated to develop 5,000 lb (2270 kg) of thrust each. Water injection increased take-off performance. Maximum gross take-off weight had risen to 115,000lb (52,300kg) compared with 105,000 lbs (47,700kg) for BOAC's Comet 1s.

Additional wing tankage provided capacity for a total of 7,000 gallons (31,800 L) of fuel and range went up by 250 miles (400 km) to 1,750 (2,800 km). It had been intended that the first of these aircraft, designated Comet 1As, would start coming off the line after the 12th Comet 1.

By May 1952 orders for 24 examples of the further improved Comet 2 had been placed. The prototype of the new variant was the sixth to come off the de Havilland assembly line. This aircraft (C/N 06006 and registered G-ALYT) was retained by the manufacturer as a development aircraft.

The Comet 2 was conceived as a trans-Atlantic airliner with a 3ft (0.92m) fuselage extension – making it the first stretched jet airliner – and Rolls-Royce Avons in place of the Comet 1's Ghosts. The slim axial flow Avon fitted easily into engine bays designed for the fatter centrifugal Ghost with only minor alterations, although the intakes and jet outlets were enlarged to provide for the increased air flow.

The Avon was to be one of the most successful of the early generation of turbo-jet engines (see box). For the Comet 2 the engine developed 6,500lbs (2,900 kg) of thrust. G-ALYT made its first flight with John Cunningham at the controls on 16

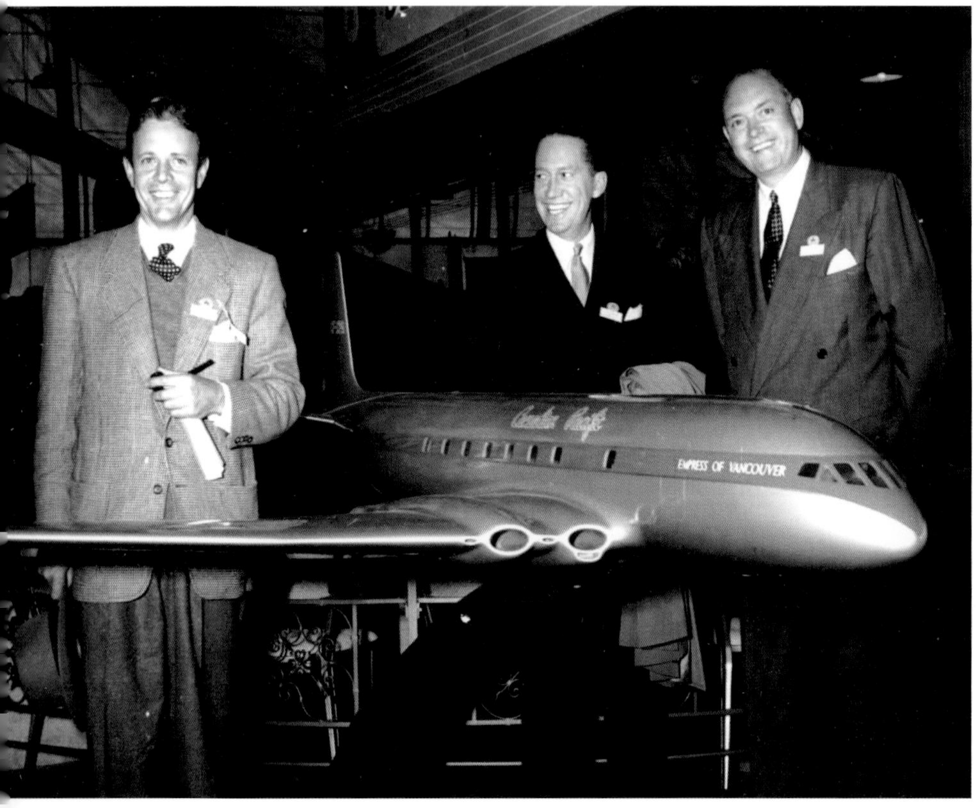
EMPRESS OF VANCOUVER

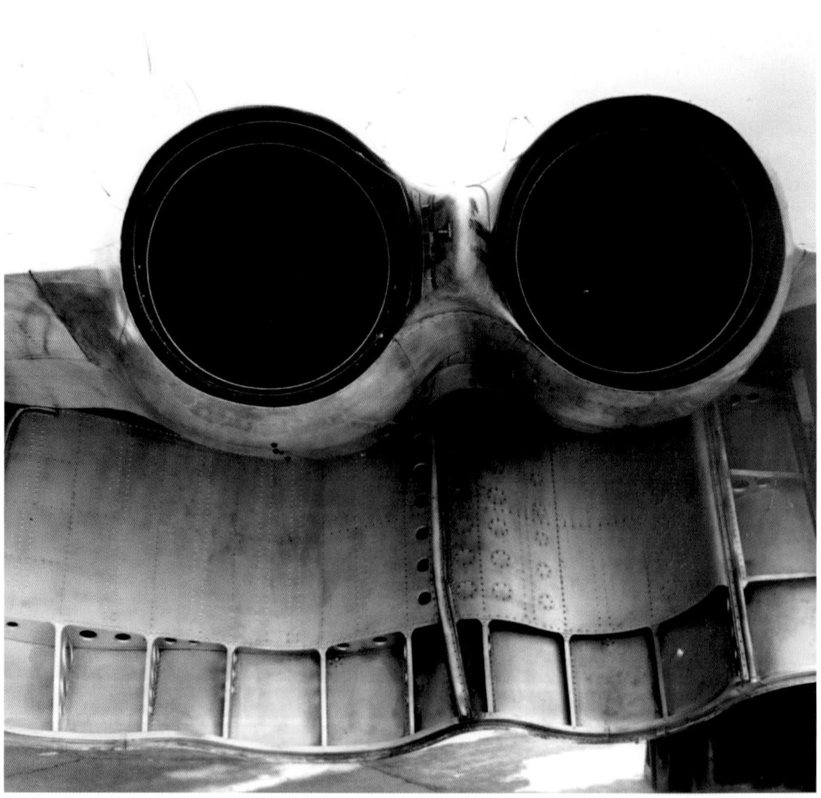

ABOVE LEFT: Canadian Pacific Airlines ordered two Comet 1As but the carrier's association with the type was not to be as happy as is suggested here by this picture of a model in its colours taken in September 1951. After the loss of the second aircraft on take-off from Karachi in March 1953, the other example was diverted to BOAC and re-registered G-ANAV.
OPPOSITE PAGE: Taken from an Air France brochure

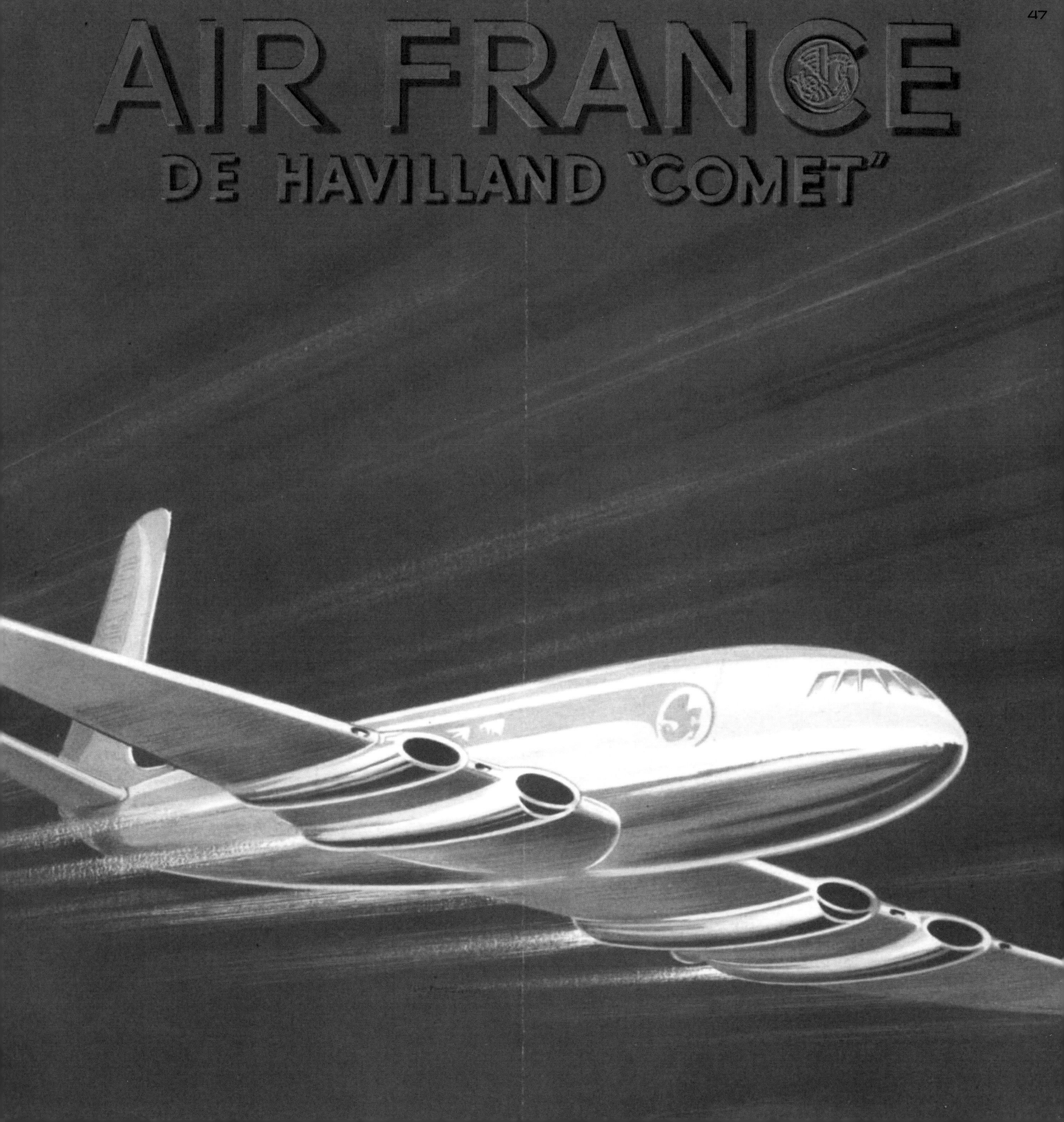
AIR FRANCE
DE HAVILLAND "COMET"

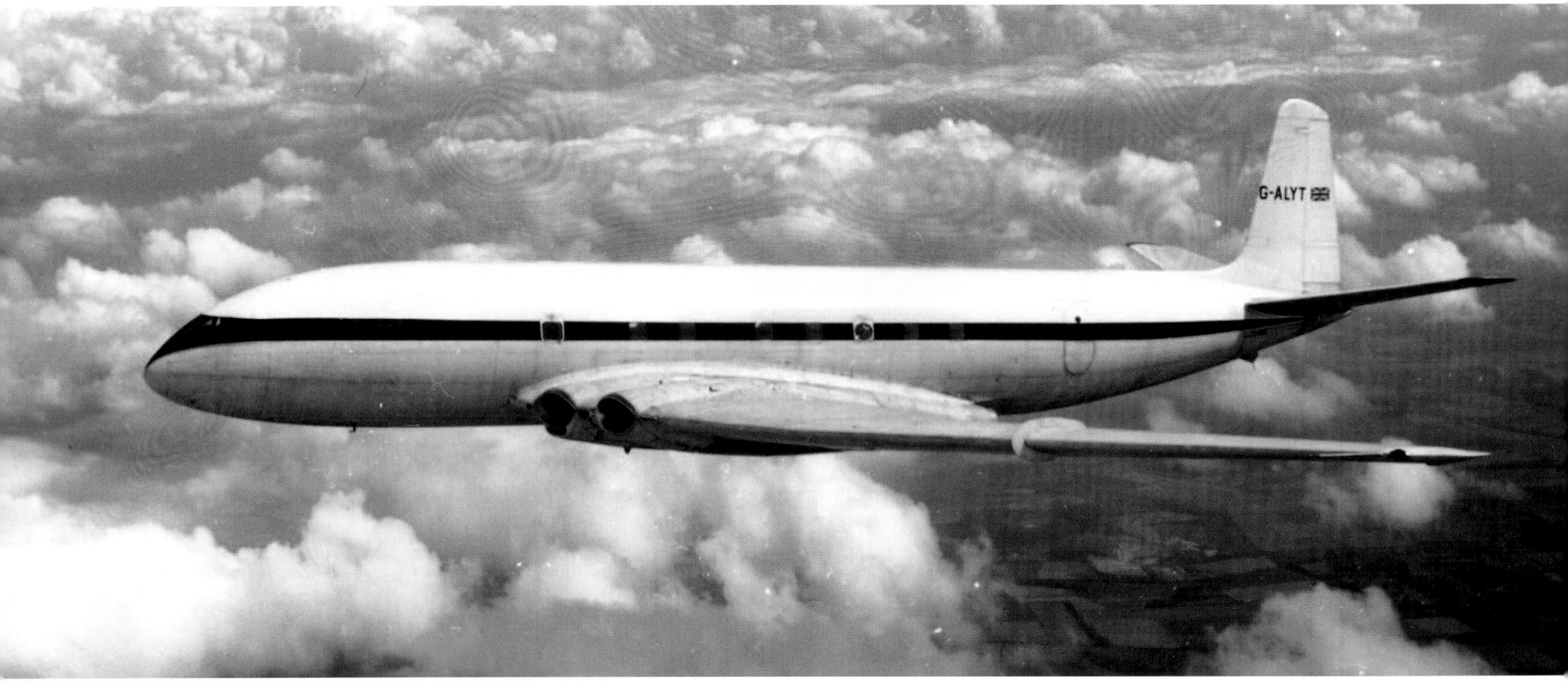
G-ALYT

February 1952. It lasted two hours during which Cunningham took the aircraft up to 25,000ft (7,700 m).

Like the 1A the Comet 2 had seats for 44 passengers but increased fuel tankage extended its range to 2,500 miles (4,000 km). Payload rose by 14 per cent. BOAC placed a launch order for 11 examples with deliveries expected to begin at the end of 1953. Further customers were British Commonwealth Pacific Airlines and also the RAF (see chapter nine).

Although also powered by the Avon engines, only one example of the long-range Comet 3 was ever built and it was to finish its life as the prototype for the most competent Comet of them all (see chapter seven).

Yet by May 1953 de Havilland's order book showed 63 Comets for airlines in eight countries. Of these, 17 were for Mk 1s or 1As, 35 for the bigger Mk 2 and 11 for the extended Mk 3. And in what was seen as a highly significant move, Pan American World Airways no less, had signed for three Mk3s.

Yet this was not de Havilland's first attempt to sell Comets to a US airline. Towards the end of 1951 the manufacturer had been trying to sell two Comet 1s to charter carrier Overseas National Airways but negotiations were halted when the Civil Aeronautics Administration refused to accept British certification of the type.

The Air Registration Board bridled at its competence to judge airworthiness being called into question and was particularly upset that its previous acceptance of US certification for types bought by BOAC had not received reciprocal treatment.

ONA's loss, however, was Air France's gain as de Havilland sold the two Comets originally earmarked for the American airline to the French flag carrier. It actually took three aircraft, the first of which was delivered in June 1953 and launched Comet services to Beirut in August. The following month it added routes to Cairo, Algiers and Casablanca.

But it was another French airline, the independent UTA (Union Aeromaritime de Transport) Aeromaritime, which became the second Comet operator after BOAC. Its first of three Comets arrived in December 1952 and the following February it launched jet services between Paris and Dakar via Casablanca. This was extended to Abidjan in April. A second African route was added to the scheduled in May with the opening of a route to Brazzaville via Kano, extended to Johannesburg in November.

Canadian Pacific Airlines ordered two Comet 1As, the first of which, delivered in March 1953, was written off after a take-off accident at Karachi the same day. The other aircraft was diverted to BOAC. The Royal Canadian Air Force also ordered two Comet 1As. They were retired in 1963 and 1964; one of them was sold and continued in operation, finally being broken up in 1975.

Comet 2 orders came from Australia, Brazil, Japan and Venezuela. But Pan Am's, for Comet 3s and in October 1952, was seen as the key one. The airline said that it intended to use the aircraft to open jet services on the prestigious trans-Atlantic route.

Opinions, however, were divided over the real purpose. Some saw the order as a wake-up call to the US aircraft industry while others believed it was a pilot purchase for a larger one to follow if the Comet met performance guarantees.

ABOVE: The first major Comet development was the Comet 2 in which Rolls-Royce Avons replaced the Ghosts of the Mk 1. G-ALYT, designated Comet 2X, was the sixth airframe off the production line and was retained by the manufacturer for development purposes.

In any case, Air India's order for Comet 3s followed a year later, although BOAC waited until February 1954.

Given the initial success enjoyed by BOAC's Comet operations the optimism seemed justifiable and shared with many people in Britain. But it was not necessarily seen that way outside the UK. According to the late Bill Gunston, one-time technical editor of Flight, the Comet prototype's first flight in July 1949 had drawn distinctly mixed feelings from the rest of the world.

"Half the air transport world refused to take it seriously," he wrote in 1961, *"and the rest took it very seriously indeed."* According to Gunston, the first category included the big American airlines. *"While acknowledging that here was a stepping stone to the future they damned it with faint praise and bought more piston-engined equipment,"* Gunston wrote.

The major US aircraft manufacturers took a similar view. They regarded the jet engine as uneconomical in its current stage of development and waited for the US military to fund the production of suitable power units in due course.

But US press coverage of the Comet's introduction into service was generally favourable. "This flight by the de Havilland Comet is jolting US airlines into the realisation that sooner or later they will have to acquire jet transports," "American airlines have been caught napping," "Our domination is seriously threatened by the British" and "Today's flight is just the beginning of Britain's effort to snatch away customers," represented typical US press comments.

The general feeling in the US towards the Comet was indifference. Congress, however, responded with four Bills, one of which was designed to subsidise US airlines which chose American-built jets in preference to foreign ones. The chief aim was, of course, to goad the nation's aircraft manufacturers to start work on rival jets but was based on the well-worn argument – still current in the 21st century – that aircraft manufacture in Europe was publicly subsidised. But some in the US industry reacted to the proposed legislation with suspicion, seeing it as the thin end of a wedge which could lead to nationalisation.

BOAC responded angrily to suggestions that its Comet operations were subsidised. In a statement issued in April 1953 it declared:

"Comets, which have been operating with high load factors, have made sufficient profit in the year to cover interest on capital. This is on a realistic costing basis, exactly applied to all the corporation's fleets, and including the cost of route-proving and training spread proportionately over the life of the aircraft. On the routes on which BOAC have been operating Comets, connecting London with Johannesburg, Colombo, Singapore and Tokyo an average load factor of 75 per cent shows a profit."

In 1950 a party of Boeing executives had visited the Farnborough air show. They were particularly impressed by the Comet. *"Appears to be a fine airplane,"* was the reaction of company president Bill Allen. Later, the Boeing party discussed the possibility of building a rival, perhaps with podded rather than buried engines and more pronounced wing sweep-back. Allen, though, kept coming back to the cost of developing a jet airliner.

He remained non-committal. When European airline bosses asked him about Boeing's plans for building a jet transport, he would only say: *"We're reviewing it."* His private view, though, was that building a jet the US airlines were not then

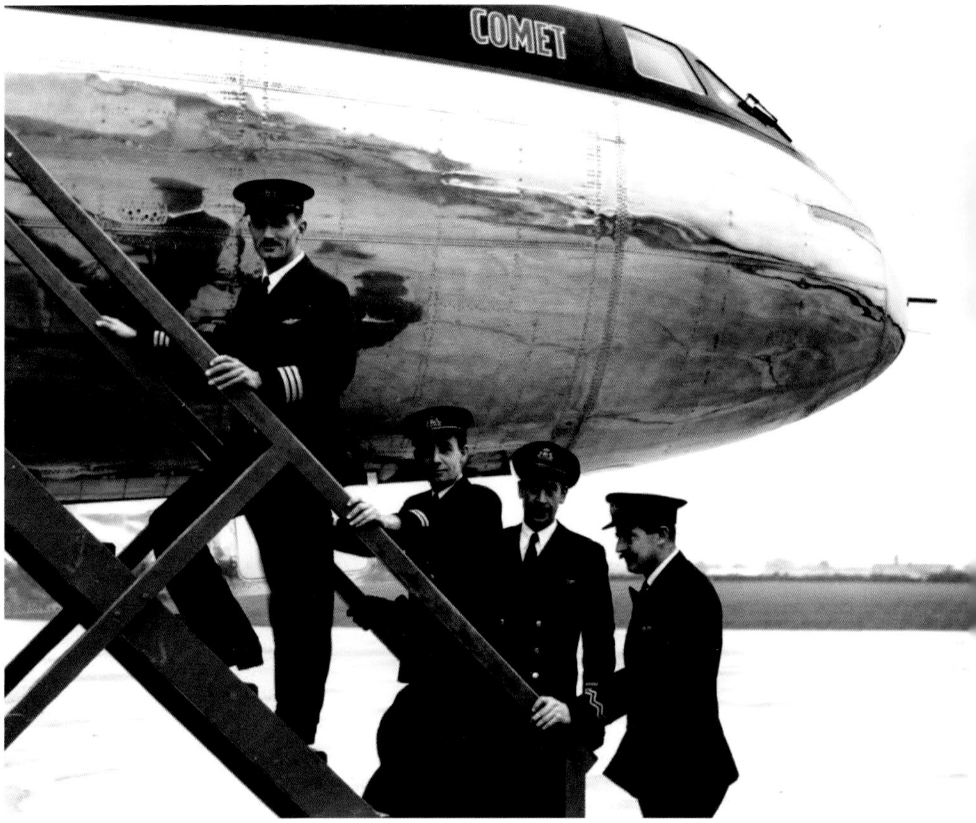
COMET

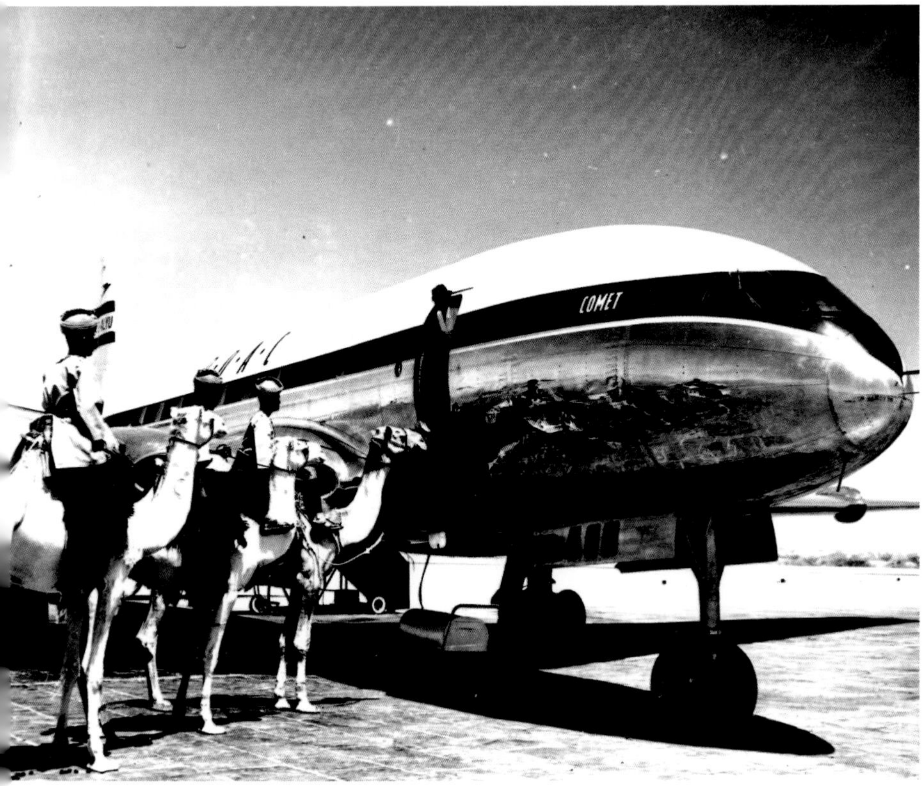
COMET

TOP: The crew of BOAC Comet G-ALYZ caught in the process of boarding for their next flight in September 1952 as the airline was extending its jet flights to the Far East.

BOTTOM LEFT: A further BOAC publicity shot taken during a North African stop by G-ALYU in 1952.

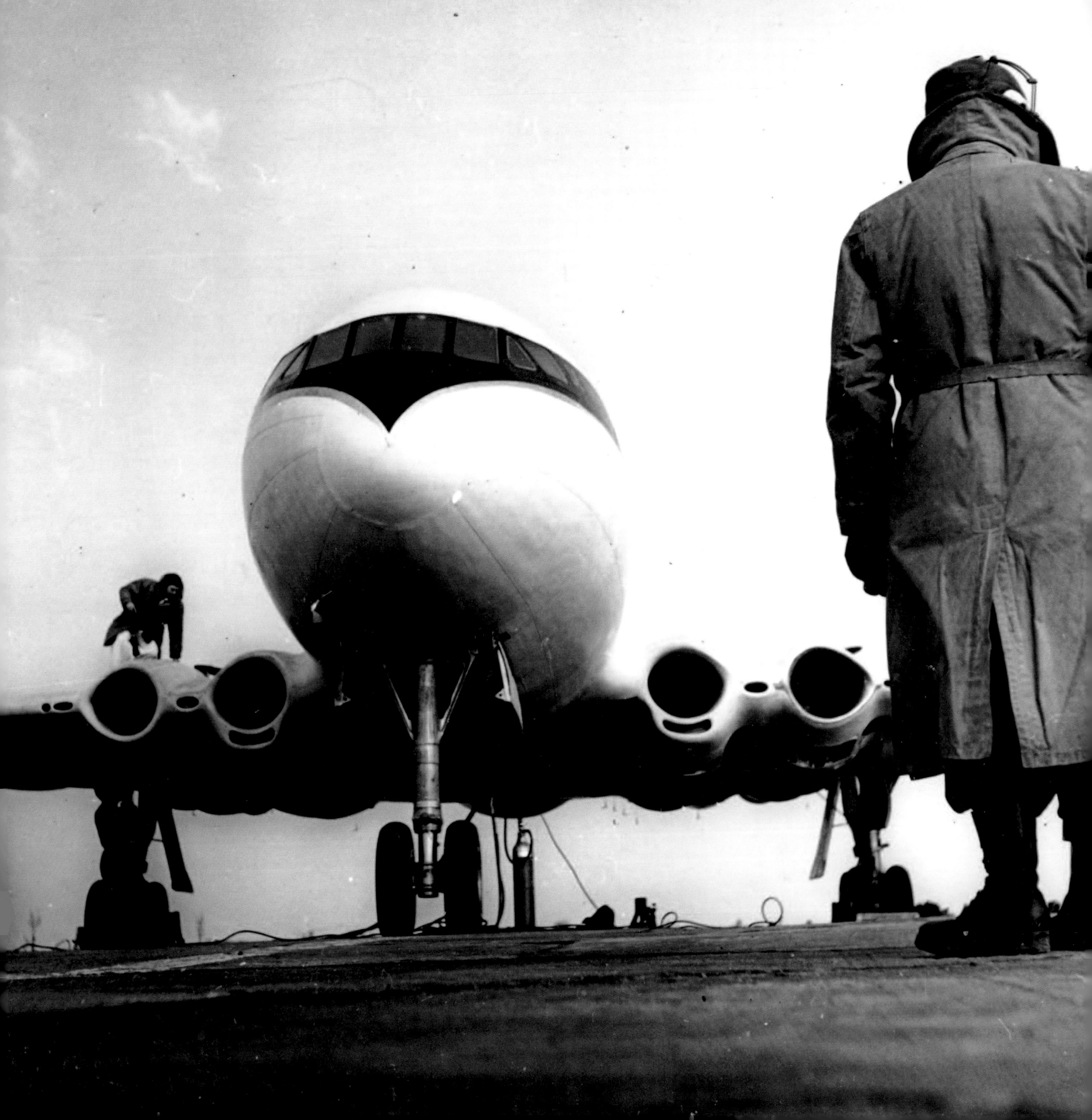

demanding might just be pouring millions of dollars down the drain. At the time the company was developing the B-47 and B-52 bombers and had just received a substantial air force order for KC-97s.

Even though Pan Am had shown its interest in the British it seemed the Americans were not ready to produce a rival to the Comet. Boeing, although busy with advanced swept-wing bombers, had offered a tentative specification for a jet airliner. But at this stage the customers were not interested. In an airliner market dominated by Douglas and Lockheed, Boeing was not then the powerhouse it later became. Yet six months before Pan Am's Comet order, Boeing's board had decided on a tangible demonstration of the company's ability by building a prototype.

Not for the first time or the last Boeing was contemplating a huge gamble. Company historian Mike Lombardi said: "Bill Allen and his team did feel the time was right but unfortunately they could not find customers who agreed - including the US Air Force. This is what makes his decision to invest all of the company's resources into building the Dash 80 one of the most important in business history. The leadership at Boeing understood that the future was in jets and staked the future of the company on that belief."

Donald Douglas was taking a cautious attitude. His DC-6 was still selling well and the DC-7, the ultimate piston-engined airliner, had yet to fly. There was no need to rush into anything. Like Lockheed and Convair, Douglas expected a gradual switch from piston engines to turbines with turboprops representing a reasonable half-way house. All three manufacturers were working on a new generation of piston-engined airliners with an eye on turboprop conversion in the

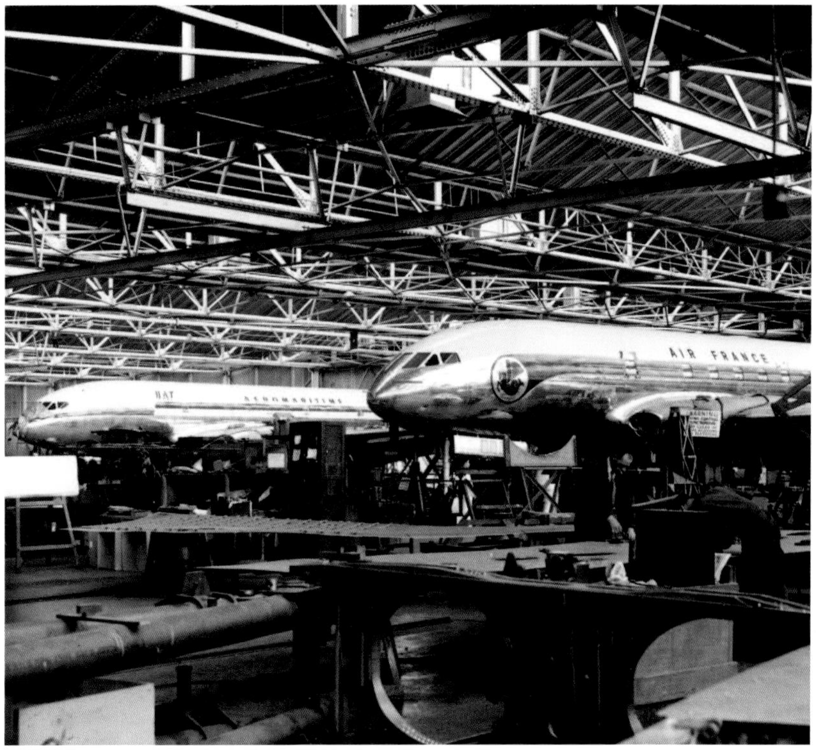
AIR FRANCE
UAT

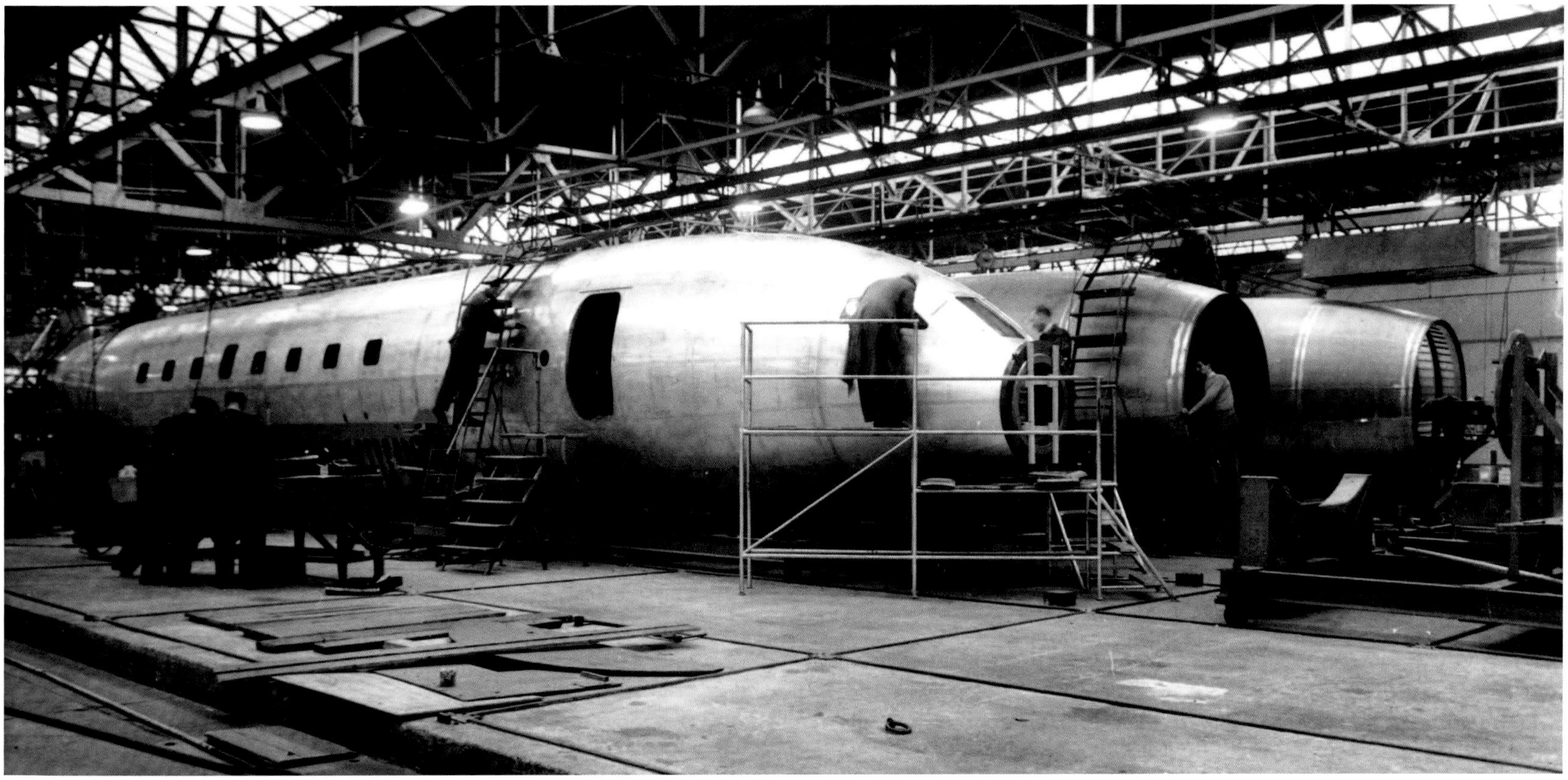

LEFT: This view of Comet 2X G-ALYT taken from an unusual angle in February 1952 clearly shows the intakes for the four Avon engines
ABOVE AND TOP: Comets under construction: (far right) 06019, F-BGSC, for UAT and 06020, FGNX for Air France in April 1953; (above) 06022, F-BGNZ for Air France, BOAC's 06024, G-AMXB and 06025, G-AMXC in January 1953.

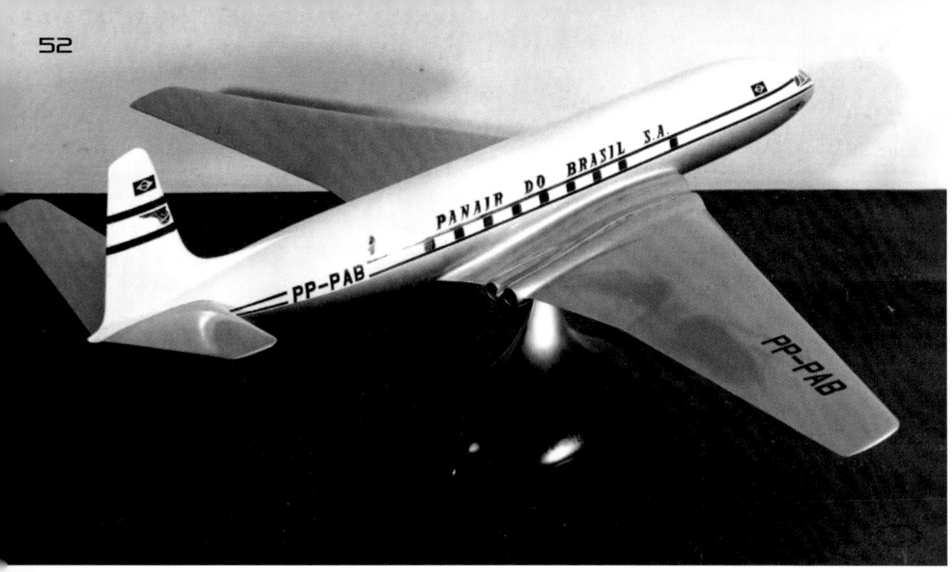
PANAIR DO BRASIL S.A.
PP-PAB
PP-PAB

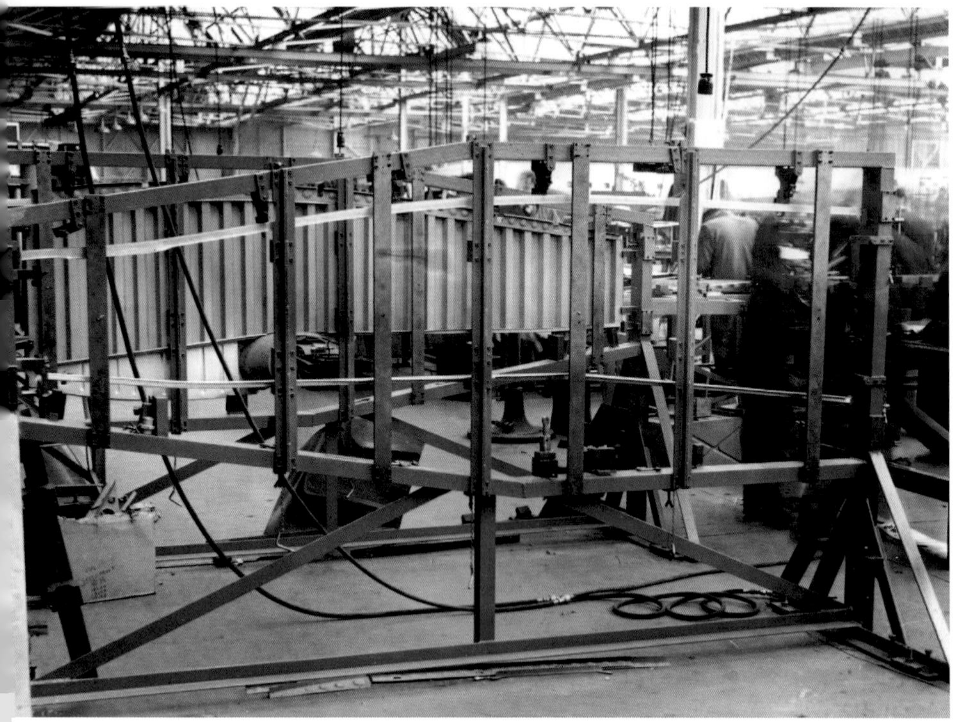

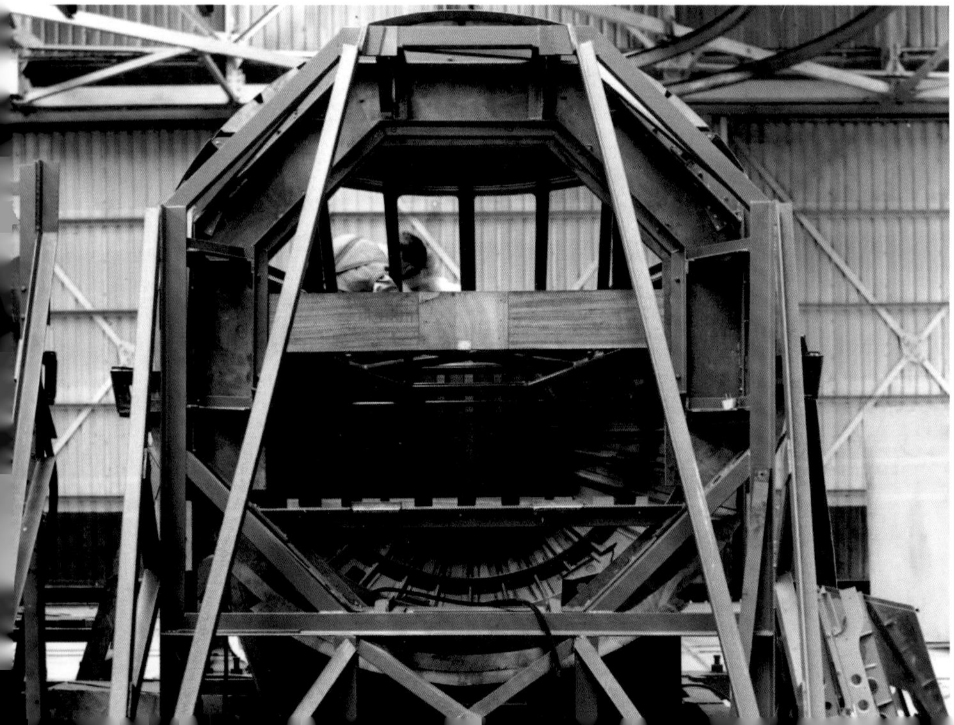

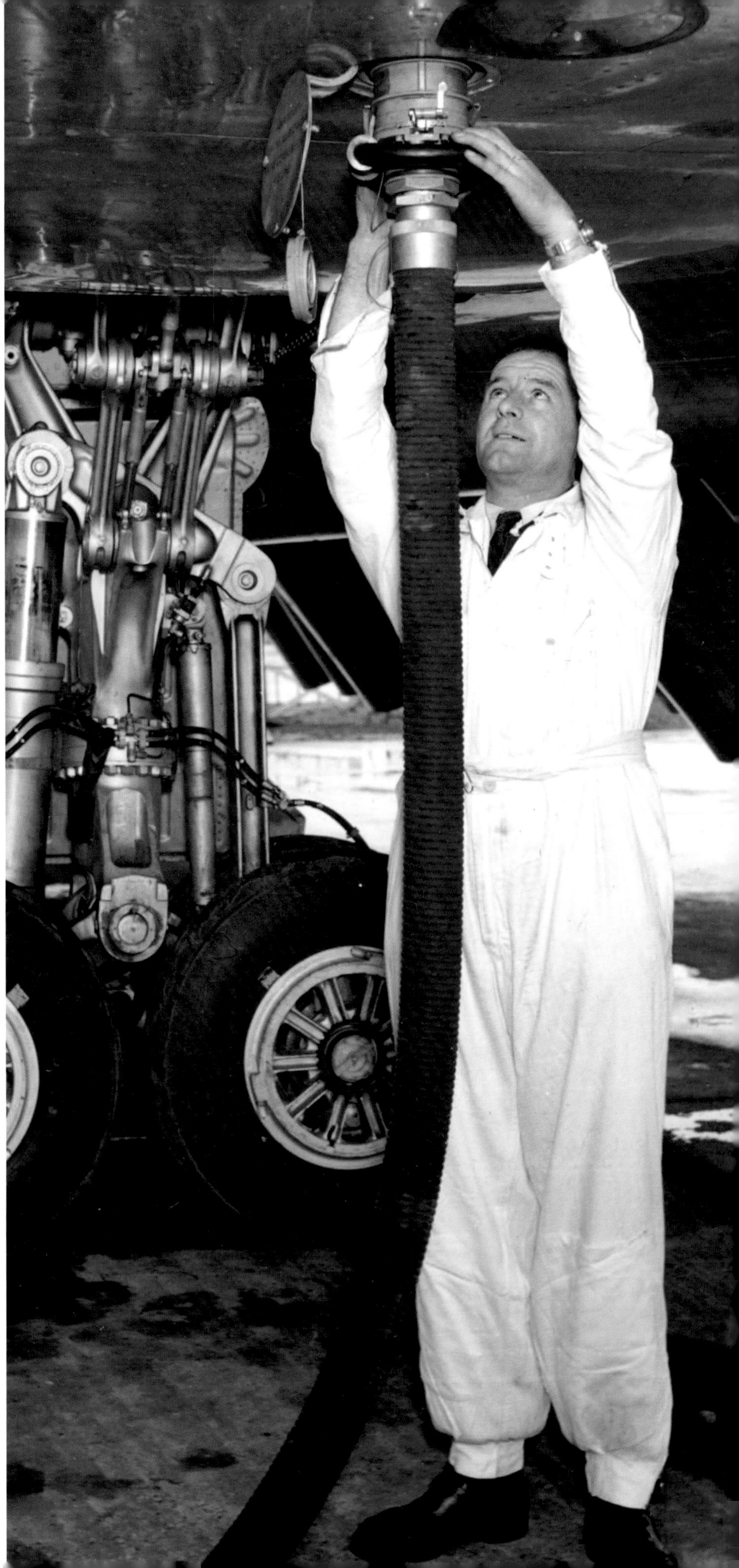

36 SEAT VERSION
COMET (SERIES II)
PASSENGER ACCOMMODATION
RADIO
CREW'S LOCKER FOR COATS & LIGHT LUGGAGE
EMERGENCY EXIT
LIGHT LUGGAGE RACK
EMERGENCY EXIT
WARDROBE CURTAIN
CREW ENTRY DOOR
EQUIPMENT BAY
LUGGAGE & FREIGHT COMPARTMENT 185 CUBIC FT.
ACCESS DOOR
ACCESS DOOR TO LUGGAGE COMPARTMENT
9 FT. 9 IN.
7 FT 0 IN
29 FT. 1·0 IN.
6 FT 6·5 IN.
17·5 IN
GANGWAY
8 FT. 11·75 IN.
FORWARD CABIN FOR 8 PASSENGERS
MAIN CABIN FOR 28 PASSENGERS
CREW ENTRY DOOR
STEWARD'S TIP-UP SEAT
CHAIRS PITCHED AT 45 IN.
CUPBOARD FOR OFFICIAL STOWAGE
GENTLEMEN'S WASH ROOM
RADIO OPERATOR
FIRST OFFICER
GALLEY
LIGHT LUGGAGE & FREIGHT
GENTLEMENS TOILET
LUGGAGE & FREIGHT HOLD 200 CU. FT
WARDROBE & HAT RACK
LADIES' TOILET
CAPTAIN
NAVIGATOR
SEAT & TABLE FOR STEWARDESS
PASSENGER ENTRY DOOR
LADIES' POWDER ROOM

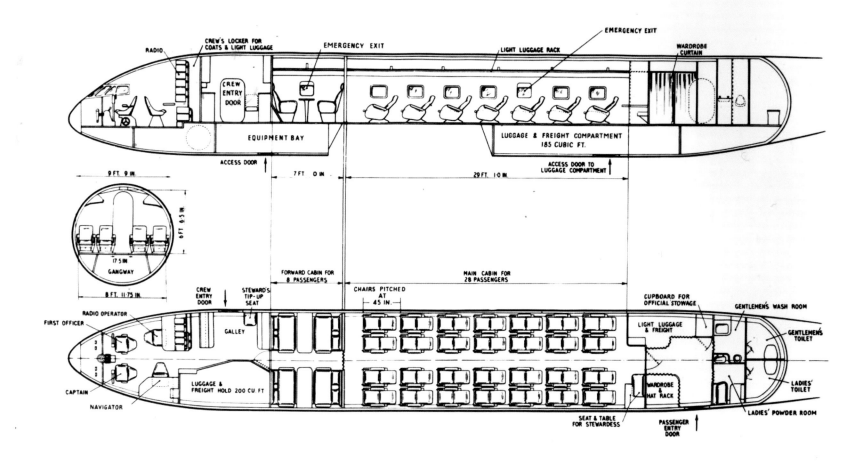

future. Douglas was still sceptical about jets in 1954.

Even after a year in service, therefore, the Comet had no rivals and none was in prospect. It seemed that BOAC and de Havilland had the world at their feet. So perhaps the biggest compliment was paid by those airlines which responded by talking down the jet, casting doubt on its operating economics and suggesting it was merely a flash in the pan.

There were other doubters. In his Empire of the Clouds, published in 2010, James Hamilton-Paterson quotes former test pilot Bill Waterton, later air correspondent of the Daily Express and co-author of a book on the Comet, as calling the first jet airliner "a brilliant conception let down by its aerodynamics, engineering and handling." It was, Waterton added, "'nothing like a one hundred per cent aeroplane." He was also dubious about the handling, recalling that in the early Comets, especially on take-off, the pilot "seemed very busy and even uneasy."

Back in April 1952 Flight had been moved to hit out at sceptics and *"saloon bar savants."* The journal declared in a patriotic editorial: *"One of the finest things this country has ever done is to build the Comet, though one would scarcely realise it to hear some of the experts talk. That BOAC should hitch their wagon to this wonderful machine and, flaunting prejudice and incredulity, throw down a challenge to the world, is apparently regarded by these gentlemen as either puerile escapism or downright dishonesty."*

OPPOSITE PAGE: De Havilland was on the verge of technical leadership when the loss of two Comet 1s in 1954 combined with the subsequent inquiry and resulting publicity changed everything. **(Top)** By the end of 1953 35 Comet 2s had been ordered including four for Panair do Brasil; **(Middle)** Comet 2 wing in its assembly jig. **(Bottom)** Comet 2 cockpit section under construction. **MAIN IMAGE:** Refuelling Comet 2X G-ALYT in January 1953.

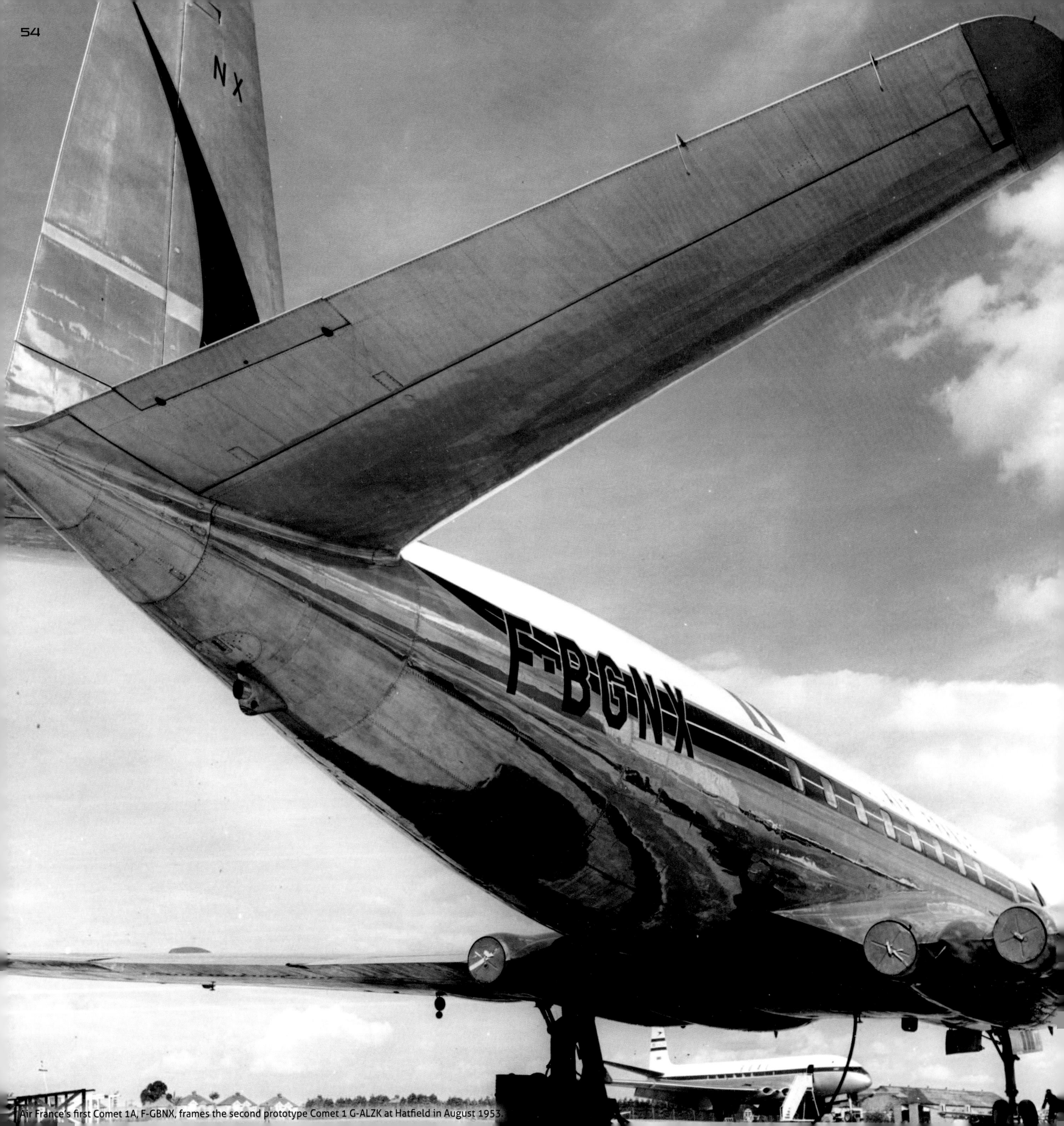
F-BGNX

Air France's first Comet 1A, F-GBNX, frames the second prototype Comet 1 G-ALZK at Hatfield in August 1953.

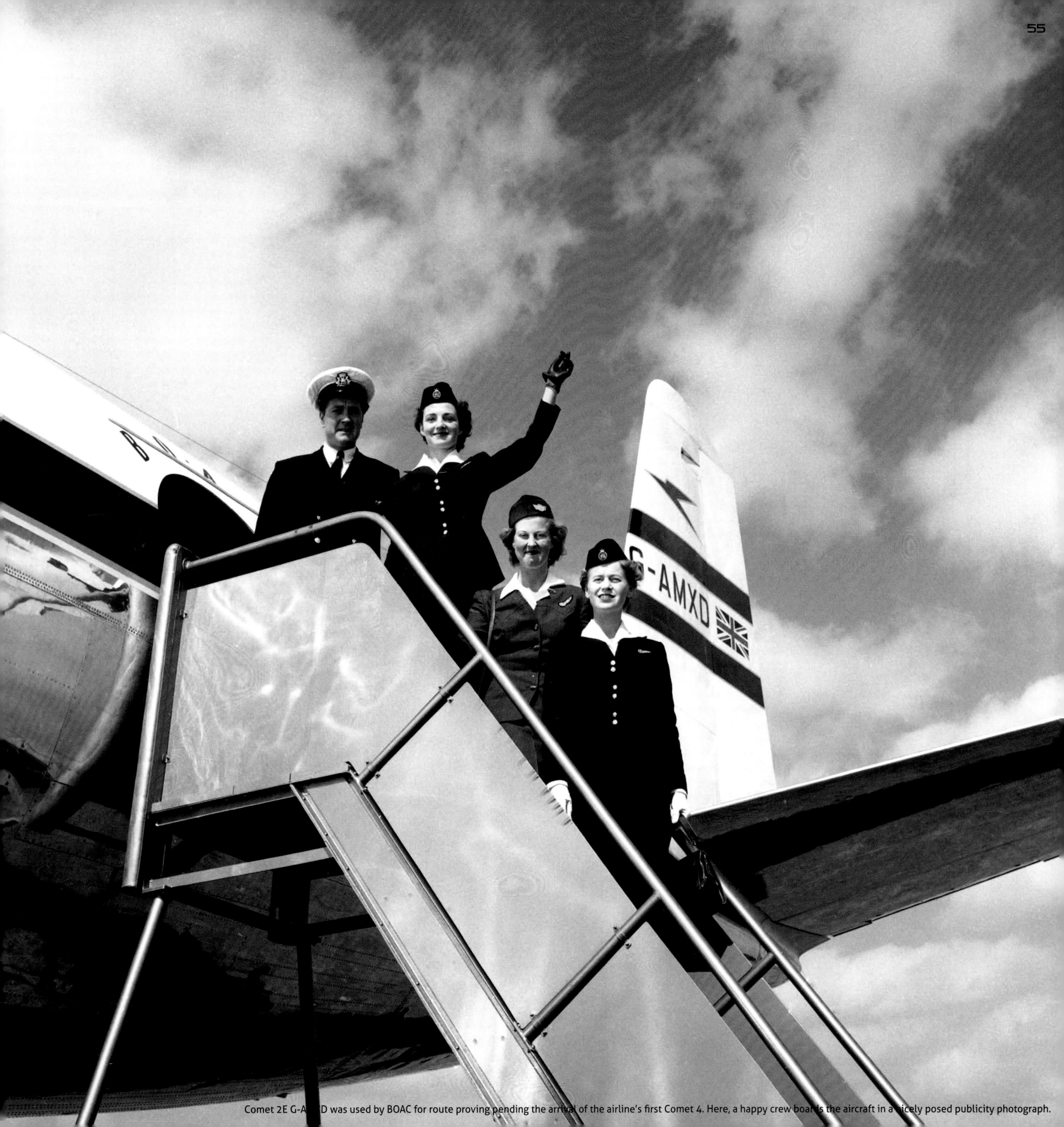
G-AMXD

Comet 2E G-AMXD was used by BOAC for route proving pending the arrival of the airline's first Comet 4. Here, a happy crew boards the aircraft in a nicely posed publicity photograph.

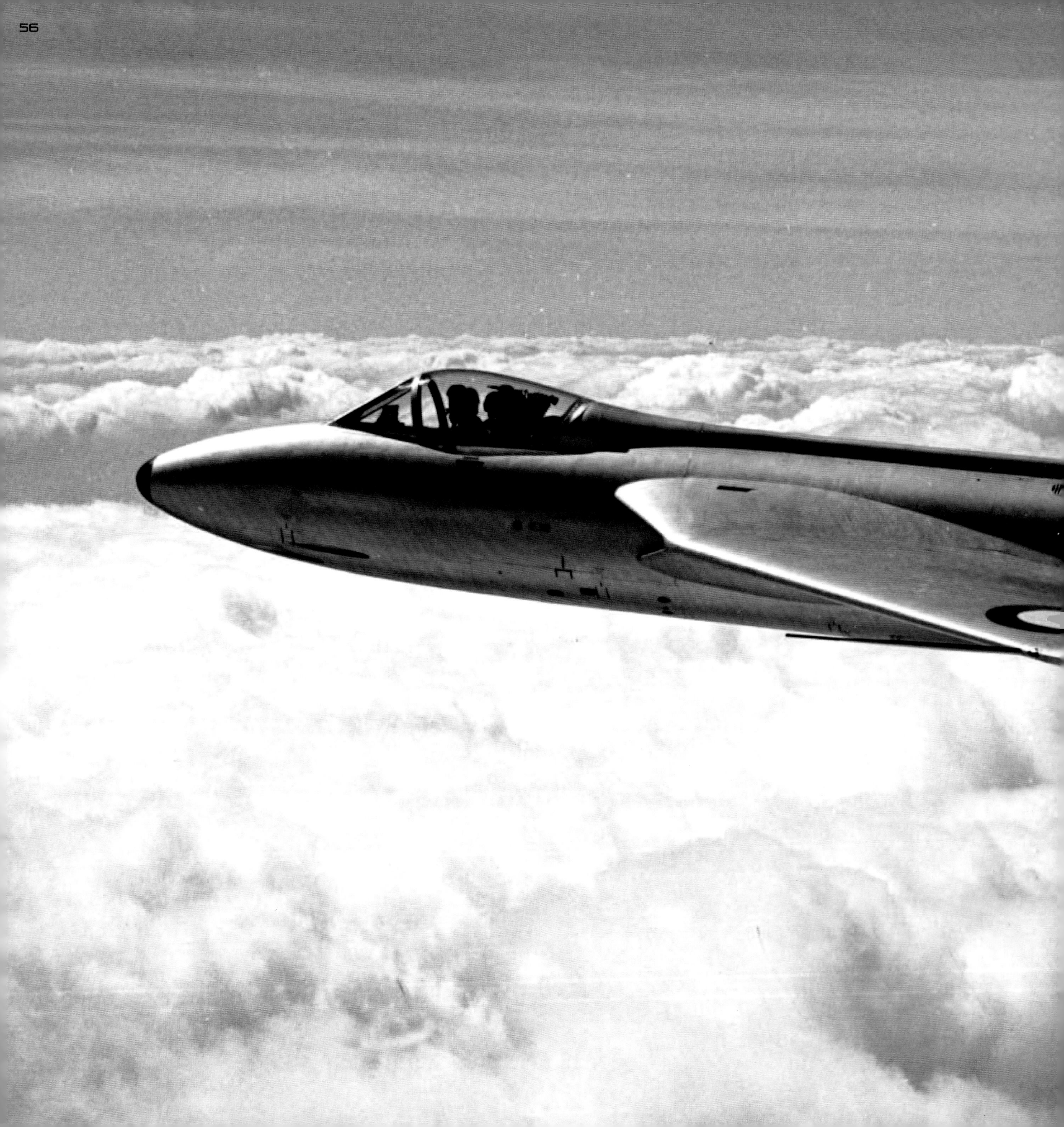

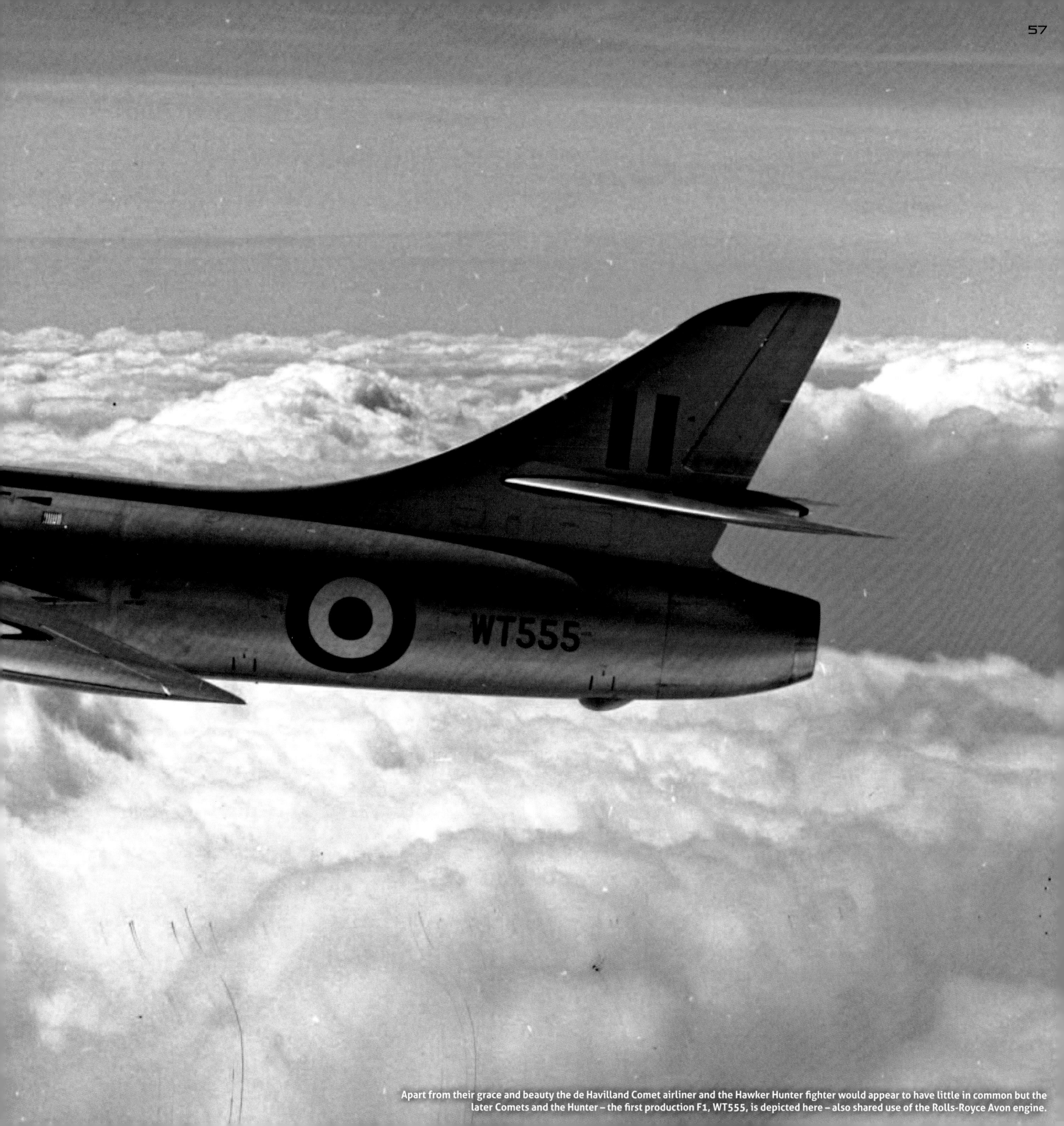
WT555

Apart from their grace and beauty the de Havilland Comet airliner and the Hawker Hunter fighter would appear to have little in common but the later Comets and the Hunter – the first production F1, WT555, is depicted here – also shared use of the Rolls-Royce Avon engine.

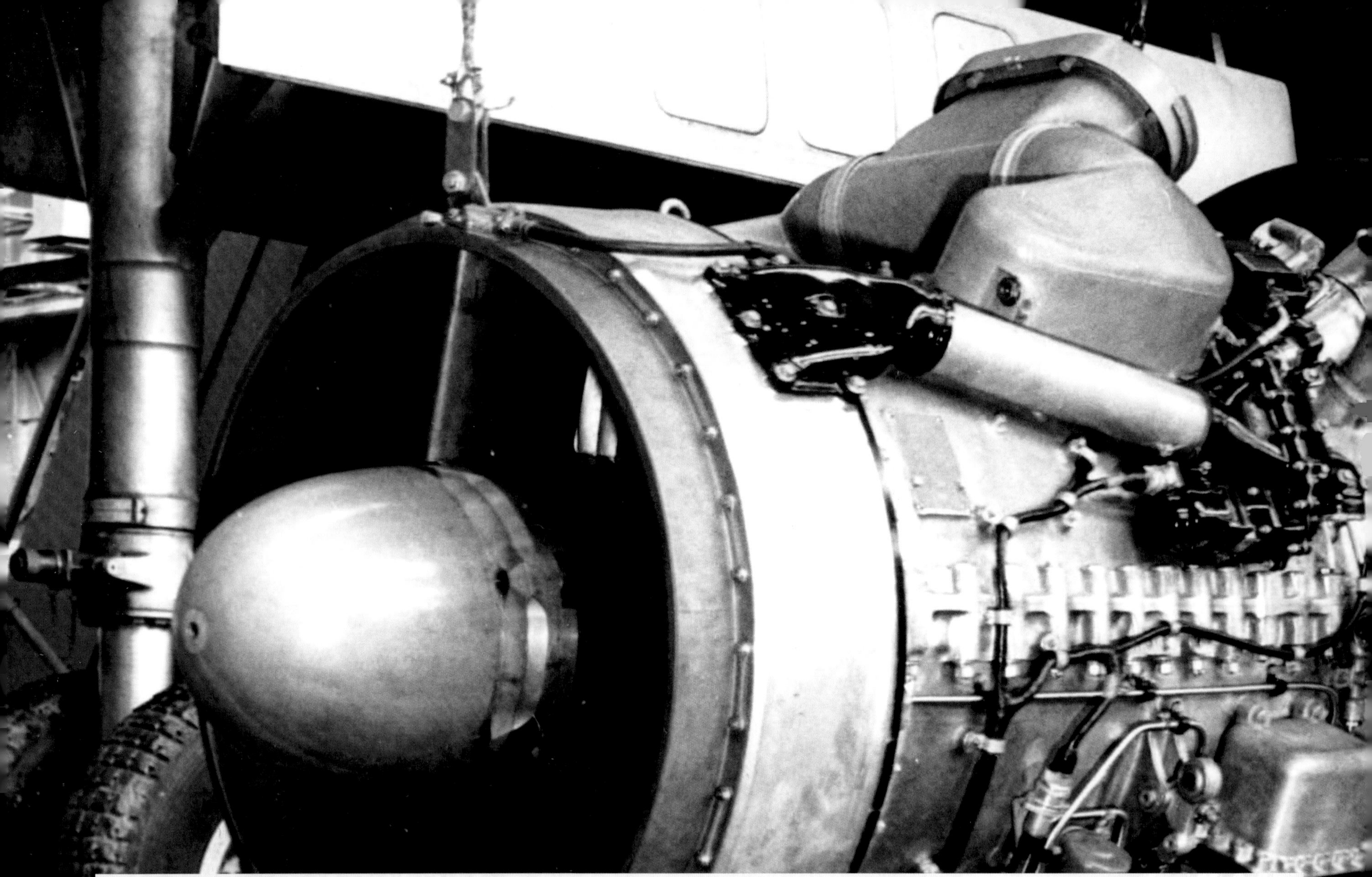

The Rolls-Royce Avon

The first axial flow power plant to be produced by Rolls-Royce, the Avon went on to become one of the manufacturer's most successful turbojet engines. It was used in a wide variety of aircraft, both military and civil, including the English Electric Canberra, Hawker Hunter, Sud Caravelle and de Havilland Comet.

The engine had originally been intended as a first venture into axial flow engines by Rolls-Royce and possibly as a replacement for the same company's Nene. The design team was led by Cyril Lovesey, who had previously been in charge of developing the Merlin piston engine which had powered the wartime Hurricane and Spitfire fighters.

The AJ.65 (axial jet, 6,500lbs of thrust) – was originally conceived as a company-funded private-venture by Dr Alan Griffith as a single spool design with eight-stage compressor. Development started in 1945 as a power plant for the Canberra bomber. The first RA.1 was bench-tested in 1947. Although it ran for two hours it was obvious there were problems with the unit.

Rolls-Royce persisted and with a ten-stage compressor began to function in a more promising way. The Avon RA.2 developed 6,000lb (2,700 kg) of thrust and two were installed in a Lancastrian test bed, which flew in 1948. By this time the Avon was receiving government funding.

The first RA.3 with two-stage turbine ran in 1949 and was displayed at that year's Farnborough show in a Meteor test bed. Full-scale production of the Avon Mk 1 began in 1950 and was cleared for use in the RAF's first Canberra squadron in 1951.

In 1950 the engine had been chosen for developed variants of the de Havilland Comet. It was still rated at 6,500lb thrust but by the time it had been installed in the Comet 2, this rose to 7,100lb (3,200 kg). When it was specified for the Comet 4 the output had reached 10,500lb (4,700 kg).

The Avon, equipped with after-burning, was also used in several high-speed aircraft including the Lightning interceptor and the Fairley Delta 2 research aircraft which set a new world air speed record of 1,132mph (1,811 kmh) in 1956.

The Rolls-Royce Avon was licence-built in a number of countries including Sweden, Belgium and Australia. A total of nearly 11,000 Avon aero engines was built by the time 24 years of production ended in 1974. But the Avon 200 industrial gas generator is still in production with 1,200 examples sold.

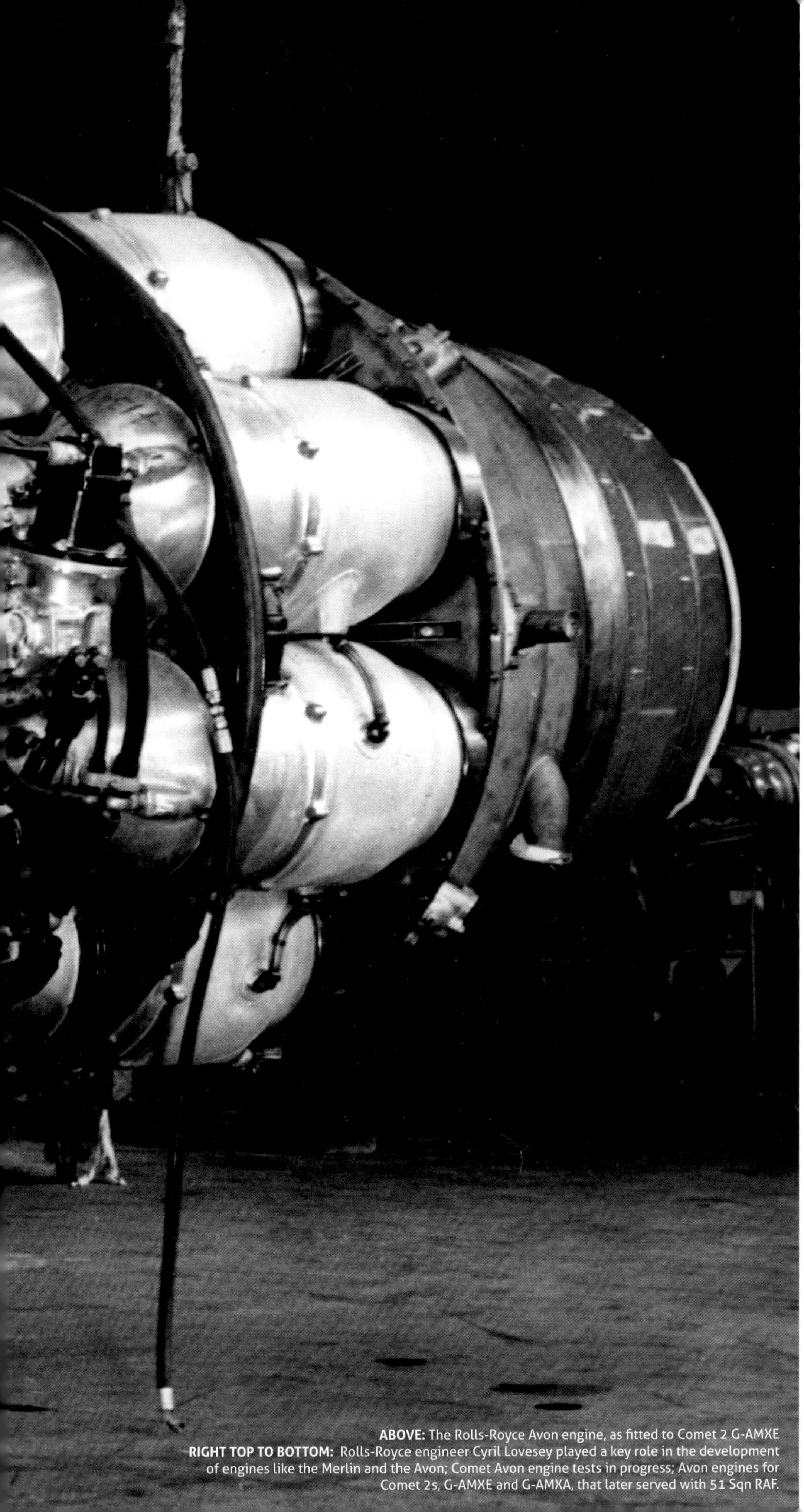

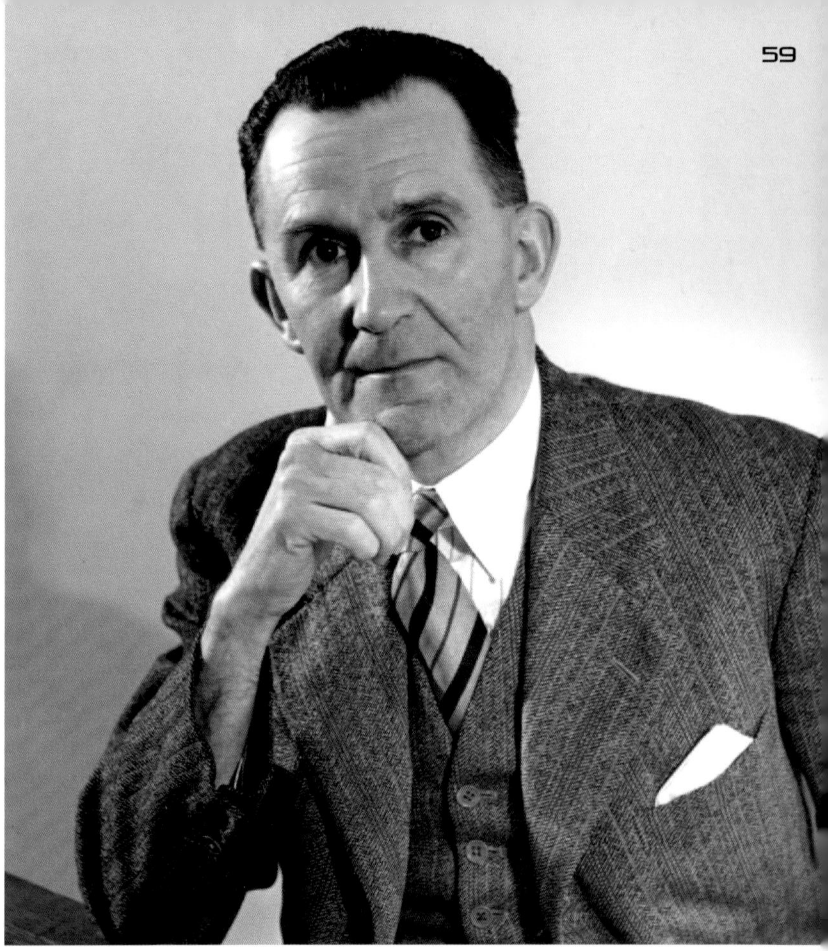

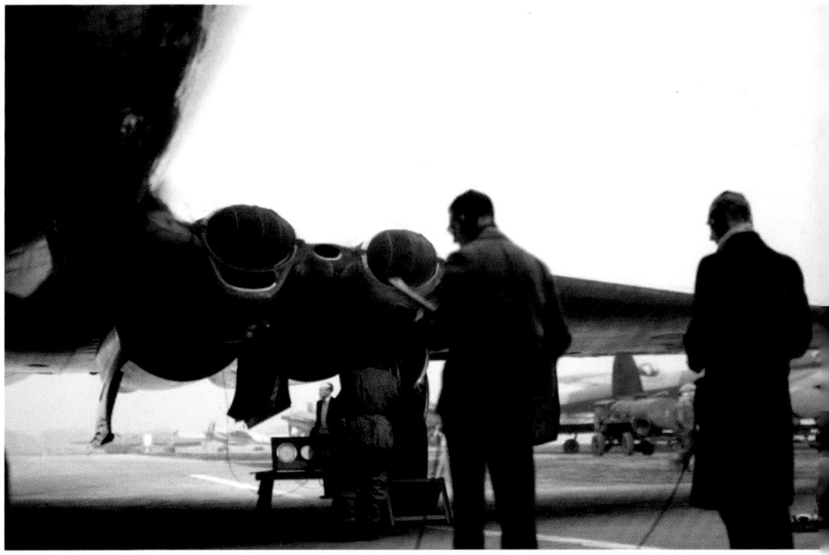

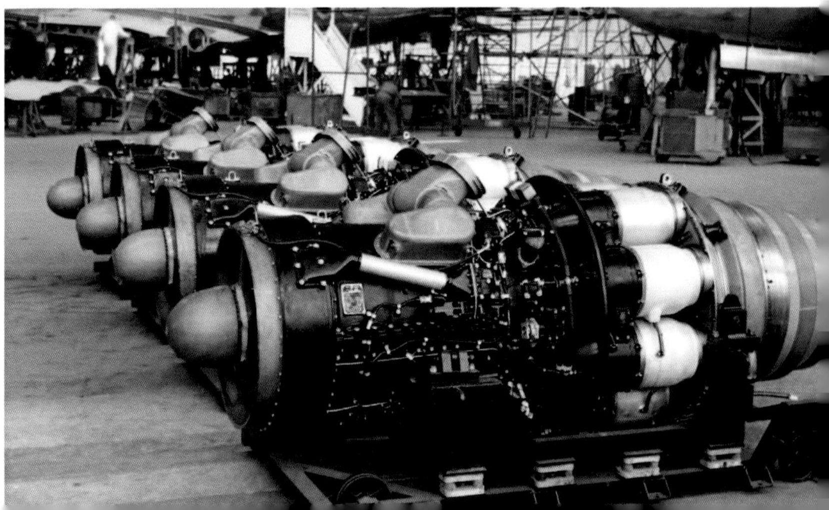

ABOVE: The Rolls-Royce Avon engine, as fitted to Comet 2 G-AMXE
RIGHT TOP TO BOTTOM: Rolls-Royce engineer Cyril Lovesey played a key role in the development of engines like the Merlin and the Avon; Comet Avon engine tests in progress; Avon engines for Comet 2s, G-AMXE and G-AMXA, that later served with 51 Sqn RAF.

John Cunningham

John Cunningham was typical of the test pilots who became heroes to countless schoolboys in the 1940s and 50s.

He was born in 1917 and was nine when he had his first flight, in an Avro 504. After school at Whitchurch, near Croydon airport, he went on to an apprenticeship with de Havilland. As a week-end flier with No 604 (County of Middlesex) Squadron, Auxiliary Air Force, he was called up for full-time RAF service shortly before the Second World War flying Blenheim fighters. But it was in a Beaufighter that he gained his first success, shooting down two Heinkel He111s on one night in 1940.

As his score mounted the story was spread that Cunningham's exceptional night vision was due to a diet of carrots. The press called him Cat's Eyes, a nickname which stuck, but the story had been invented to cover the real reason for the success: airborne intercept radar. Later he reflected that eating carrots might have been easier, such was the hard work involved in perfecting radar-guided interception. But in April 1941 Cunningham and his radar operator Jimmy Rawnsley destroyed three enemy bombers in a single night and in 1943 he became CO of 85 Squadron with Mosquito night fighters. By the war's end he had a score of at least 20 and at just 26 was a group captain.

Cunningham re-joined de Havilland and, following the death of Geoffrey de Havilland Jr, became its chief test pilot. He was a key member of the team which developed the Comet and he earned a place in aviation history when, on July 27 1949, his 32nd birthday, Cunningham made a 35-minute maiden flight in the world's first jet airliner.

When in 1954 two BOAC Comets broke up in flight over the Mediterranean within a few months of each other Cunningham immersed himself in the investigation. During a world tour with the revised Comet 3 in 1955 President Eisenhower presented him with the prestigious Harmon Trophy for service to aviation. Three years later the Comet 4 went into service on the North Atlantic route and Cunningham gained a seat on the de Havilland board.

With Hawker Siddeley he became involved with the Trident programme. After its certification in 1964 the focus shifted to smoothing its way into service, delivering aircraft and training crews. But in 1975, while demonstrating an HS 125 executive jet to a party of Chinese visitors, Cunningham had his most serious accident. On take-off from Dunsfold the engines ingested birds and the aircraft hit a car killing four occupants. Although Cunningham sustained crushed vertebrae none of his passengers was hurt.

He continued as chief test pilot after the formation of British Aerospace, becoming an executive director. He retired in 1980. His talents had been summed up by Sir Geoffrey de Havilland who called him "test pilot, demonstration pilot and ambassador all in one and has made some sensational flights. He can do thousands of miles for many days and at the end of the flight can be charming, unruffled and apparently as fresh as ever when discussing points raised by a host of officials, pressmen and others."

Among many honours, Cunningham was appointed OBE in 1951 and CBE in 1963. Wartime service earned him the DSO with two Bars and the DFC and Bar.

He died in 2002 aged 84.

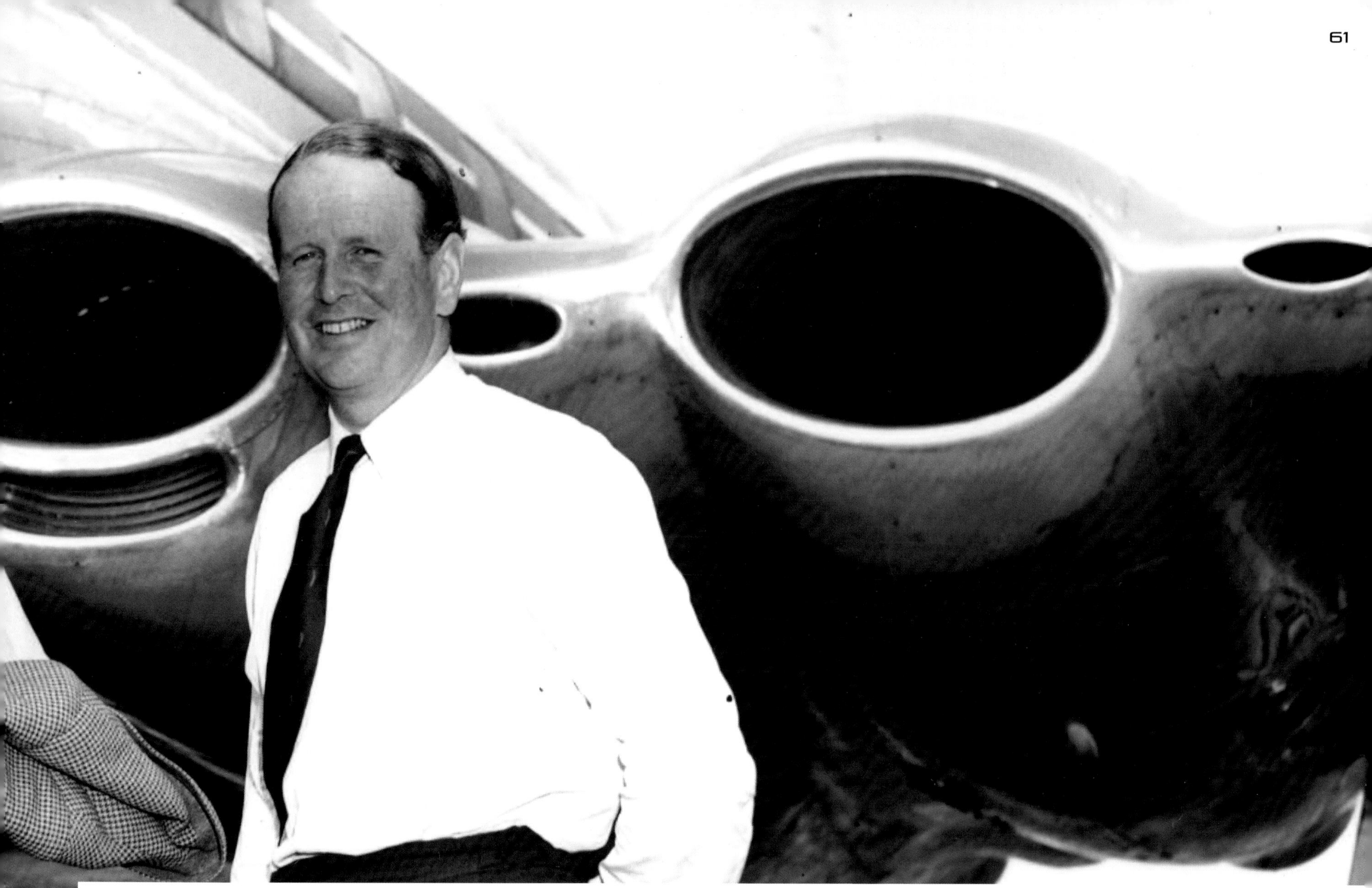

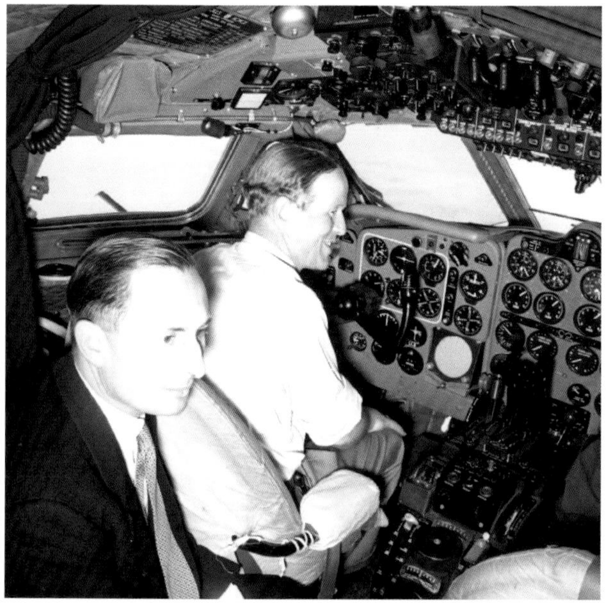

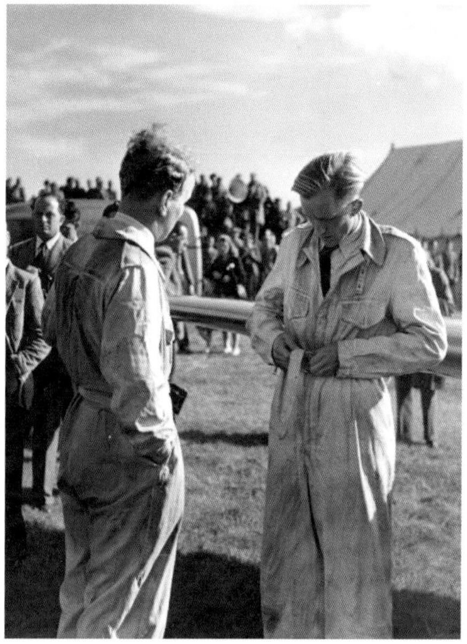

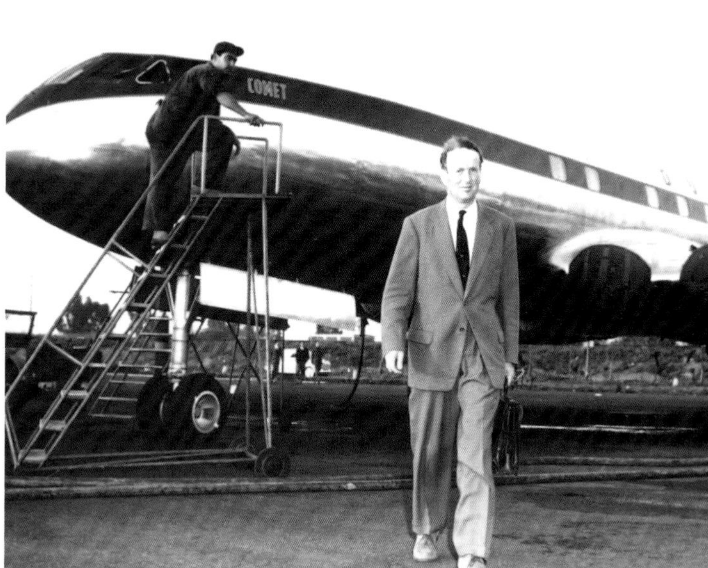
COMET

Images from the life of de Havilland chief test pilot John Cunningham.
MAIN IMAGE: In front of Comet 1XB, 5301, one of two operated by the Royal Canadian Air Force
3 INSET IMAGES: (left) on the flight deck of BOAC Comet 4 G-APDA, June 1958; (middle) with John Derry; (right) striding away from Comet 2 G-AMXD, October 1955.

THE 1954 COMET LOSSES

From Triumph to Tragedy to Triumph

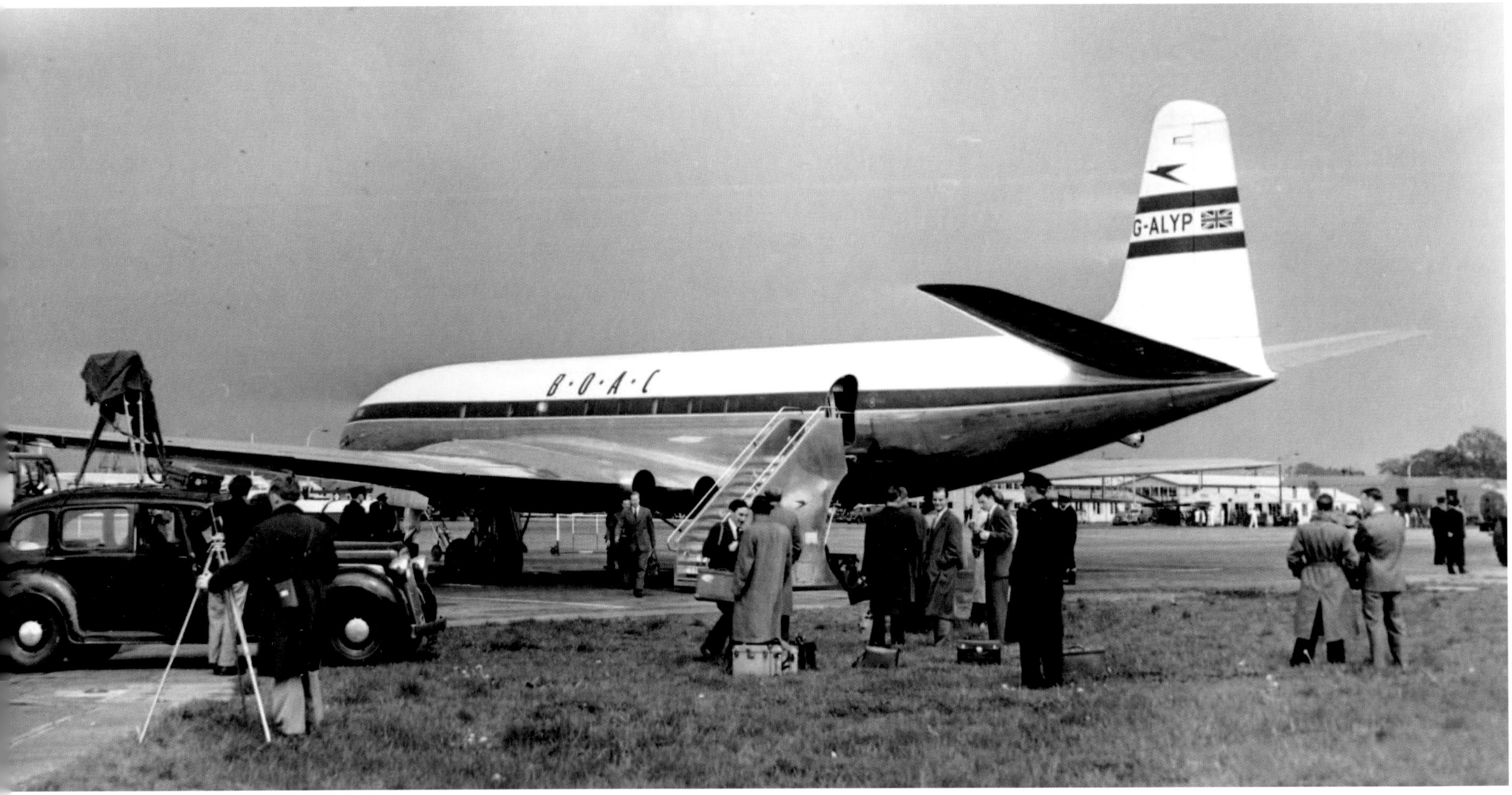
G-ALYP
B·O·A·C

It came out of a clear blue sky as such things often do, shocking and without warning.

In the case of BOAC's Comet Yoke Peter it was a blue Mediterranean sky but the location was of secondary importance for what happened that day in 1954 forced the industry to make profound changes in its approach to the technology it had introduced.

The de Havilland Comet was nearing the start of its second year in service by January 1954. The jet airliners had been setting new standards of speed and passenger comfort when G-ALYP, the very aircraft which had inaugurated commercial jet operations in May 1952, simply disappeared.

Captain Alan Gibson and his crew – First Officer Bury, Radio Officer Macmahon, Flight Engineer Macdonald, Steward F L Saunders and Stewardess Jean Cark – took over the aircraft at Rome for the final leg of its journey from Singapore to London.

Everything appeared normal. Capt E E Rodley, BOAC's Comet Flight Captain, was later to describe Gibson as a commander who had shown himself to be *"extremely capable"* of dealing with any emergencies which might arise. The other crew members were similarly experienced on the Comet.

The aircraft had arrived at Rome's Ciampino airport from Beirut at 0830hr on January 10. It took off to operate Flight 781 to London just over an hour later. The aircraft climbed rapidly in accordance with its flight plan which called for it to level off at 36,000ft (11,000 m). From then on the aircraft sent a stream of routine position reports to Ciampino.

At 0950hr Gibson radioed that the Comet was flying at 26,500ft (8,150 m) over the Orbetello beacon and still climbing. As soon as this message had been transmitted, Capt J R Johnson, pilot of a BOAC piston-engined Argonaut, which had left Rome 12 minutes before the Comet, received a message from Gibson who had earlier promised to tell him the height at which he could expect to break out of the clouds.

At this point the Comet was probably crossing the Italian coast on its way to Elba at about 27,000ft (8,300 m). Its message began: "George How Jig from George Yoke Peter, did you get my......?"

The message was never finished. It was the last anyone heard from the Comet.

Bobbing in his boat five miles below on the Mediterranean Ninuccio Geri was busy with his fishing nets. *"I heard a heavy roaring noise like thunder,"* he would say later. *"I turned in the direction of the noise and saw a globe of fire rotating as it came down into the sea."*

Ashore, farmer Vasco Nomellini heard the sound of a passing aircraft but ignored it. Then he too heard a sudden *"roaring sound in the air"* coming from

TOP: From triumph to tragedy: BOAC Comet 1 G-ALYP, pictured on the day it operated the world's first commercial jet flight, was lost in January 1954 when it broke up over the Mediterranean.

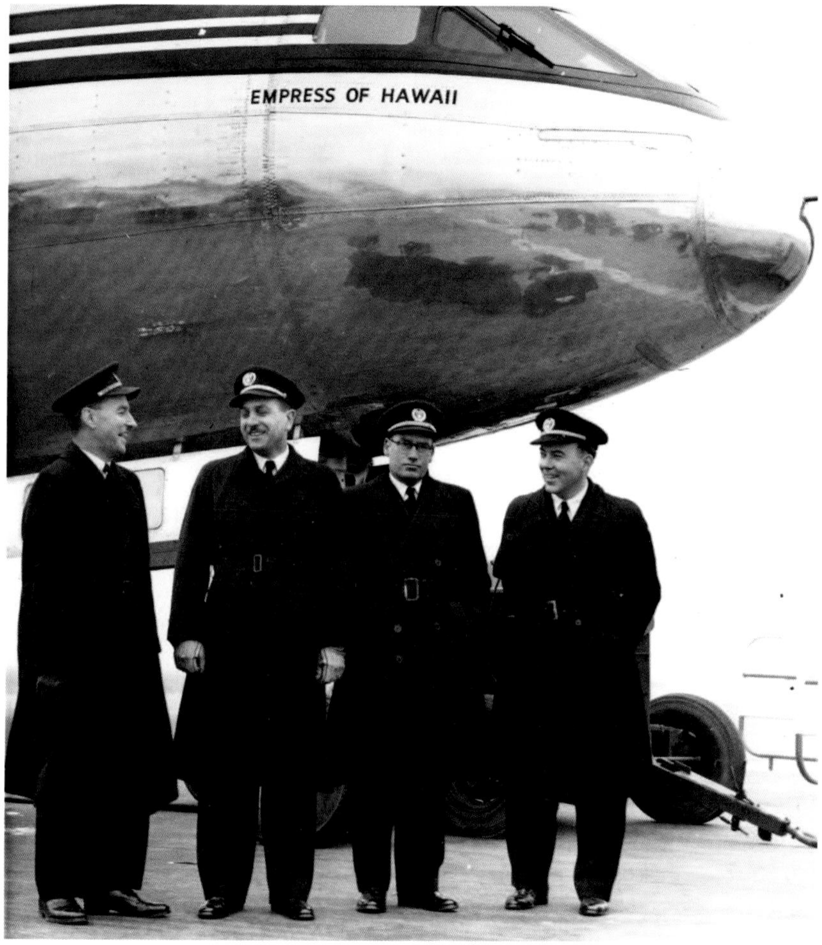
EMPRESS OF HAWAII

the same direction as the passing aircraft. Looking up he saw *"two pieces of an aircraft, the smaller in flames, falling in almost parallel lines into the sea.* "Leopoldo Lorenzini, a driver, also noticed the roaring sound from the sky. Then he saw a red flame falling into the sea, followed by a coil of smoke.

The authorities were notified and Lt Col Guiseppe Lombardi, head of the harbour authority at Porteferraio, Elba put in hand an immediate and extensive search and rescue operation involving ships and aircraft.

The loss of Yoke Peter and the lives of the 35 passengers and crew naturally came as a massive shock to BOAC. There had been accidents before and three aircraft had been written off overshooting the runway. These accidents were attributed to pilot error but a drooped leading edge was fitted to the wings of all Comets to improve take-off performance. Far more serious, however, was the loss near Calcutta of G-ALYV which broke apart in the air during a tropical storm.

Following the accident to Yoke Peter BOAC grounded its Comets to enable a detailed examination of the aircraft to be made in collaboration with the Air Registration Board and the manufacturers. The airline appointed a committee under Charles Abell, deputy operations director (engineering).

It had to reach its findings without the benefit of any substantial body of wreckage. Accordingly it blamed the Comet's loss on a range of causes: flutter of the control surfaces; primary structural failure with particular emphasis on the possibility of abnormally high loads caused by gusts; malfunctioning of the power controls; fatigue; explosive decompression and engine trouble with particular emphasis on possible causes of fire.

The committee also called for a number of inspections and tests to existing airframes to be made. It was found that cracks had appeared near the edge of the wheel wells on the under surfaces of the first prototype's wing which was then under test at Farnborough. At the time of the accident it had completed the equivalent of 6,700 flying hours compared with Yoke Peter's 3,681.

The committee considered the possibility of fatigue affecting the wings much more likely than failure of the pressure cabin due to the same cause. Accordingly, its list of recommendations specifically directed at fatigue related to the wings. A large number of other modifications was requested together with inspections of the surviving fleet. Around 60 precautionary modifications were recommended.

On 19 February 1954 BOAC chairman, Sir Miles Thomas, forwarded the Abell committee's report to the Government. Lord Brabazon, then chairman of the ARB, agreed with Thomas' view that there was no reason *"why passenger services should not be resumed."*

Sir Frederick Bowhill, chairman of the Air Safety Board, recommended that the Comets should go back into service following incorporation of the recommended modifications and completion of the testing called for by the Abell committee.

Although he had not revoked the Comet's Certificate of Airworthiness, the minister of Transport and Civil Aviation, Alan Lennox-Boyd, gave permission for a resumption of Comet operations from 23 March.

Far from losing confidence in the new jet many observers were convinced that sabotage was the most likely cause of Yoke Pete's loss. Yet this suggestion was soon forgotten just two weeks later when it happened again. For BOAC it was the stuff of nightmares.

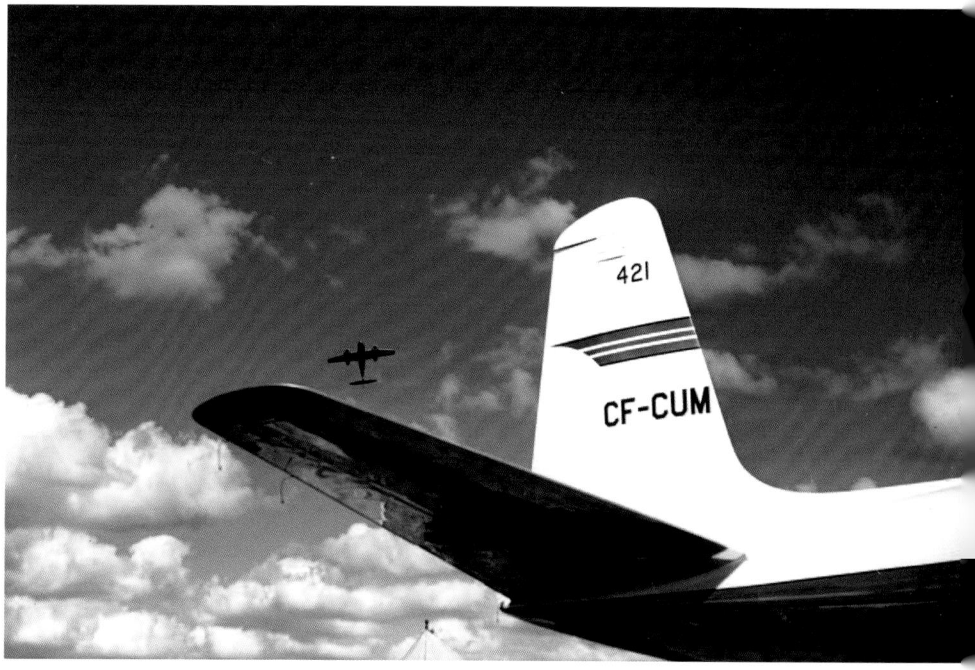
421
CF-CUM

TOP LEFT: The first Comet to be lost in an accident was Canadian Pacific Airlines' 1A CF-CUN Empress of Hawaii was written off after failing to take-off from Karachi in March 1953.
BOTTOM RIGHT: Although CF-CUM Empress of Vancouver was one of two Comet 1As ordered by Canadian Pacific Airlines it was not delivered and transferred instead to BOAC as G-ANAV. It is pictured here at the 1952 Farnborough Air Show, its tail framing a Meteor fighter.

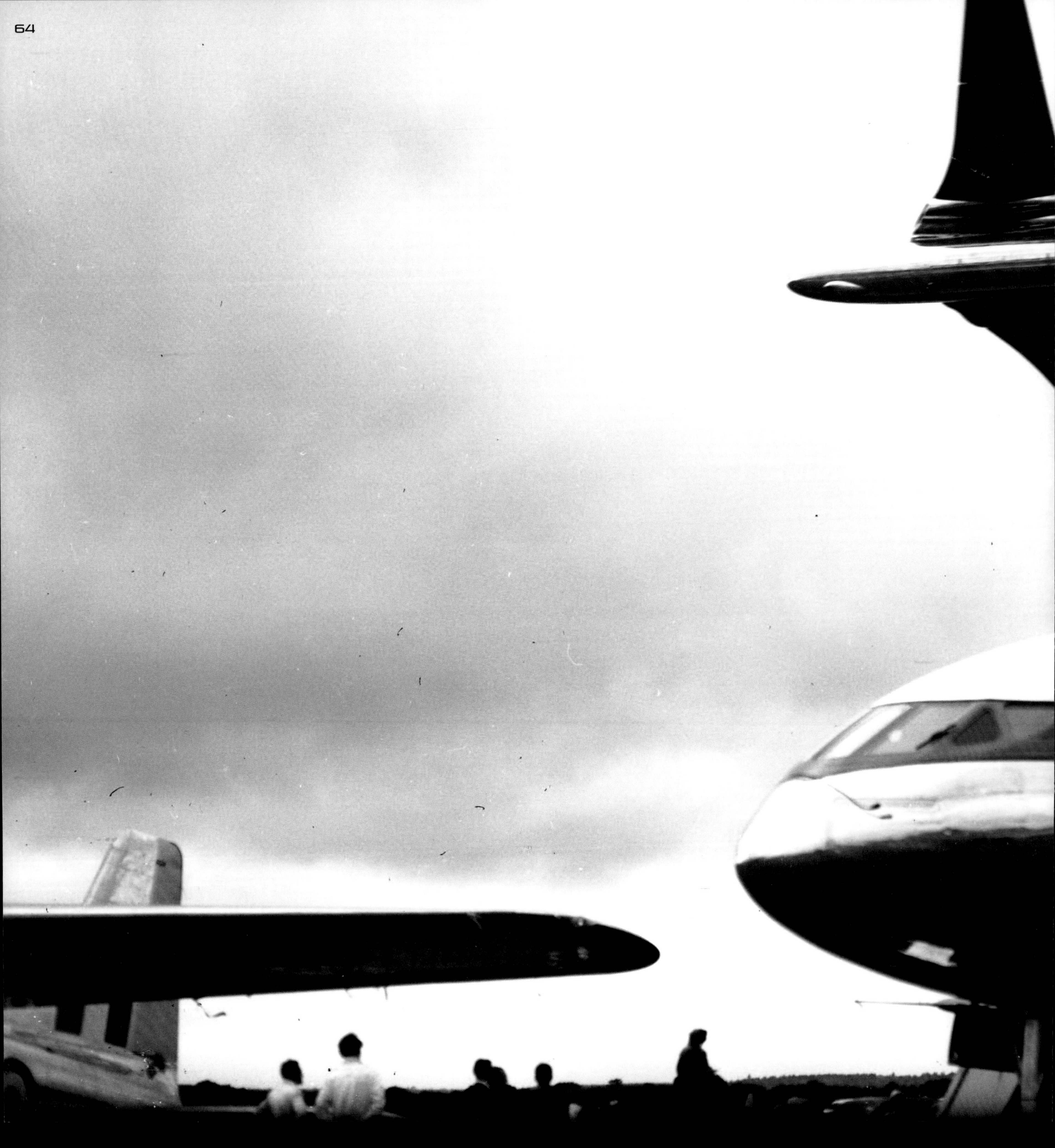

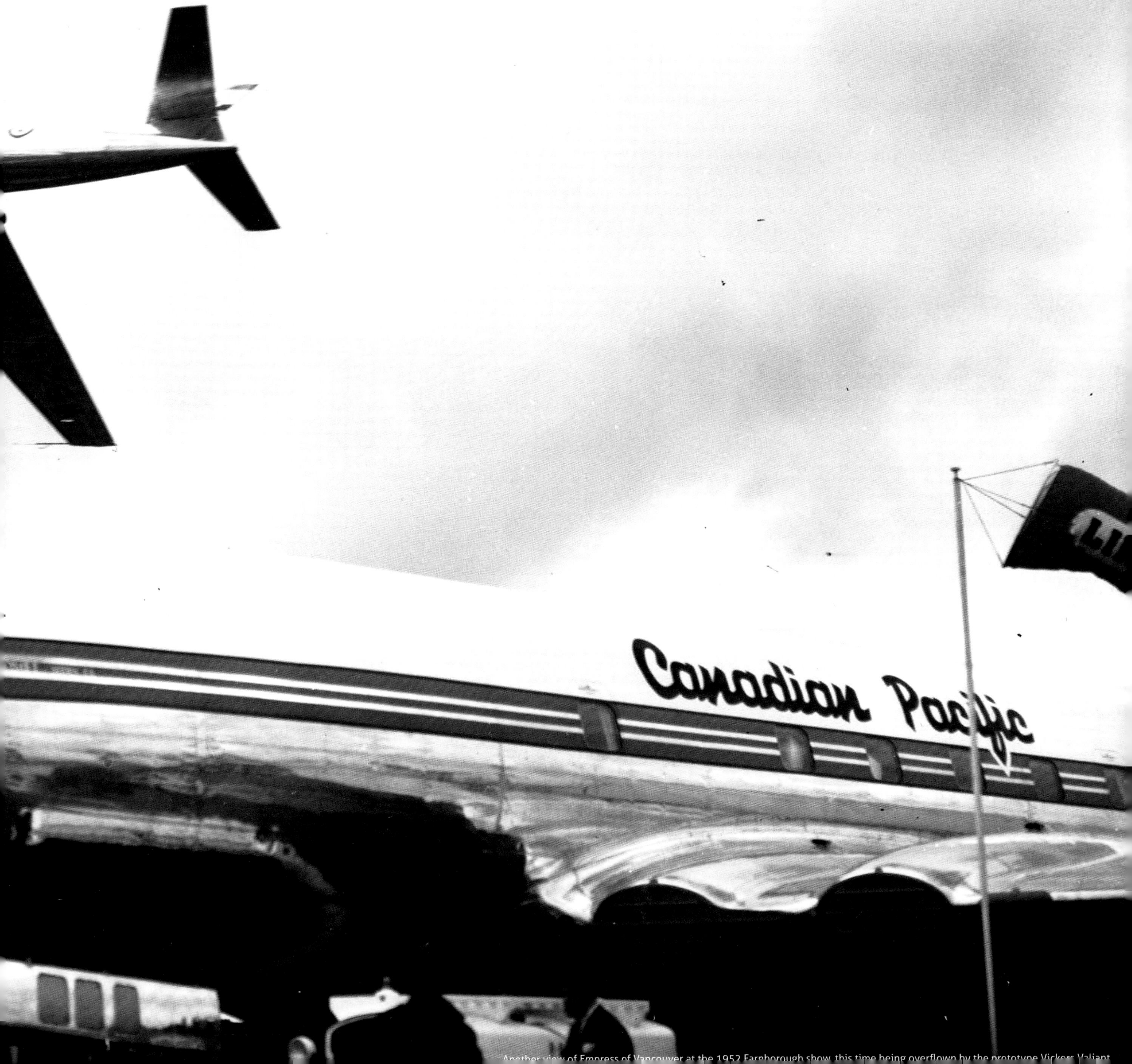
Canadian Pacific

Another view of Empress of Vancouver at the 1952 Farnborough show, this time being overflown by the prototype Vickers Valiant

G-ALYY was on charter to South African Airways when, on 8 April, it was operating Flight 201 from London to Johannesburg when it disappeared. It was soon obvious that the aircraft had plunged into the Mediterranean near the island of Stromboli off the southern Italian coast. All 21 passengers and crew on board were lost with the aircraft.

The aircraft had arrived in Rome at 1755hr on 7 April and taken off at 1832hr the following day. There was no reason to connect the delay with the aircraft's loss. The last message from Yoke Yoke was received at 1905hr. The pilot said he was climbing to 35,000ft (10,700 m), the cruising height predicted by the flight plan. He was asked to report when he reached this altitude but nothing further was heard from the aircraft.

There were no eyewitnesses but the emergency services were alerted that evening and by morning five bodies and some wreckage were retrieved. The similarity between the losses of the two Comets could hardly be ignored. BOAC halted Comet services and the aircraft's Certificate of Airworthiness was withdrawn. On 12 April Lennox-Boyd instructed Sir Arnold Hall, director of the Royal Aircraft Establishment at Farnborough, to use all the resources at his disposal to make a comprehensive technical investigation of the Comet.

The resulting report would later be hailed at the subsequent court of inquiry as *"one of the most remarkable pieces of detective work ever done."* The salvage

work done by of the Royal Navy was crucial to this success. It had been ordered by Prime Minister Winston Churchill, who instructed that, *"The cost of solving the Comet mystery must be reckoned neither in money nor in manpower."*

As a result Operation Elba Isle was launched to recover as much Comet wreckage from the bottom of the sea as possible. By this time Yoke Peter was thought to be lying on mud 400ft (123 m) below the surface. Its position, according to Cdr Gerald Forsberg RN, the officer in charge of the operation, "was only vaguely estimated from conflicting reports.

HMS Wrangler, an anti-submarine frigate used its Asdic detection gear to survey the sea bottom. By 25 January it was joined by HMS Barhill and the Royal Fleet Auxiliary salvage vessel Sea Salvor. Among the equipment these ships brought to the site was a television camera that had been flown out from England. Sea Salvor also had an oxygen-equipped diving bell.

For most of this period the weather was unfavourable with high winds and rough seas. But it improved on 12 February and Sea Salvor was able to make a square search of the area, trailing the TV camera along the sea bottom to sweep a 12ft (3.7 m) wide path. It was slow work. It had to be, Forsberg wrote later, as otherwise *"the camera would have come flying off the bottom like a kite on a string."*

Initial sightings revealed many small pieces of wreckage. *"The bottom of the*

ABOVE: Anti-submarine frigate HMS Wrangler was one of the fleet of vessels used by the Royal Navy to search for wreckage of Comet 1 Yoke Peter. Wrangler's Asdic detection gear was employed to survey the sea bottom.

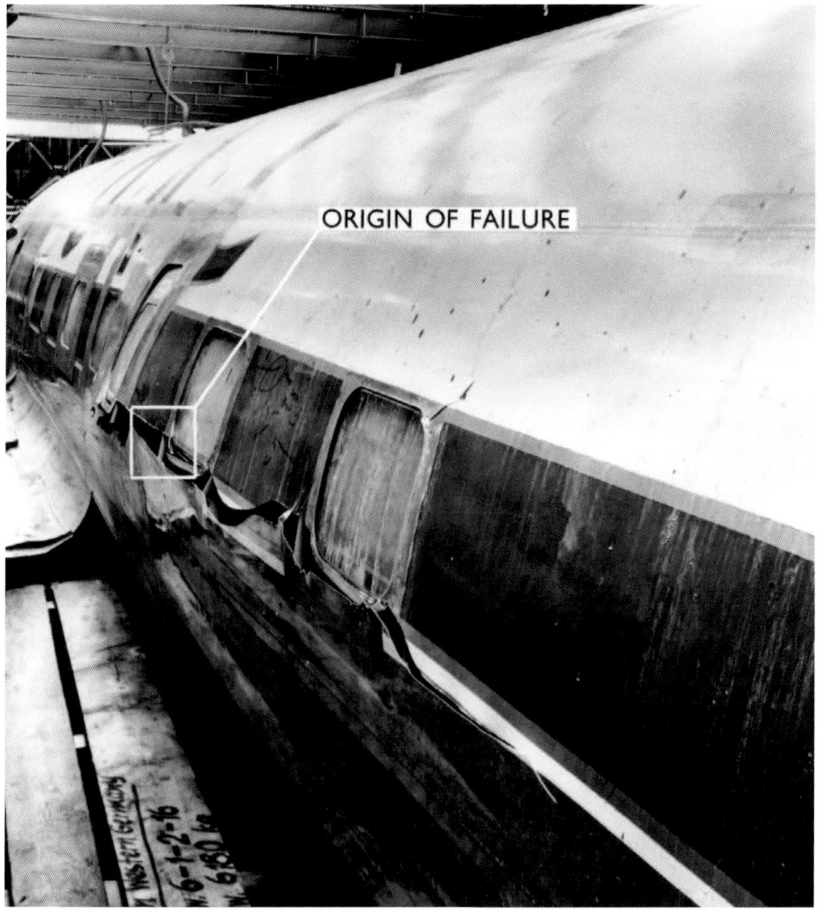
ORIGIN OF FAILURE

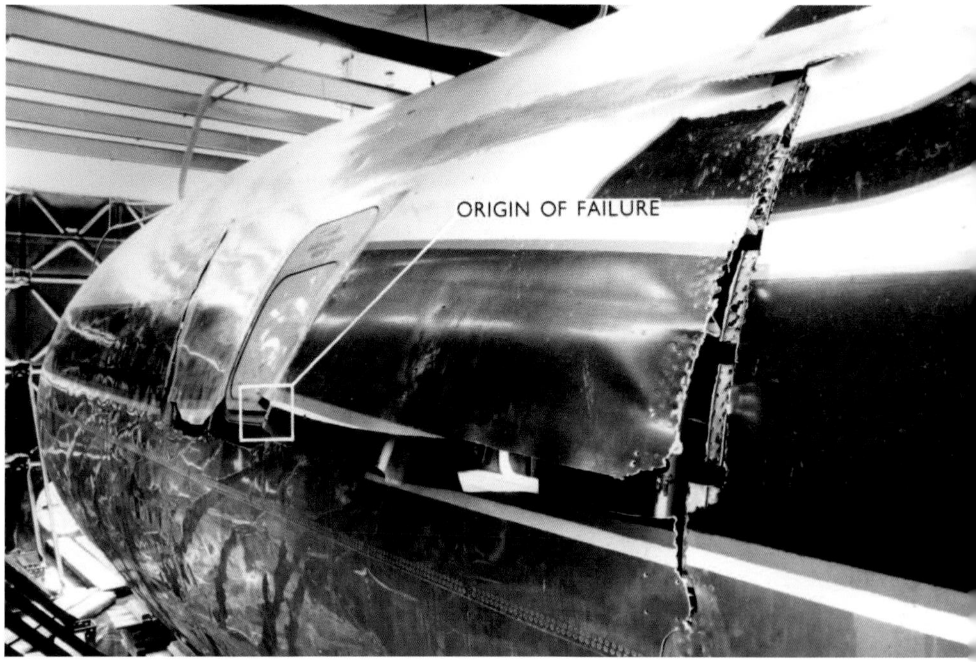
ORIGIN OF FAILURE

sea looked as though someone had up-ended a waste-paper basket," Forsberg reported. The next day brought a howling gale and it was not until the 19 February that the weather improved enough for the operation to resume. Diver John Galpin followed a mooring wire down straight to a substantial section of wreckage. Down went another diver, Tom Bray, to guide the grab to retrieve it.

There was no further success over the next three days and the salvage team was starting to lose heart. Then a chain was lowered on the off-chance. Forsberg wrote later: *"The chain caught round a chair from the Comet, the chair caught round some electric cables, the electric cables were attached to the after pressure dome. We carefully dragged the whole issue to within 20ft [6.15 m] of the surface. Then, fearing to push our luck another inch, an ordinary soft-suited diver was sent down to get a stout sling round it. Within an hour it was safely on deck. We had rescued the ladies' and gentlemen's toilets from 400ft [123 m] below the surface. It was with curious feelings that we read familiar English trade names and notices."*

That week the navy brought up 12 grab loads of wreckage, all from the aft fuselage. Then the gales return and the ships had to run to harbour for shelter. On 15 March one of the divers went down again and reported finding the largest piece of wreckage yet. When it finally surfaced it was seen to be a section of wing 65ft (20 m) long. The next piece was even bigger. Sea Salvor's deck was loaded with wreckage but the diver now reported finding two of the engines.

Over the next few days more and more wreckage was brought to the surface culminating in the biggest find of all – the entire forward fuselage back to the wings. On 9 April Forsberg was due to sail for Malta when he was handed a signal from the commander-in-chief. It read: "Proceed to search for BOAC Comet G-ALYY missing on flight from Rome to Cairo."

The operation had exceeded expectations in terms of the amount of wreckage recovered. It was sent to Farnborough where it was painstakingly assembled over a framework representing the Comet's fuselage. On 21 April the engines were finally recovered. When the crates containing them arrived at de Havilland Engines in the small hours of the morning the engineers, who had been waiting with a growing feeling of suspense, soon discovered that they had been running when the aircraft broke up.

By this time 70 per cent of the aircraft's empty weight had been recovered, although very little of Yoke Yoke was to be recovered since it had plunged into much deeper water.

Three days earlier Hall had decided on several separate lines of inquiry. The first involved a study of the wreckage, although at this stage it was far from clear how much of it would be recovered. Initially, therefore, the primary thrust would involve an examination of general theoretical considerations and the integrity of the Comet's basic design. There would also be comparative tests of other Comets both on the ground and in the air. The fourth line to be followed would involve experiments with models, test specimens and other items.

The Royal Aircraft Establishment reasoned that the apparent similarity of the two accidents, which had happened when the aircraft had reached the top of their climbs - plus the fact that the post-Elba modifications appeared to rule out many other possible causes – pointed to pressure cabin failure.

TOP LEFT & RIGHT: Two views of the fuselage of Comet 1 G-ALYU which was installed in a water tank at Farnborough in 1954 for pressure testing under controlled conditions. The result was that metal fatigue, a hitherto little understood phenomenon, was discovered on the test specimen, as indicated here.

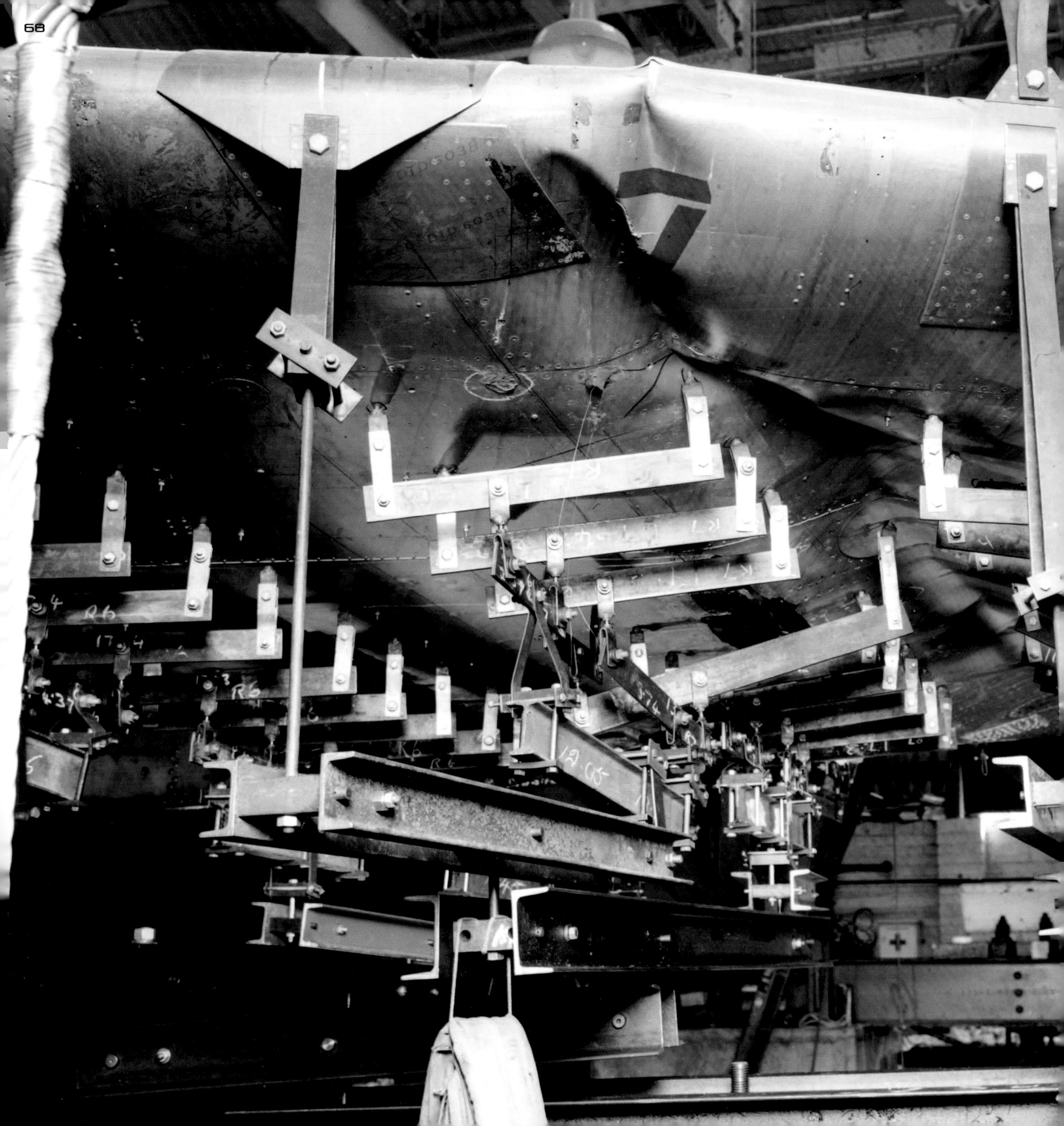

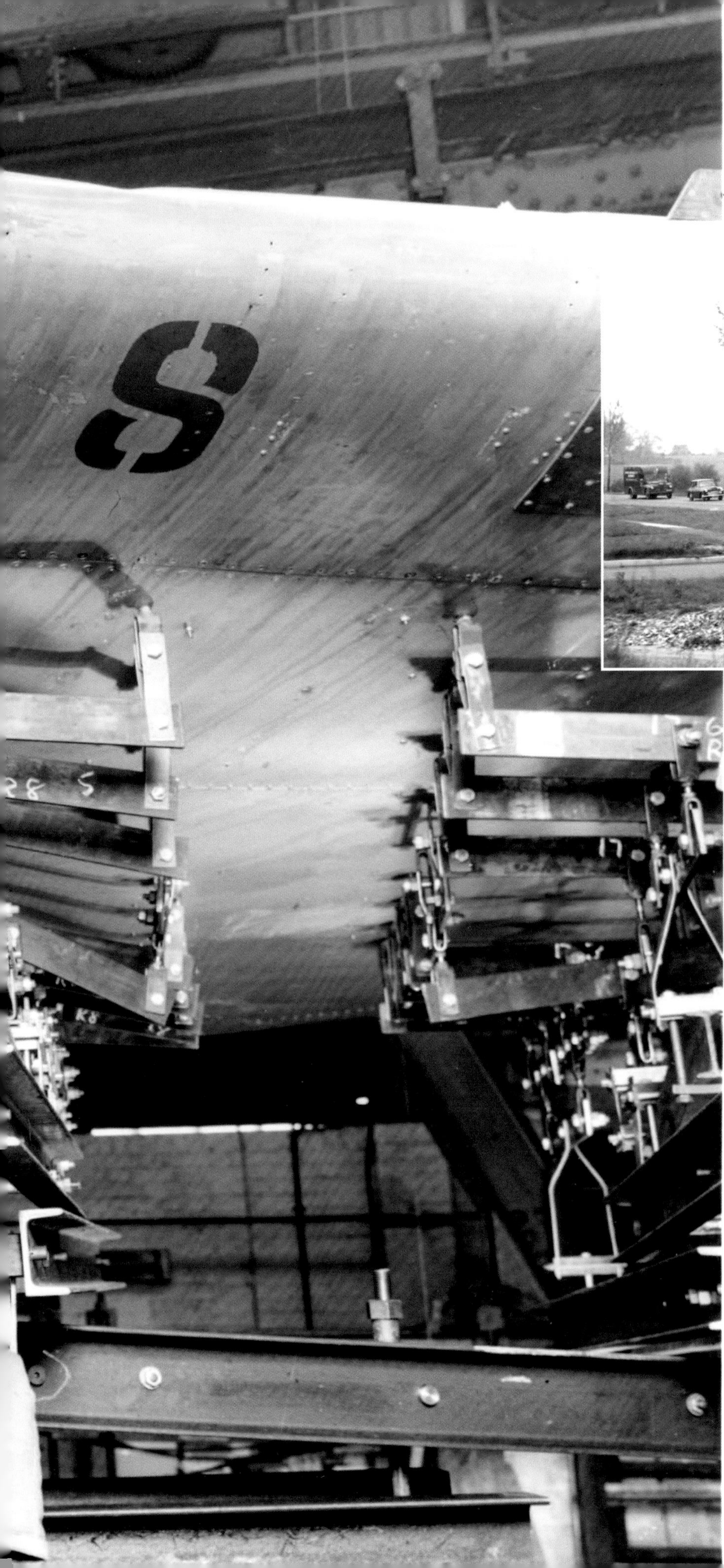

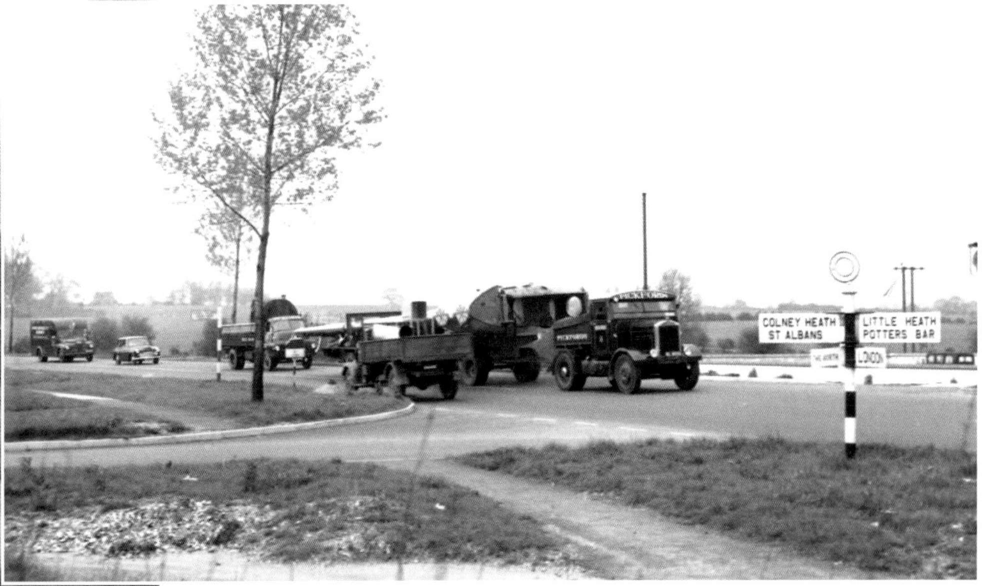
COLNEY HEATH
ST ALBANS
LITTLE HEATH
POTTERS BAR
LONDON

Comet G-ALYU was therefore installed in a water tank at Farnborough for pressure testing under controlled conditions. These repeated loading tests began in June. Fluctuating loads were applied to the wings with one application of cabin pressure for each simulated flight. At the end of each of 1,000 "flights" there was a proving test in which the pressure was raised to 1.5 times the normal value (11 lbs/sq in).

Before the test Yoke Uncle had made 1,230 pressurised flights. After a further 1,830 the cabin structure failed. The failure started at the corner of one of the Comet's square cabin windows. This suggested that the most likely cause of Yoke Peter's loss was the bursting of the pressure cabin. Close examination of the wreckage so far recovered appeared to confirm this but more samples were needed. As a result instructions were passed to the salvage team of Elba to re-orientate the area of search still in progress.

The tank test also showed that the pressure cabin had a considerably shorter fatigue life than had been thought. Yoke Uniform was therefore repaired and the tests resumed but this time strain gauges were placed near the corners of windows. Again it was discovered that the stress was much higher than previously believed.

The metallurgical jigsaw puzzle yielded further significant information. Marks believed to have been made by the parts of the cabin as it had burst catastrophically five miles above the Mediterranean were found on parts of the port wing. This suggested that the failure had happened near the front wing spar.

Further examination narrowed down the source of failure to a window. This was also the location of the aerial for the aircraft's automatic direction finder, part of its navigation system. There were several possible starting points: a countersunk hole near the starboard rear corner of the window, which showed distinct evidence of fatigue, and a small hole drilled during the manufacturing process and actually intended to prevent cracks spreading from the port forward corner of the same window.

The investigators concluded that the aircraft had then broken apart, probably

LEFT: The prototype Comet 1, G-ALVG was also used in the structural testing at Farnborough in 1954
INSET, TOP RIGHT: The wing of test specimen G-ALYU on its way to Farnborough.

into six main pieces: the nose and tail sections, the centre section with the engines, the two wing tips and the top of the fuselage. *"That was a preliminary judgement,"* Hall told the subsequent court of inquiry. It matched the impact damage and also lined up with the plot of the wreckage on the bed of the sea."

Other tests conducted by Hall and the RAE team were intended to investigate other possible causes. During the early stages they set out to satisfy themselves that structural failure had not been the cause. Tests were therefore made and de Havilland's previous work reviewed. Other possibilities had to be eliminated such as explosion in the cabin due, say, to ignition of hydraulic fluid or even a bomb. Had there been a leakage of fuel or had the pilot lost control for some reason?

Flight tests were made using Comet G-ANAV to check if vibration or flutter, other aerodynamic issues or fuel venting had caused the crashes. *"We operated it at all times in company with a Canberra aircraft which flew behind it to keep general observation on it,"* Hall noted later.

Forensic evidence yielded by examination of bodies recovered from the sea tended to confirm the theory that the aircraft had burst apart. Prof Antonio Fornari of the Institute of Forensic Medicine at Pisa University examined 15 bodies and concluded that the cause of death in each case had been violent displacement and sudden impact with part of the aircraft, explosive decompression and deceleration. They had not been the victims of an explosion, nor had they drowned. These findings were confirmed by an eminent Harley Street pathologist.

On Tuesday 19 October 1954 a court of inquiry opened to review the evidence and reach a conclusion on what had caused the loss of the two Comets and the 56 people who had been aboard. It sat at Church House, Westminster until 24 November with Lord Cohen as commissioner assisted by two assessors, Sir William Farren and Air Cdre A H Wheeler. In 22 days of sittings they received evidence from 68 witnesses either in person or by affidavit. The transcripts of proceedings would run to 1,600 pages and about 800,000 words.

The key piece of documentation placed before the inquiry was an investigation report the size of a telephone directory containing tens of thousands of words of detailed explanation supported by hundreds of diagrams and photographs. Maurice Smith, editor of Flight, said that its *"exhaustive deductions and eliminations"* had led *"stage by stage to a coherent account of unseen events."*

In his opening address to the inquiry, Sir Lionel Heald QC for the Crown, summarised the key elements of the evidence to be put before it. He noted that science applied to the service of humankind had not infrequently led to a radical new departure which had resulted in a disaster costing many lives and which seemed to suggest the forces of nature seemed too strong to be controlled. But history had shown that there had been no shrinking from re-examination in the light of more recent knowledge and research.

Such accidents, Heald went on, might be regarded as the price of progress and their results were not merely negative. Already the Comet had undergone elaborate and searching tests which would have been far beyond the means of any single organisation. No aircraft in history had ever been subjected to such an examination. The results should benefit not just the industry but the whole world by enabling high speed travel to be developed with increased safety and efficiency.

Heald said that Arnold Hall had taken personal charge of the investigation. The result, he said, would be generally regarded as one of the most remarkable pieces of scientific detective work ever done. Right from the start Hall had thought that Yoke Peter must have broken up at a great height, probably around 30,000ft (9,230 m), and that as the amount of wreckage pulled from the sea increased a picture started to emerge of what had happened.

"It was quite clear," Heald declared, *"that there had been an almost instantaneous and tremendously powerful forward force generated inside the pressure*

ABOVE: Another view of G-ALVG under test at the Royal Aircraft Establishment, 1954.
OPPOSITE PAGE: Close-up of the Comet fuselage nose section in the Farnborough water tank where it was subjected to over 16,000 pressurisation cycles, equivalent to 40,000 hours of flying.

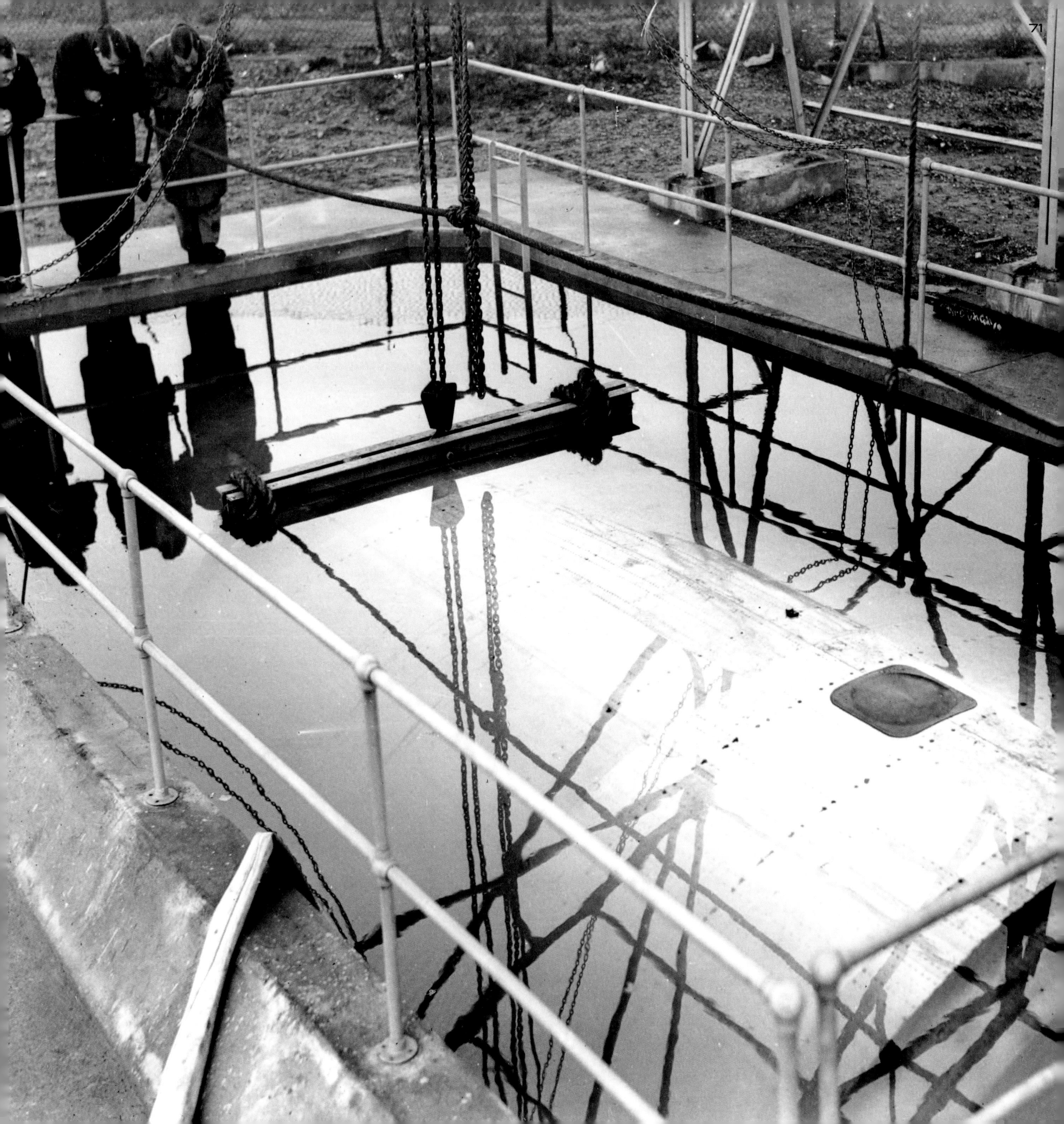

cabin which had thrown most of the passengers and their seats forwards and upwards against the roof. But it must also have driven some of them clear right out of the aircraft without touching anything at all because in the case of some of the bodies it was clear that they had an initial impact and in other cases they had not."

Even Heald's precise phraseology could not fail to conceal the full horror of the events that had followed the bursting of the cabin. It would, though, have been brief for those subjected to it. *"Within one-third of a second of the accident taking place,"* Heald went on, *"the cabin was apparently empty."*

This conclusion had been drawn from the results of experiments conducted with a one tenth scale model of the Comet's pressure cabin. Forensic evidence of the bodies had confirmed that there was evidence of decompression of the lungs consistent with sudden loss of pressure.

"It is not clear on general principles that if a fracture of any substantial size – not merely a perforation or a bullet hole – occurs in the wall of a tube or vessel which is under 8lbs/sq in pressure, a large hole will immediately open up and the tube will at once become what the layman might describe as a compressed air gun," Heald told the inquiry. A terrific blast of air will force anything and everything out of the hole and will tend to throw the aircraft into violent contortions and so tear the whole of the fuselage to pieces,"

Using a model Comet Heald then explained the sequence in which RAE's experts believed Yoke Peter had broken up. "The first thing that happened was a violent disruption of the centre part of the pressure cabin." He then removed a small piece of the model near the ADF aerial windows. *"The fuselage aft of the rear spa, the nose and the outer port wing fell away....thirdly the main part of the wing separated and caught fire...the fuselage aft of the rear spa with the tail unit still attached fell into the sea with the open end first and the tail plane last. Last of all, the main part of the wing, still on fire, hit the water in an inverted position..."*

It was a dramatic moment. Heald's audience in Church House must have sat spellbound as the eminent QC continued his reconstruction of disaster. The sequence of events, he went on, could only have been triggered by a sudden disruption of the pressure cabin and that was most likely to happen when the aircraft was reaching its maximum height and the pressure cabin was at the point of greatest stress.

After elimination of other possible causes only one remained. *"There is what is called fatigue – metal fatigue. In other words, "a structure which had an ample reserve of strength when it was new might fail under its normal working load after a certain length of time."*

It had previously been thought that the maximum stress concentration due to pressure loadings under operational conditions would be about up to 50 per cent of the material's ultimate stress. But RAE's testing had shown that there was as much as 70 per cent in the Comet's pressure cabin. The key points had been near the corners of the windows. This could not have been known in 1946 or even in 1951: clearly the question of stress concentration was underrated.

Turning to the *"life"* at which failure could occur, Heald said that the water tank specimen had failed at an equivalent life of 9,000 flying hours, compared with the 3,681 hours flown by Yoke Peter. That was now considered to be within reasonable scatter, and the 2,701 of Yoke Yoke was also within that area.

Heald concluded by commenting that RAE's explanation based on the reconstruction work would be *"generally acceptable."* He added: *"As regards Naples, of course, we are in the area of surmise."*

Cohen agreed. The inquiry's report was submitted on 1 February 1955 and published 12 days later. Its major finding was that the loss of Yoke Peter was structural failure of the pressure cabin brought about by metal fatigue. The reason for Yoke Yoke's loss, however, could not be definitely established but the explanation of the Elba's accident's cause appeared to be applicable to the second. In neither cause was there evidence of wrongful act, default or negligence.

The report rejected other causes including the suggestion that failure of the Redux bonding had been to blame. Lord Cohen also discounted reservations expressed by Walter Tye, ARB chief technical officer, about the failure of the two Comets after only 1,000 flights while `YU achieved the equivalent of 3,000. *"I have unhesitatingly come to the conclusion that the RAE were right,"* Cohen concluded. He also rejected criticism of the manufacturer which had produced the Comet in accordance with what was then regarded as good engineering practice.

In his report Cohen also made recommendations aimed at ensuring the lessons of Yoke Peter and Yoke Yoke would be applied to future operations. To ensure a safe life well above the minimum acceptable to an airline methods would have to be devised to ensure that design, combined with a reasonable programme of testing could guarantee pressure cabins would be entirely safe.

"When these methods have been applied and the tests completed," the report noted, de Havillands will no doubt ask ARB to recommend the grant of a Certificate of Air Worthiness to the re-designed Comet aircraft." *Cohen said he hoped that the public would be reassured about the integrity of pressure cabins "and will justify Sir Arnold Hall's confidence that the Comet aircraft will fly again."*

History has come to regard the probe of the 1954 Comet accidents as a watershed in air accident investigation which led not only to revised Comets but also to the more successful Boeing 707 and Douglas DC-8 which were really to revolutionise air transport and ultimately to the airliners in use today. The results of the investigation were published and widely discussed within the aviation community.

Flight's editor Maurice Smith chose to accentuate the positive aspects of the investigation in his journal's editorial published on 29 October 1954, ten days after the inquiry opened. Calling it the *"most remarkable and most momentous inquiry in aviation history,"* he wrote: *"This report on the investigation may, in fact, be described as one of the few pleasing matters arising from the whole unhappy affair for it confirms beyond doubt the capacity and remarkable knowledge and ability of our scientists. It gives the promise that in spite of the imperfections of all man-made machines, and in spite also of the many unknowns, it is not beyond the ability or knowledge of our technicians to design and produce air transports of the new order that will be both safe and reliable."*

Smith added: *"There are some who would say that it was naïve to expect successfully to double transport speeds and operating heights in a single stage. Yet every new step, especially if it is a bold and enterprising one, involves a calculated risk. Everyone knows this well enough, and fortunately, we believe, very few are so lacking in spirit that they stand still or condemn others for pressing on."*

OPPOSITE PAGE: Overhead view of Comet G-ALYU in the water tank at Farnborough.

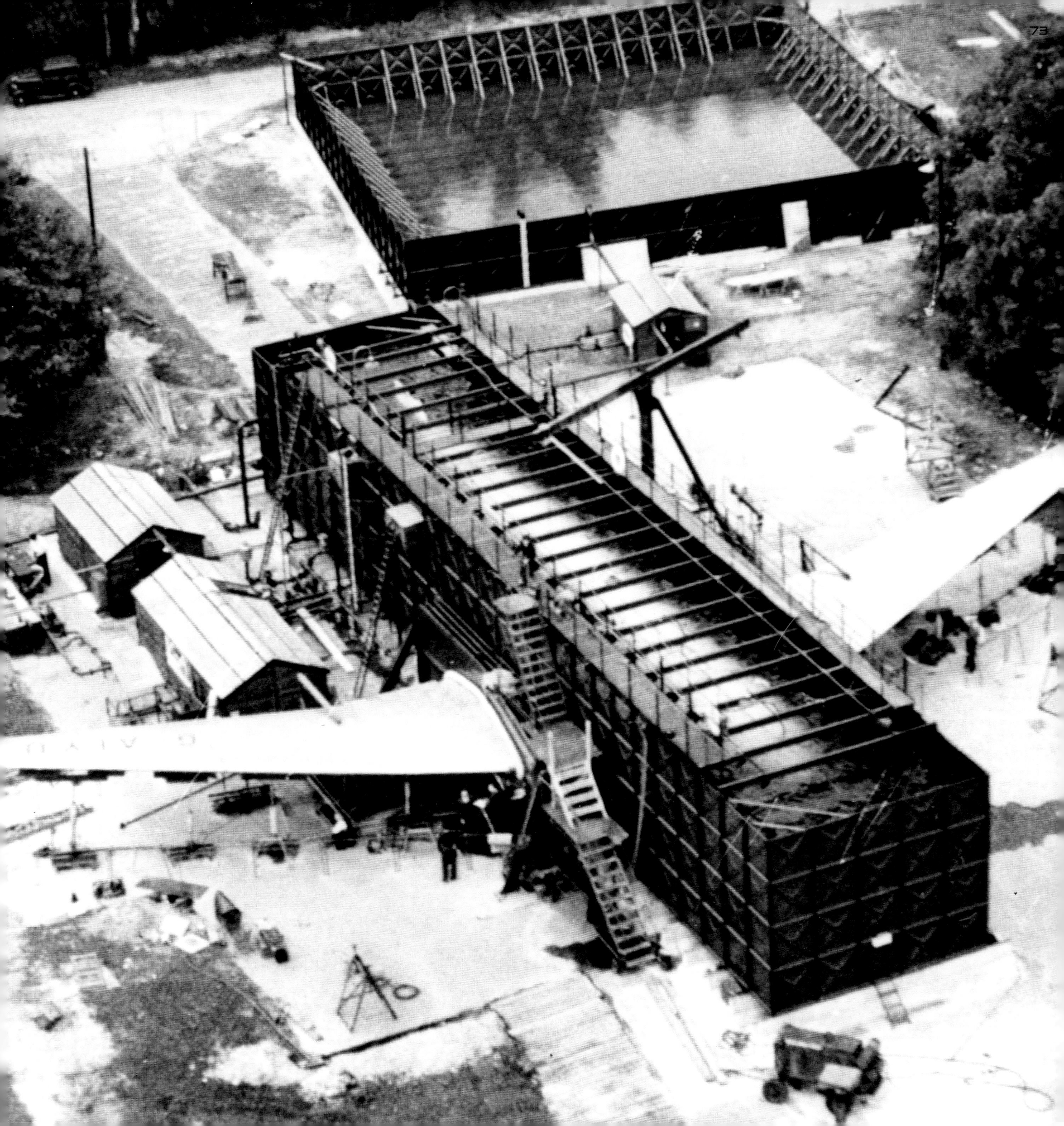

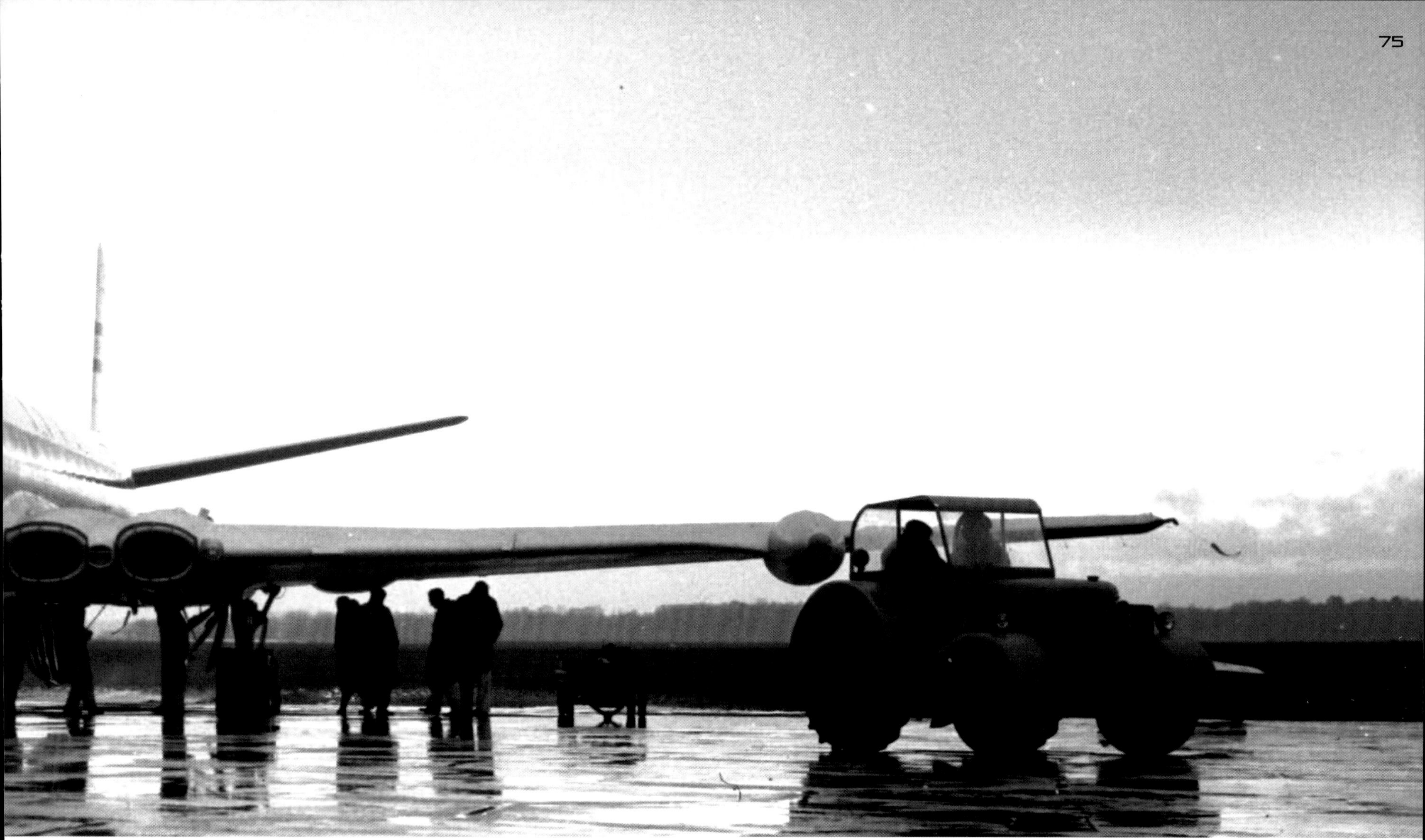

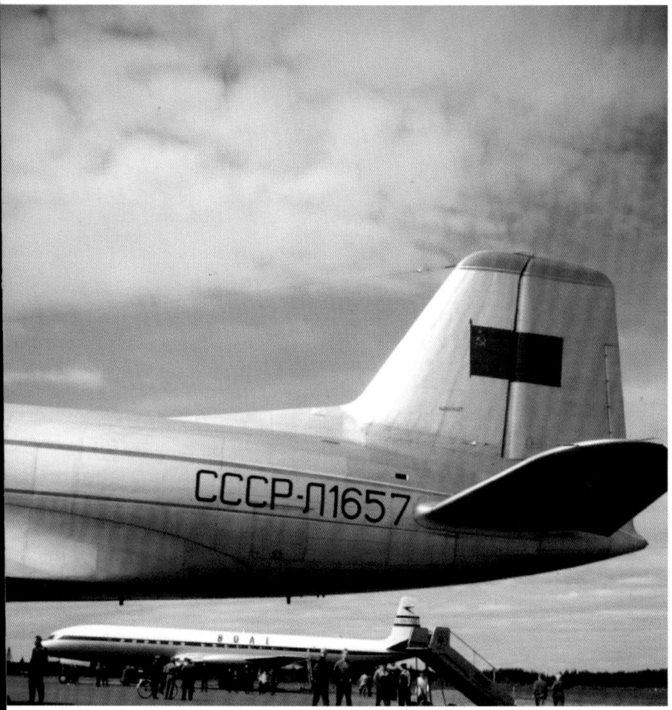
CCCP-Л1657
BOAC

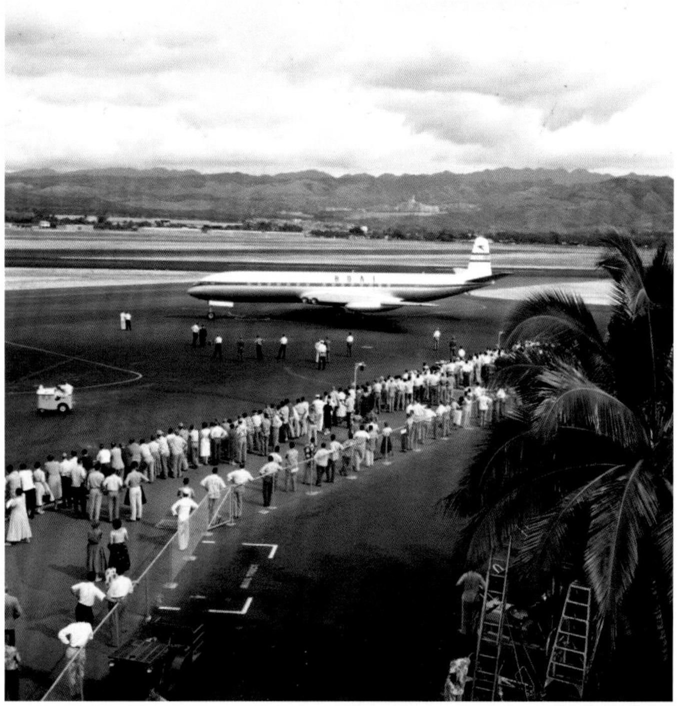

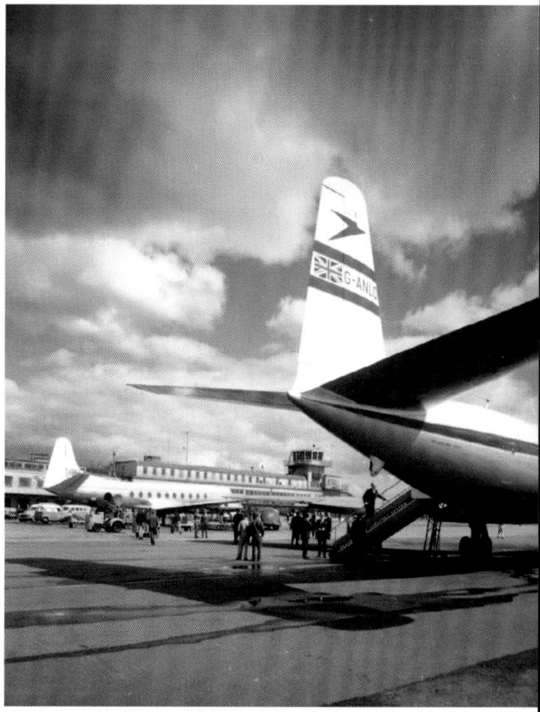
G-ANLO

MAIN IMAGE: Before the 1954 accidents, de Havilland had high hopes of the long range Comet powered by Rolls-Royce Avons and it was hoped that an order by Pan American World Airways would represent a breakthrough. The sole prototype G-ANLO is pictured here in February 1957.

INSET IMAGES: G-ANLO made a major contribution to the Comet 4 development programme and this included a round-the world flight with John Cunningham in command in December 1955. The aircraft is pictured (left to right) at Bombay, 1955; again, Bombay, 1955; Stockholm, 1957; Stockholm, framed by an Aeroflot Il-14; Honolulu, 1955.

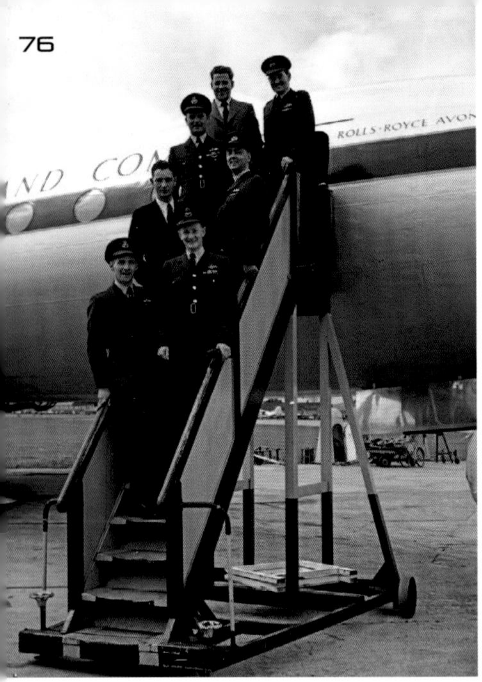
ROLLS-ROYCE AVON

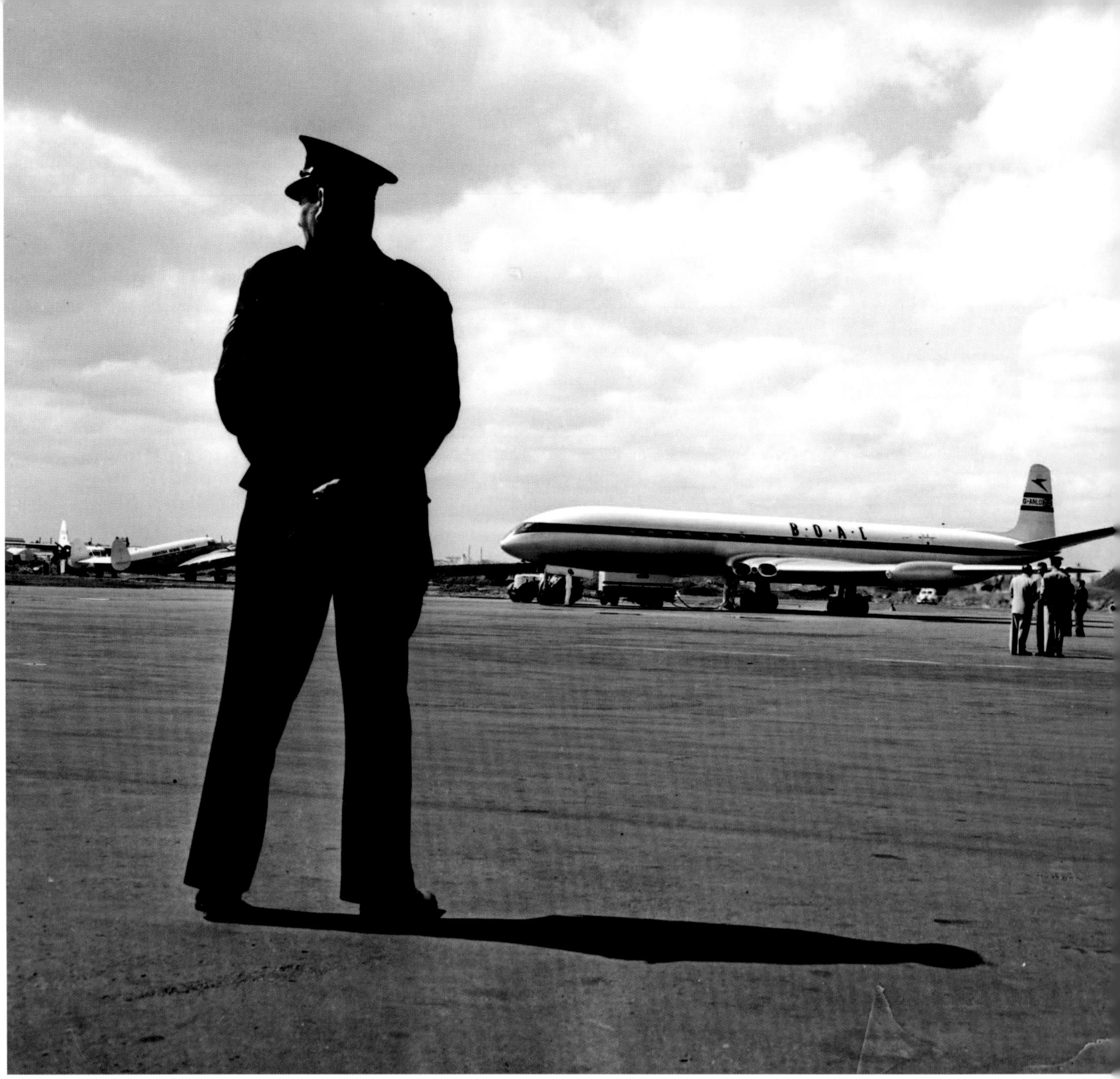

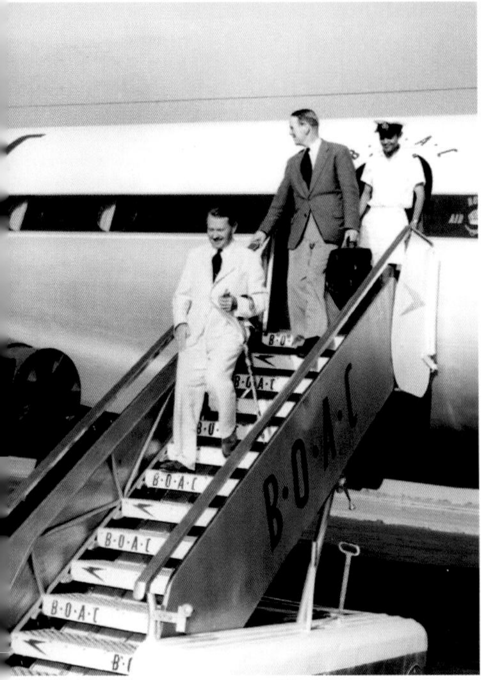
B·O·A·C
B·O·A·C
B·O·A·C
B·O·A·C

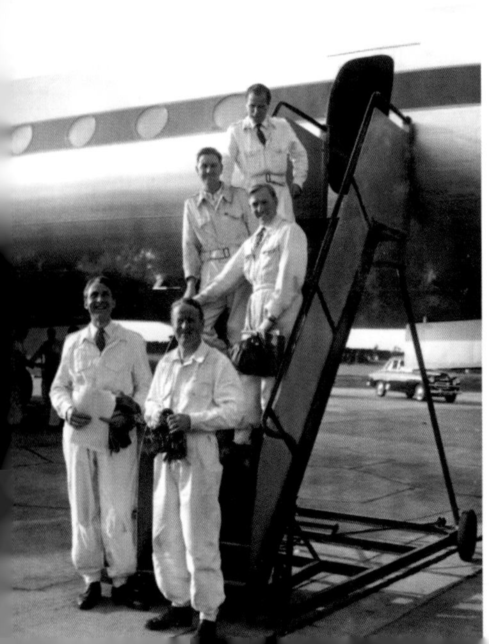

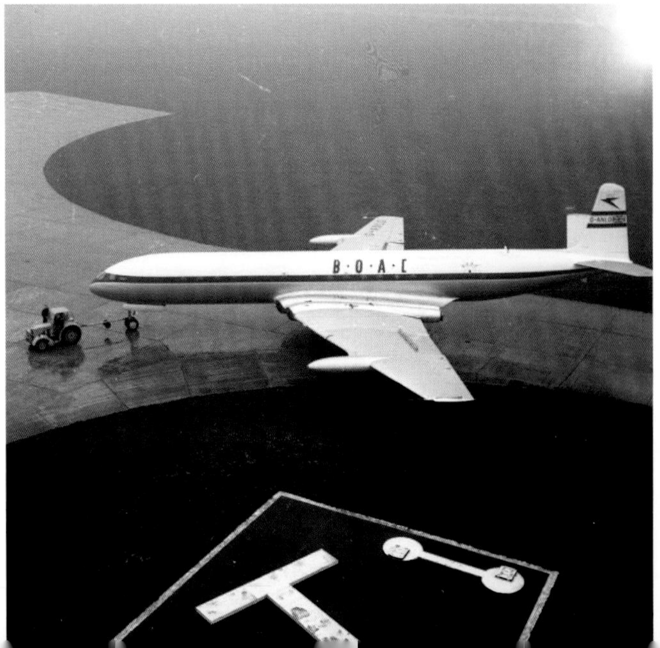
B·O·A·C

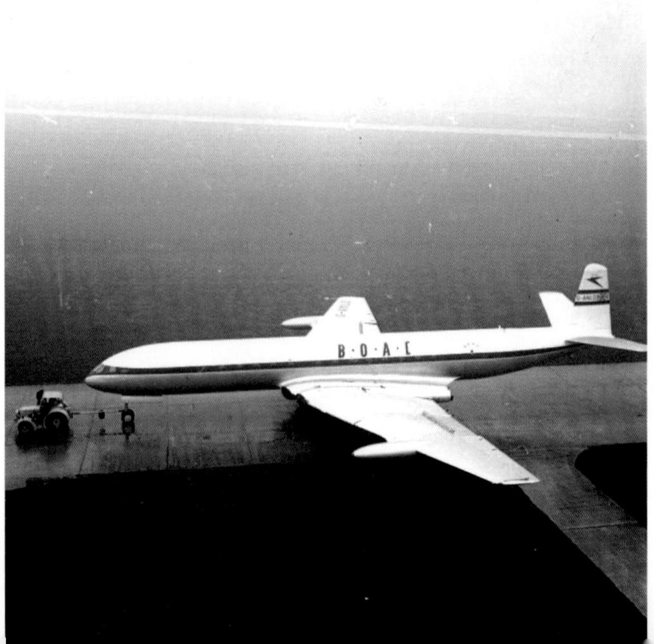
B·O·A·C

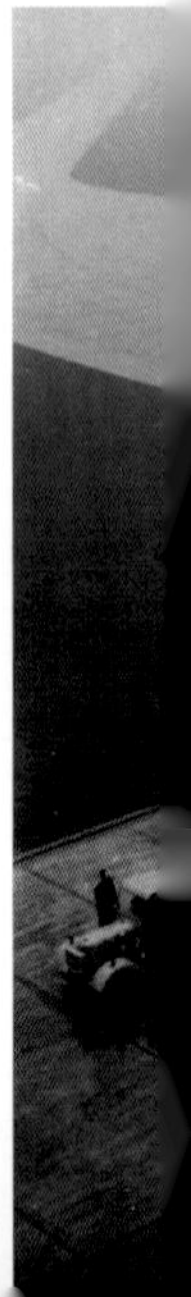

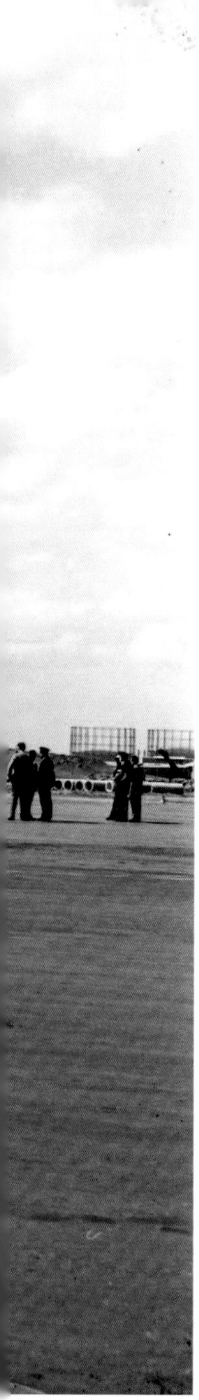

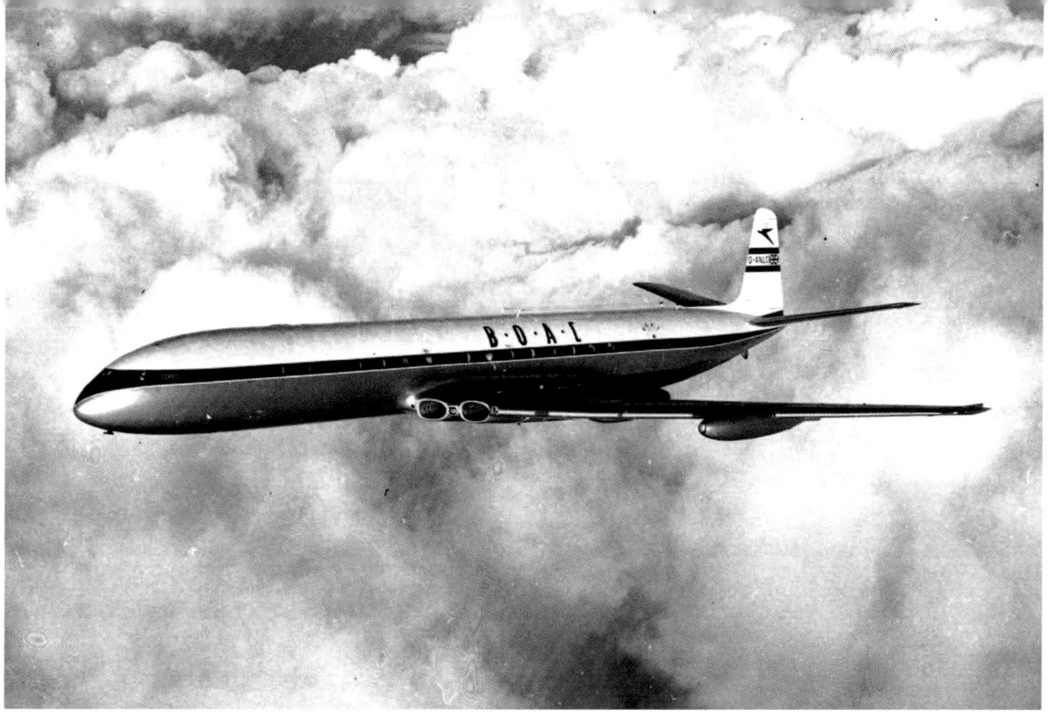
B·O·A·C

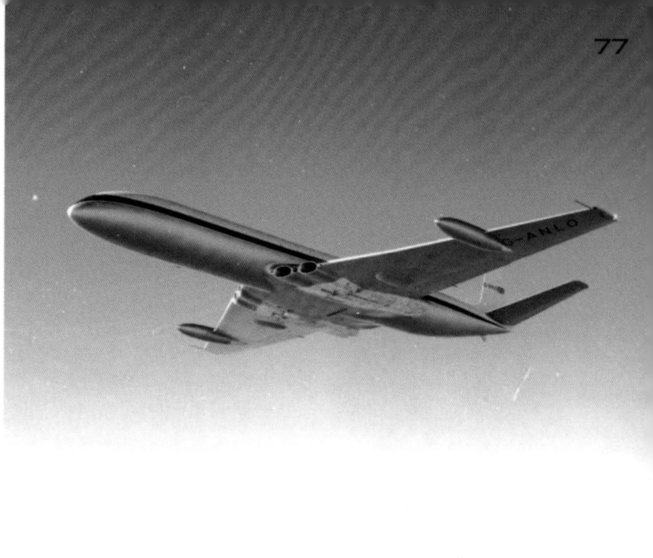
G-ANLO

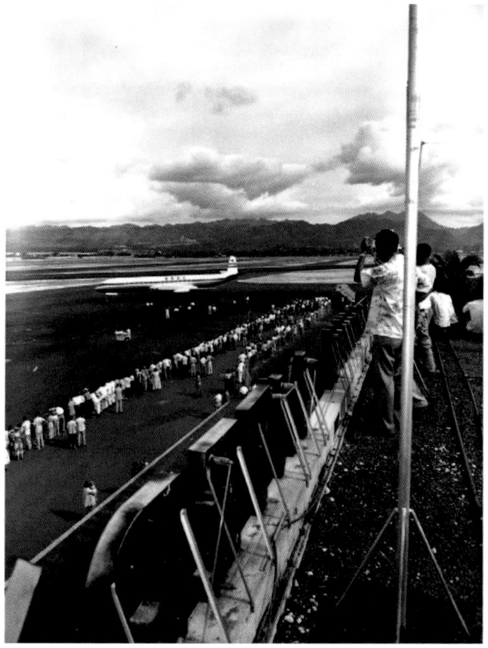

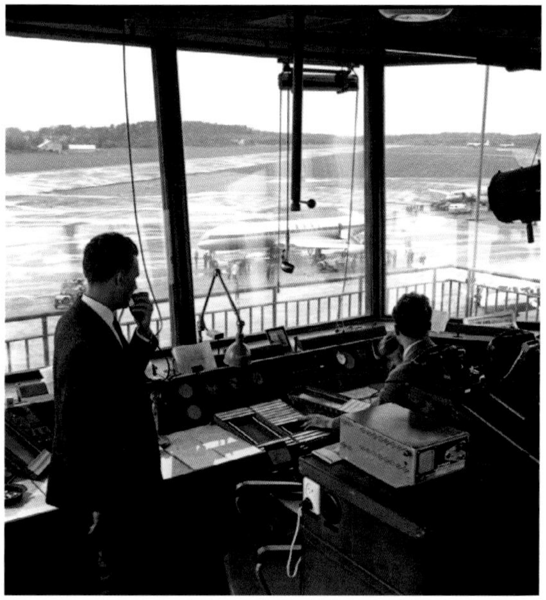

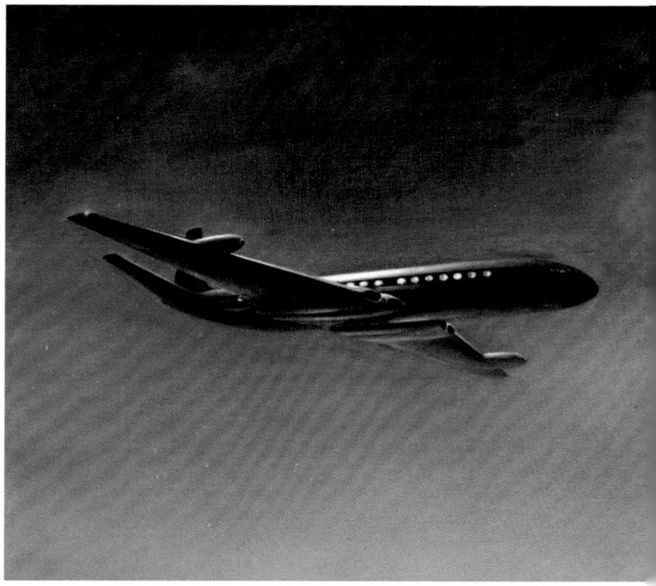

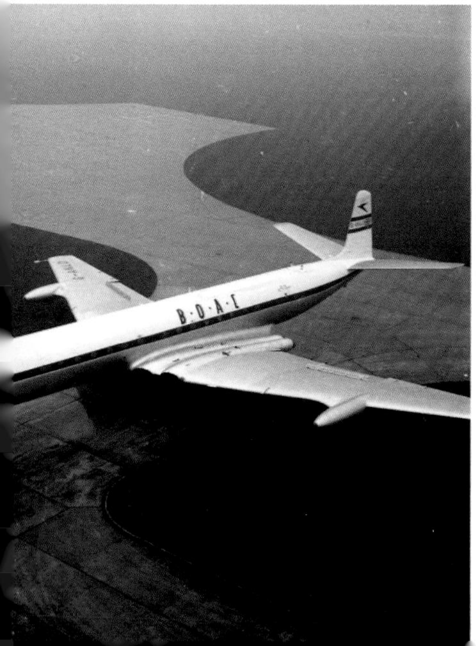
B·O·A·C

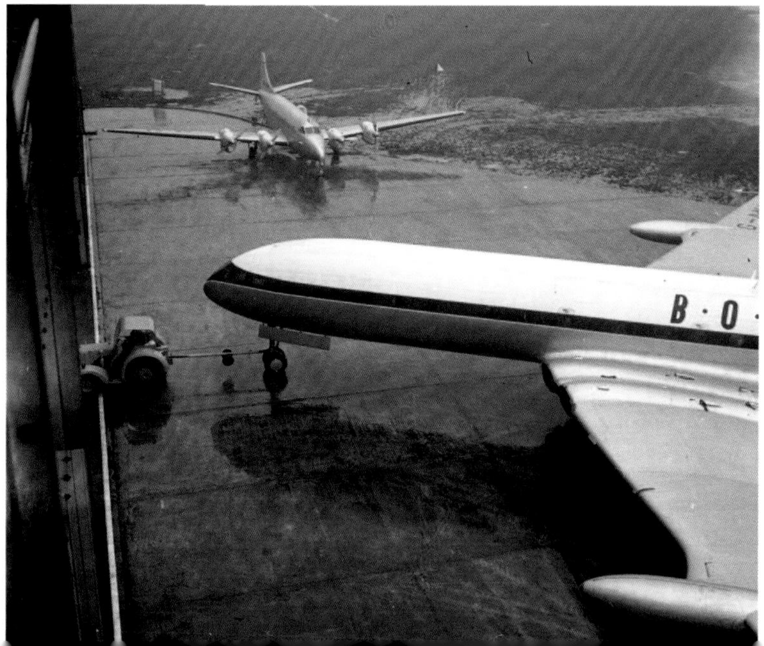

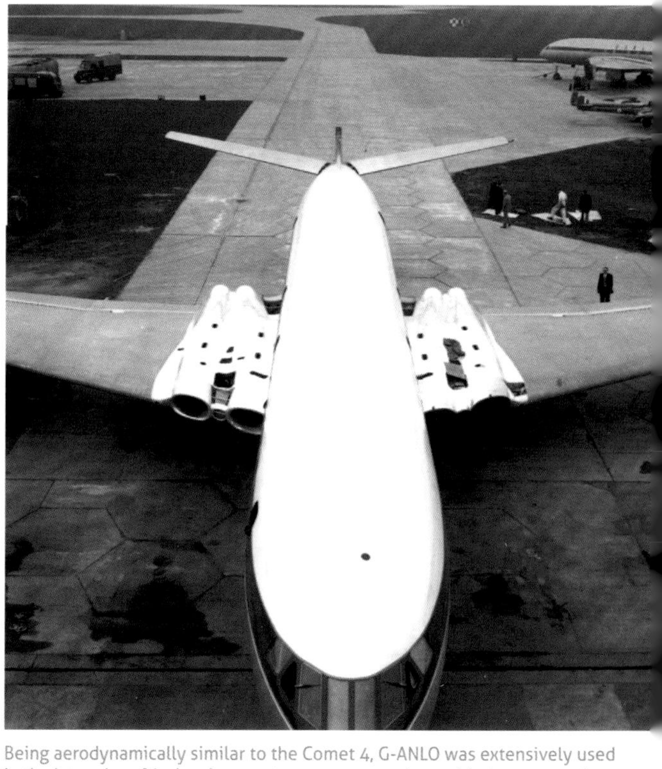

Being aerodynamically similar to the Comet 4, G-ANLO was extensively used in the later aircraft's development programme and was able to save much valuable time in the Comet 4's introduction into BOAC service. `LO's route in 1955 was: London-Cairo-Bombay-Singapore-Darwin-Sydney-Perth-Melbourne-Sydney-Auckland-Fiji-Honolulu-Vancouver-Toronto-Montreal-London.

THE COMET 4

Bigger and Better

It was not just the tone of Pathe News' reporting that had changed in the eight years since that record-breaking flight to Rome in 1950.

On the eve of the first trans-Atlantic commercial service British cinema audiences were told that

"...... this is one of the smoothest airliners flying. Yes, in comfort as well as speed the Comet 4 is a powerful challenge to the world. The rivalry with the Boeing will be particularly interesting because BOAC, in its urgent need for jets, has Boeings on order as well."

The aircraft was still designated the DH 106 and still called Comet but, compared to the airliner with which BOAC had launched the world's first jet airliner services in May 1952, the Comet 4 was very different even if it looked similar. Indeed, it was suggested that the name should be changed to reflect this but both de Havilland and BOAC rejected the idea on the grounds that they wanted to restore the Comet's reputation not bury it.

The new aircraft had different engines offering a total of 135 per cent more power, could carry 125 per cent more passengers over a 115 per cent greater range, it was 20 per cent bigger and 12 per cent faster. And what would ultimately be the high capacity, shorter-ranged 4B, which later became the backbone of the holiday charter business, could carry 101 passengers compared with the 36 of the original variant.

From an early stage in the Comet's development the Rolls-Royce Avon engine had been seen as the type's definitive power unit. The first production aircraft was retained by the Ministry of Supply to form the basis of the Avon-powered Comet 2. This aircraft, G-ALYT, first flew in February 1952. BOAC ordered 12 production examples, with 3ft (0.92m) longer fuselage and seating 44 passengers for use on its South American routes.

The first production aircraft was busy on route-proving when it was grounded, like the rest of the Comet fleet, in 1954 after the loss of Yoke Peter and Yoke Yoke. All remaining Comet 1s and 1As were either scrapped or modified, while production Comet 2s were modified to remove fatigue risk. BOAC cancelled its order but the RAF acquired 10, which went on to serve with No 216 Squadron as Comet C2s (see chapter eight).

The bigger, longer-ranged Comet 3 was also to fly with Avon power and at one stage there were hopes that this variant, able to carry up to 78 passengers, would attract an order from Pan American World Airways. In fact Pan Am's order for three, announced in October 1952, was the first for the Comet 3. BOAC's, also for three, came a year later.

Although only one Comet 3 was actually built it formed the basis for the Comet 4. It had the same fuselage but larger span wings and accommodation for 106 passengers. It would cruise at 503mph (805kph). BOAC ordered 19 in March 1955 and the first (G-APDA) made its maiden flight in April 1958. A new production line was established at Hawarden (Chester) and the first examples enabled BOAC to begin an extensive series of route-proving flights.

Publication of the Cohen Committee's report had signalled the start of the Comet's re-birth. With less than two years of airline service behind it the aircraft and its manufacturers now faced a hiatus. It would be over four years before commercial services with the revised and enlarged Comet 4 would resume. And so began the long and uphill task of re-establishing confidence in the type and embodying the lessons learned from the 1954 accidents.

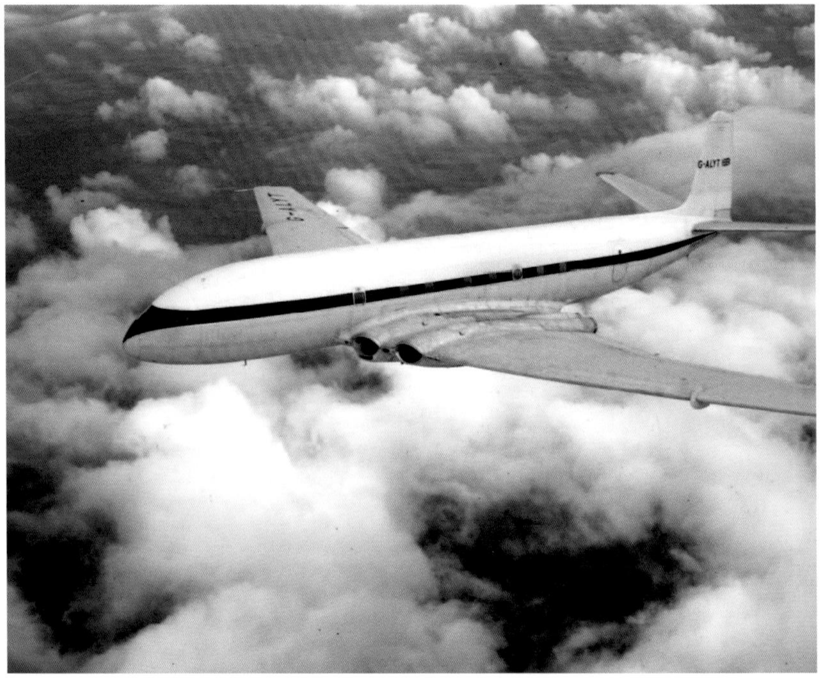
G-ALYT

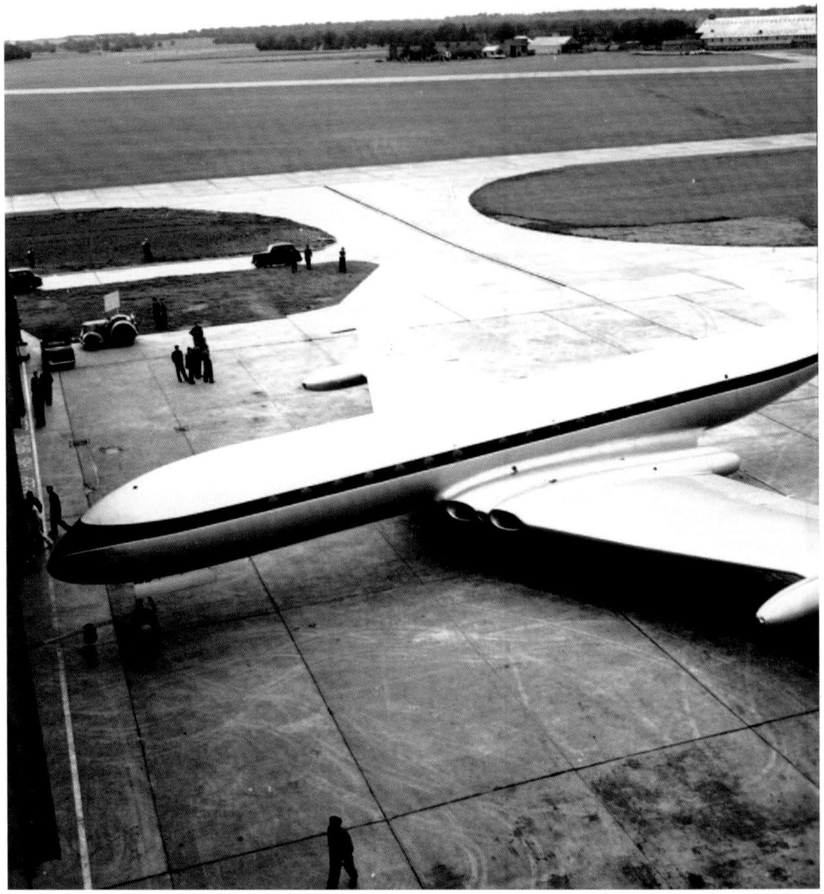

Prototypes both: **(Top)** G-ALYT, the Comet 2 prototype, first flew in February 1952 and is pictured here in July of the same year; **(bottom)** G-ANLO, the sole Comet 3, made its maiden flight in July 1954.

With its promise of intercontinental range, the Comet 3 raised high hopes at Hatfield. It was powered by the Rolls-Royce Avon 502 axial flow engine developing 10,000lb of thrust and de Havilland's experimental department had assembled the prototype which was rolled out for engine runs just as the Cohen Committee was beginning its deliberations.

The aircraft featured an extended fuselage with accommodation for up to 78 passengers. With a 20,000lb payload it could fly stage lengths of 2,400 miles or 2,600 miles with a slightly lower payload. It was expected to cruise at 500 mph. Apart from its extra size there were two particular recognition features, the torpedo-shaped pinion fuel tanks which protruded from the outboard wing leading edges and the oval windows which had been specified even before the 1954 accidents and subsequent investigation.

The aircraft, registered G-ANLO, made its first flight in the hands of John Cunningham and Peter Bugge on 19 July 1954. On this occasion the aircraft flew for 1hr 25min and appeared in public, in company with a Comet 2, at that year's

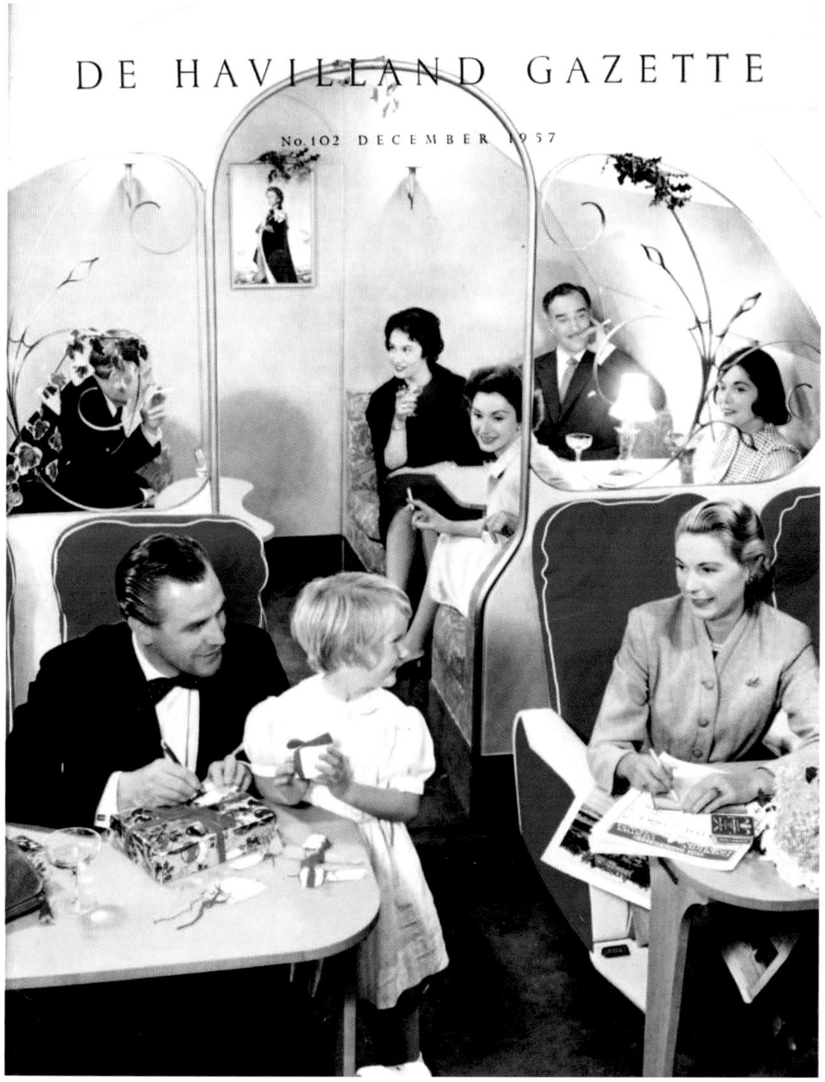
DE HAVILLAND GAZETTE
No.102 DECEMBER 1957

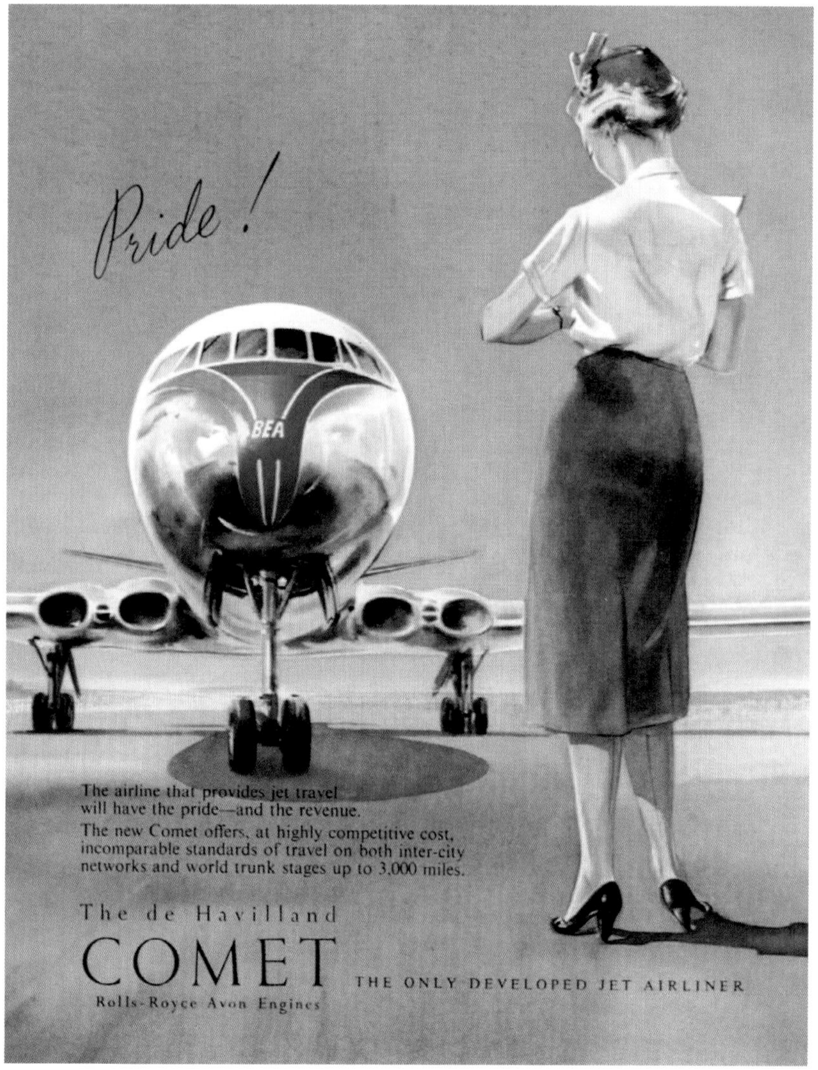
Pride!
BEA
The airline that provides jet travel will have the pride—and the revenue.
The new Comet offers, at highly competitive cost, incomparable standards of travel on both inter-city networks and world trunk stages up to 3,000 miles.
The de Havilland
COMET
THE ONLY DEVELOPED JET AIRLINER
Rolls-Royce Avon Engines

Farnborough display.

All the orders for the Comet 3 were cancelled but the disappointment was slightly eased by the aircraft's reception when it made a round-the-world flight in December 1955. From London the aircraft flew to Cairo, Bombay, Singapore, Darwin, Sydney, Perth, Melbourne, Auckland, Fiji, Honolulu, Vancouver, Toronto and Montreal before returning to London. It had covered 30,000 miles (48,280km). One of the highlights of the tour had been the crowd of 35,000 which turned out to greet the aircraft at Sydney.

The aircraft was subsequently used for aerodynamic and performance testing as part of the Comet 4 programme. In 1956 it was fitted with Avon RA.29 engines and many of its systems brought up to Comet 4 standards. With the availability of the new aircraft G-ANLO's outer wings were removed and replaced by shorter span sections without the pinion tanks to test the wings for the planned Comet 4B for British European Airways. In this guise it was known as the Comet 3B, flying for the first time in August 1958 as the first Comet to display BEA livery. In 1961 it

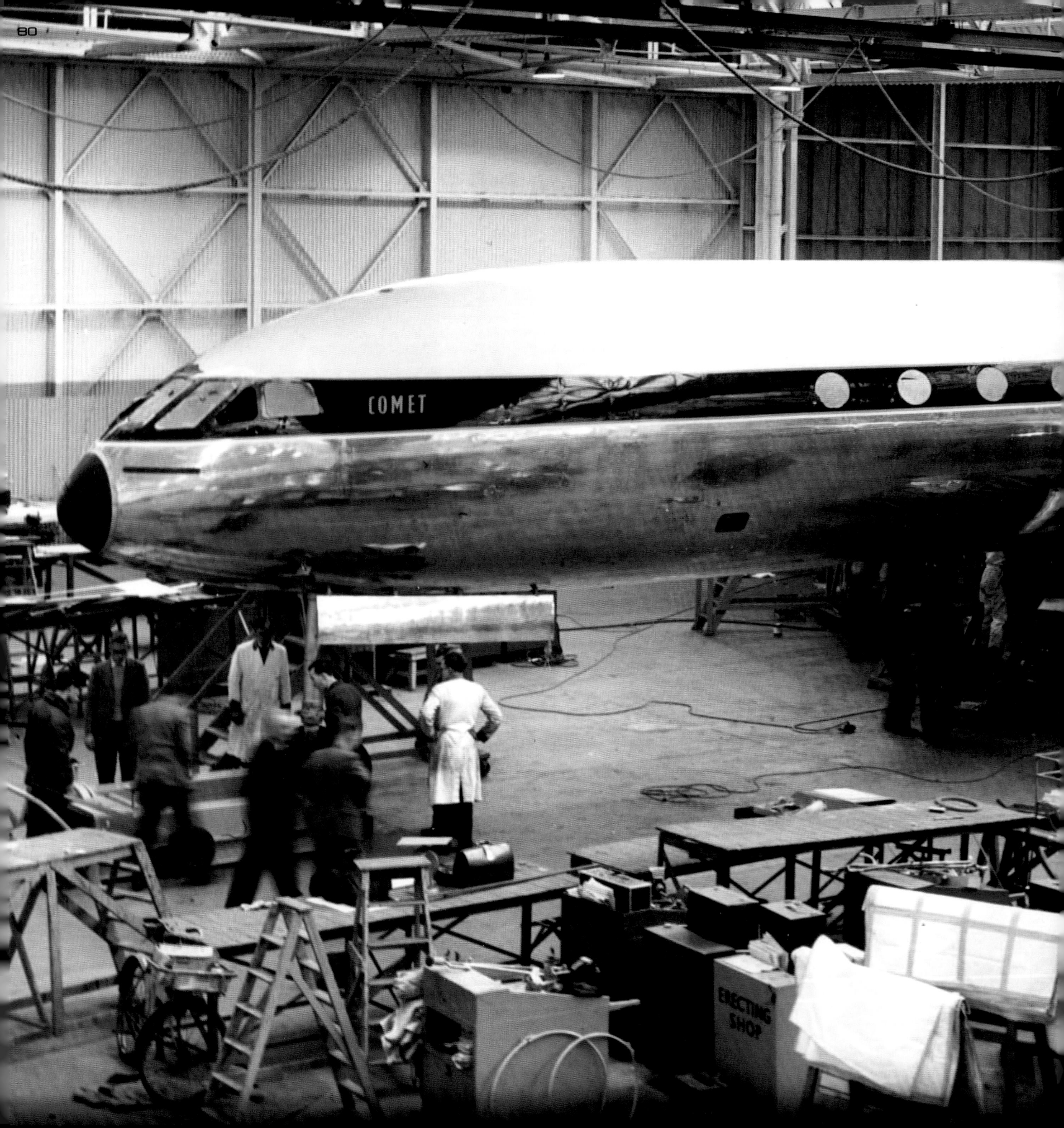
COMET
ERECTING SHOP

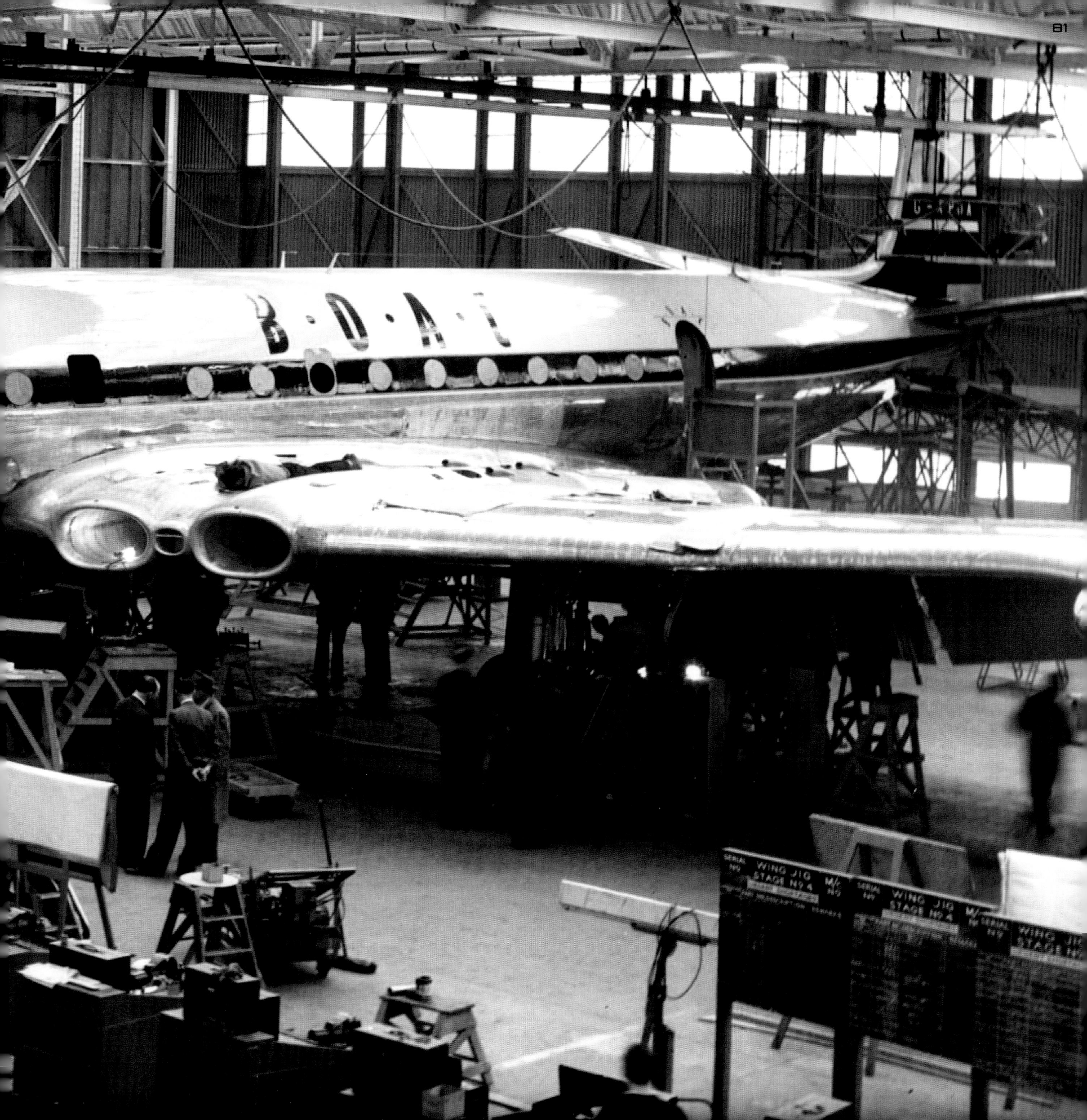
B·O·A·C
SERIAL No
WING JIG
STAGE No 4
M/C No

G-APDA, shown here under construction at Hatfield, was the first Comet 4 to fly, taking to the air in April 1958. It was delivered to BOAC the following February.

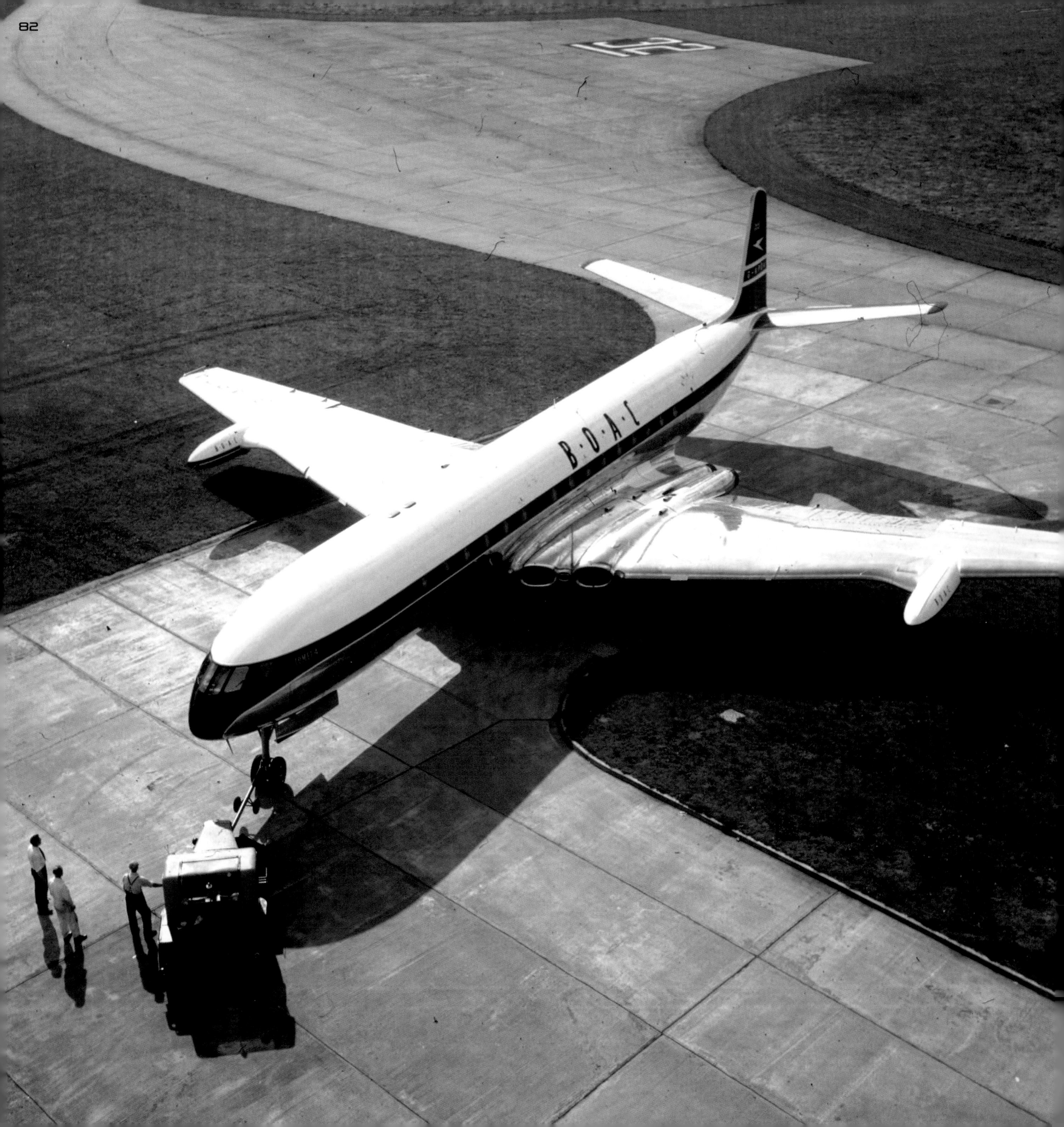
B·O·A·C

was delivered to the Blind Landing Experimental Unit at Bedford for the Autoland programme. There it flew in military markings as XP915. It was eventually dismantled and its fuselage used as a Nimrod mock-up.

Meanwhile two Comet 2s were modified with a pair of Rolls-Royce Avon 524s, each rated at 10,500lb of thrust, in each of the outer wing bays in place of the Avon 504s offering 7,330lbs. These aircraft, registered G-AMXD and G-AMXK, were designated Comet 2Es and used by BOAC in 1957 and 1958 for route proving for what was to be the definitive Comet.

It was in March 1955 that de Havilland announced what was to be the most successful Comet variant. This was followed a month after the publication of the Cohen inquiry's report by BOAC's order for 19 Comet 4s with the more powerful Avon RA.29s and accommodation for up to 81 economy class passengers in five abreast or 63 in a mixed four abreast layout.

This variant incorporated the structural knowledge gained from the investigation. Indeed, a rig testing programme had been in progress since the early summer of 1954. Its purpose was twofold: to form the basis of research into materials and design methods to establish a new formula for the avoidance of fatigue as well as to conduct applied research into components designed to these new principles.

Structurally this variant was virtually a new design. Most of its features differed from those of the Comet 1. All that remained the same was the external shape, allowing for the changed proportions. The basic structure was strengthened to the extent that nobody would ever call a Comet 4 flimsy.

The rear fuselage was modified to withstand the jet blast even though, as on the Comet 2, the jet pipes of the inner engines were splayed outwards to minimise

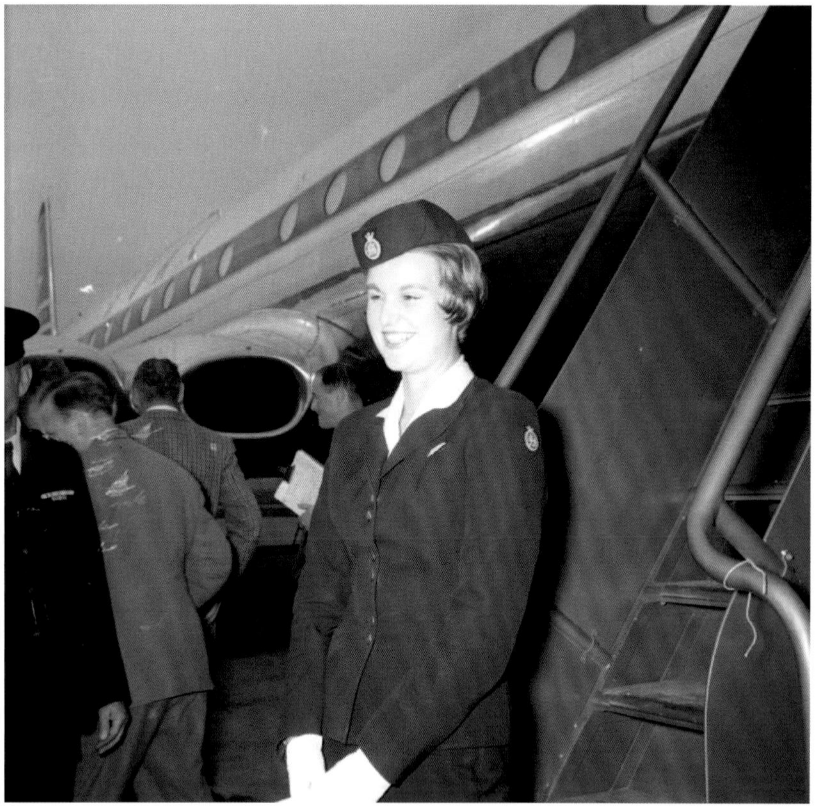

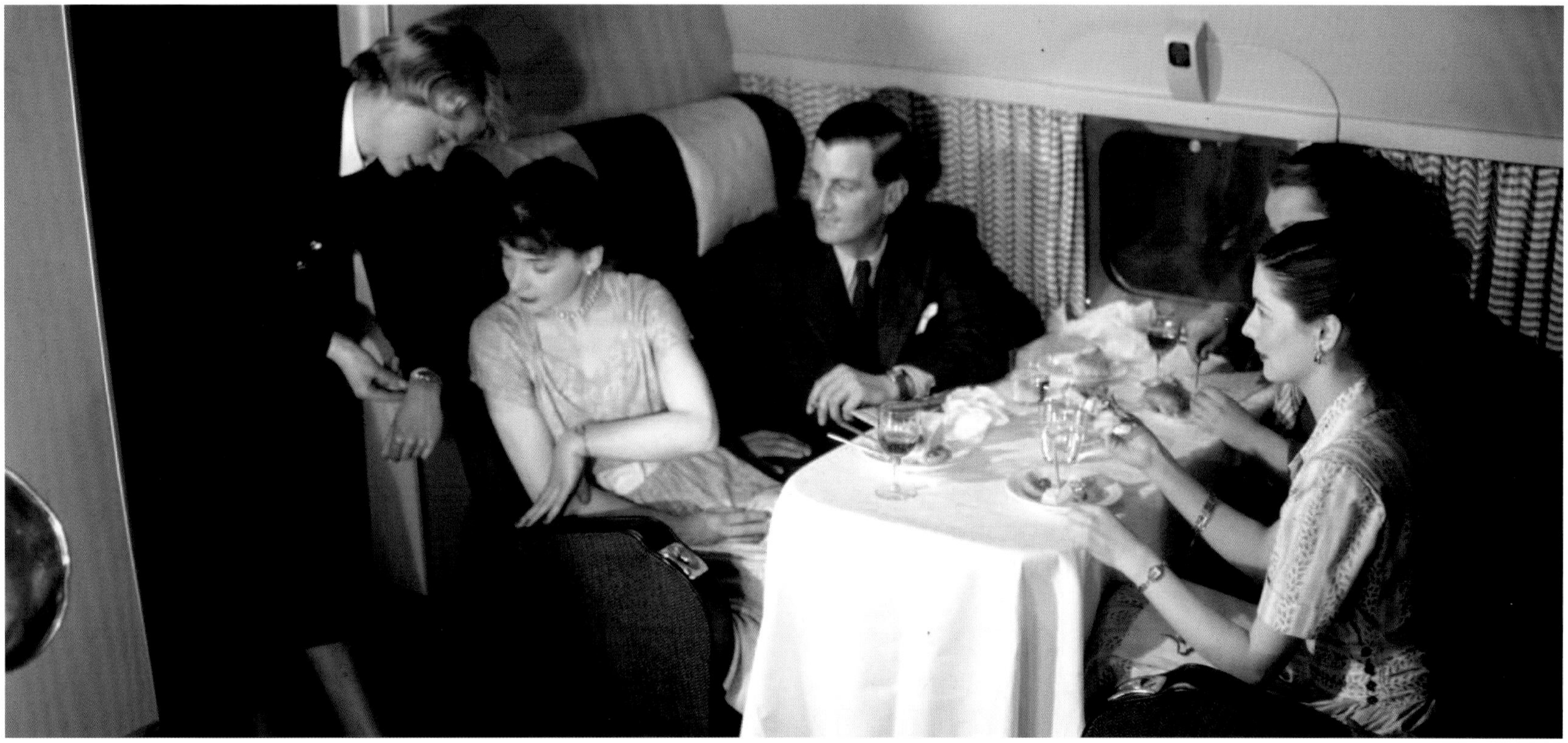

LEFT: Comet 4 G-APDA pictured in August 1958, a month before Comet 4 deliveries to BOAC began.
TOP LEFT: Dawn on 14 September 1958: A stewardess from the crew of Comet 4 G-APDA prepares for her 7.925 miles non-stop flight from London to Hong Kong.
ABOVE: Dinner time on a BOAC Comet 4, mocked up for promotion

blast. The horizontal tail surfaces were re-designed with thicker skins and doubled up ribs to handle the effects of jet noise. Specially-treated American specification aluminium alloy called 24ST was used on the wing surfaces and fuselage, while steel was employed on the key forgings used for the attachment of wings and horizontal tail.

As with the structure, main systems like the electrical supply, cabin air and flying controls were modified in the light of experience with the Comet 1 and later developments. An example was the complete separation of electrical and hydraulic system components. The electric power distribution system was duplicated to deal with any expected power failure scenario.

A major system change was the introduction of a flying control system incorporating artificial feel proportional to air loads. This power-operated "Q-feel" system was of de Havilland design and considered to be remarkably compact. It gave Comet 4 pilots control feel proportional to airspeed.

The Comet 1 was criticised for its heavy controls. A force of 18 to 20lb was required to displace the control column but on the Comet 4 this was reduced to 10lb mainly through the elimination of friction in the system and by the addition of automatic cable tension compensators. Trimming was also automatic on the Comet 4 when the Smiths SEP 2 autopilot was in use. An electric motor in the trim circuit sensed changes of load in the autopilot.

There was an artificial stall warning using a stick-shaker which operated before airframe shake could warn the pilots of an impending stall. It was programmed to operate at a speed 12 per cent above the stall whatever the aircraft's aerodynamic configuration.

A speed sensor in the elevator control circuit, which had originally been installed on the French and Canadian Comet 1As was fitted to automatically apply up-elevator at a speed of Mach 0.77. The elevators and ailerons also featured duplicated power boosters. There were three completely separate hydraulic systems for the flying controls.

Compared with the Comet 1 the Comet 4 featured more effective ailerons with increased chord, while the inner split flaps were given 20-degrees more movement. The rudder circuit incorporated a yaw damper. At that time the Comet 4 and the French Sud Caravelle twin-jet, whose control system was based closely on the Comet's, were the only airliners to feature power-operated flying controls.

The Comet 4's cabin pressurisation and air conditioning systems were considerably simpler to operate than those on the Comet 1, being virtually fully automatic. Once the required altitude setting was selected other values, such as temperature, mass flow, recirculation and climb rate were varied automatically.

De-icing arrangements were also revised on the Comet 4 having been extensively tested on a Comet 2 as well as a Lincoln bomber with a special spray rig. The Lincoln was flown with a section of Comet tail incorporating a Napier Spraymat system was mounted on the top of its fuselage.

The even though pilots praised the Comet 1's flight deck layout the Comet 4 incorporated operational experience provided by BOAC crews. The most obvious change was the incorporation of American-style grey panels in place of the previous black. Instruments were easier to read.

The Comet 4's fuel system was comprehensively re-engineered, the main requirement being the simplification of the pressure-refuelling blow-off valves. There was also an independent fuel feed to each engine so that none of the fuel

pipes was common to pairs of engines as was the case with the Comet 1.

A key event in the Comet's rehabilitation was the long hoped-for order from a US airline. In July 1956 Capital Airlines ordered four Comet 4s and ten of a short-haul development with reduced wingspan and 40-inch fuselage stretch to accommodate 92 passengers in five abreast seating. This version was designated Comet 4A. But it was not to be. Capital's acquisition by United Airlines in 1961 meant that the order was cancelled and the 4A was not built.

Before this happened the Comet 4 came under close scrutiny by the US regulator, the Civil Aeronautics Administration. One aspect of the aircraft's design which came in for particular attention was the buried engines. The CAA had no objection in principle to such an installation but needed to be satisfied about fire safety.

As a result Rolls-Royce constructed at Hucknall a special rig establishment which contained a Comet 4 stub wing complete with engines. Different scenarios were replicated and proved the value of encasing the engine's combustion zone in titanium. Graviner Firewire fire detectors were fitted.

Special attention had also to be paid to noise suppression to satisfy New York Port Authority requirements in particular. A thrust reverser system was also developed and although it had been hoped to install it in BOAC's first Comet 4 the equipment had to be retro-fitted. Ground tests were conducted with a Comet 2 before being flight tested on the Comet 3's two outer engines.

While the Comet I's interior furnishings had been considered tasteful by 1958 the traditional dark blue and grey was seen as "rather dull." The Comet 4's décor was thought to be more in keeping with the jet age and well able to match BOAC's American rivals.

Although BOAC's first two Comet 4's (G-APDB and G-APDC) did not arrive until September 1958, the airline had by then accumulated a considerable amount of experience with the Avon-powered aircraft. The flight testing programme was already well advanced by the time the first production aircraft (G-APDA) first flew in April. By this time the modified Comet 3 prototype, now dubbed Comet 31/2, had accumulated 830 flying hours in over 580 flights.

Had this aircraft not been available, de Havilland would probably have faced a two-year test flying programme with the Comet 4. Indeed, it was estimated that availability of the Comet 3 may well have enabled the manufacturer to reduce the total Comet 4 development programme by a year with the reduction in testing that had been possible.

The airline had not wasted time either. The return flight from Heathrow to Beirut of a BOAC Comet on 16 September 1957 signalled the airline's return to the jet airliner business. Although the tragedies of 1954 and the subsequent grounding of the Comet I fleet stunned the airline its staff did not lose their faith in the aircraft. They were well aware that there was a "Comet effect", as there was later to be with Concorde decades later. The jet was popular with crews and passengers and it had enhanced the airline's reputation.

At that stage the key route envisaged for the new Comet was that to Australia. The Kangaroo route was due to be flown in partnership with rival Qantas which had ordered Boeing 707s. It was planned to operate four times a week from February 1959, replacing the Bristol Britannia 102s. The Australia service would be followed by others, to Tokyo – in June 1959 - and South Africa the following June.

OPPOSITE PAGE: Dramatic head-on view of an unidentified BOAC Comet 4 taken in October 1958 by which time the first three examples had been delivered.

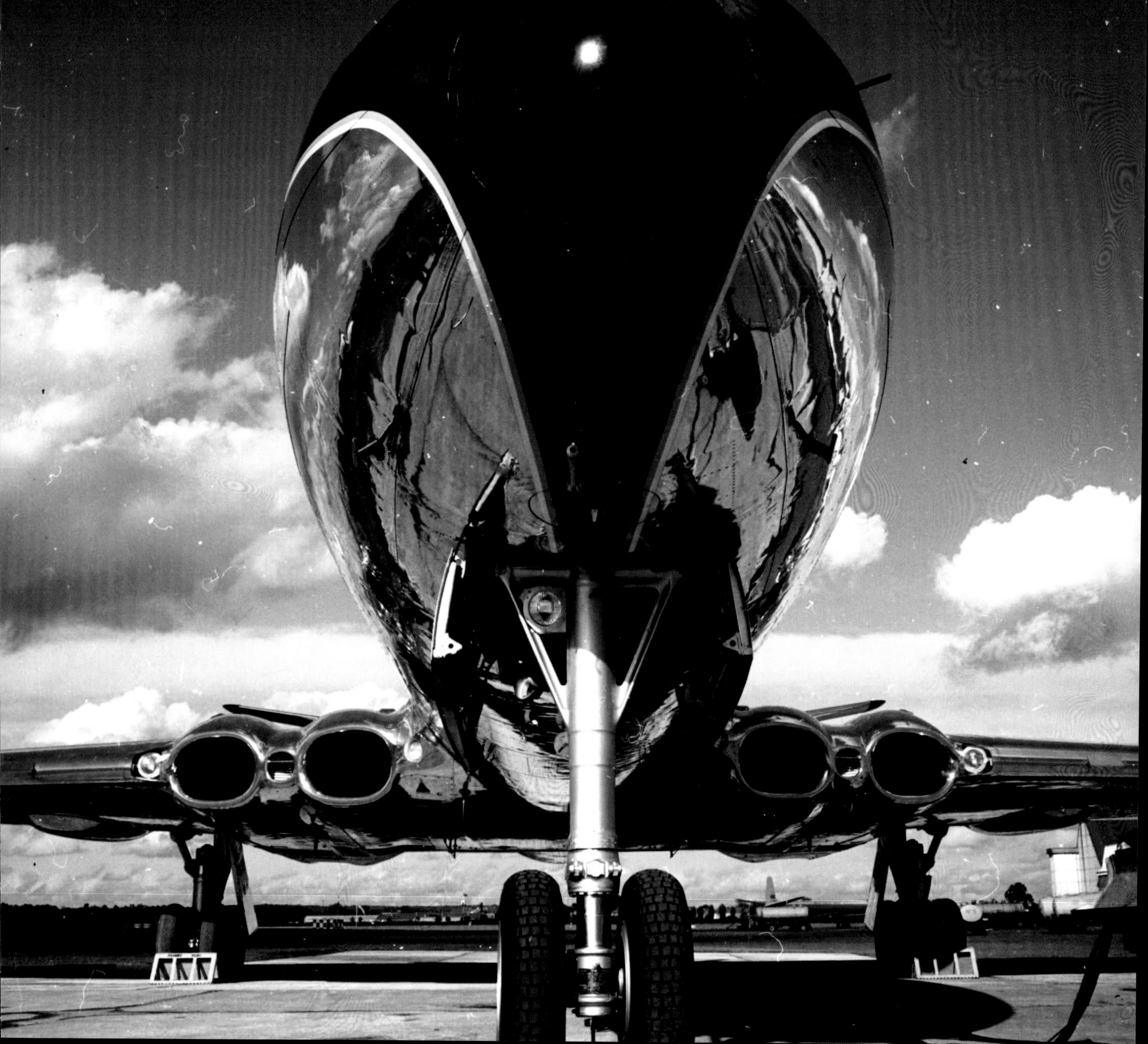

But by early 1958 Pan Am had announced its intention of opening trans-Atlantic 707 services that October. BOAC, which had not originally intended to use its Comet 4s on the route, declined to be drawn on speculation that it was changing its mind. The journal Flight commented: *"No doubt it would be a proposition as a prestige operation but the corporation is not likely to be easily persuaded – however great the political pressures – from its cautiously laid plans for introducing Comets on the Commonwealth routes."*

BOAC maintained that it would need to accumulate 1,500hr with the new aircraft between September 1958 and the target in-service date of 1 February 1959. By that time it planned to have at least six aircraft. The last would be in service in December by when it expected have its first Boeing 707-320. A total of 117 fully trained crews would be required for the Comet fleet and 24 would be available for the start of services. Each crew would comprise two pilots, a navigator and an engineer.

Training was conducted from Heathrow. The idea of using Hurn, Bournemouth was rejected because it was an hour's flying time away from London at a time when jet fuel cost 1s 5d (18p) a gallon.

The Comet 2Es played a vital role in BOAC's preparations for the resumption of Comet operations. Two (G-AMXD and G-AMXK) were delivered to BOAC in August 1957 with the original intention of clearing the Avon RA 29s for a 500hr overhaul life before the start of Comet 4 operations. During 1957 and 1958 the two aircraft were busy on route-proving operations. By the first quarter of 1958 the engines was cleared to 750hr with 1,000hr in prospect.

With the delayed delivery the airline had to raise the tempo of its Beirut flights from eight to 11 and sometimes 13. As a result, the Comets were flying 125hr per week with a daily utilisation rarely falling below 9hr. The intense programme also helped air traffic controllers, then employees of the Ministry of Transport and Civil Aviation, refresh their skill at integrating the jets into the UK's air traffic pattern.

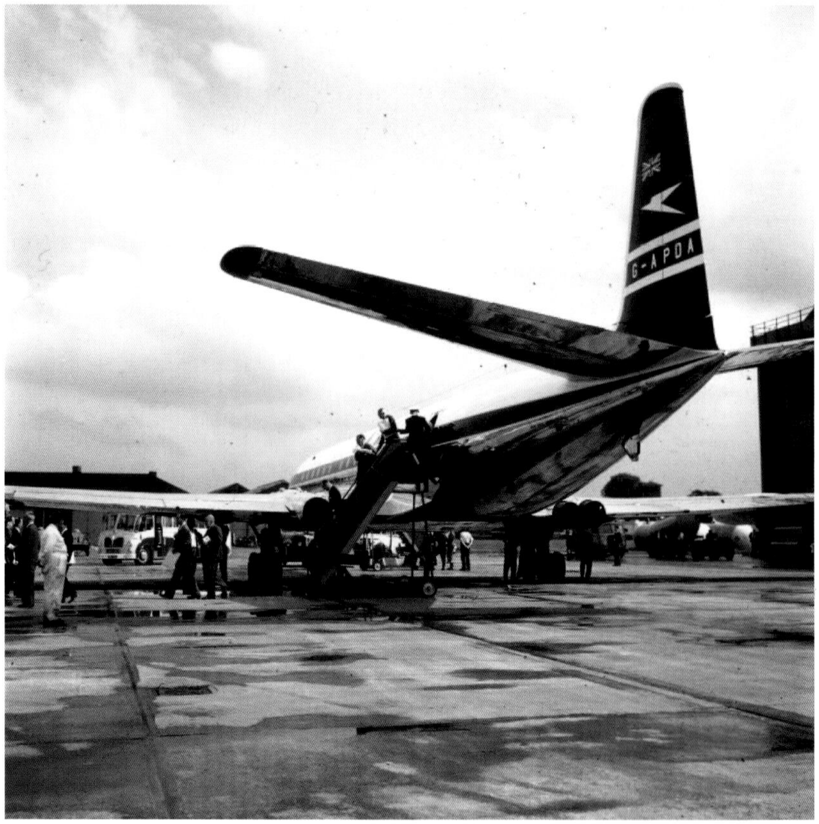
G-APDA

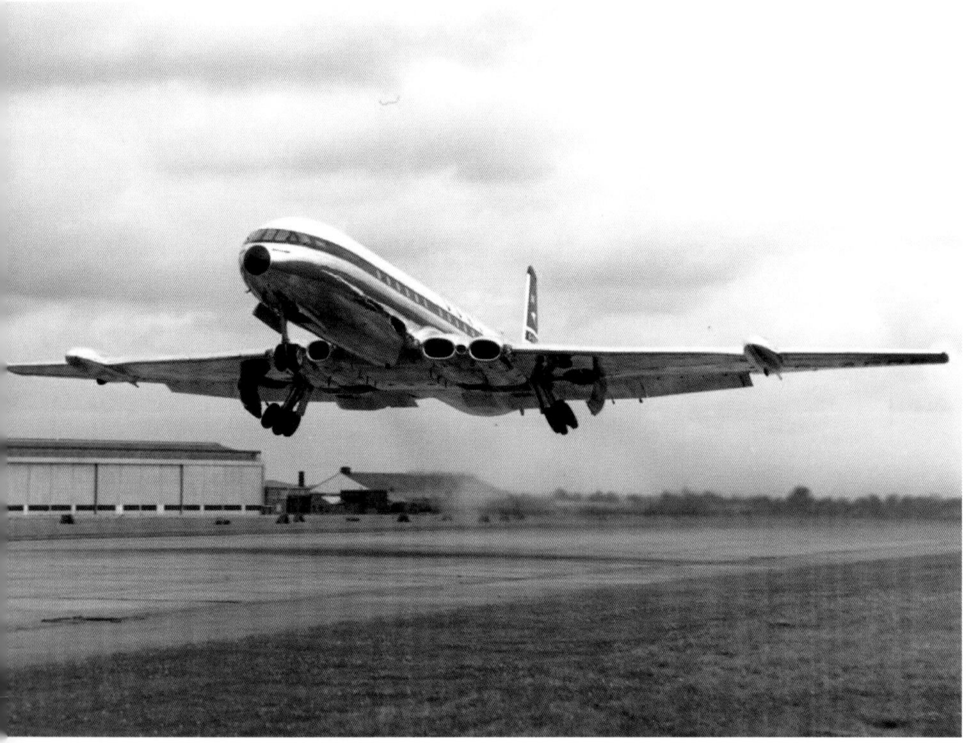

ABOVE: Two of BOAC's Comet 4's are pictured in this spread in 1958. (Top, right) G-APDA; (bottom left) G-APDB was one of the first two delivered, on 30 September;

OPPOSITE PAGE: (top and bottom right) `DA again.

Despite BOAC's planning and previous intentions the chance of beating Pan Am and the Boeing 707 to the honour of flying the first trans-Atlantic jet passenger service and salvage some of Britain's aeronautical prestige was clearly too good to miss. On 4 October 1958, BOAC Comet 4 G-APDC, resplendent in its tasteful white, blue and silver colour scheme, left Heathrow to inaugurate the first jet service between London and New York.

History shows that the Comet beat the 707 by 22 days. But Pan Am powered ahead in August 1959 when it introduced the bigger and faster 707-320 series on the route. It offered greater frequency than BOAC could manage. A point, though, had been made. One of the first American lady passengers to fly the Comet exclaimed: "Isn't this the dreamiest?" Her reaction to the jet's cabin décor was noted by Flight's Mike Ramsden, the de Havilland apprentice turned journalist.

He flew on one of the early trans-Atlantic services and described the Comet's interior as *"a work of art, a masterpiece of design so subtle that print can but inadequately convey the pleasure which it gives."* Ramsden commented in particular on the variations in colour between the linen headrests and cushions and the upholstery. The seats were pronounced *"most comfortable"* but high standards were expected: BOAC's Monarch service had become a byword on the north Atlantic. *"Its refinements could not have had a more appropriate setting than the aesthetically pleasing and physically tranquil cabin of the Comet,"*

Ramsden added.

All this came at a price, of course. Passengers who chose de luxe travel occupied 16 seats in the forward – and quietest – section of the cabin which enjoyed 56in pitch. The aft cabin accommodated 32 first class passengers who paid £155 for the round trip. The deluxe surcharge was £18, almost double the average weekly wage in the UK at the time.

One aspect of the Comet 4 compared with the Comet 1 that was particularly noticeable was the additional power offered by the new variant. Compared with the piston-engined airliners then flying the route the Comet seemed effortless and the power offered by the four Avons promised ample reserves for *"hot and high"* operations in Asia and Africa. By this time overhaul intervals of 1,000hr had been approved by the Air Registration Board with 1,500hr in prospect.

When BOAC had its complete Comet 4 fleet available it was able to extend its jet services to girdle the globe. Soon all six continents would hear the whine of the Avons as the airline's Comets flew to 46 cities in 36 countries. By 1960 the original plans to serve Australia (Darwin and Sydney), the Far East (Singapore, Hong Kong and Tokyo) and South America (Rio de Janeiro, Buenos Aires and Santiago) had been realised. In North America, Montreal had joined New York.

Meanwhile the Comet 4 family was expanding. The short-range 4B was developed from the projected 4A (see chapter eight.) The 4C was basically a 4 crossed with a 4B. The Comet 4's wing and larger fuel tankage mated to the 4B's longer fuselage and higher capacity produced an intermediate version combining the 4B's superior operating economics with a payload-range capability not far short of the baseline Comet 4's. The 4C flew for the first time in October 1959 and was to prove popular with smaller airlines.

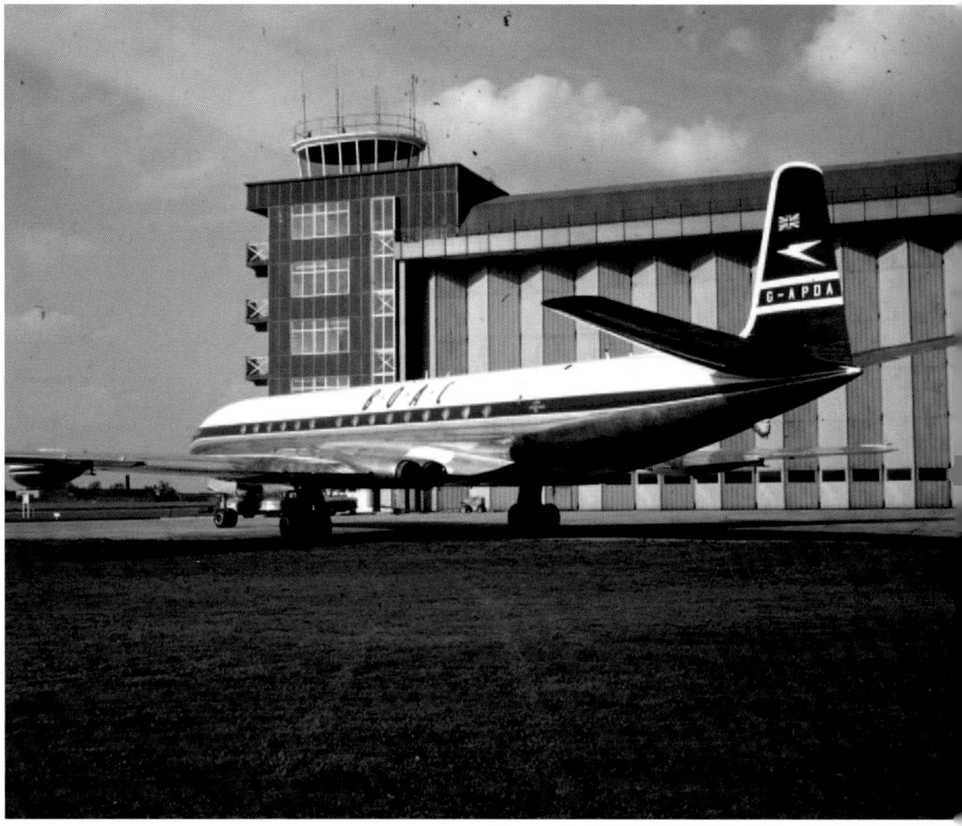
G-APDA

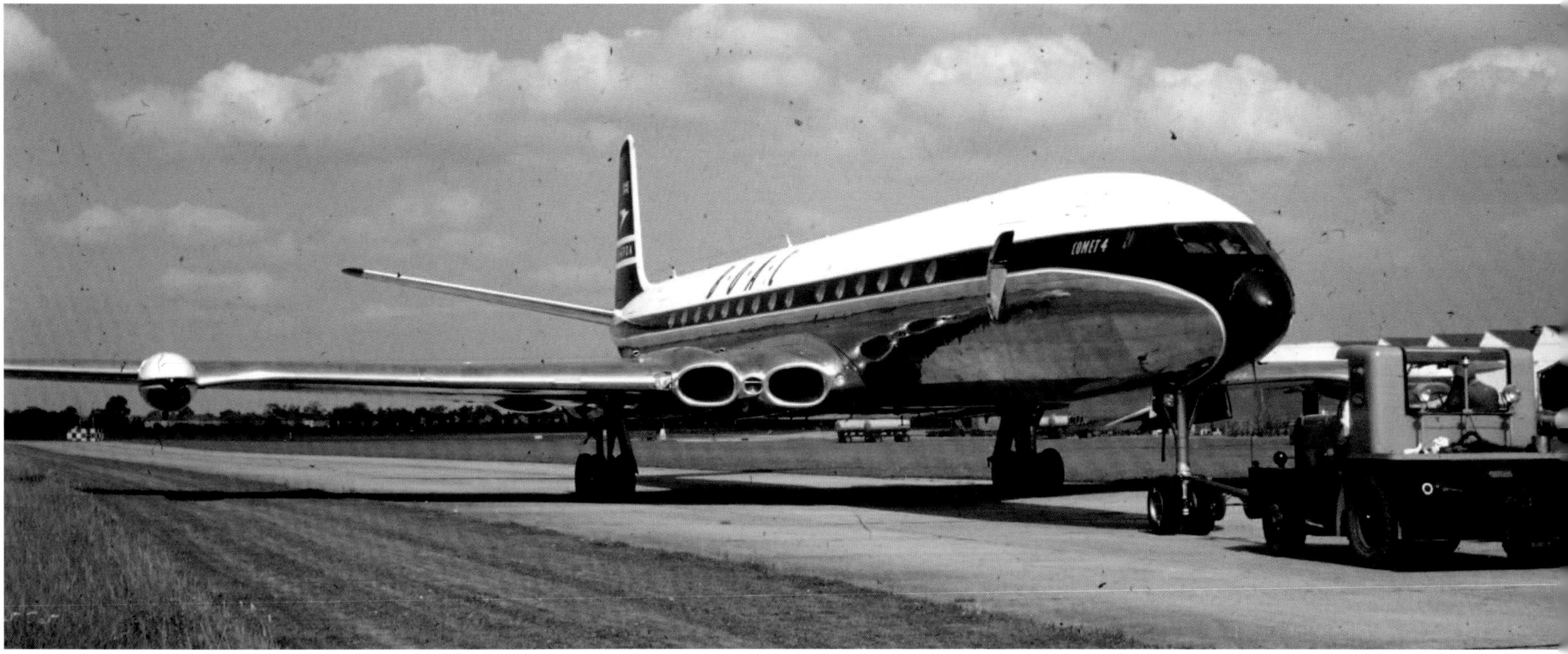
COMET 4

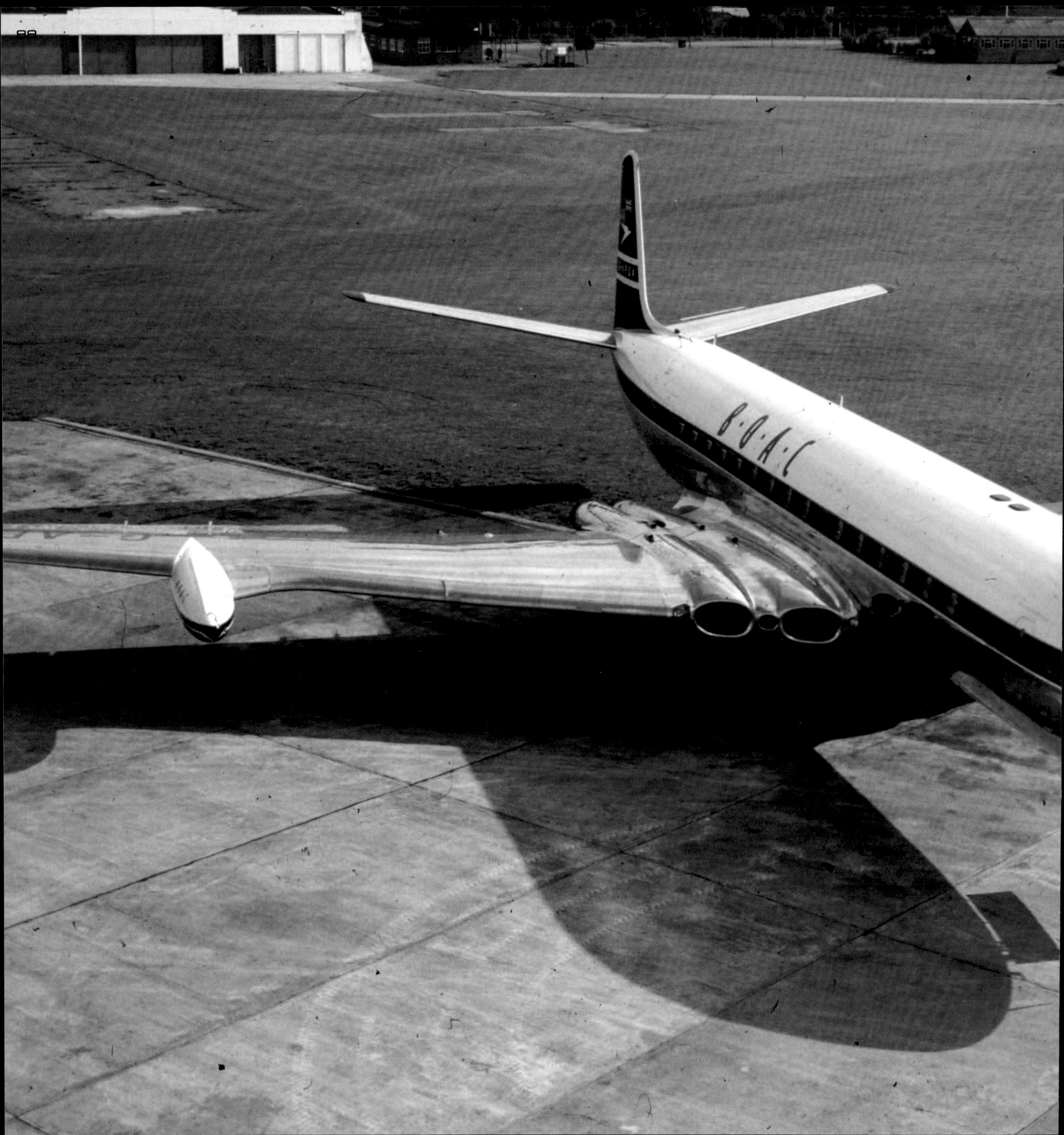
B·O·A·C

By that time the Comet club had expanded. Aerolineas Argentinas acquired seven Comet 4s (including one 4C), which were delivered between March 1959 and April 1962. The airline used the aircraft to open South America's first jet service, from Buenos Aires to Santiago, in April 1959. A month later it pioneered jet services across the South Atlantic to Europe, to Lisbon, Madrid, Paris, Rome, Frankfurt and London. In June 1959 it linked North and South America with the first jet services by flying between Buenos Aries and New York.

Another Latin American Comet 4 operator was Mexicana, which received two Comet 4s and three 4Cs between July 1959 and October 1960. The aircraft flew a mix of domestic and International services from Mexico City. Los Angeles, Miami and Chicago were among the US destinations.

East African Airways had three Comet 4s delivered in 1960 and 1962. The airline, based in Nairobi, Kenya, also represented Uganda, Tanganyika (now Tanzania) and Zanzibar. Between 1960 and 1971 the airline's Comets operated a network of services within Africa and also to India and Europe. Their use of high altitude airports demonstrated the Comet's ability to cope with a variety of runways as well as hard use. Daily utilisation often reached 11. After the airline received Super VC10s in 1967 the Comets were used for charter operations.

Other Comet 4C operators included Sudan Airways whose pair of aircraft was delivered in 1962. They operated from Khartoum to European, Middle Eastern and African destinations. In 1972 one of the aircraft flew the final scheduled Comet service into Heathrow.

Seven years earlier when BOAC had retired its Comet 4s five of the earlier examples, including G-APDC, which had flown the first jet trans-Atlantic service, were acquired by Malaysia Airways, later to become Malaysia-Singapore Airlines. Until 1970 the aircraft flew services from Kuala Lumpur and Singapore to destinations in Asia as well as Australia.

United Arab Airlines, formerly Misrair, the national carrier of Egypt, had nine aircraft, which were delivered between 1960 and 1964. The airline used them until 1976 on an extensive route network within the Middle East, Africa, the Mediterranean region and Europe. Beirut-based Middle East Airlines ordered four aircraft for use within the Middle East and as far afield as London and Bombay. Three aircraft were written off on the ground in December 1968 during an Israeli attack on Beirut. Aircraft were leased from Kuwait Airways in an attempt to continue operations but the Comets then flying in MEA colours were withdrawn in 1971.

Before they were leased to MEA, Kuwait Airways' pair of Comets were delivered in 1963 and 1964. The purpose had been for the airline to gain experience of jet airliners before the delivery of Trident 1Es. It was the last Comet customer. Its aircraft, though, like other Middle Eastern Comets, would return to Europe for a new life.

A Comet 4C featuring a VIP cabin was supplied to Saudi Arabia for use by King Ibn Saud but the aircraft crashed in the southern Alps in March 1963.

BOAC's last Comet service, from New Zealand, arrived at Heathrow in November 1965. By that time the airline had already begun to dispose of its fleet, five going to Malaysia, two to MEA, seven to Dan-Air, two to Mexicana and two to Aerovias Ecuadorianas. BOAC also leased aircraft to airlines like Air Ceylon, East African Airways, MEA, and Nigeria Airways.

Superb overhead view of BOAC's Comet 4 G-APDA, which was delivered to the airline in February 1959.

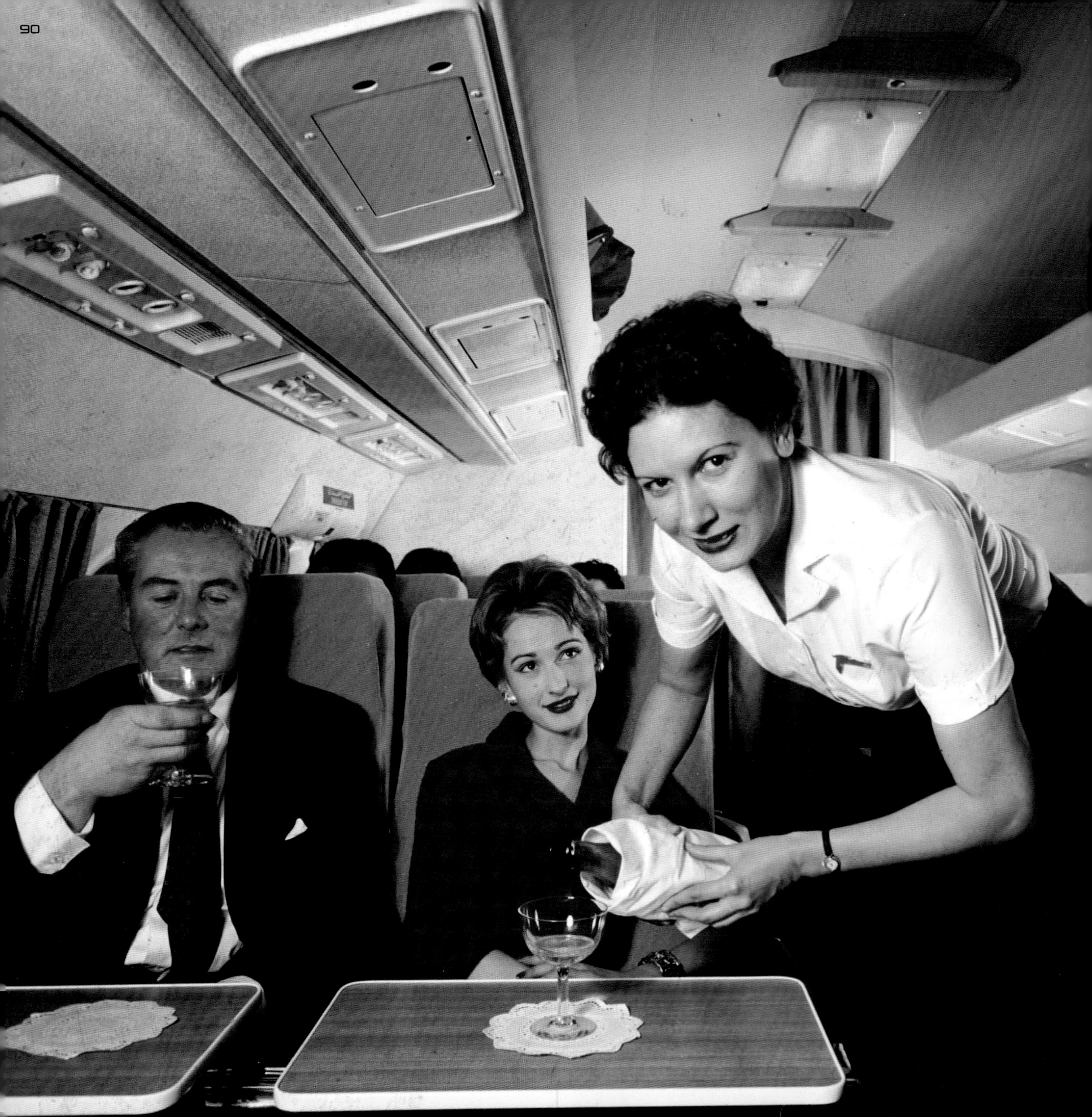

BOTH PAGES: On board a Misrair Comet 4C in 1960. The airline, later re-named United Arab Airlines took delivery of its first three of nine aircraft in 1960, the year it introduced the type on the Cairo-London route.

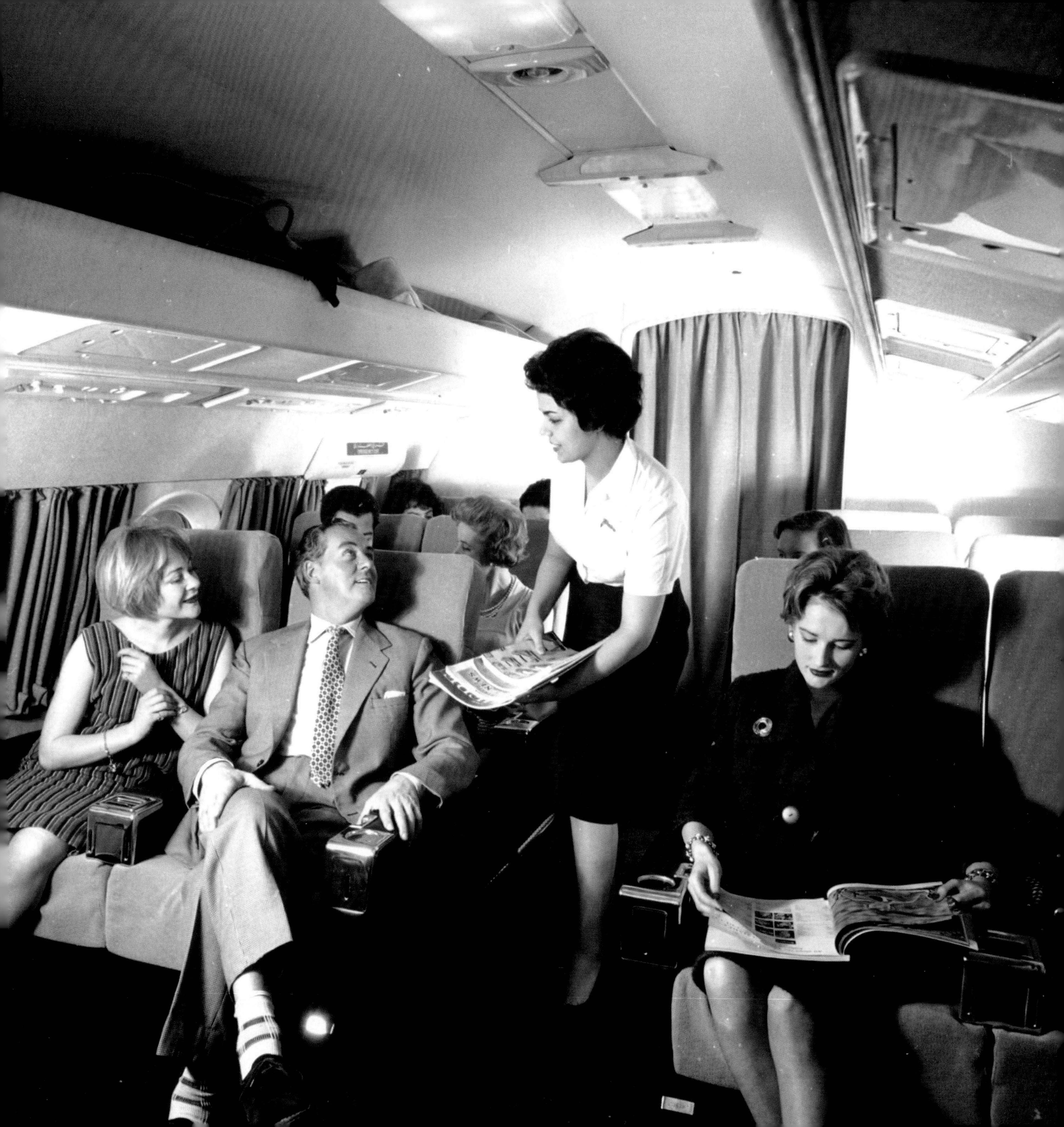

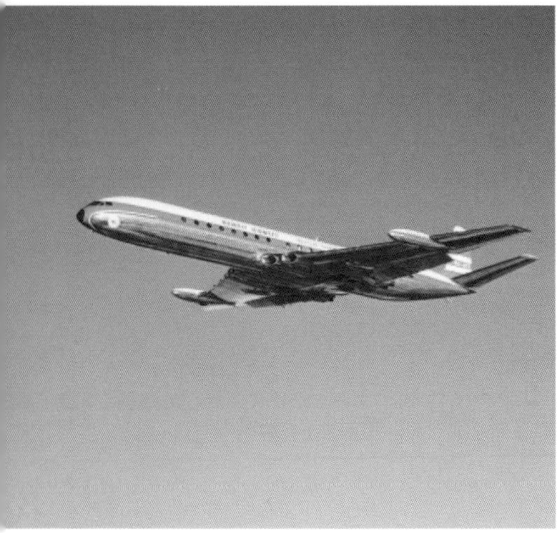

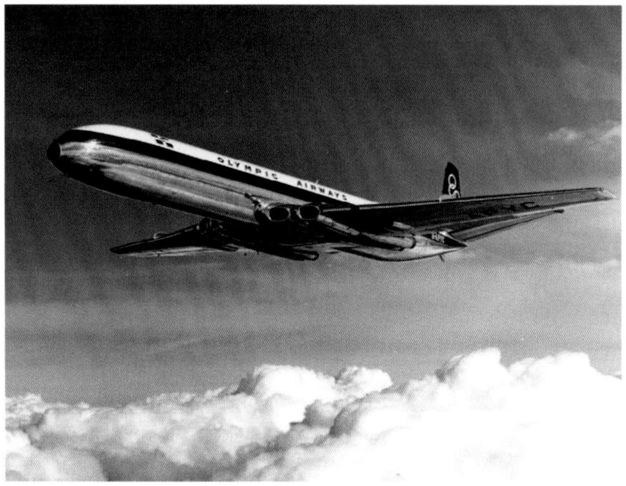
OLYMPIC AIRWAYS

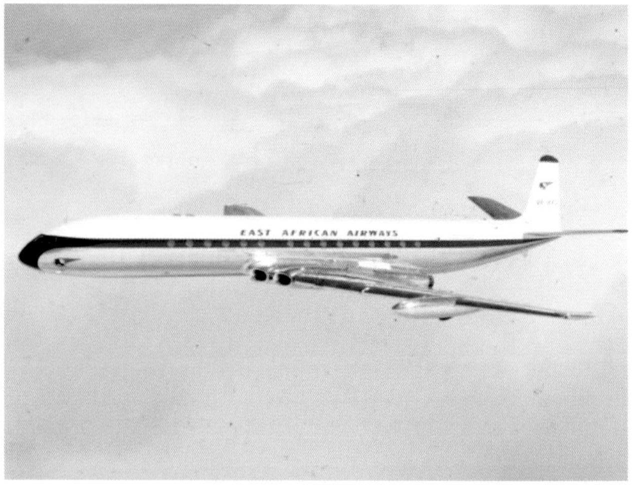
EAST AFRICAN AIRWAYS

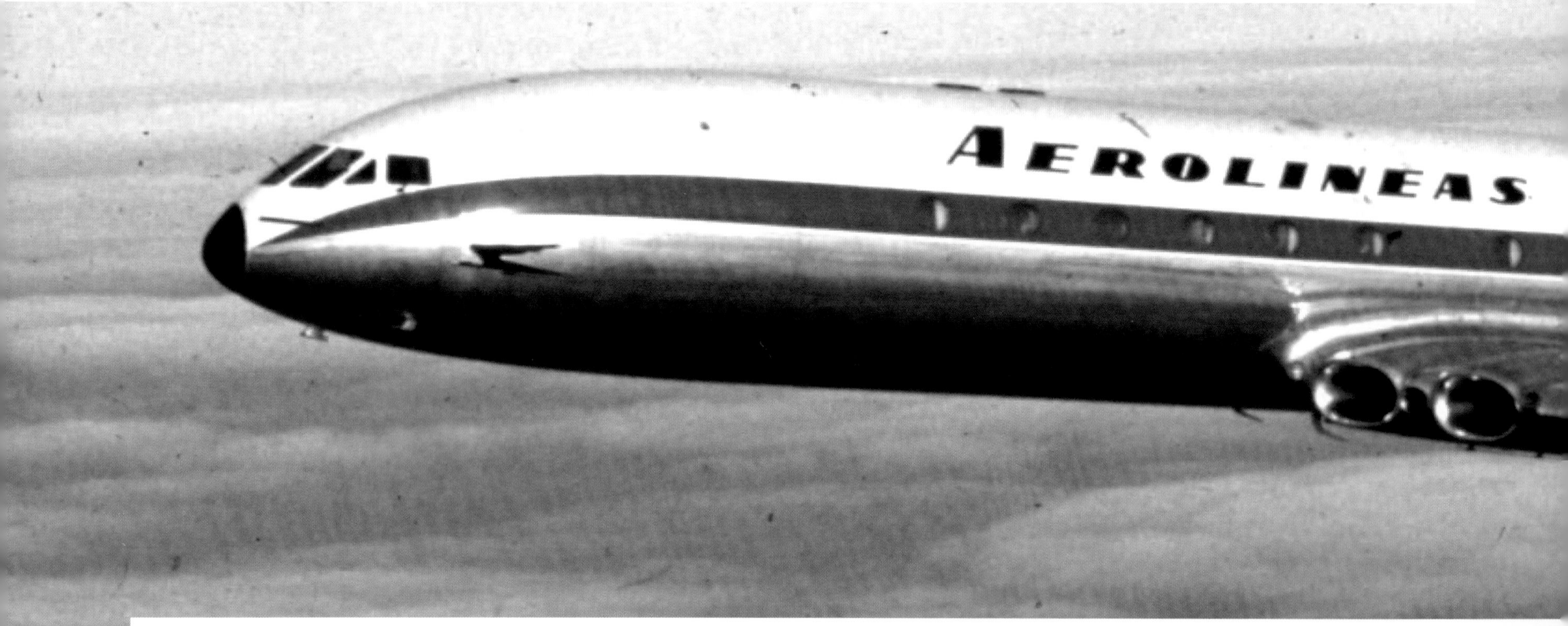
AEROLINEAS

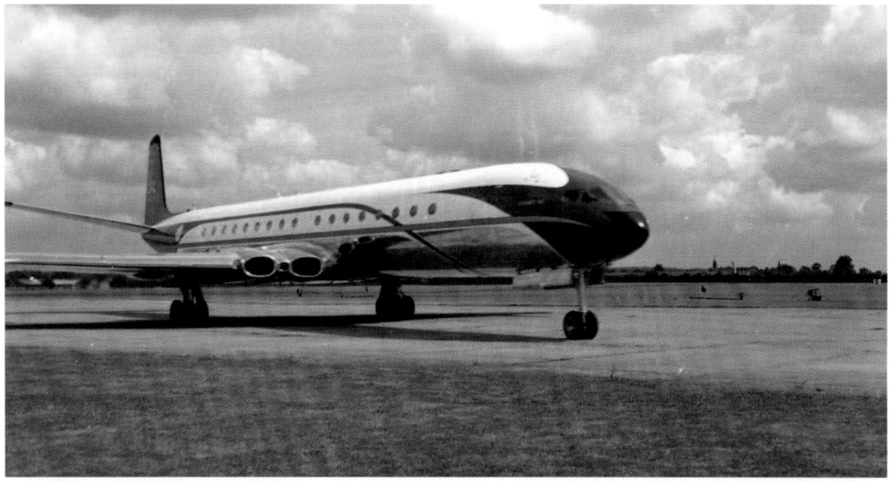

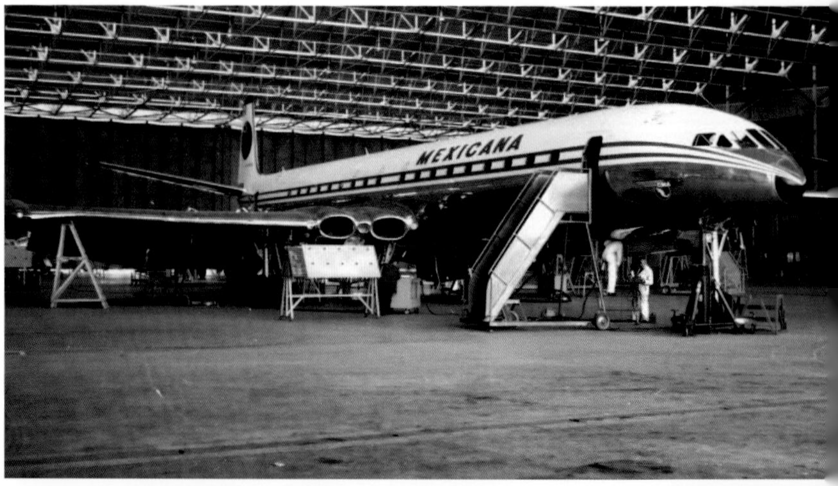
MEXICANA

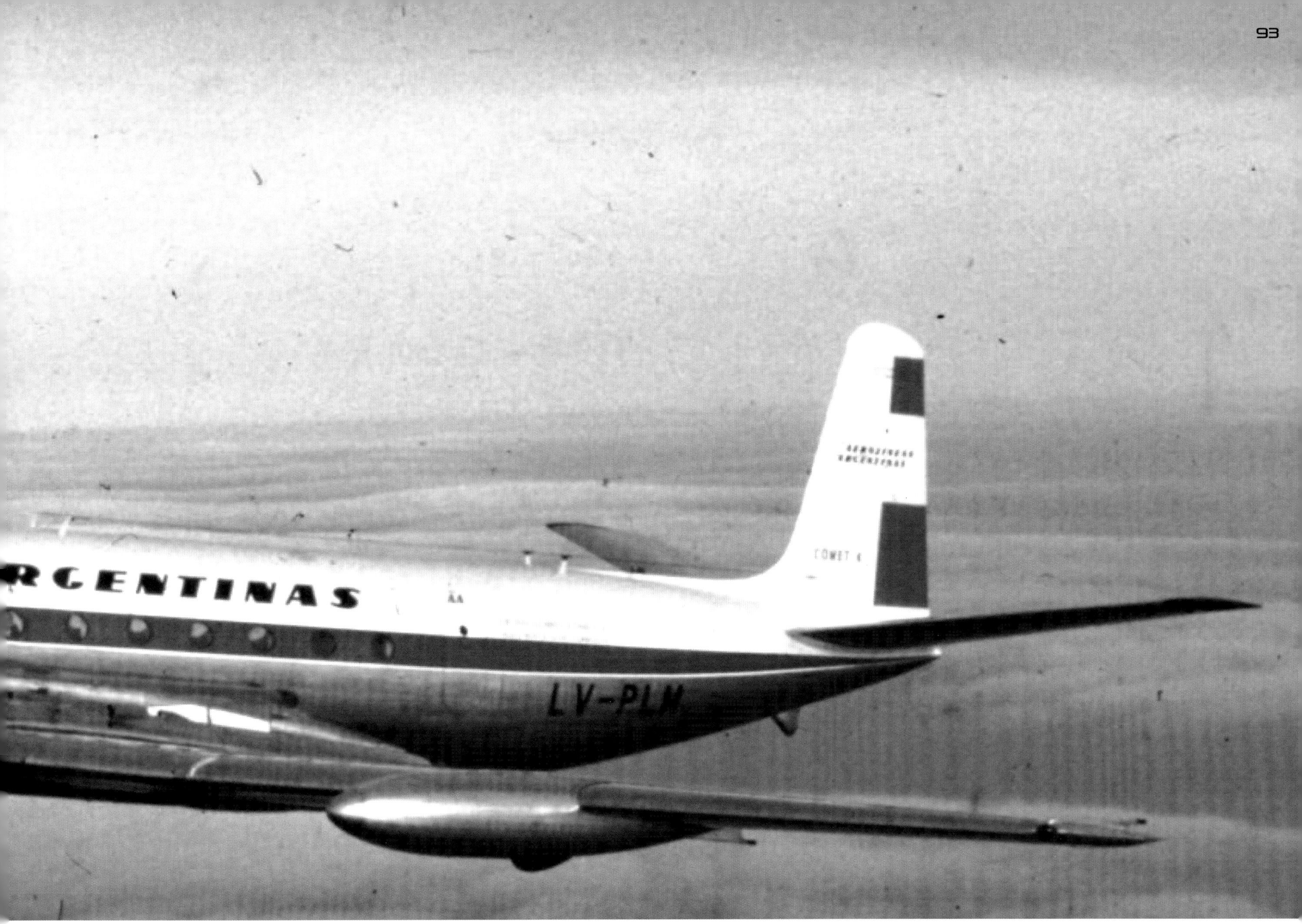
RGENTINAS
COMET 4
LV-PLM

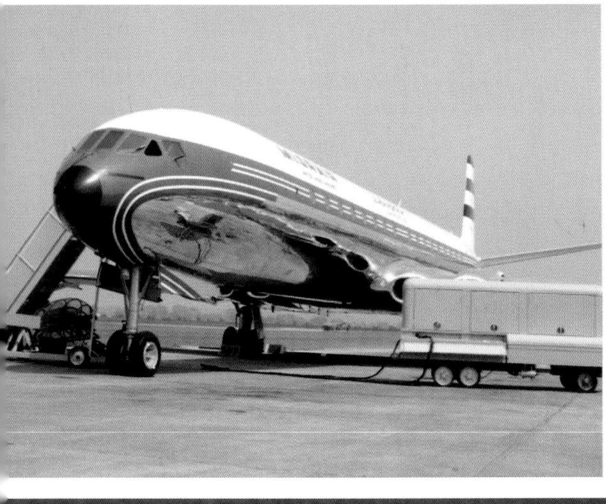

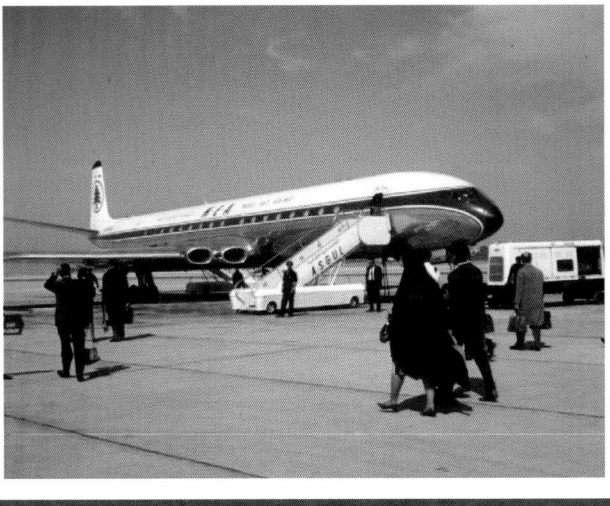
MEA

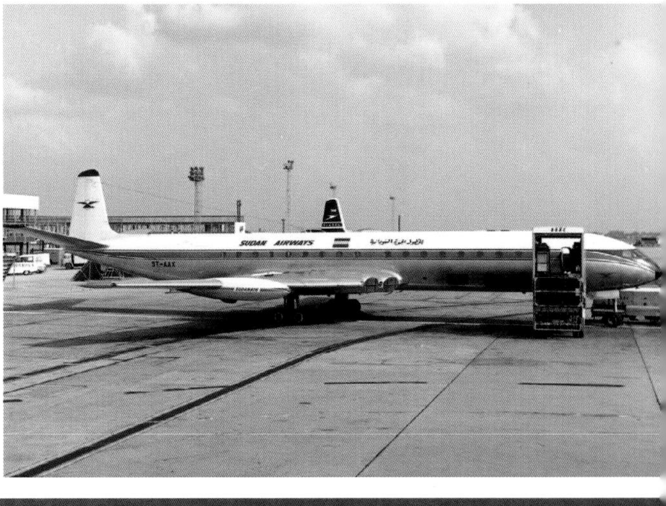
SUDAN AIRWAYS

Nine overseas airlines placed orders for Comet 4s and examples are depicted on this spread.

MAIN IMAGE: Aerolineas Argentinas ordered seven and the first, LV-PLM, was delivered in March 1959. A month later the type was introduced on the Buenos Aires-Santiago route. Other operators were **TOP, LEFT TO RIGHT:** Kuwait Airways; Olympic Airways; East African Airways. **BOTTOM, LEFT TO RIGHT:** Saudi Arabian Royal Flight; Mexicana; Misrair; Middle East Airlines; Sudan Airways.

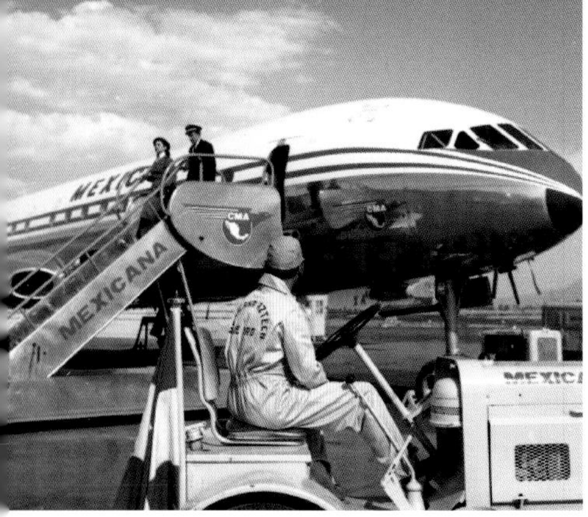
MEXICANA

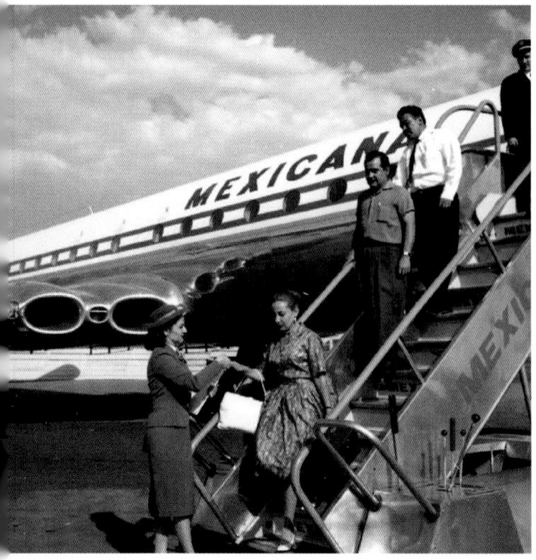
MEXICANA

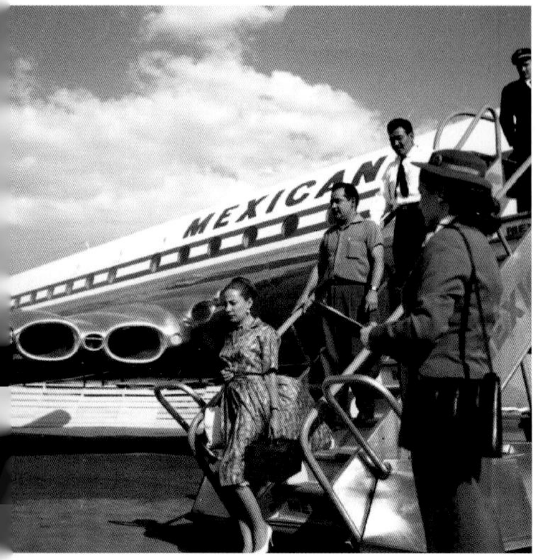
MEXICANA

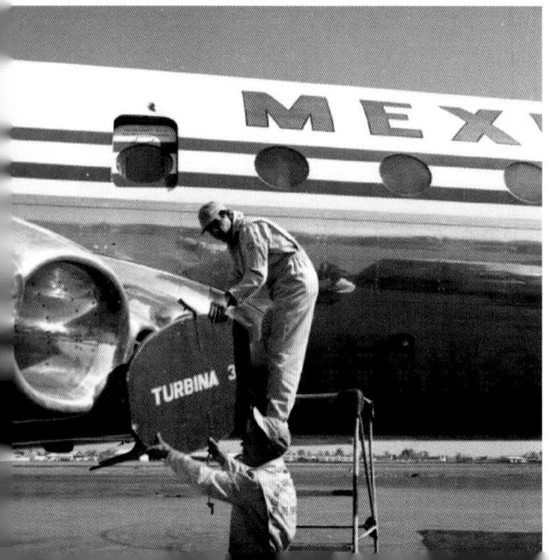
TURBINA

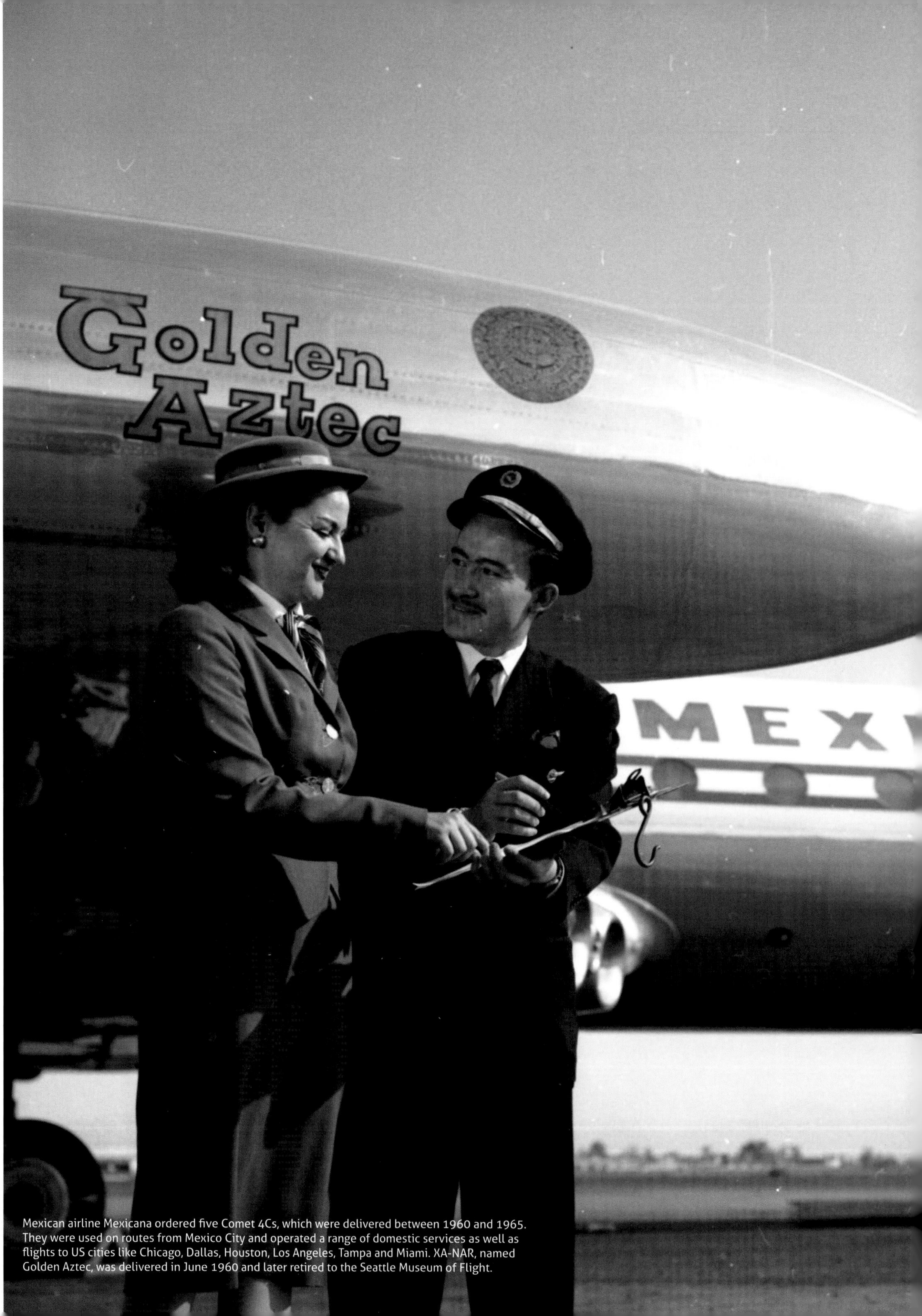
Golden Aztec

Mexican airline Mexicana ordered five Comet 4Cs, which were delivered between 1960 and 1965. They were used on routes from Mexico City and operated a range of domestic services as well as flights to US cities like Chicago, Dallas, Houston, Los Angeles, Tampa and Miami. XA-NAR, named Golden Aztec, was delivered in June 1960 and later retired to the Seattle Museum of Flight.

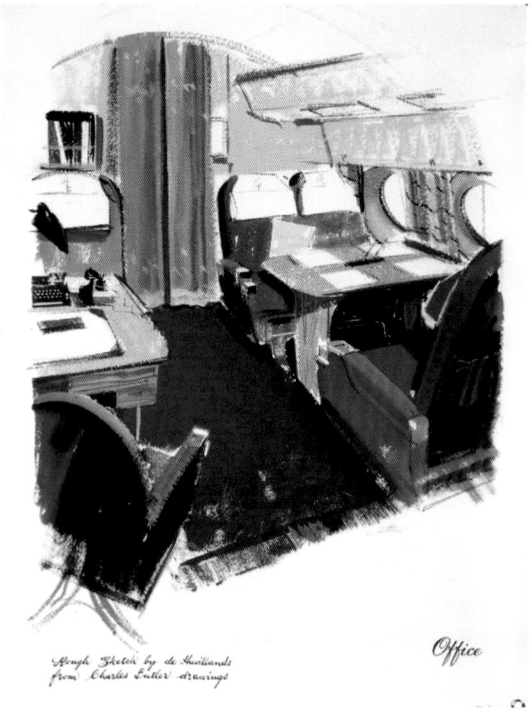
Rough Sketch by de Havillands from Charles Butler drawings
Office

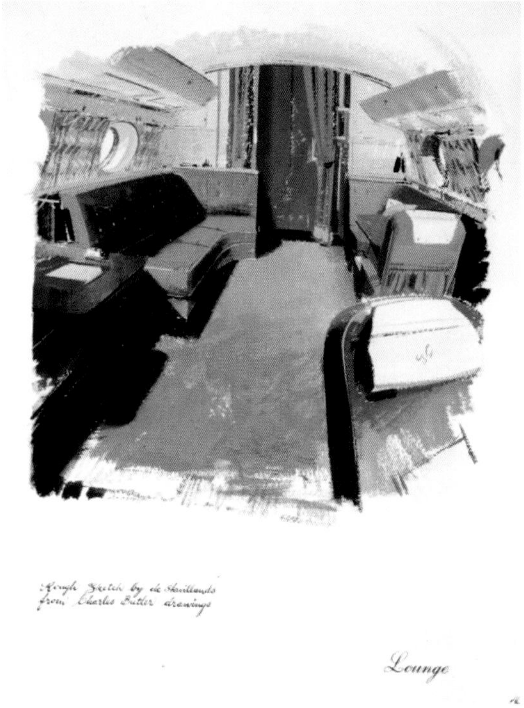
Rough Sketch by de Havillands from Charles Butler drawings
Lounge

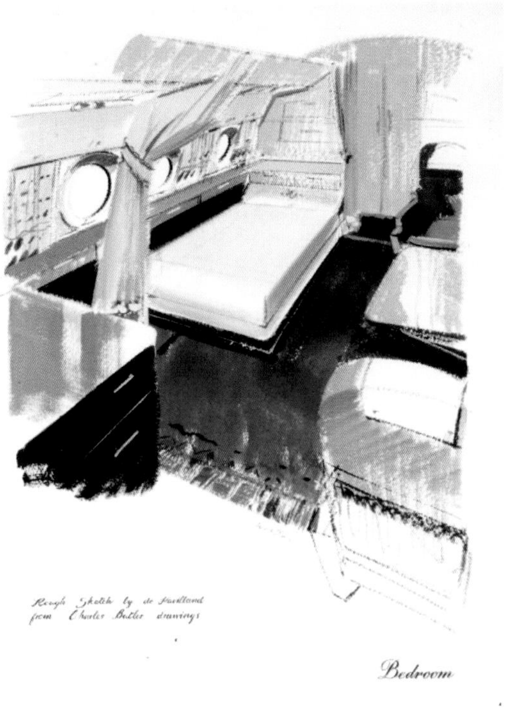
Rough Sketch by de Havilland from Charles Butler drawings
Bedroom

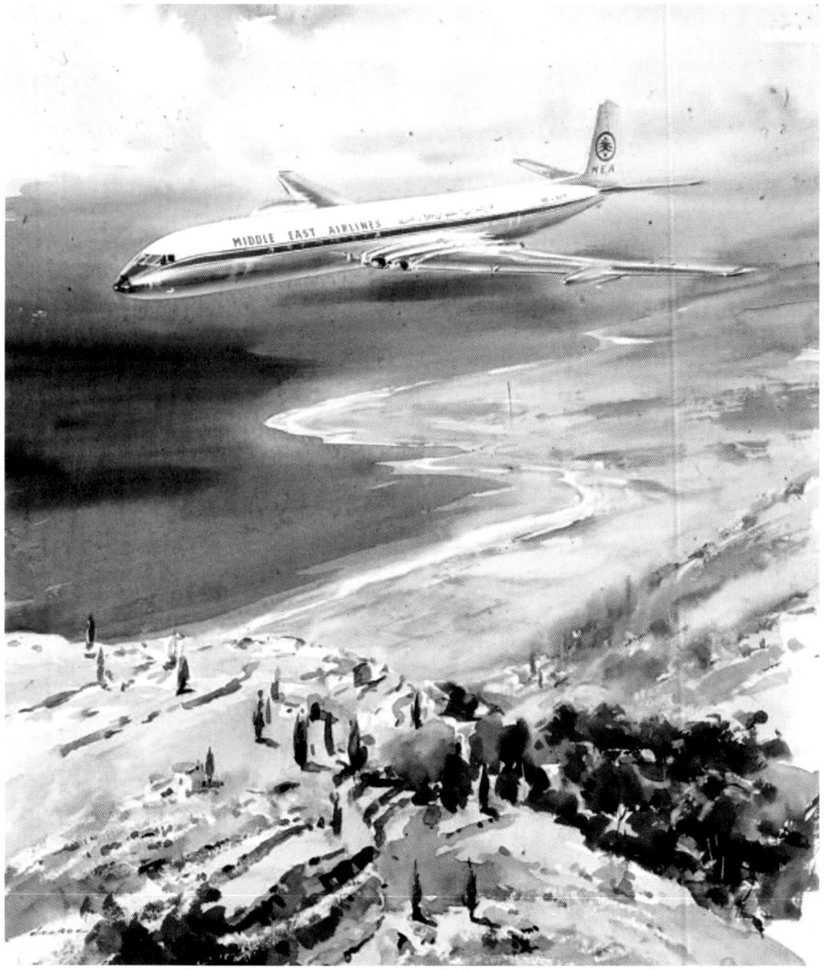
MIDDLE EAST AIRLINES
MEA

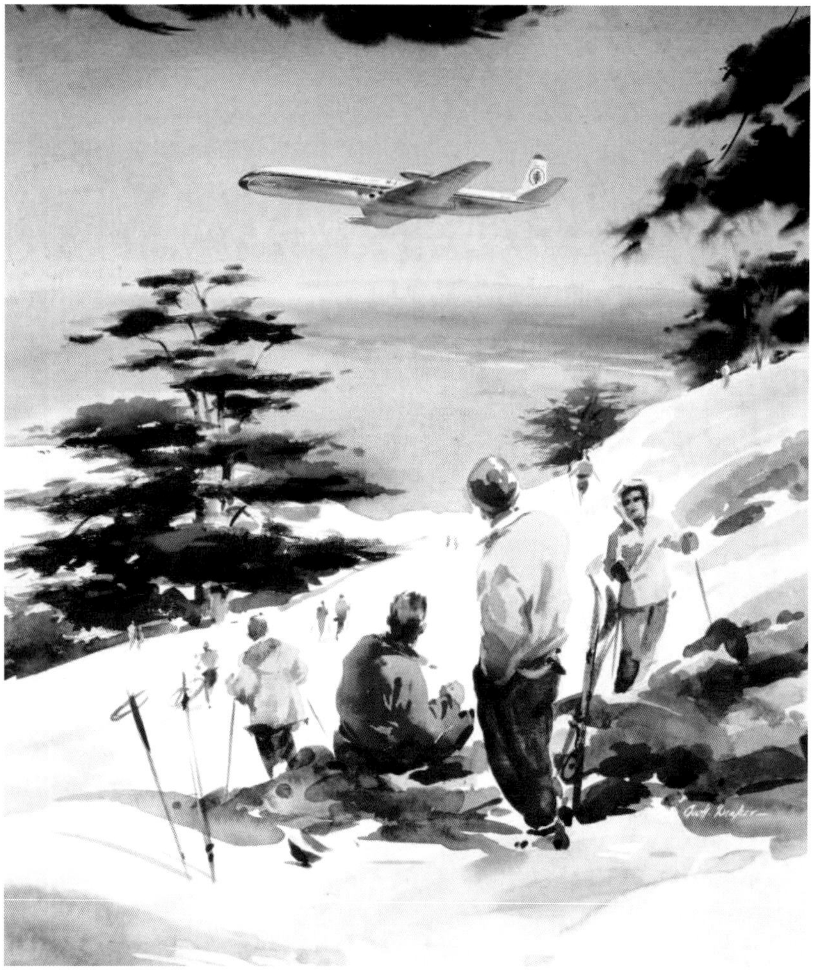

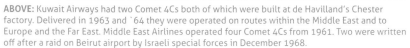

ABOVE: Kuwait Airways had two Comet 4Cs both of which were built at de Havilland's Chester factory. Delivered in 1963 and `64 they were operated on routes within the Middle East and to Europe and the Far East. Middle East Airlines operated four Comet 4Cs from 1961. Two were written off after a raid on Beirut airport by Israeli special forces in December 1968.

INCLUSIVE TOUR OPERATIONS

Fun Flights

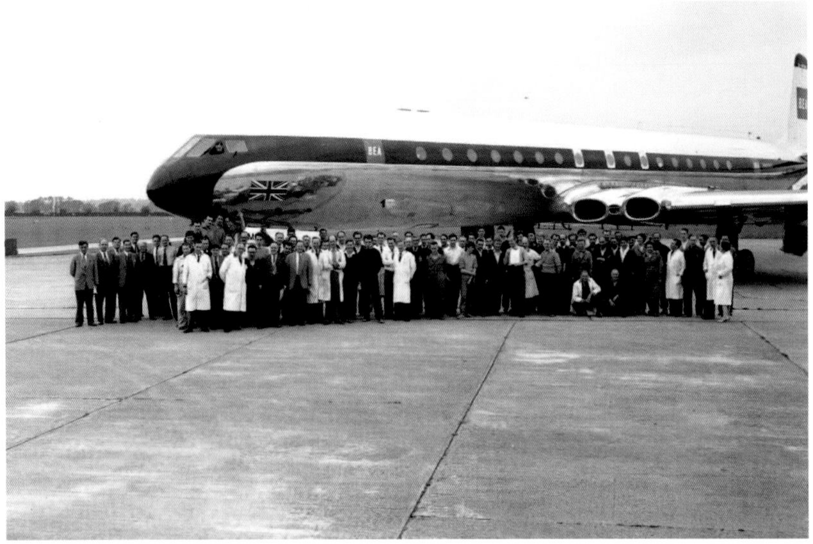

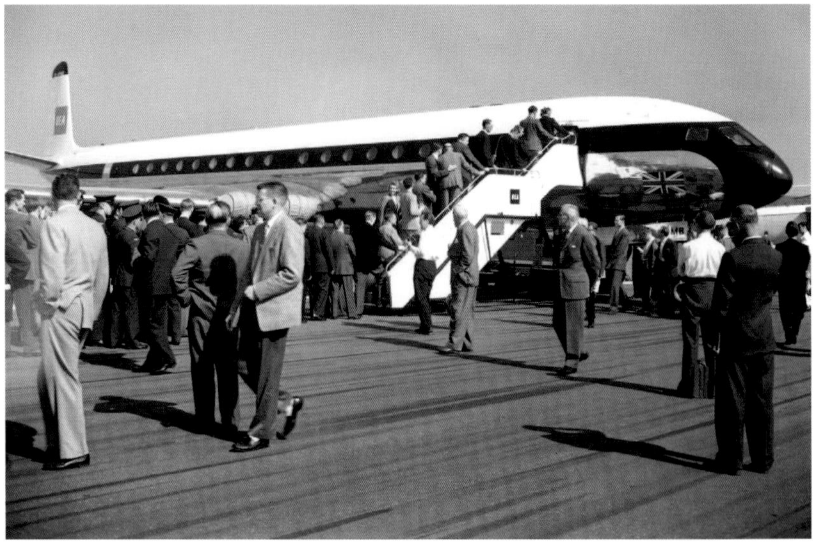

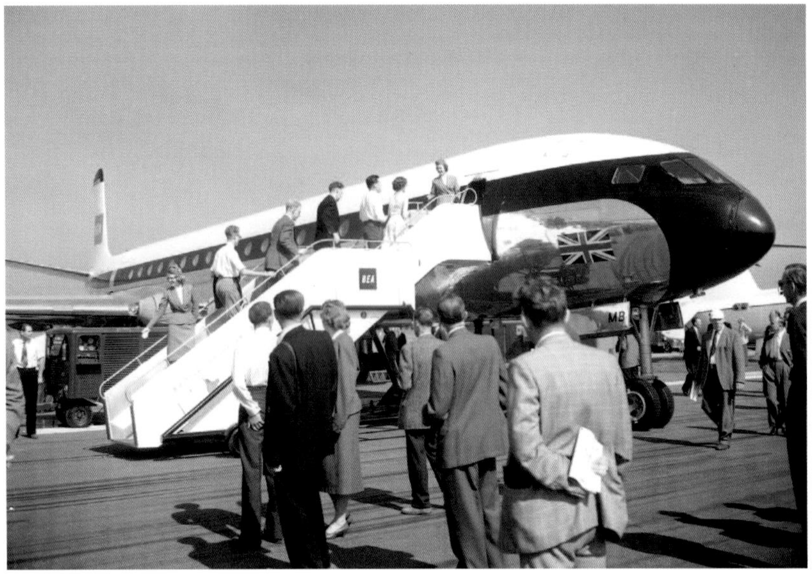

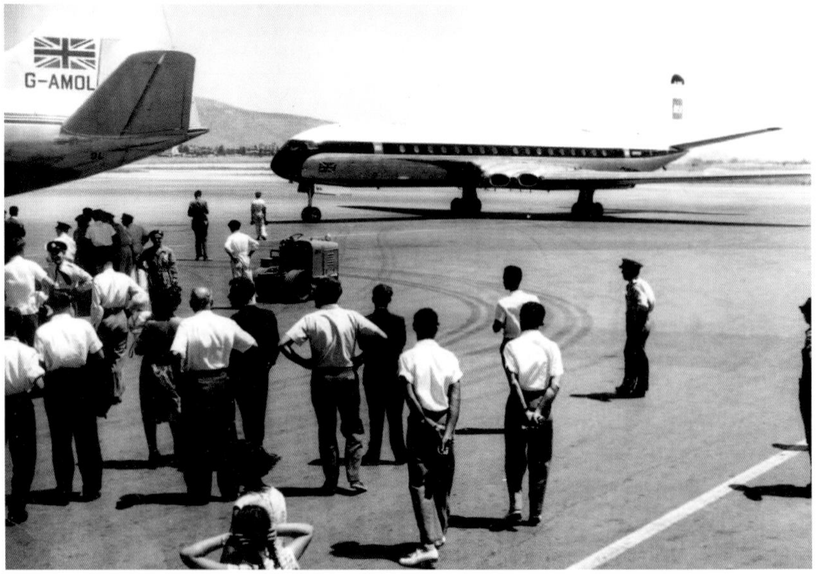
G-AMOL

During its lifetime Dan-Air operated a wide variety of aircraft and among them was the largest fleet of de Havilland Comets. None was bought new and some were third-hand never mind second-hand but for Dan Air the Comet 4s were the right aircraft at the right time.

The Comet 4As were not built but the variant formed the basis of the Comet 4B for British European Airways. With a 38-inch fuselage stretch the 4B could accommodate 102 passengers in a fuselage 6ft 6in bigger than the baseline Comet 4.

This new variant carried three times more passengers than the original Comet 1. BEA ordered six aircraft in 1958 and by taking up all its options ended up with 14. The Comet 4B flew for the first time on 27 June 1959. By that time the state-owned British European Airways was the continent's largest airline and one of the world's most powerful carriers. But Air France's decision to order the Sud Caravelle twin-jet at a time when BEA was pinning its faith on the turbo-prop Vickers Vanguard meant that it risked falling behind in the race for technological leadership.

Consequently its call for a medium-range jet had been answered by de Havilland and its projected DH121. The first of the tri-jets was ultimately to enter service as the Trident. But with the Vanguard delayed until 1961 and the Trident not due until 1964 the Comet 4B therefore represented something of a stop-gap for BEA. But it was a surprisingly successful one considering it had originally been designed as a long-haul airliner.

BEA took delivery of its first Comet in November 1959, although G-APMA in BEA livery had taken part in the Daily Mail London-Paris air race in July. The

BOTH PAGES: Although the Comet 4 was not originally designed for short to medium haul operations British European Airways' 4Bs were to become a familiar sight at European and Middle Eastern airports from Oslo to Las Palmas and from Moscow to Cairo between 1960 and 1966. On this spread are pictured G-APMA and `MB, two of BEA's 14-strong fleet.

airline launched Comet operations on 1 April 1960 with services from London to Moscow (by G-APMF), from London to Nice (by G-APMA) and by Tel Aviv to London (G-APMB) and back by G-APMD. Although the Comets were mainly operated on BEA's longer routes they were also used on some of its shorter services such as London-Paris, London-Edinburgh and London-Glasgow.

The only other customer for the variant was the Greek national airline Olympic Airways. It operated two aircraft which it leased from BEA in 1960 and operated in a pooling arrangement with the British airline. They remained on the UK Register but Olympic later ordered two aircraft of its own. From Athens the airline operated the Comet 4Bs to destinations in Europe and the Middle East.

The late Capt Pete Jarvis had been a BEA Comet co-pilot and transferred to BEA Airtours when the charter subsidiary was established to continue flying an aircraft which he "absolutely loved."

The Comet may have been a pilot's aeroplane but the accountants were not so keen because it was becoming increasingly uncompetitive in terms of revenue generation. And it was economic factors which prompted BEA to consider setting up its own charter operation. Concerned that it was losing revenue to the charter operators the state-owned carrier decided in 1969 to establish its own inclusive tour arm. Based at Gatwick, BEA Airtours began operations with Comets transferred from BEA. On 6 March 1970 Comet 4B G-ARJL took off for Palma on BEA Airtours' first operation.

It had been something of a rush to get ready, particularly as the first flight was brought forward several weeks at the behest of the client, a tour operator called Sunair run by Harry Goodman. Goodman's International Leisure Group, which included the airline Air Europe, was to collapse spectacularly two decades later.

Airtours was reported to have paid its parent £150,000 each for the Comets but the aircraft had to be adapted to their new role. For one thing the galleys had to be re-configured. Cabin services manager Ronald Thorburn had to work out specifications for new catering and bar boxes as well as designs for meal trays, cutlery, cups and glasses. The meals themselves represented a departure for BEA-trained staff who had to seek the advice of their charter airline competitors.

Jarvis clearly enjoyed his time with Airtours. He described it as *"the St Trinian's of the airline world."* Before his death in 2014 he explained the comparison with the legendary but fictional girls' school created by cartoonist Ronald Searle. He said: *"We attracted a lot of very individual characters and the cabin crew in particular seemed to be keen to look after our passengers and entertain them in their own way. They were individualistic in their approach to how we ran the airline and that really permeated the whole of Airtours. The St Trinian's*

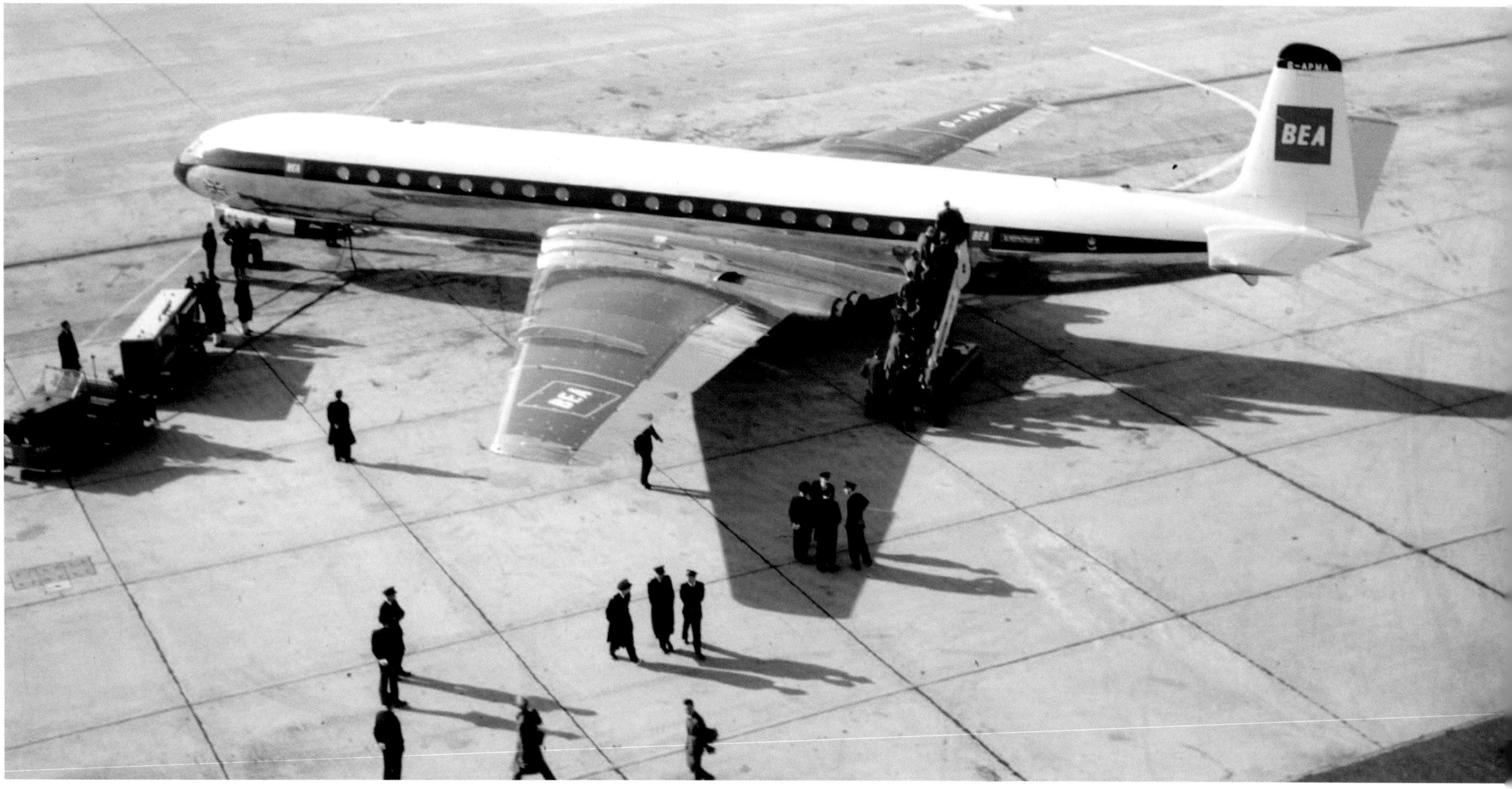
BEA

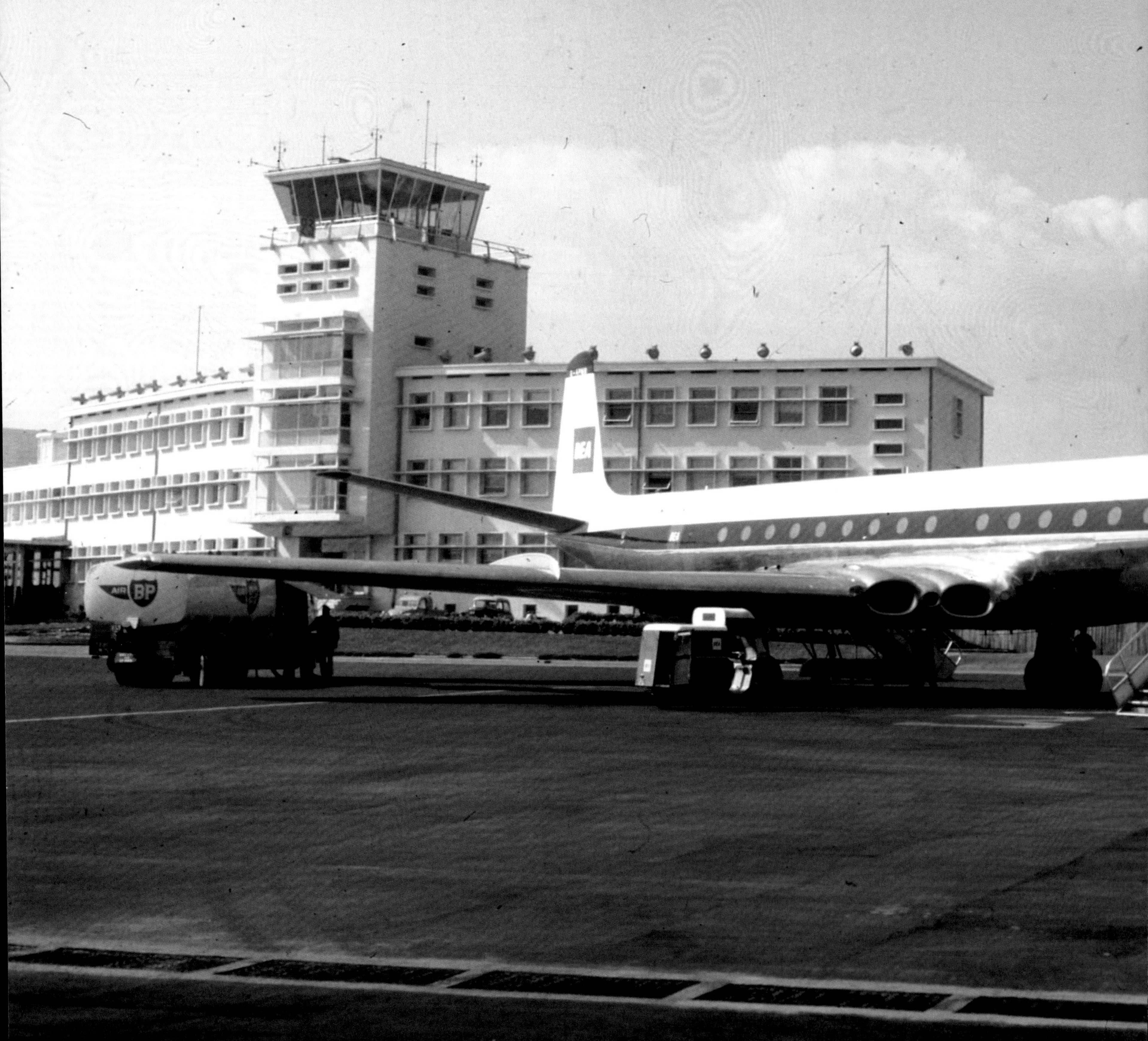
BEA
AIR BP

approach was something we adopted and were happy to go along with."

"We thought we were on a step ladder on which we were at least two rungs above BEA because of their stuffiness and we reacted against it. We were labelled by BOAC as the cowboy outfit, which didn't disturb us at all. It wasn't the way our passengers perceived us. They were very happy with our service, both on the flight deck and from the cabin crew."

In the early days of the Airtours operations the standard of catering was fairly basic. An account of those days by Capt Peter Howard indicates that outbound passengers received two sandwiches and an Eccles cake, while those on the inbound leg were served two sandwiches and a Penguin chocolate biscuit. The food came in a plastic tray specially designed to facilitate stacking and distribution.

Airtours general manager, flight operations, Capt Bill Baillie, also wanted a simplified ticketing system that could be operated by a minimum of staff and would reduce processing time. The system he inspired worked so well that it was copied by rivals, some of whom, according to Howard, tried to claim the credit for devising it.

Among the passengers on that first flight was a group of Sunair hostesses who would be looking after the company's clients in resort and they seem to have added an additional festive air to the occasion. In command was Capt Peter McKeown, a senior BEA training captain who had been appointed Airtours' flight manager. On the flight deck with him were two co-pilots, Pete Jarvis and Geoffrey Evans. Stewards were Eric Winsper and Ray Short. The other flight attendants were Maggie Read and Pauline Pool, both of whom were married to Airtours co-pilots.

Before take-off McKeown told his crew: *"This is a very special occasion, so let's calm down, do things slowly and make sure we get things right."* After the speeches, BEA personality girl Heather Angus cut the ribbon at the foot of the aircraft steps and Airtours' first passengers stepped aboard. Just before 1400hr the tower radioed the Comet's flight deck: *"Beatours 243, you are cleared for take-off."*

During its first season, the new airline made around 900 flights to Palma. Peter Jarvis recalled: *"That was remarkable. At one stage, I believe, there were six Airtours aircraft sitting on the hard-standing at Palma. The authorities there thought we were a major airline, but they were six of the only nine aircraft we had."*

By the end of its first year's operations Airtours was able to report carrying 650,000 passengers to 84 destinations for 63 different charterers. On four occasions the client had been Manchester City football club. The Comets had shown themselves ideally sized for transporting soccer clubs to European tournament games. But it was not long before something bigger was required and the Comets were being passed on.

The 48 acquired by Dan-Air Services represented 40 per cent of total Comet production even if ten of them were bought specifically as spares sources. The airline's first two examples were ex-BOAC Comet 4s bought in 1966. They were the first jets bought by a British airline specifically for inclusive tour charter operations. Later acquisitions included G-APDC which had operated the first trans-Atlantic scheduled operation back in 1958.

Dan-Air converted the ex-BEA aircraft to 99-seaters. They had been acquired relatively cheaply and at the right time: the market was on the brink of major

The 101-seat Comet 4B entered BEA's service on 1 April 1960. Pictured here in the same year is G-APMB, which flew with the airline until it was acquired by Channel Airways.

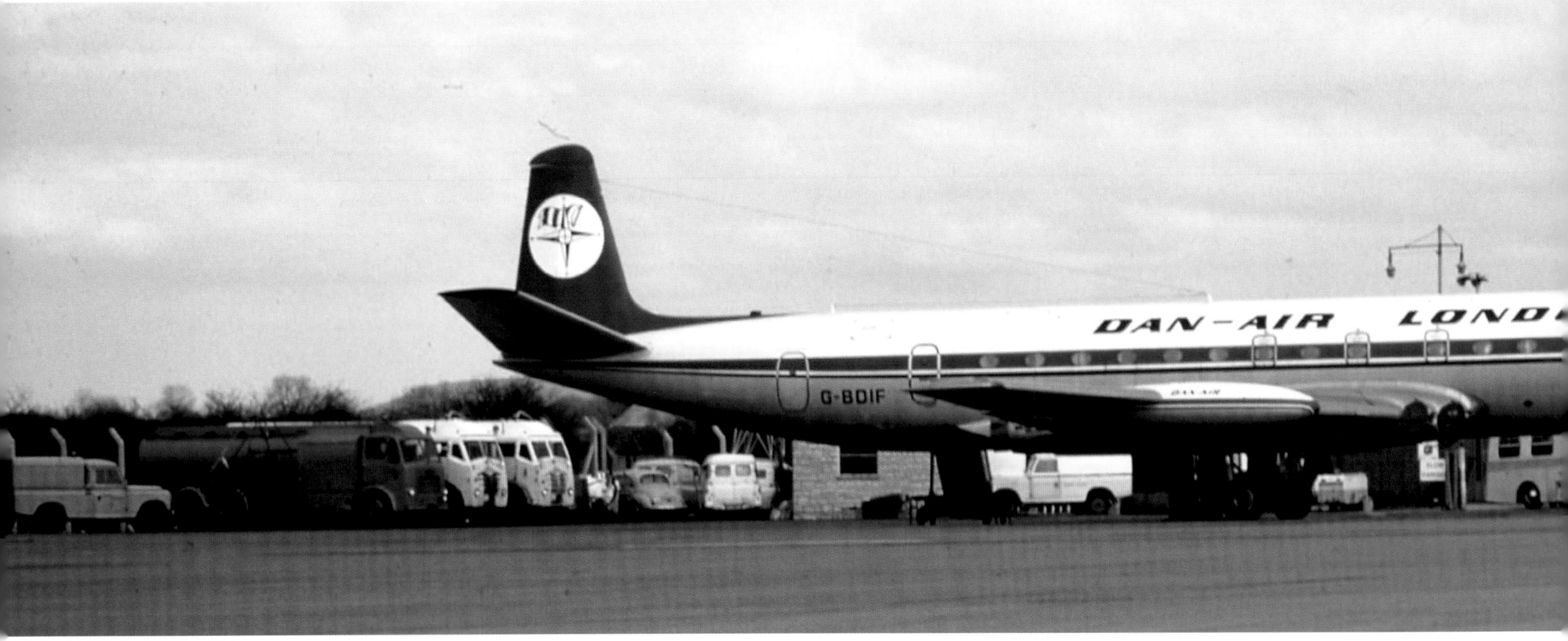
DAN-AIR LOND
G-BDIF

expansion and the Comets would form the backbone of Dan-Air's charter fleet. It comprised 11 aircraft by the end of the decade. In 1969 a Comet 4 operated Dan-Air's first trans-Atlantic flight, to Trinidad.

One of Dan-Air's Comet pilots was Yvonne Sintes. For two years she had been a first officer on an aircraft she found *"wonderful to fly."* One day in June 1970 was a particularly long one for her and Capt Bob Atkins. They left Gatwick for Akrotiri, Cyprus with a full passenger load and Sintes was handling the return leg when she was instructed to divert to Izmir, Turkey to pick up passengers from another Dan-Air Comet which had *"gone technical."*

Sintes, who had joined the airline in 1969 as a Bristol-based DC-3 pilot, recalled later: *"We were not allowed to start because we hadn't as yet been given permission to land by the aviation authority. So we had to sit there quietly fuming on the tarmac for nearly another hour while the paperwork `caught up' and we were officially declared 'landed' and could therefore 'depart.' We all put in 15 hours duty that day."*

Dan-Air's sales director managed to persuade German tour operators to take advantage of the low rates it was able to offer with its Comet fleet which derived from its status as an Allied airline permitted to operate into West Berlin. On 31 March 1968 a Comet took off from Berlin's Tegel airport for Malaga, the first of almost 300 flights on behalf of German tour operators. It was also the start of a 25-year association between airline and airport.

For Dan-Air the Comet's low acquisition costs meant that the aircraft could be operated at low utilisation rates without economic penalty. Even the fuel crisis of late 1973 when the price of oil quadrupled, hitting the leisure market particularly hard, failed to spell the end of Dan-Air's Comet operations.

Although they burned twice as much fuel as more modern types like the BAC One-Eleven the Comets offered longer range. Dan-Air was therefore able to develop the growing demand for winter breaks in places like the Canary Islands. The Comets were also used to open up services from UK regional airports where operations were usually concentrated at week-ends and which enabled the Comet's impressive airfield performance to come into its own.

Dan-Air's Comets were also used for scheduled flights. In 1974 the airline used them on its newly-launched twice-daily Gatwick-Newcastle service. It could not last, of course. Dan-Air's Comet fleet peaked in the early 1970s and by 1980 was down to just four examples. Indeed, when the airline flew its last Comet flight on 9 November 1980 it was also the type's last-ever commercial flight. The aircraft used, G-BDIW, was one of Dan-Air's most recent acquisitions, an ex-RAF 216 Sqn Comet C4, which had entered the airline's service in September 1975.

Southend-based Channel Airways was another early 1970s Comet operator. During 1971 and 1972 it leased five stored ex-BEA and Olympic Airways Comet 4Bs. The jets were based at Stansted, which was more suitable than Southend for jet operations. They also operated from Manchester. The aircraft retained their original liveries although they also displayed Channel Airways titles.

The operation was to be short lived. Channel Airways, run by inclusive tour pioneer Jack Jones, went bust and ceased operations on 1 February 1972. The four Comets it was operating at the time were acquired by Dan-Air in April.

Independent airline Dan-Air was to operate the biggest Comet fleet between 1966 and 1980.

TOP LEFT: 4C G-BDIF was delivered to the airline in 1975 and retired four years later; It is pictured here at Bristol, Lulsgate airport in April 1976.

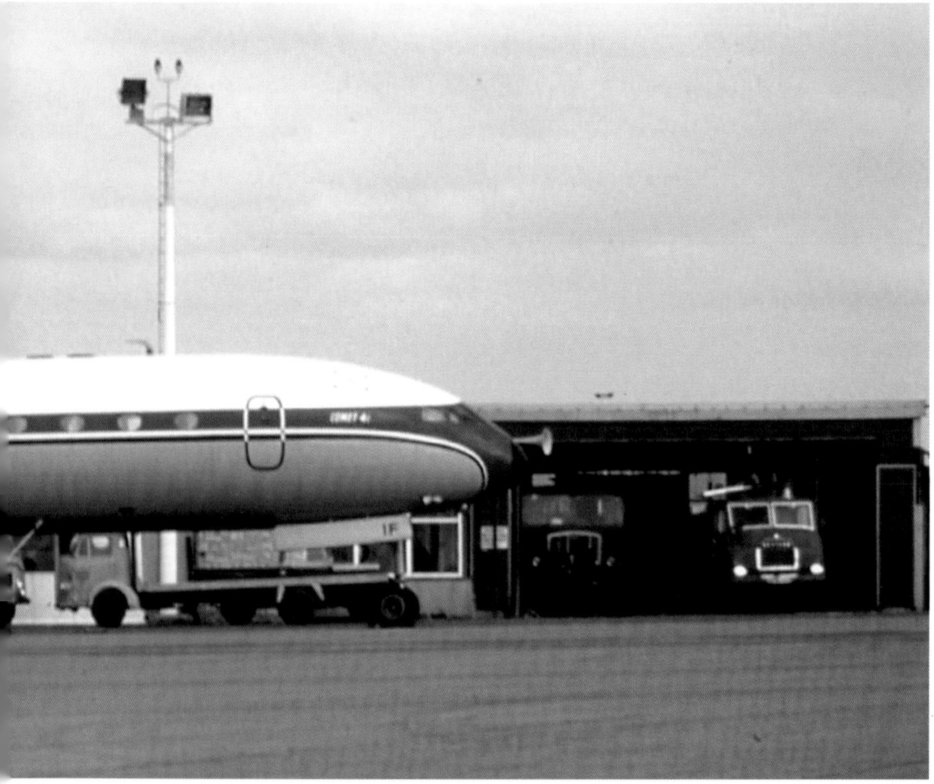

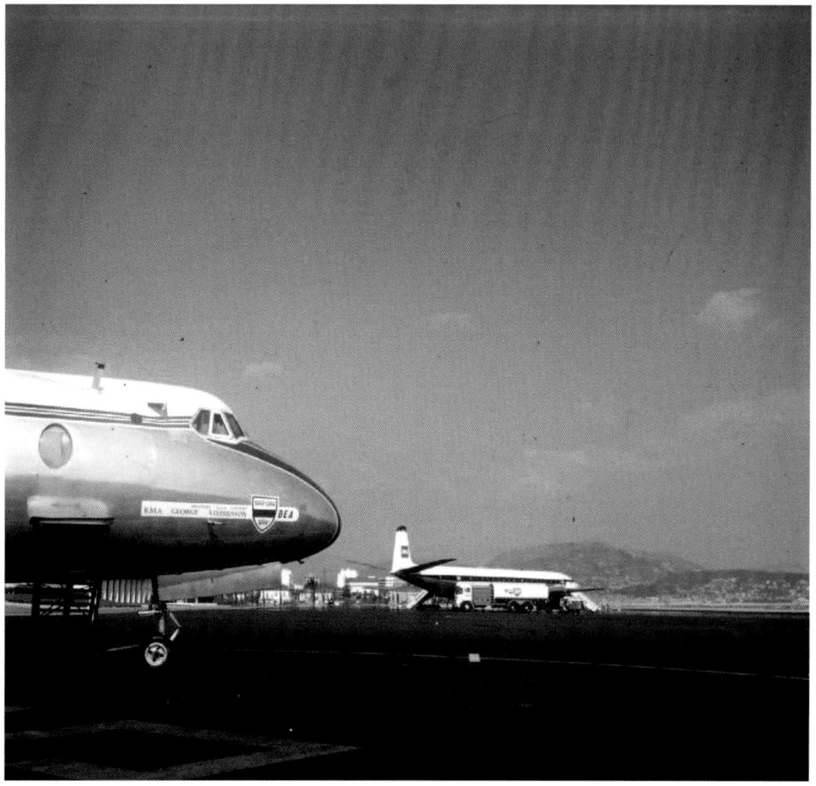

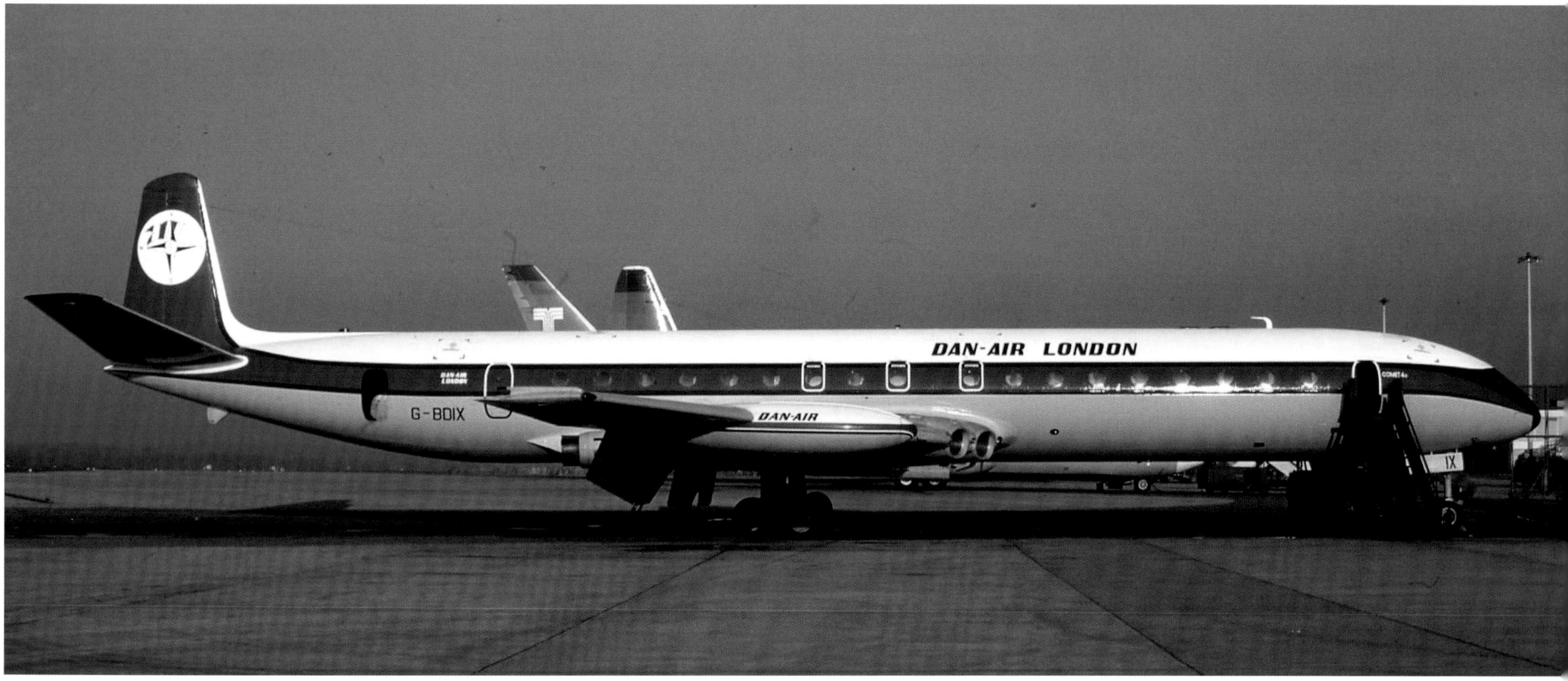
DAN-AIR LONDON
G-BDIX
DAN-AIR

TOP RIGHT: BEA's 4B G-APMB in 1960 with the nose of one of the same airline's Viscounts in the foreground.
BOTTOM RIGHT: G-BDIX was operated by Dan-Air between September 1975 and October 1980; it was retired to the Scottish Museum of Flight, East Fortune.

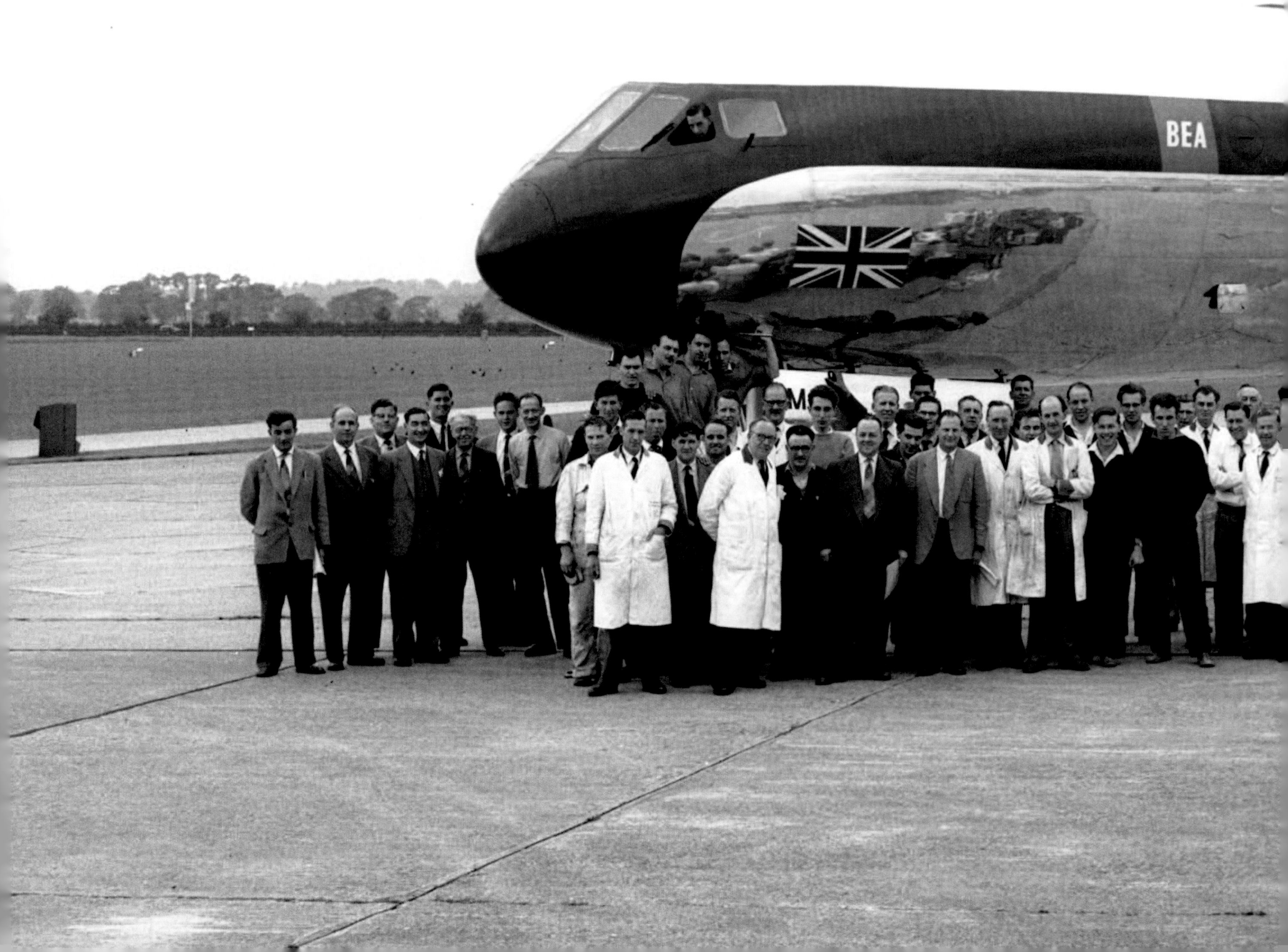
BEA

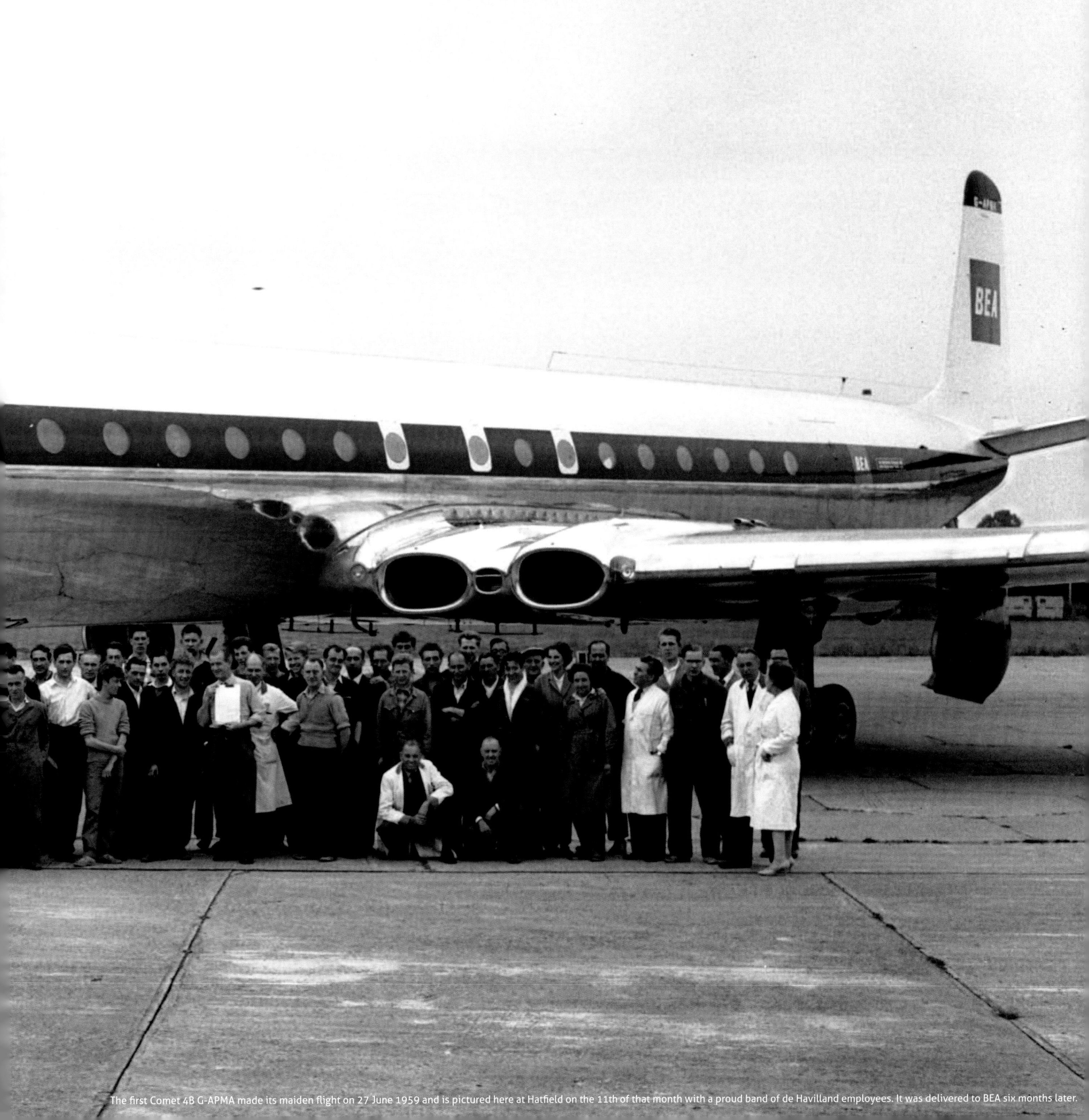
BEA
G-APMA

The first Comet 4B G-APMA made its maiden flight on 27 June 1959 and is pictured here at Hatfield on the 11th of that month with a proud band of de Havilland employees. It was delivered to BEA six months later.

British European Airways

From 1945 until it merged with BOAC to form British Airways, BEA was Britain's state-owned short-haul airline. Formed by Act of Parliament it offered international and domestic scheduled services and from 1970 its subsidiary BEA Airtours provided leisure charters for a growing number of holiday-makers.

From the start the airline set out with vigour to establish a commanding presence in the marketplace and it soon had a network of routes from Stockholm to Gibraltar and from Belfast to Istanbul. Douglas DC-3s and de Havilland DH 89s provided the initial backbone of its fleet but it soon had its first post-war design the twin-engined Vickers Viking.

By 1950 BEA had built its main base, the London airport of Northolt, into the busiest in Britain if not Europe, handling a quarter or all UK flights. But BEA was losing money and a new managing director was appointed to keep tighter control of costs and boost revenue. Peter Masefield also brought a relentless determination to generate high loads and among his innovations were budget fares. Monthly earnings reached £1 million.

New aircraft were introduced. The Airspeed Ambassador, introduced as the Elizabethan class, brought new standards of comfort but it was soon eclipsed by the turboprop Vickers Viscount which entered service in 1953. By 1958 the airline had 77 Viscounts in service, including the bigger Series 800.

The 1960s saw new jets join the fleet, first the three-engined Trident and later the BAC One-Eleven twinjet. But by now BEA was becoming exasperated by the high cost of its support for Britain's aircraft industry. The airline's 1962/63 annual report noted that the introduction of the Vanguard and Comet 4B had cost it over £6 million over two years. It was, BEA noted, *"a heavy financial burden."*

Having found that the Trident, originally designed to meet BEA's needs, was now too small the airline sought government permission to buy Boeing's 150-seat 727. It also wanted the smaller 737. But the Labour government refused and after much delay also declined to provide development funding for the 208-seat BAC 2-11. Later BEA was instructed to buy the stretched Trident 3, an injunction it considered an encroachment on its commercial freedom. Nevertheless, in 1968 BEA ordered 26 Trident 3s at a cost of £83 million.

Going into the new decade BEA was celebrating it's biggest-ever profit. It was Europe's biggest airline and for a while carried more passengers than any other in the western world outside the USA. But in 1969 a government-appointed committee called for a unified board to run both Britain's state-owned airlines. The next move was inevitable and on 1 April 1974 BOAC and BEA merged.

Meanwhile, concern at the revenue being lost to the holiday charter airlines prompted BEA to launch its own non-scheduled operation. The rest of the industry viewed this development with alarm and saw the state-owned BEA Airtours as unfair publicly-subsidised competition.

Having started with Comet 4Bs transferred from its parent Airtours found them too small for its needs within a few years. Its original plan had been to acquire ex-American Airlines Boeing 707-123Bs which offered larger capacity and longer range compared with the Comets. But although the government approved the deal, the corporations were far from happy, insisting that Airtours should source its aircraft from existing BOAC and BEA fleets.

The result was that it ended up with seven aircraft having a seating capacity greater than that required and powered by Rolls-Royce Conway engines of an older generation to the Pratt and Whitney JT3D turbofans of the 707-120s. The higher operating costs were reflected in the purchase price, although the BOAC aircraft came with spares including engines. The first of the 174-seaters entered service in 1971 with the last arriving two years later. Altogether Airtours was to operate 15 707s including one leased from Dan Air, which was to acquire most of Airtours' Comets.

The operation continued after the merger, although its name changed to British Airtours. However in 1985 its image was to be tarnished by an accident to one of its aircraft on the ground at Manchester. The Boeing 737-200 suffered an uncontained engine failure and 55 passengers and crew died in the resulting fire.

In the late 1980s Airtours disposed of its associated tour operating businesses and when BA absorbed British Caledonian the charter operation was re-branded. BA finally sold Caledonian Airways in 1995.

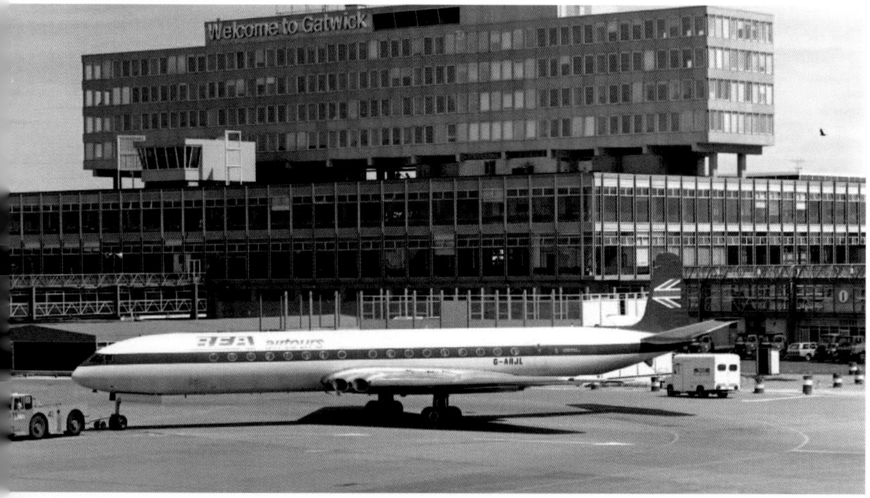
Welcome to Gatwick

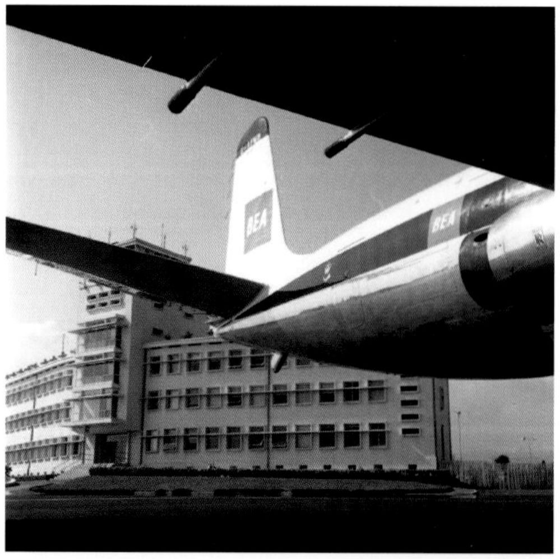
BEA

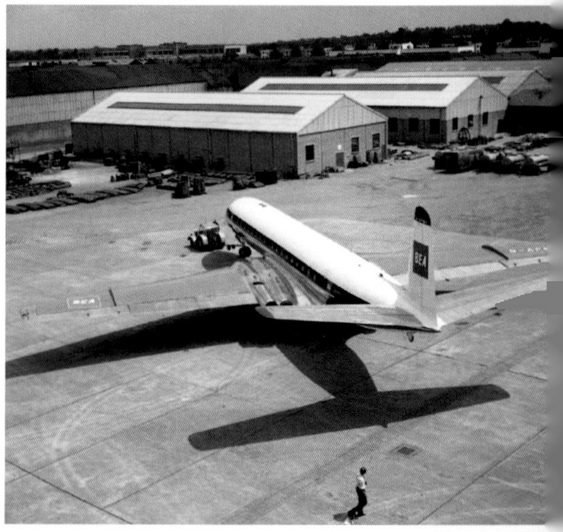

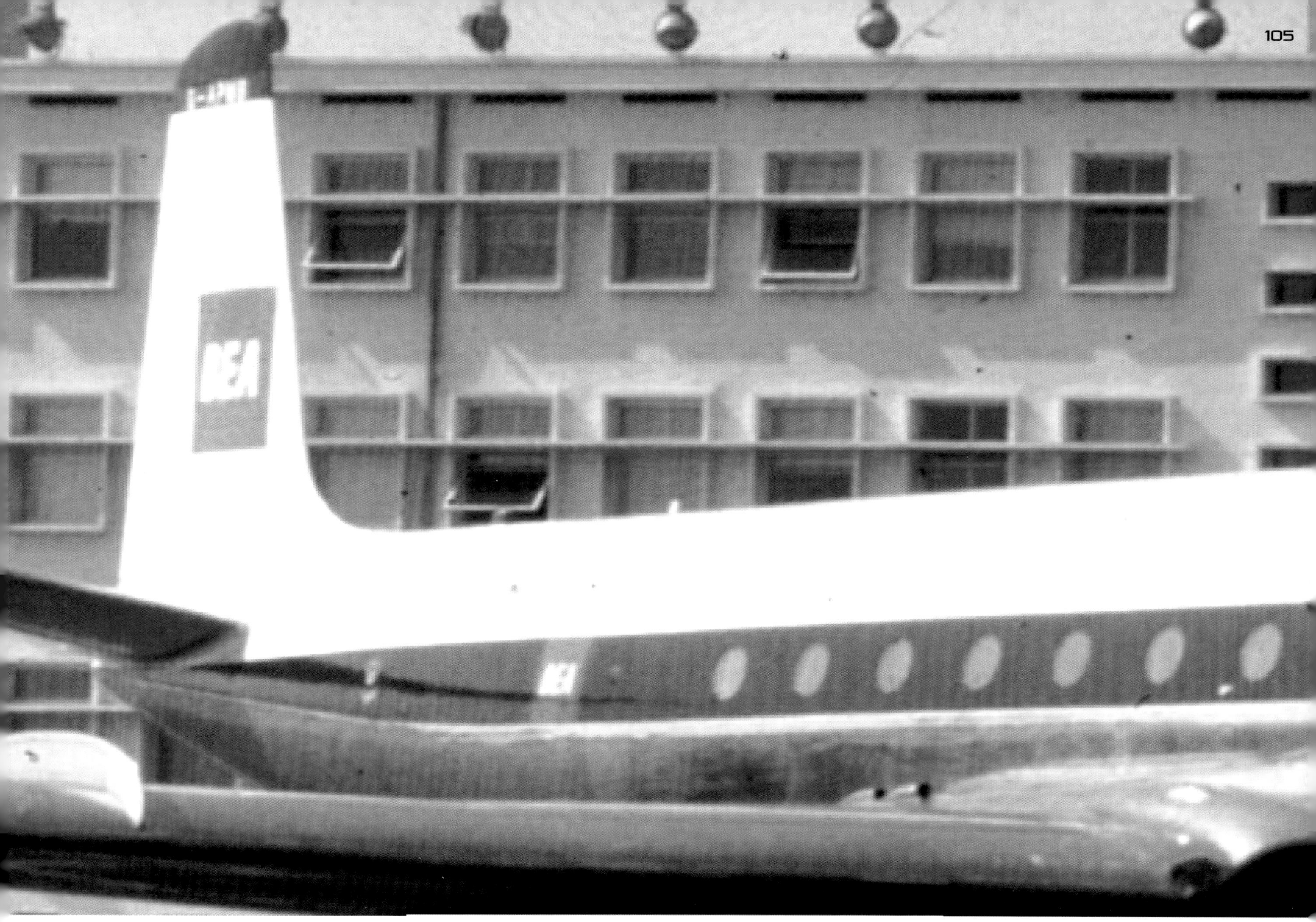
BEA

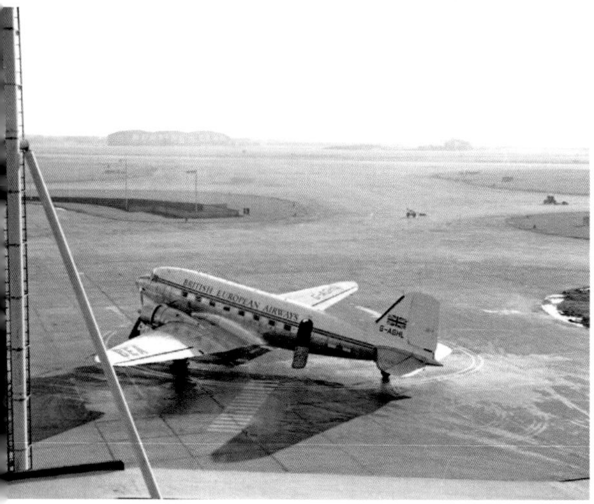
BRITISH EUROPEAN AIRWAYS
G-AGHL

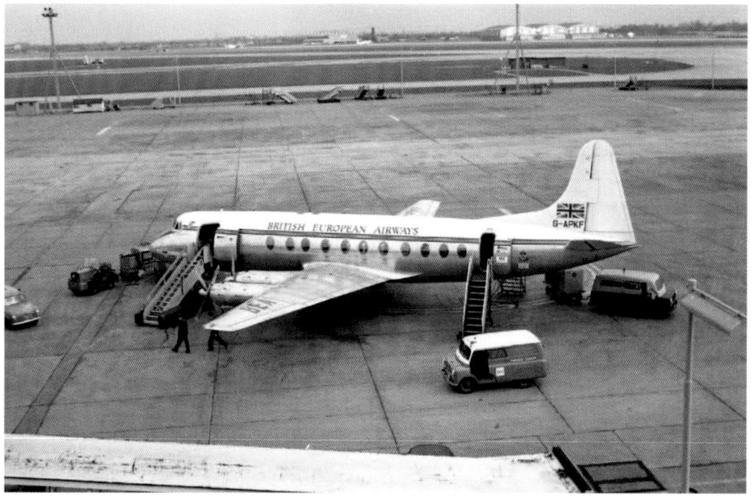
BRITISH EUROPEAN AIRWAYS
G-APKF

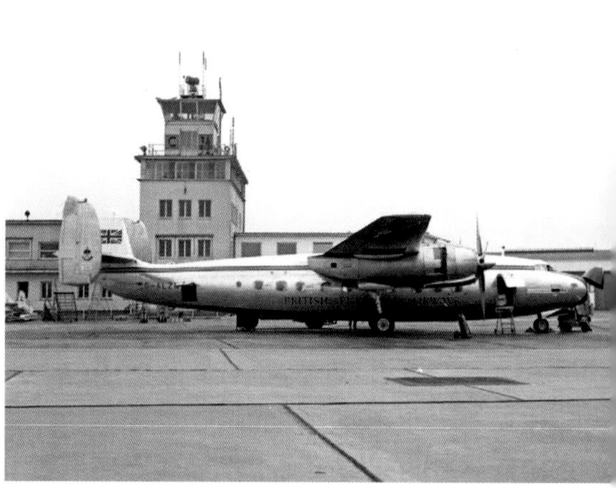

MAIN IMAGE: Another image of BEA's G-APMB
BOTTOM LEFT TO RIGHT: BEA Airtours' Comet 4B G-ARJL at Gatwick, 1972; Comet 4B G-APMB; `MB again; DC-3 G-AGHL; Viscount 806 G-APKF Michael Faraday; Airspeed Ambassador/Elizabethan G-ALZN.

Dan-Air

It was originally a shipping company which only became an airline because of the aircraft it acquired in settlement of a debt.

That may have been why the red and white painted airliners operated by Davies and Newman, which were to become such familiar sights at British and Continental airports up to the early 1990s, all displayed "Dan-Air London" titles, like ships proclaiming the association with their home port.

Despite its "Dan Dare" image Dan-Air was profitable for 37 of its 40 years. From May 1953 when Dan-Air Services received its Air Operator's Certificate it operated a mixture of scheduled and charter flights.

Within two years it was operating two DC-3s and a trio of ex-RAF Avro Yorks. It was then based at Blackbushe and had just established an engineering base at Lasham. In 1956 the airline launched its first scheduled service, from Blackbushe to Jersey. With newly-acquired Ambassadors it was able to start operating inclusive tour holiday flights from Manchester on behalf of Horizon Holidays.

By 1960 Dan-Air was carrying an annual 100,000 passengers as well as freight on contract to BEA. When Blackbushe closed Dan-Air moved to Gatwick and business continued to grow. By the mid-1960s Dan-Air was approaching a turning point as it was becoming clear that continuing with the IT business would require a switch to jets. *"The problem was solved,"* Fred Newman wrote,*" when we purchased two Comet 4s from BOAC."*

Despite its long association with the Comet the airline also had Boeing equipment and became the only UK airline to operate the 727 tri-jet. Again, they were acquired at a time when their cost was low. At one point Dan-Air was operating Comets, 727s and BAC One-Elevens so was able to choose the optimum aircraft type for a particular route. At the other end of the scale Hawker-Siddeley Hs 748 turboprops were operated to support offshore oil activities.

But by 1989 Dan-Air was posting a £3 million loss despite carrying 6.2 million passengers, many of them on the short-haul scheduled routes it had acquired following British Caledonian's departure from the market in the late 1980s.

The banks insisted on the appointment of a company doctor and he was forced to undertake some drastic pruning. But it was not enough. The downturn in air travel demand of the early 1990s was a crisis too far for Dan-Air. In late 1992 with the creditors poised to appoint a receiver a deal was done with British Airways to acquire Dan-Air for a token £1.

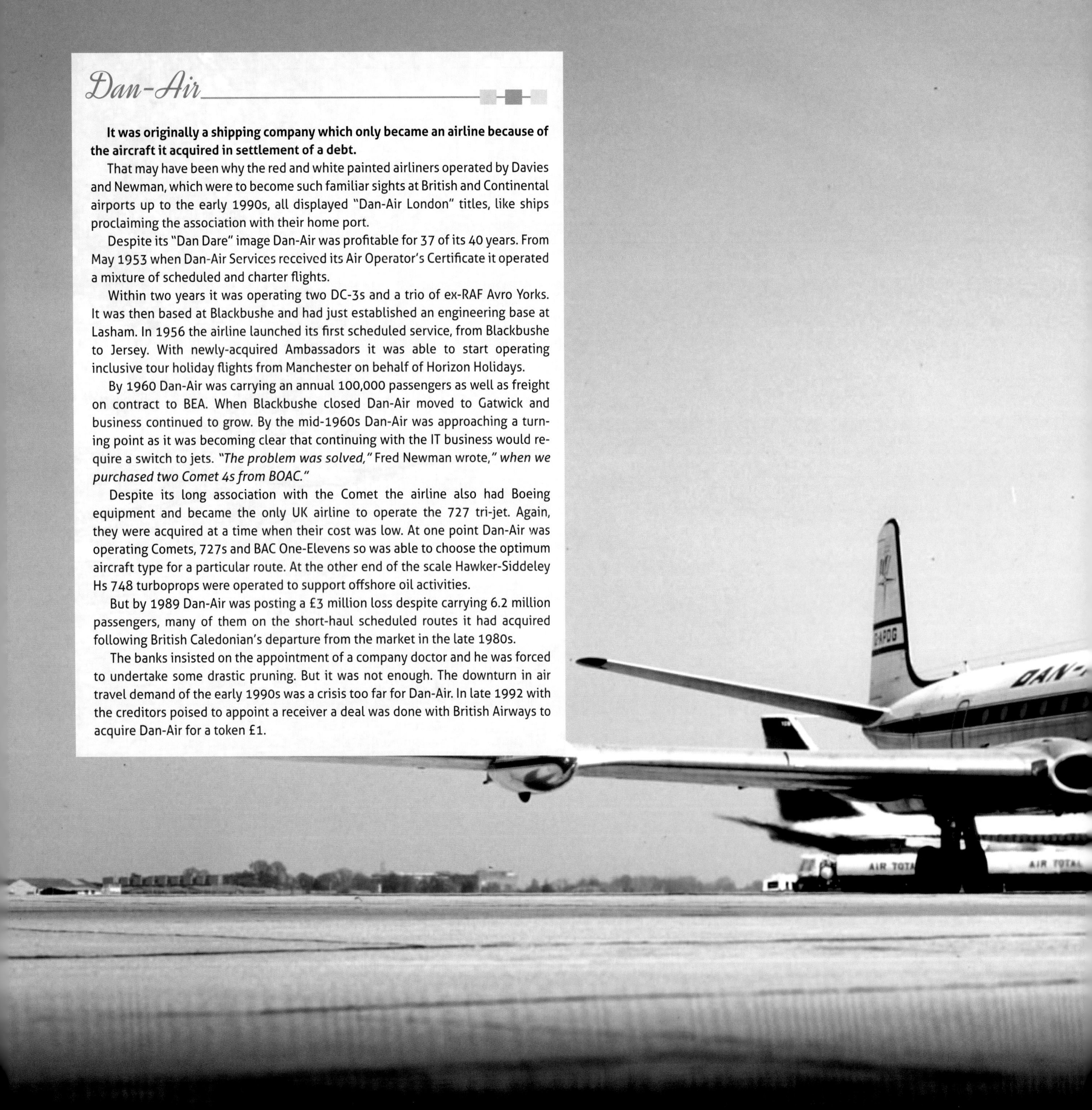
AIR TOTAL

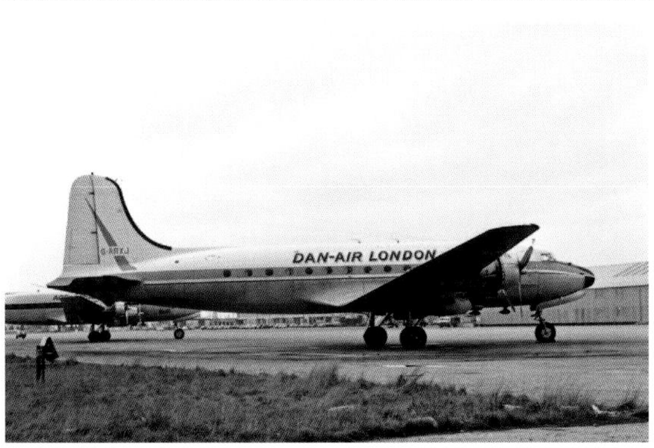
DAN-AIR LONDON
G-ARXJ

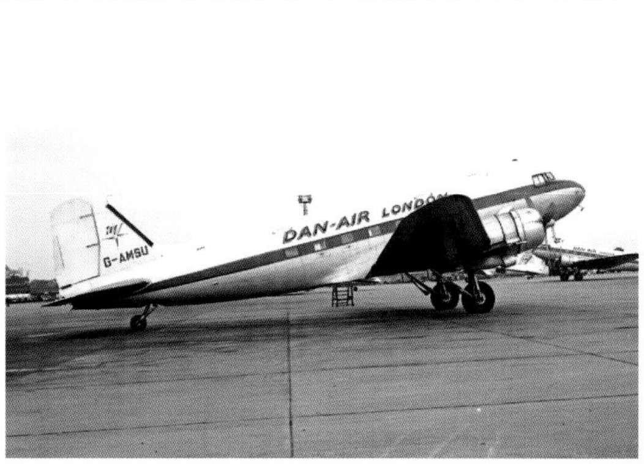
DAN-AIR LONDON
G-AMSU

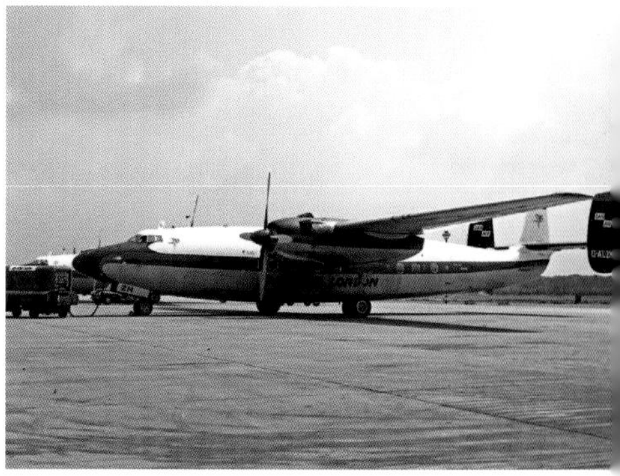

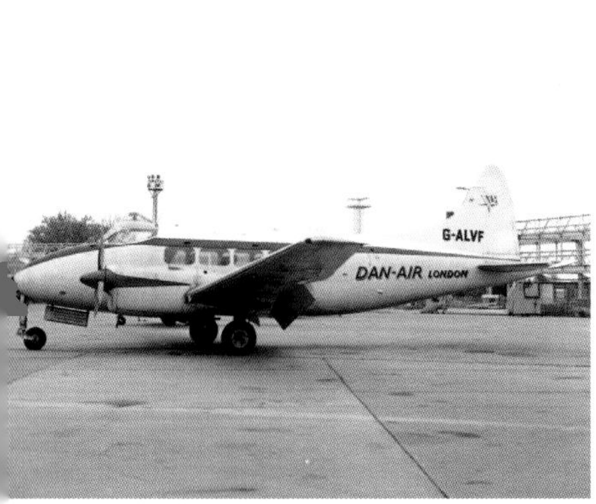
G-ALVF
DAN-AIR LONDON

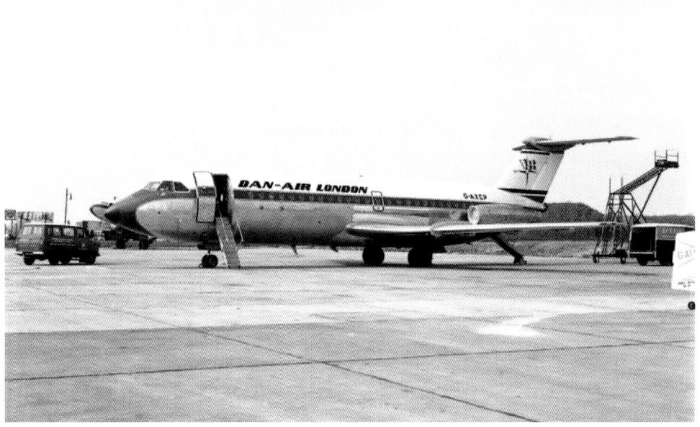
DAN-AIR LONDON

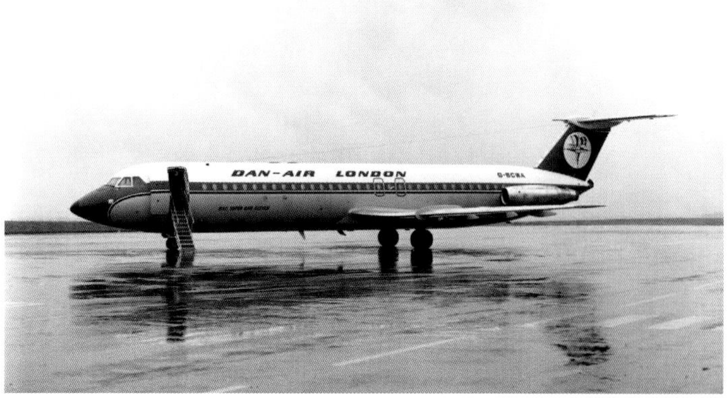
DAN-AIR LONDON

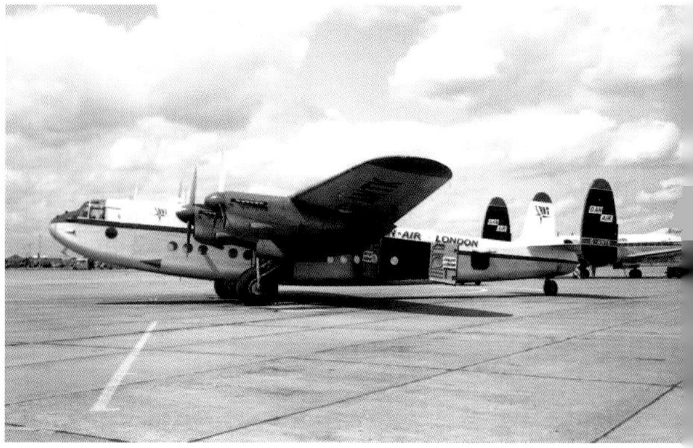
LONDON

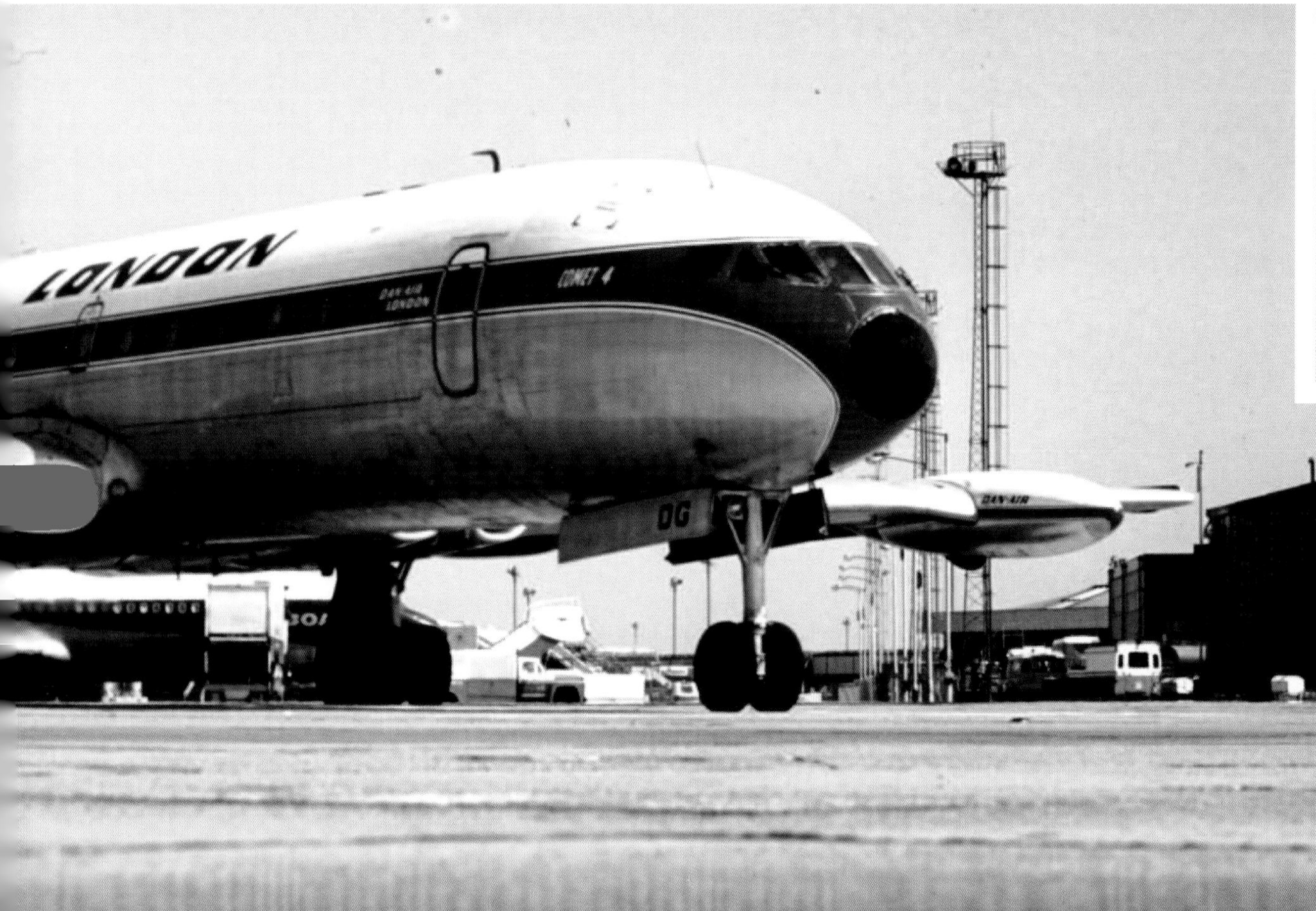
LONDON
DAN-AIR LONDON
COMET 4
DG
DAN-AIR

Dan-Air operated a variety of aircraft including the biggest fleet of Comet 4s.

MAIN PICTURE: G-APDG was operated by Kuwait Airlines and Middle East Airlines before joining Dan-Air in 1970. It was scrapped in 1974. Other types included **TOP ROW, LEFT TO RIGHT:** DC-4 G-ARXJ, pictured at Heathrow, 1965; DC-3 G-AMSU, also Heathrow 1965; Airspeed Ambassador G-ALZN, Perpignan, 1962. **MIDDLE, LEFT TO RIGHT:** de Havilland Dove G-ALVF, Gatwick 1964; BAC 1-11 Series 401 G-AXCP,

MILITARY SERVICE

Comets in Uniform

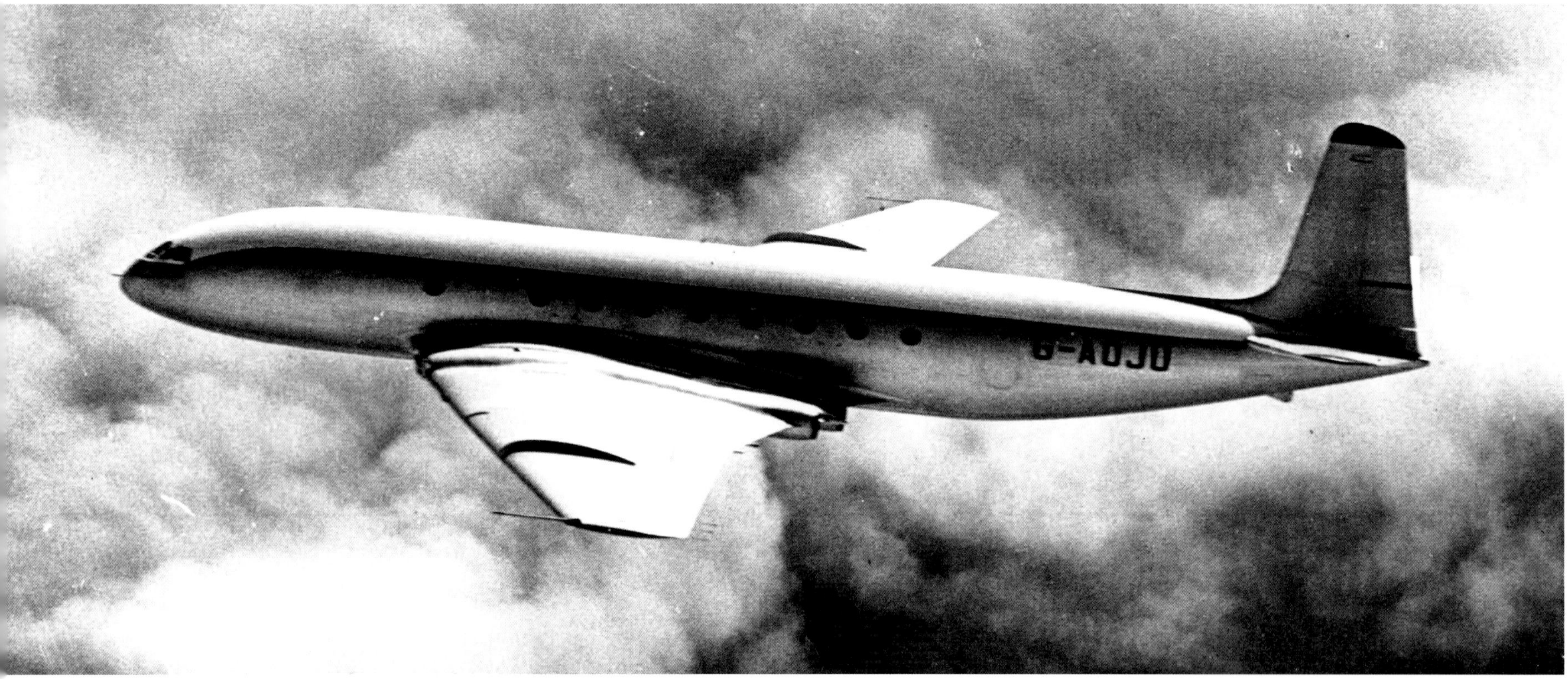
G-AOJU

If BOAC was the world's first jet airline then RAF Transport Command's 216 Sqn was its military counterpart, except that the unit was intended to be an all-jet one right from the start.

In fact, the comparison with an airline is an apt one. While operating Comets, C2s at first followed later by C4s, 216's crews took pride in going by the book, in this case the Air Registration Board's flight manual.

But even though it was obviously not a commercial undertaking, 216 was in the business of flying scheduled services. And for a while 216 operated the world's only jet airline. It transported personnel and equipment around the globe in the days when Britain still had world-wide military commitments. Its Comets looked the part too with white cabin tops and silver fuselages divided by smart blue cheat lines.

From its base at RAF Lyneham the squadron linked Britain with its bases in Malta, Cyprus, Aden, Africa and the Far East. The Comets also flew to Christmas Island and Woomera, Australia to support Britain's nuclear weapons programme.

As it happened, though, the RAF was not the first military Comet operator. The Royal Canadian Air Force took delivery of two Comet 1As in March and April 1953, not quite a year after BOAC had operated the first-ever commercial jet services.

Following the 1954 accidents the aircraft were returned to de Havilland's Chester factory to have their cabins strengthened. When they emerged they were designated Comet 1XBs and, operated by 416 Sqn, they were finally retired in 1963 and 1964 respectively.

The background to the RAF's acquisition of Comets was less conventional. The Comet 2 had been planned as a developed Comet 1 with a longer fuselage and increased fuel tankage. To handle the increased gross weight of 120,000lb (54,500 kg) new engines were specified. The Comet 2 was therefore the first variant to be powered by the Rolls-Royce Avon axial flow turbojet.

Production was well in hand and several aircraft had flown when commercial operations were suspended following the 1954 accidents. BOAC had ordered 11 Comet 2s but the order was cancelled and de Havilland took the decision to concentrate on the further improved Comet 4. For financial reasons, therefore, it was decided to complete 16 Comet 2s using many parts already manufactured. The aircraft were virtually re-built with strengthened fuselages using heavier-gauge material. Oval windows replaced rectangular ones.

Of these aircraft ten were allocated to RAF Transport Command as C2s and T2s, three to No 51 Sqn for special duties (as 2Rs) and two 2Es which were used by BOAC for route proving ahead of Comet 4 deliveries. One was used as a test example. The majority of C2s were delivered during 1956 and 1957. The first to arrive, in mid-1956, was a pair of T2s to be used for conversion training; the first full standard C2 was delivered in August 1956.

The C2s arrived at a time when Transport Command was being re-equipped with propeller-driven Britannias and Beverleys and now it found itself with the world's biggest fleet of military transport jets. The T2s were direct adaptations of existing civilian aircraft and were equipped solely for passenger transport.

One of them took an RAF delegation to Moscow for the 1956 Soviet Aviation Day celebrations. The T2s were later returned to de Havilland to be converted to C2 standard. The first proving flights, to Aden, were made in September 1956 followed by Singapore a month later. Regular monthly flights began in November

TOP: This Comet 1A was among the first of the breed to wear military markings, although in this picture, taken near Hatfield in September 1957, it was displaying the civilian registration G-AOJU. It had started life as Air France's F-BGNY and was later allocated the military serial XM829 and operated by the Aircraft and Armament Experimental Establishment, Boscombe Down. It ended its days at the Fire Training School, Stansted in 1970.

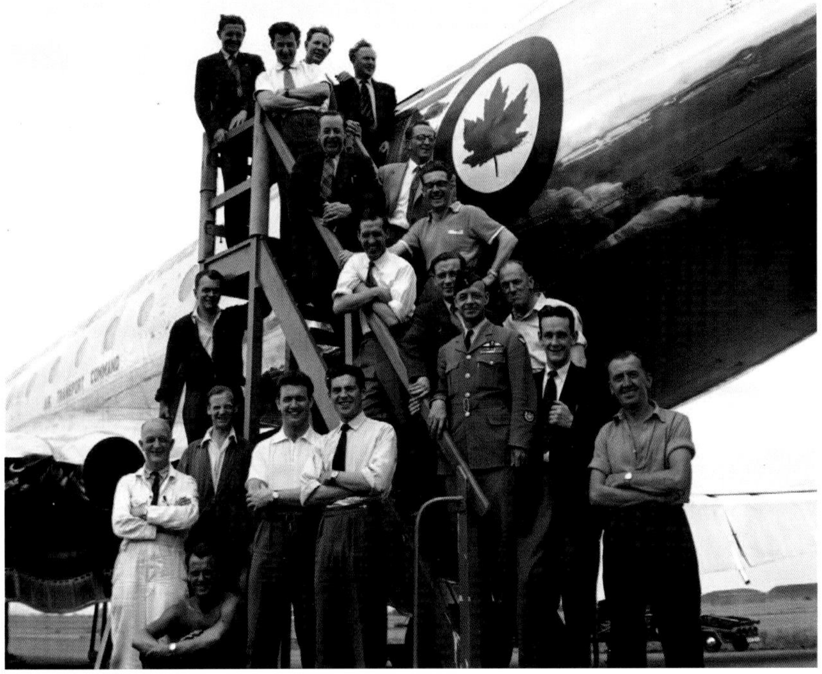

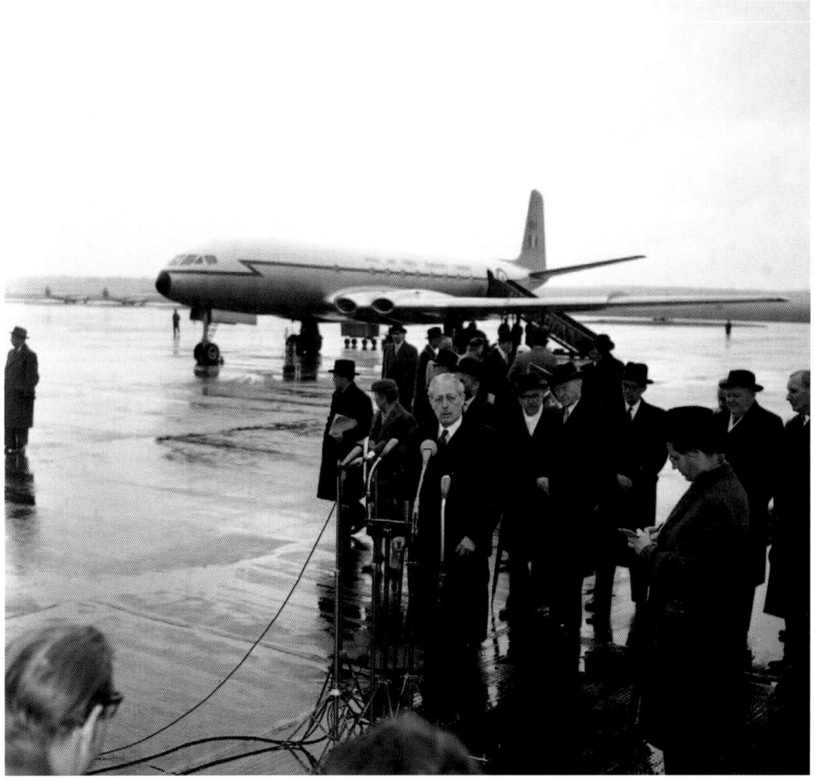

with the dual purpose of establishing the best operational techniques and to give intermediate staging posts experience in handling the jets.

During the Suez campaign in late 1956 Comets ferried aircrew to Malta, making the round trip from Lyneham in nine hours. Cyprus was another regular destination during this period. A pair of 216's Comets supported Bomber Command Valiants when they visited Accra for Ghana's independence celebrations.

Full scale transport operations began in June 1957 to support "V" bomber crews, carry troops and Royal Navy ship's crews. They also transported VIPs such as government ministers and senior officials, and on occasions members of the Royal Family.

As the unit's experience with the jets accumulated Comet services were extended across the North Atlantic and, from October 1957, to Christmas Island via San Francisco and Honolulu. It was a 19,000-mile (30,400 km) round trip that occupied over 45 flying hours and was operated on a weekly basis. Trips to the Woomera guided missile range were operated in stages of up to 2,000 miles (3,200 km) or just over four hours, with night stops at Singapore. Initial experience showed that Comet operations were far less tiring than comparable journeys in piston-engined aircraft.

One typical VIP operation was that described by the internal Air Ministry publication Air Clues which reported on a trip to Argentina made by George Ward, Secretary of State for Air, to attend the inauguration in May 1958 of the nation's new president. The Comet, specially fitted-out for the role with what were described as "VIP fittings" and BOAC-pattern seats, travelled to Buenos Aires via Gibraltar, Dakar, Recife and Rio de Janeiro in company with two Vulcans from No

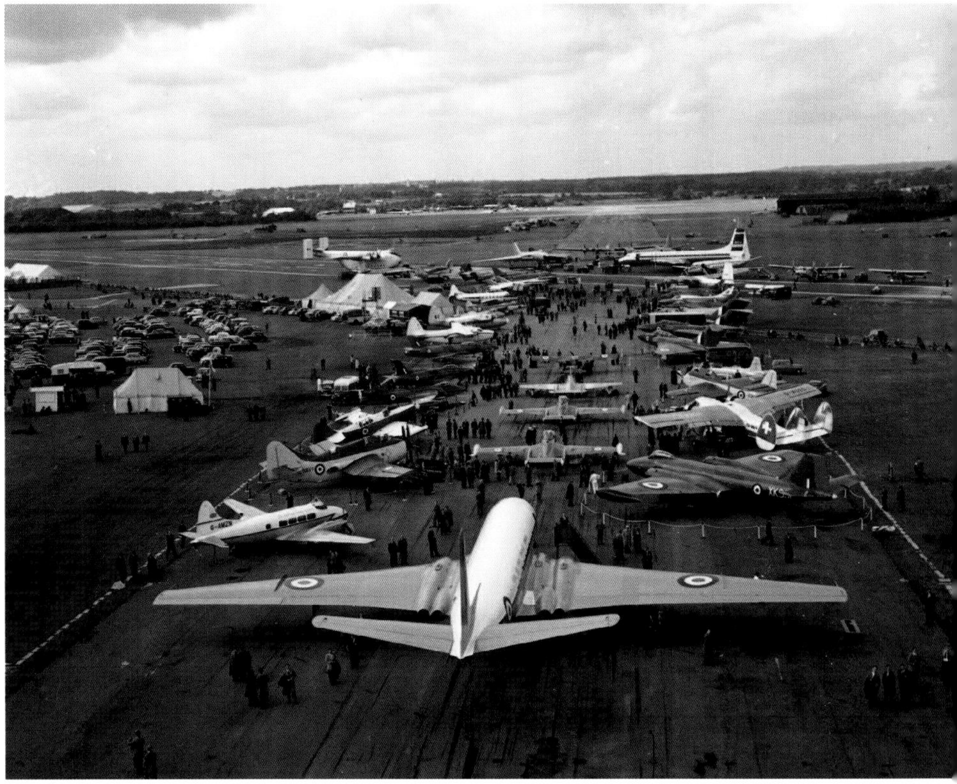

TOP LEFT: Comet 1A 5302, one of two operated by the Royal Canadian Air Force between 1953 and 1963.
TOP RIGHT: RAF Comets frequently acted as VIP transports and here C2 XK695 of 216 Sqn RAF provides the background for prime minister Harold Macmillan, 1957.
BOTTOM RIGHT: XK695 again, at the 1956 Farnborough Air Show.

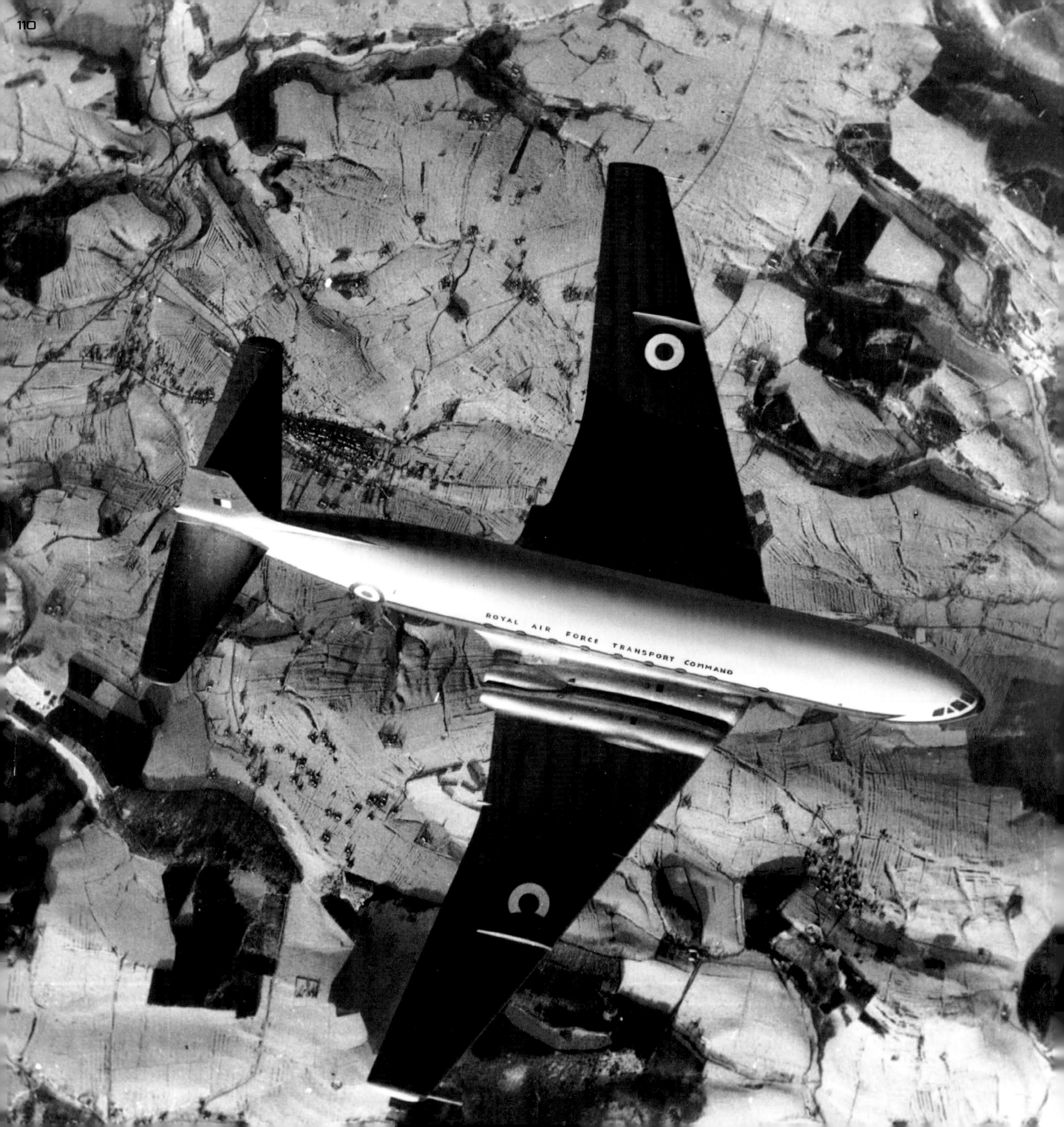
ROYAL AIR FORCE TRANSPORT COMMAND

83 Sqn. Flying time was 16hr 50 min and average speed 477 mph (763 kmh).

Air Clues reported that *"hundreds of thousands of people"* saw the three RAF machines, which joined Argentine air force aircraft in a flypast over Government House in "V" formation with the Comet leading. Earlier, local dignitaries had joined journalists in a series of flights on the Comet.

The vice-president of Aerolineas Argentinas, which had ordered three Comet 4s, handled the controls for a time. On his return to Lyneham, where the Argentine ambassador to Britain was among the welcoming party, Ward said he believed the Comet's 100 per cent serviceability record during the trip had not only created a favourable impression of the British aircraft industry but also confirmed Argentina's desire to be the first South American country to operate jets. Nearly a quarter of a century later Argentina had other reasons to remember the Vulcan.

The Comets were intended to carry passengers as well as freight and were equipped with nose radar. The main cabin featured nine rows of double rearward-facing seats similar to those fitted to the Beverley. The reclining seats were set at 39-inch (99 cm) pitch and the general level of furnishing conformed to the original BOAC standard. The Comet, therefore, set new standards of comfort for Transport Command.

The main cabin was divided from the forward cabin by a non-structural bulkhead. With the two rows of seats removed, this area could carry up to 11,200lb (5,000 kg) of freight. There was an under-floor luggage bay located aft of the wing.

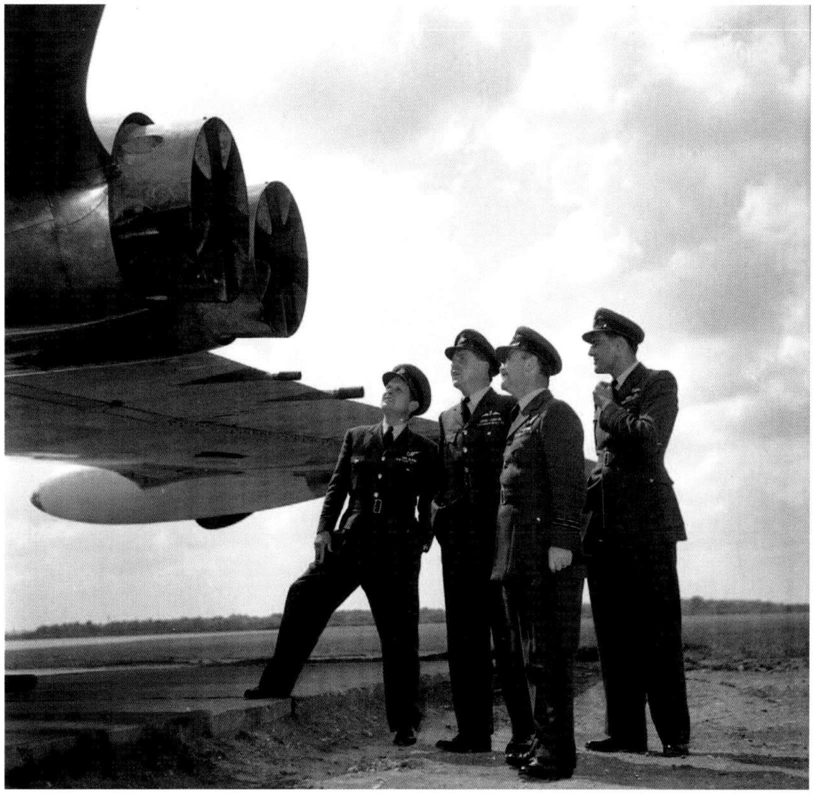

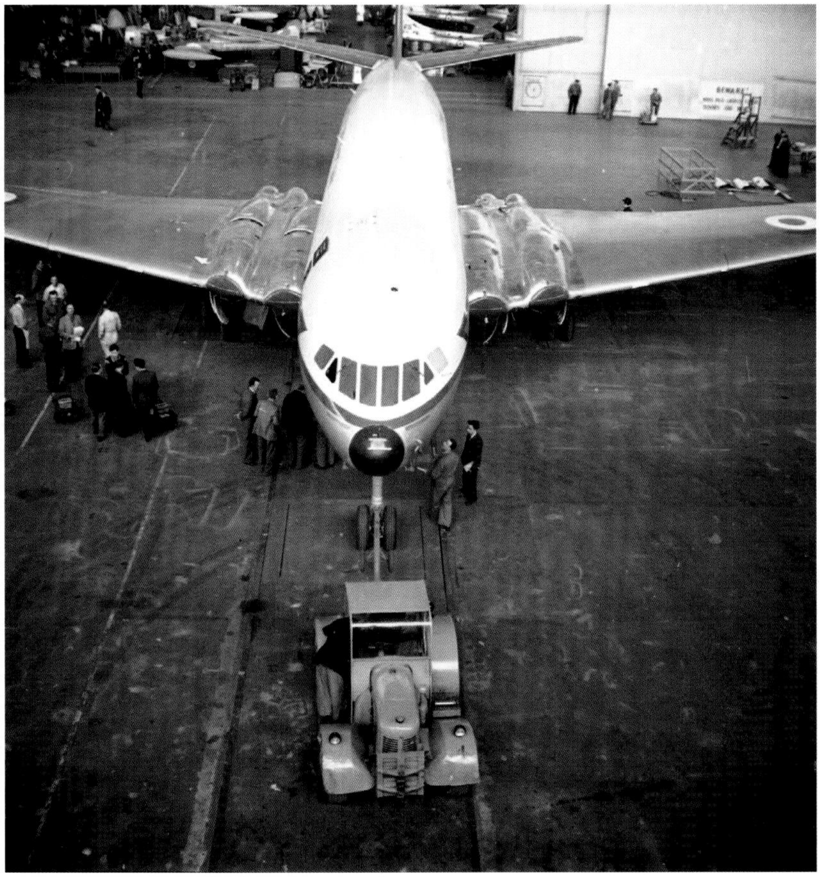

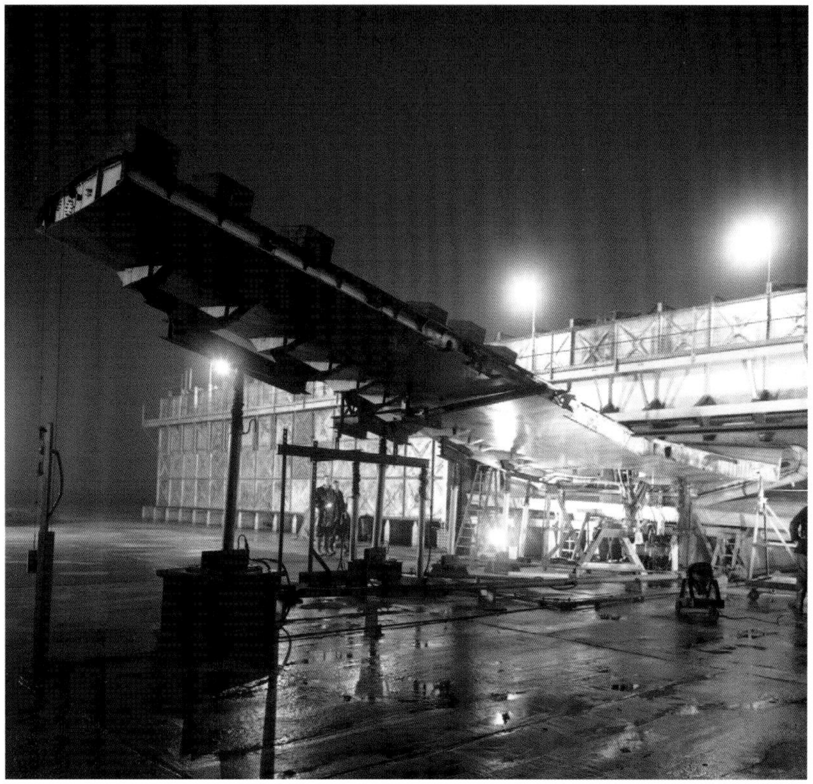

OPPOSITE PAGE: Dramatic overhead shot of an RAF Comet C2. These aircraft were used for global operations, making regular flights to destinations as distant as the weapons testing range, Woomera, Australia. They were also used as VIP transports for government ministers and carried members of the Royal Family. In the first two years of Comet operations 216 Sqn flew 5.5 million miles and 12,000 flying hours.

ABOVE LEFT: Comet C2 XK716 pictured at Broughton in May 1957
TOP: RAF officers examine BOAC Comet 4 G-APDA, June 1958
ABOVE RIGHT: Comet T2 06036 was used as a structural test specimen.

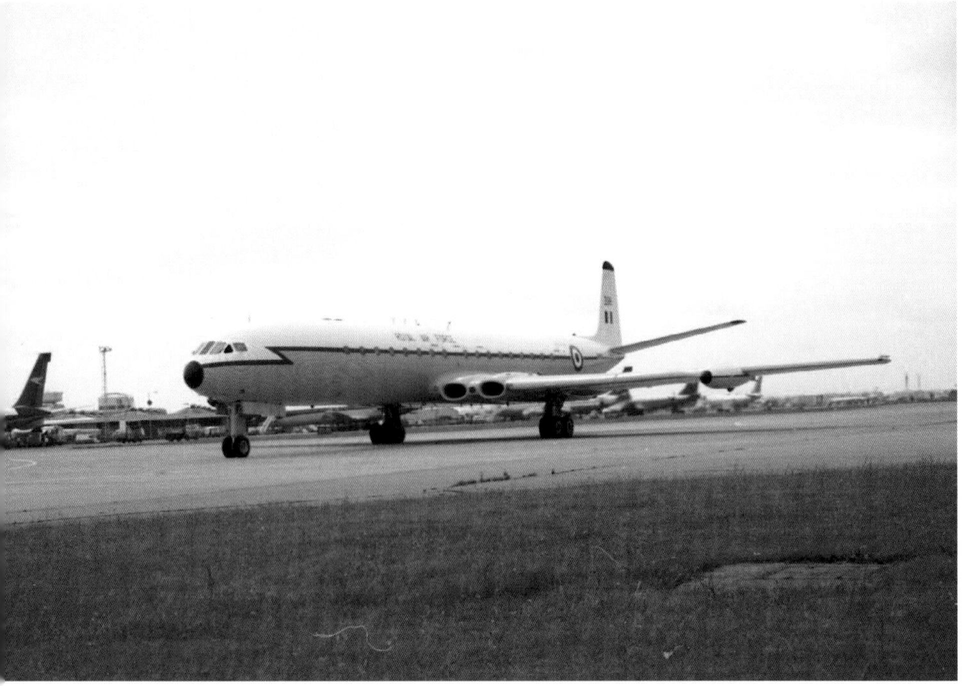

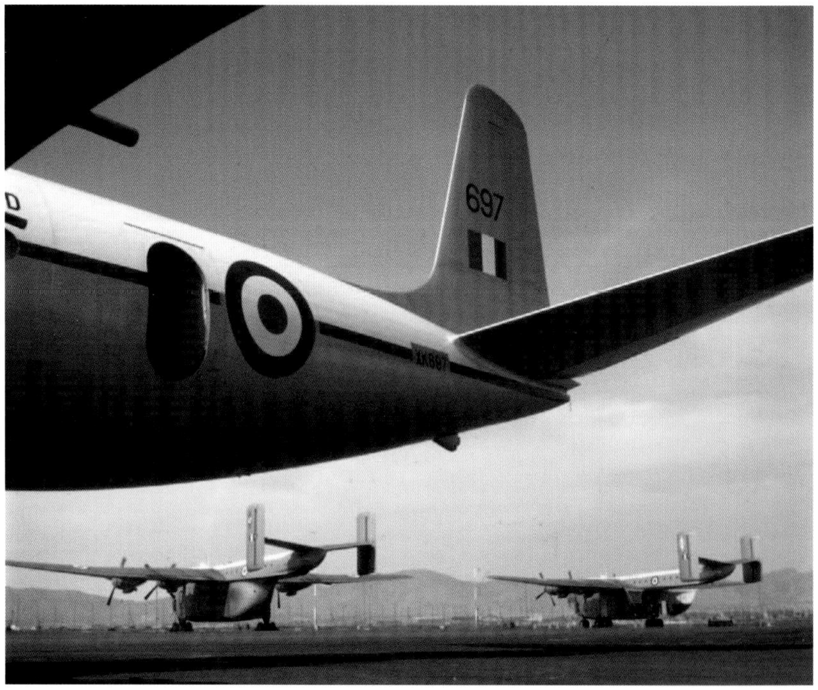
697
XK697

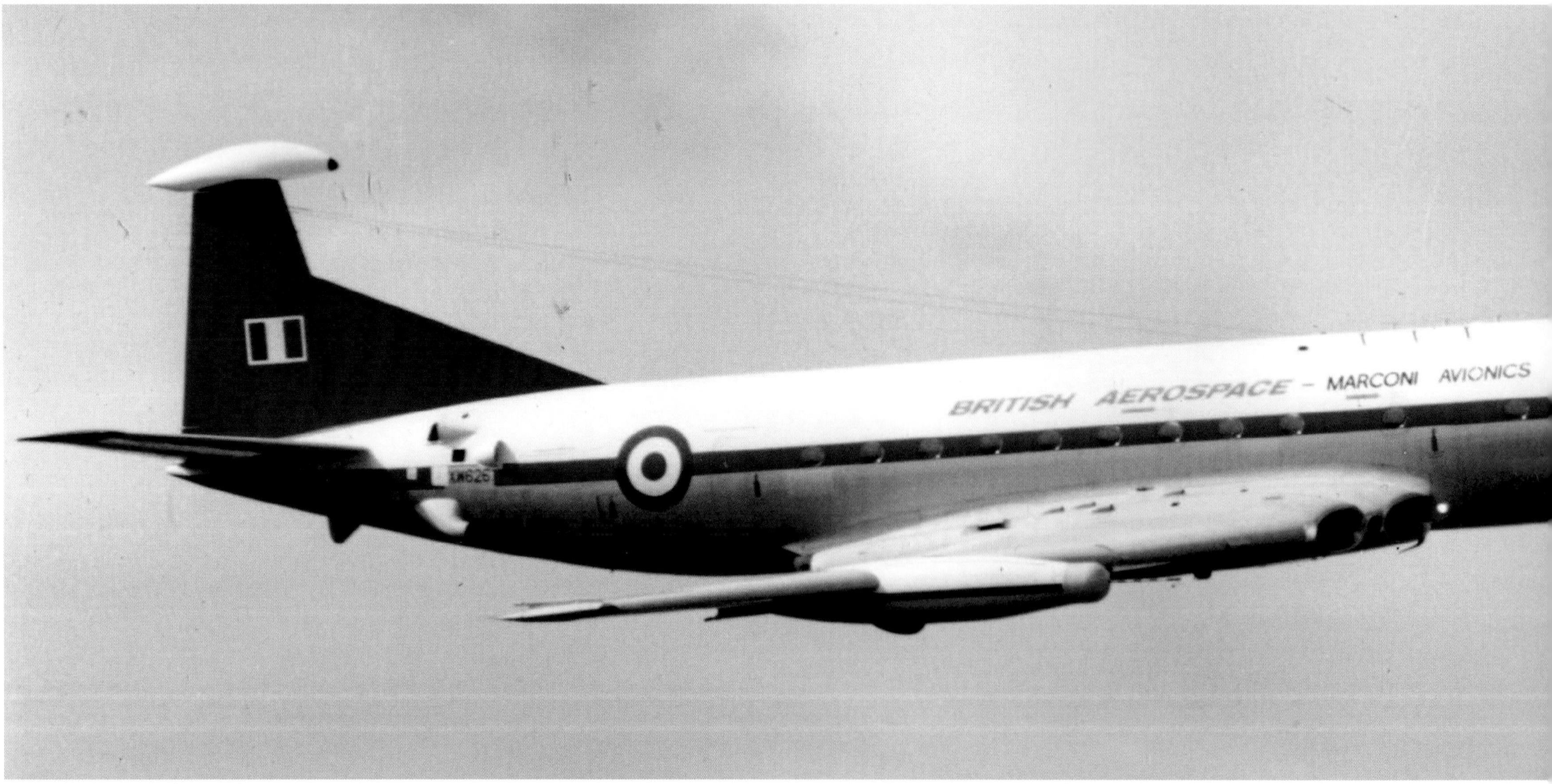
BRITISH AEROSPACE - MARCONI AVIONICS
XW626

TOP LEFT AND RIGHT: Comet C4 XR398 of 216 Sqn; C2 pictured at Nicosia, Cyprus with a pair of Beverleys.
ABOVE LEFT AND RIGHT: Two views of Comet 4 XW626 after conversion as a trials aircraft for the Nimrod AEW 3 programme.

A normal maximum payload of 13,300lb (6,000kg) could be carried over stage lengths of up to 2,300 miles (3,680 km).

The Comet could be configured as an air ambulance capable of carrying up to 36 patients, including six stretcher cases in the forward cabin, plus medical attendants and other accompanying passengers.

A normal flight crew comprised captain, co-pilot, navigator, engineer and signaller together with one or more air quartermasters. The majority of pilots came to the unit with "above average" ratings. Average experience levels were well over 3,000hr. Jet conversion was accomplished by 25hr on Meteors followed by a short period on Canberras.

Candidates then had to undergo intensive courses on the airframe and engine together with a programme of circuits, instrument and cross-country flying as well as instruction in operational procedures, emergencies and diversions. All this was rounded off by a series of overseas flights.

In its first two years of Comet operations 216 flew 5.5 million miles and 12,000 flying hours. Journeys varied from 200-mile (320 km) hops to Paris to 30,000-mile (48,000 km) around-the-world flights with matching temperature variations. On this basis Transport Command considered the Comet to be the least troublesome aircraft it had ever operated.

The C2s had proved outstandingly successful. The aircraft were not withdrawn from service until April 1967 by which time they had flown over 60,000hr or about 25 million miles with 216 and carried 380,000 passengers including VIPs and royalty.

They were replaced in 216 service by five Chester-built Comet C Mk 4s, these being the RAF's version of the 4C. The RAF order for the type was announced in September 1960 and the first aircraft made its maiden flight in November 1961. Following acceptance and crew training at Hatfield the first aircraft arrived at Lyneham in February 1962 with all five in service by June.

For the next five years the C4s were operated the alongside the C2s but on longer routes. Like the C2s the C4s featured rearward-facing seats and were used on Transport Command's regular services and also for trooping flights. They remained operational until June 1975 when 216 was disbanded. One of the Comets, XR395, made a commemorative flight from Lyneham via Heathrow and Hatfield to Leconfield, Yorkshire, home of 60MU where they awaited new owners.

The least publicised military Comet operations were those of the RAF's 51 Sqn. Three of the Hatfield-built Comet 2s ordered by BOAC were later fitted out for highly secret signals intelligence gathering at the height of the Cold War. Eventually seven aircraft were operated in this role.

Designated R2 the aircraft replaced piston-engined Lincoln and Washington bombers in the gathering of electronic intelligence. In addition to the normal flight crew the R2s carried up to 10 specialists working in the main cabin where they operated the monitoring and recording equipment to gather information

on the frequencies of Soviet and Warsaw Pact radars and weapons systems. Intelligence gathered was shared with the US and the Comets frequently operated in conjunction with USAF RDB-47s.

The first R2s were flown unpressurised and retained the original square windows. The fuselages also featured cut-outs with radomes covering the special antennas. The aircraft were delivered to No 192 Sqn at RAF Watton during 1956 and 1957. The unit became 51 Sqn in 1958. One of the aircraft was destroyed in a hangar fire at Watton in 1959 and replaced by a 216 Sqn C2. The R2s were replaced in the intelligence gathering role by Nimrod R1s in May 1974.

A number of Comet 1s and 2s acquired military serials after the 1954 accidents and were used for experimental work. G-AMXK, for example, was used for testing the Smiths triplex Autoland. Two Comet 2Es were fitted as engine test-beds with 10,000lb (4,500 kg) thrust RA.29 Avon 524s in the outboard positions, this being the Avon intended for the Comet 4. As described in chapter seven they were used to help BOAC prepare for the arrival of the Comet 4.

Some Comets were used for weapons research. XM823, acquired from Air France by the Ministry of Supply, was converted to 1XB standard at Chester and used to test infra-red guidance systems for Red Top and Firestreak as well as the TV guidance system of the Martell missile being developed by Hawker Siddeley Dynamics.

A number of ex-BOAC Comet 4s wore military markings during their time as flying laboratories. G-APDF was acquired by the Ministry of Technology as XV814 and operated from RAE Farnborough for radio and communications equipment development. It displayed a colourful white, blue and red livery and remained in service until 1992 when it was used as a spares source for what was to be the last Comet still flying. Along the way XV814 acquired a distinctive Nimrod fin and rudder and the inevitable nickname of "Conrod." It was finally scrapped in 1997.

Dan-Air's G-APDP became XW626 when it was acquired by RAE Farnborough in 1973 and given a new identity as XX944. It was used for equipment testing until 1976 and later broken up. The Ministry of Technology acquired G-APDS in 1969 as

XW626. It later joined the Nimrod AEW3 programme and in revised configuration with Nimrod nose radome, first flew in June 1977. It was retired in 1981, flown to Bedford and scrapped in 1994.

The last of the Comets never flew with an airline or with the RAF. A 4C, it was delivered straight from the Chester production line to the RAE at Boscombe Down in December 1962. Its cabin had been fitted out with racks for navigation equipment and at that stage it had a distinctive bath-shaped radome under its fuselage to cover aerials. This was later removed.

Given the military serial XS235 and called Canopus, the aircraft was used as a flying laboratory to test navigation equipment. For the next 33 years it led a relatively sedate life amassing just 8,200 flying hours during which time the airframe had been subjected to a high level of monitoring and non-destructive testing. But by late 1997 two of its Avon engines were close to reaching their normal life expectancy and by that time there were no overhaul facilities available.

The aircraft was withdrawn from service and made its final operational flight on 14 March 1997. On board was John Cunningham, the man who had taken the first Comet into the sky 48 years earlier. There were two further, shorter flights, culminating in a final landing at Boscombe Down.

There was, though, plenty of life left in the Comet design. The Hawker Siddeley Nimrod, the world's first jet maritime reconnaissance aircraft, was based on the well-proven Comet 4 but powered by four Rolls-Royce Spey engines. The RAF initially ordered 38 Nimrod MR 1s in 1965. Comet production had, however, not been completed. The last two 4Cs on the Chester production line were converted into development aircraft.

The Nimrod was withdrawn from service following the coalition government's security and defence review of 2010.

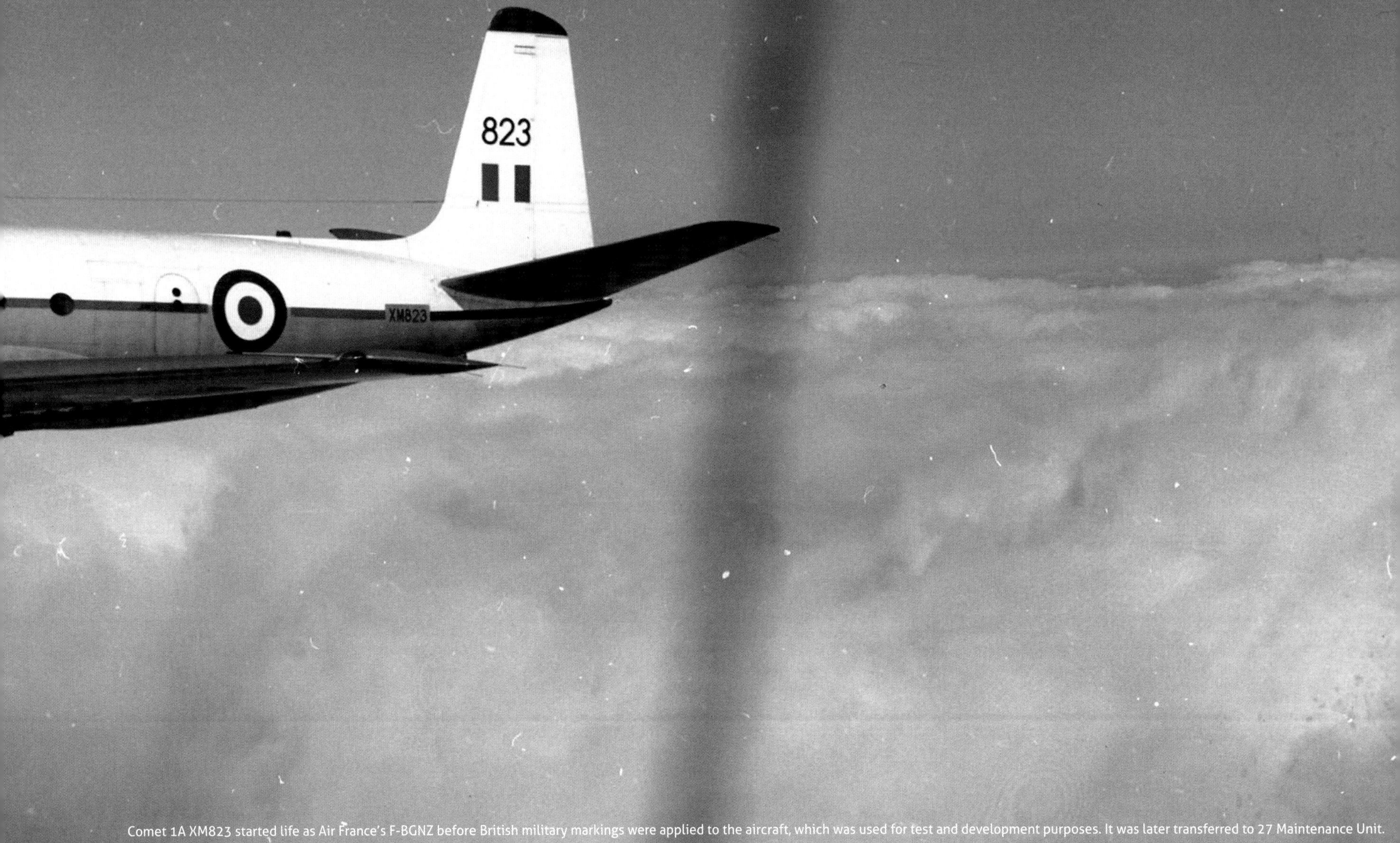
823
XM823

Comet 1A XM823 started life as Air France's F-BGNZ before British military markings were applied to the aircraft, which was used for test and development purposes. It was later transferred to 27 Maintenance Unit.

COMET ACCIDENTS

Sabotage!

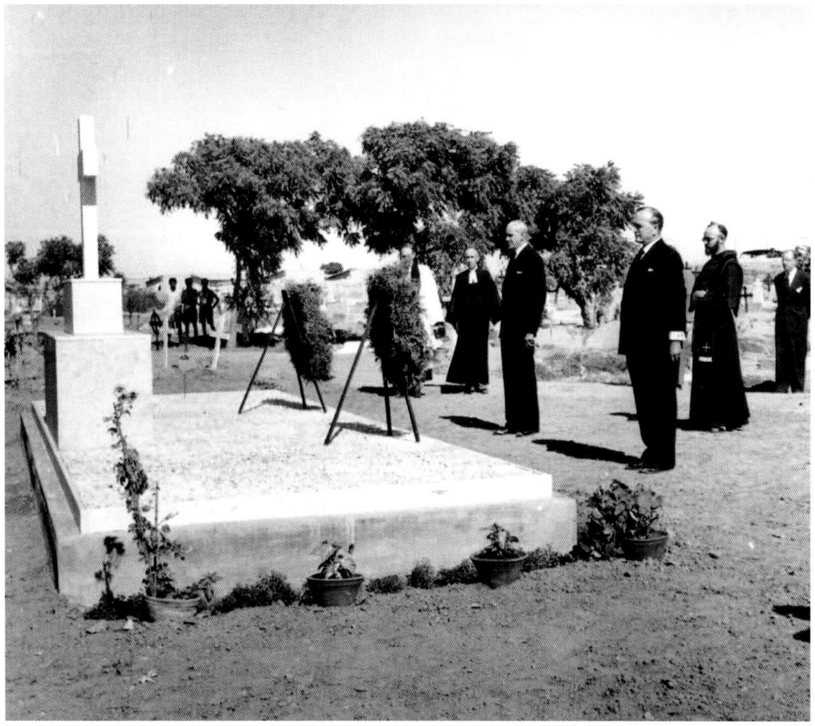

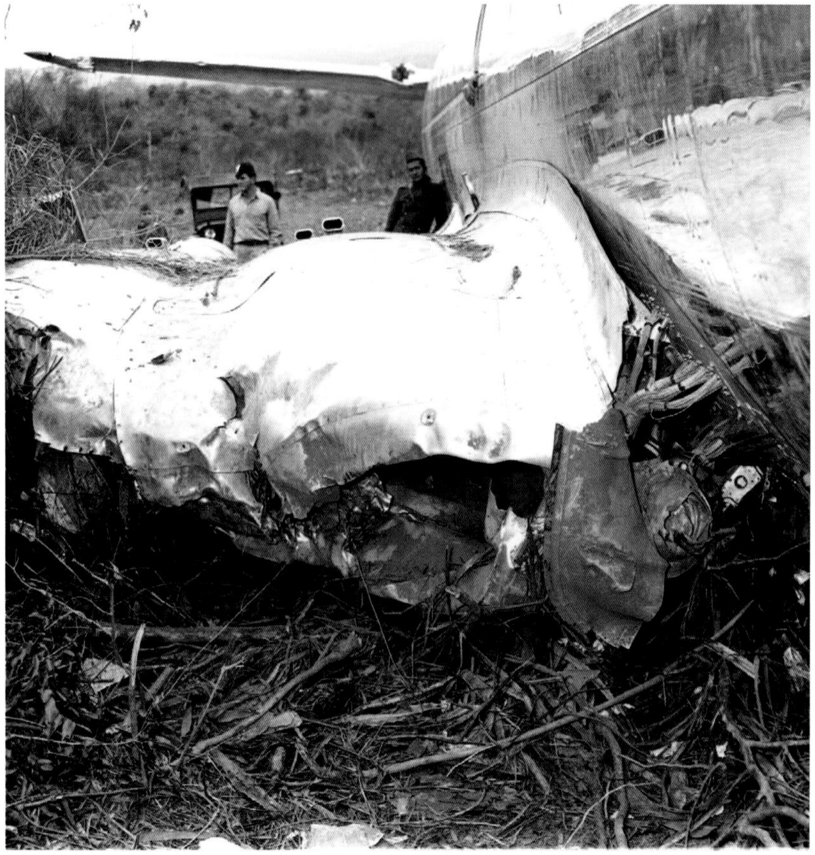

Languishing in the dust on top of a grey-painted metal cupboard in the press office on the seventh floor of the Department of Trade and Industry building in London's Victoria Street during the 1970s was a shapeless piece of foam rubber.

Enquires revealed that it had been part of a seat from a British European Airways Comet that that been blown up over the Mediterranean in the late `60s. Quite why it was there nobody seemed able to say.

But the fact remained that this same seat cover had formed a central part of a classic piece of detective work by the department's Accidents Investigation Branch. Possibly it had been part of the explanation given to media representatives at a press conference when the cause of G-ARCO's loss was

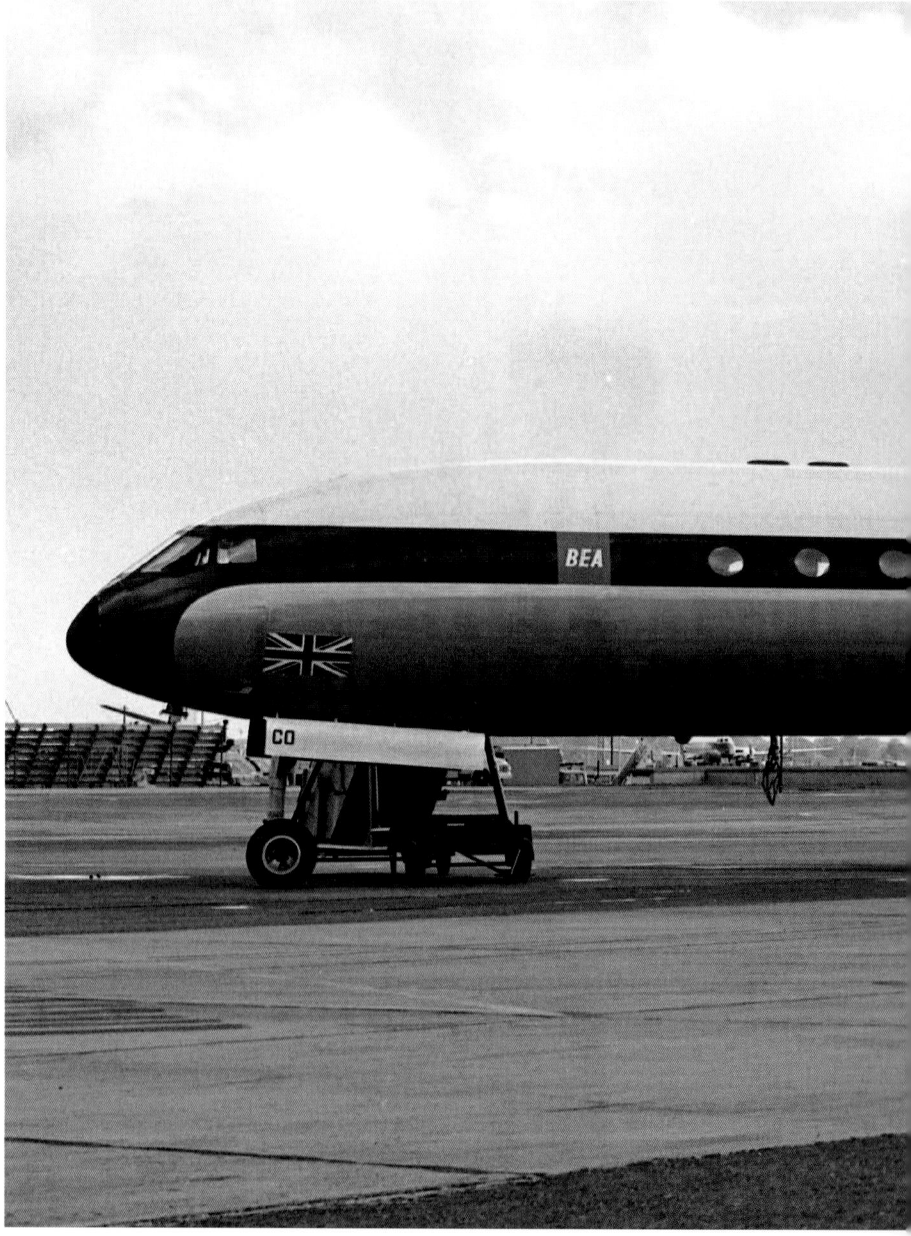
BEA
CO

TOP LEFT: A memorial to remember the 11 victims of the fatal crash of . Canadian Pacific Airways Comet 1A, CF-CUN, Empress of Hawaii.
ABOVE LEFT: Aerolineas Argentinas was the first overseas customer for the Comet 4 and it eventually operated seven including one 4C. LV-AHP, El Lucero del Alba, was delivered in May 1959 but damaged beyond repair three months later near Asuncion. There were two fatalities.

announced. It was certainly a fact, though, that the BEA Comet had been one of four lost during the decade to acts of terrorism or the response to such acts.

It's probably fair to say, however, that a decade earlier most of the Comet losses had been, at least partly due to the novelty of the jet airliner concept. Of the nine Comet 1s built five were lost in accidents; of the 10 Mk 1As built three crashed.

Eminent airline historian the late Ron Davies wrote in 1964 that the Comet accidents of a decade earlier had come as a great shock to all those who had come to respect the new type's reliability record. Even though there had been some criticism of the Comet's *"handling difficulties"* during take-off and landing, the initial accidents had been regarded as *"teething troubles."* Three aircraft had been lost as a result of runway accidents.

"So great was the generally held confidence in the aircraft," Davies wrote, *"that the suggestion that the aircraft was basically at fault was received with incredulity."* After the first of the two BOAC losses of 1954 there were, he reported, many people prepared to believe sabotage had been to blame.

Even the loss of G-ALYV in a tropical storm near Calcutta in circumstances *"never fully explained"* despite a full inquiry, were regarded as *"part of an acceptable penalty for breaking entirely new ground not only in performance but in air traffic control and cruising procedures."* The Comet, after all, cruised at twice the average altitude for piston-engined airliners.

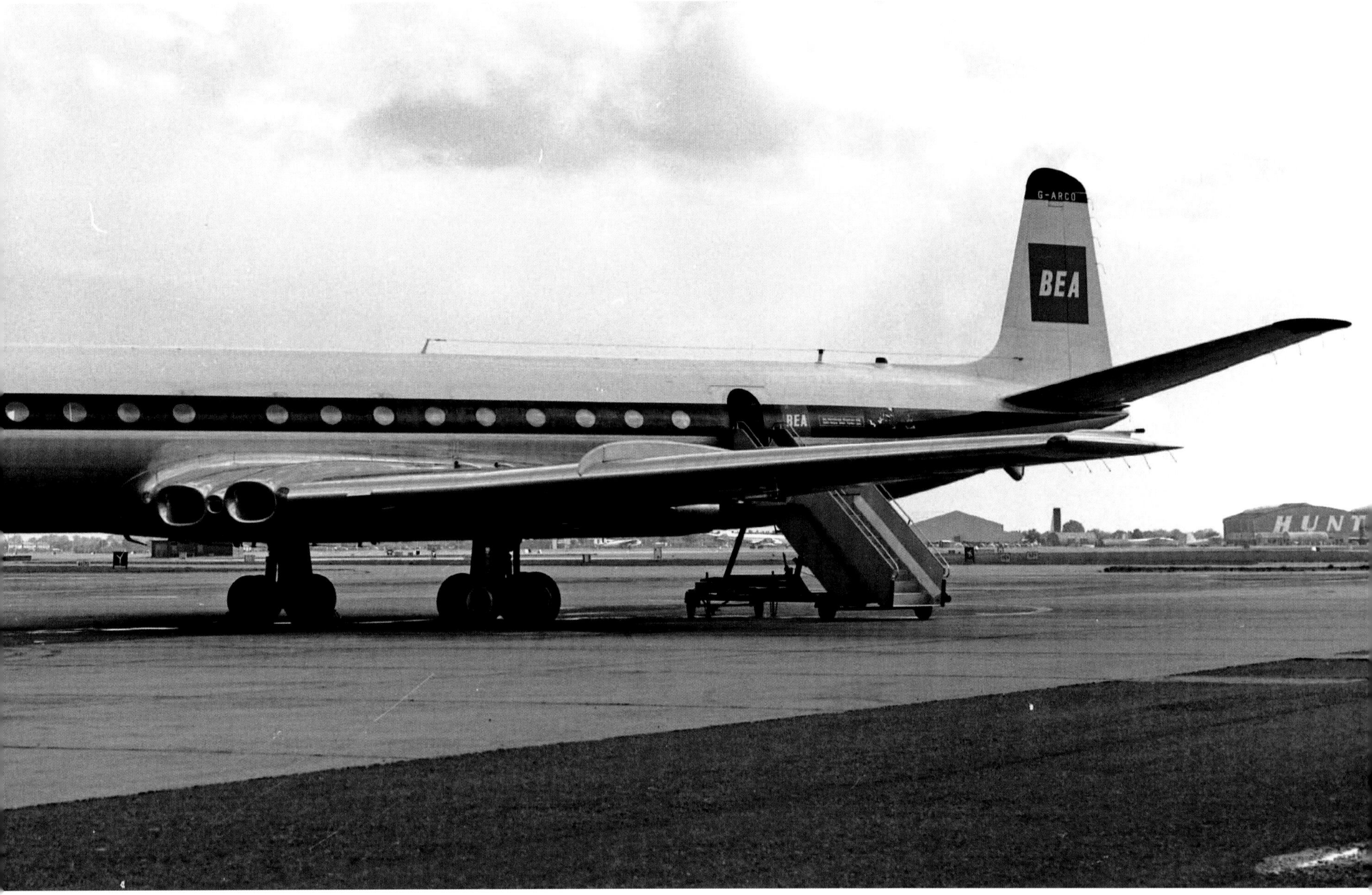
G-ARCO
BEA
BEA

ABOVE: BEA Comet 4B G-ARCO which was blown up by a terrorist bomb on 12 October 1967

They were, of course, far from being the only Comet losses. Of the seven delivered to Aerolineas Argentinas, for example, three were destroyed, one during a crew training accident, another damaged beyond repair at Asuncion, Chile and the third crashed at Sao Paulo, Brazil. Three Middle East Airlines Comet 4Cs were among a dozen aircraft written off after being heavily damaged in an assault on Beirut airport by Israeli special forces, following a terrorist attack on an Israeli aircraft.

The unique Comet 4C operated as a luxuriously-appointed VIP transport by the Saudi Arabian government was destroyed on its first overseas trip in March 1963. It had been delivered the previous June and had flown just 168 hours. The aircraft had left Hatfield bound for Geneva with de Havilland personnel accompanying the Saudi crew.

The aircraft hit an Alpine ridge near Cuneo, south of Turin in the early hours of the morning. All on board were killed. The aircraft was so near the crest of the ridge that much of its wreckage was found beyond the impact point.

Dan-Air, the operator of the biggest Comet fleet, lost two of its aircraft in 1970. In July G-APDN, an ex-BOAC airliner, was operating a charter flight from Manchester to Barcelona with 105 passengers and seven crew on board. On approach to the airport the aircraft hit trees on the north-east slope of the Los Angudes peak in the Sierra del Montseny. All on board were killed.

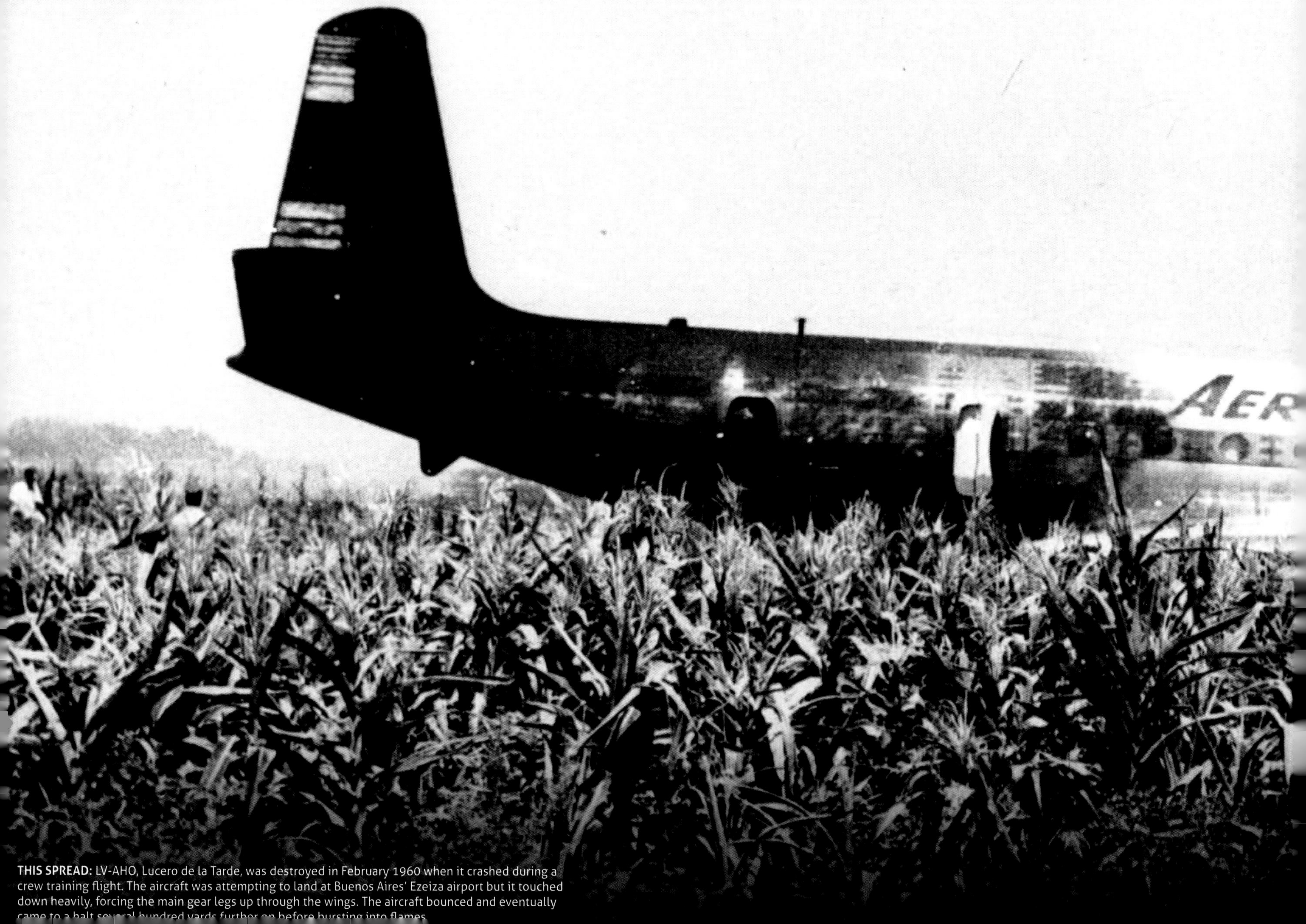
AER

THIS SPREAD: LV-AHO, Lucero de la Tarde, was destroyed in February 1960 when it crashed during a crew training flight. The aircraft was attempting to land at Buenos Aires' Ezeiza airport but it touched down heavily, forcing the main gear legs up through the wings. The aircraft bounced and eventually came to a halt several hundred yards further on before bursting into flames.

AEROL
INAS

INAS

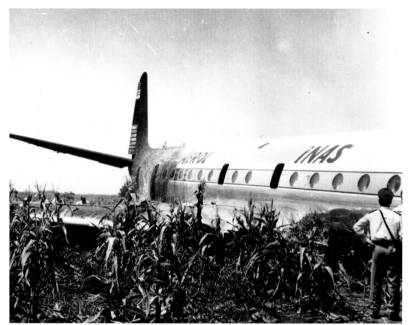

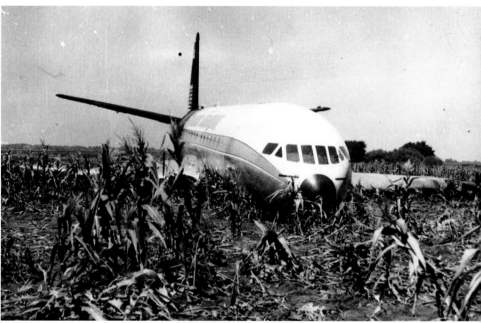

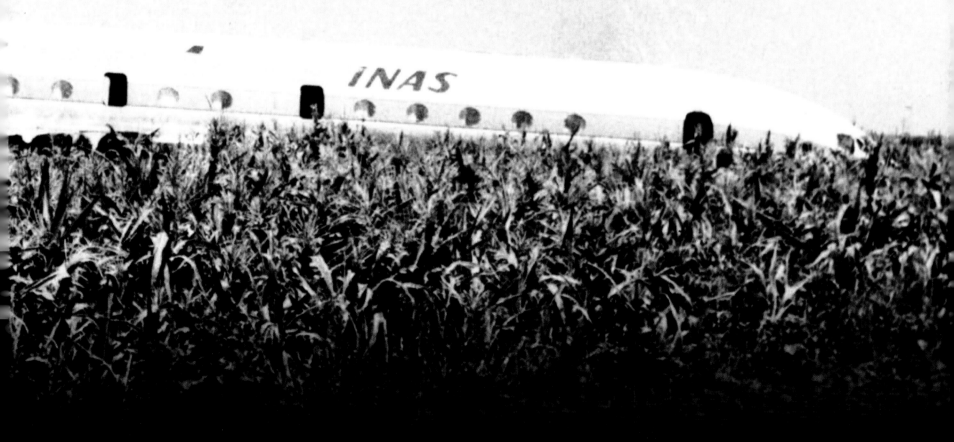

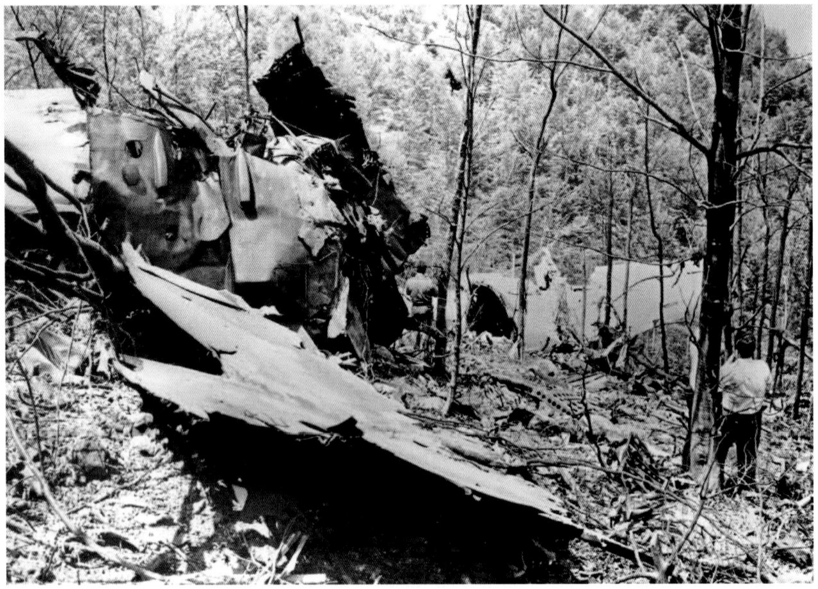

It had been a classic *"controlled flight into terrain"* accident resulting from a combination of navigational errors. In fact, of all the fatal Comet accidents it was the most costly in terms of human life.

Dan-Air's other Comet loss, also an ex-BOAC machine, resulted from a wheels-up landing at Newcastle airport. The nine occupants all survived. The cause was attributed to the failure of the crew to carry-out pre-landing checks.

BEA's G-ARCO was operating on behalf of Cyprus Airways when it crashed into the Mediterranean off Demre, Turkey in October 1967. All 59 passengers and seven crew members were killed.

The aircraft had left Heathrow as BEA Flight 284 to Athens. When it arrived at the Greek capital six passengers disembarked and 27 joined what was now Cyprus Airways Flight CY284 bound for Nicosia and then Cairo. After take-off the aircraft made its routine position reports before radioing that it was abeam of Myrtou, Cyprus. The message was received by another, westbound, BEA Comet and relayed to Athens ATC which cleared `CO to change to the frequency of Nicosia ATC.

Immediately after its crew contacted Nicosia at 0515hr all contact was lost. Later 51 bodies were recovered from the sea. Most were wearing lifejackets. Some had wristwatches that had stopped at 0525hr. Investigators estimated that the

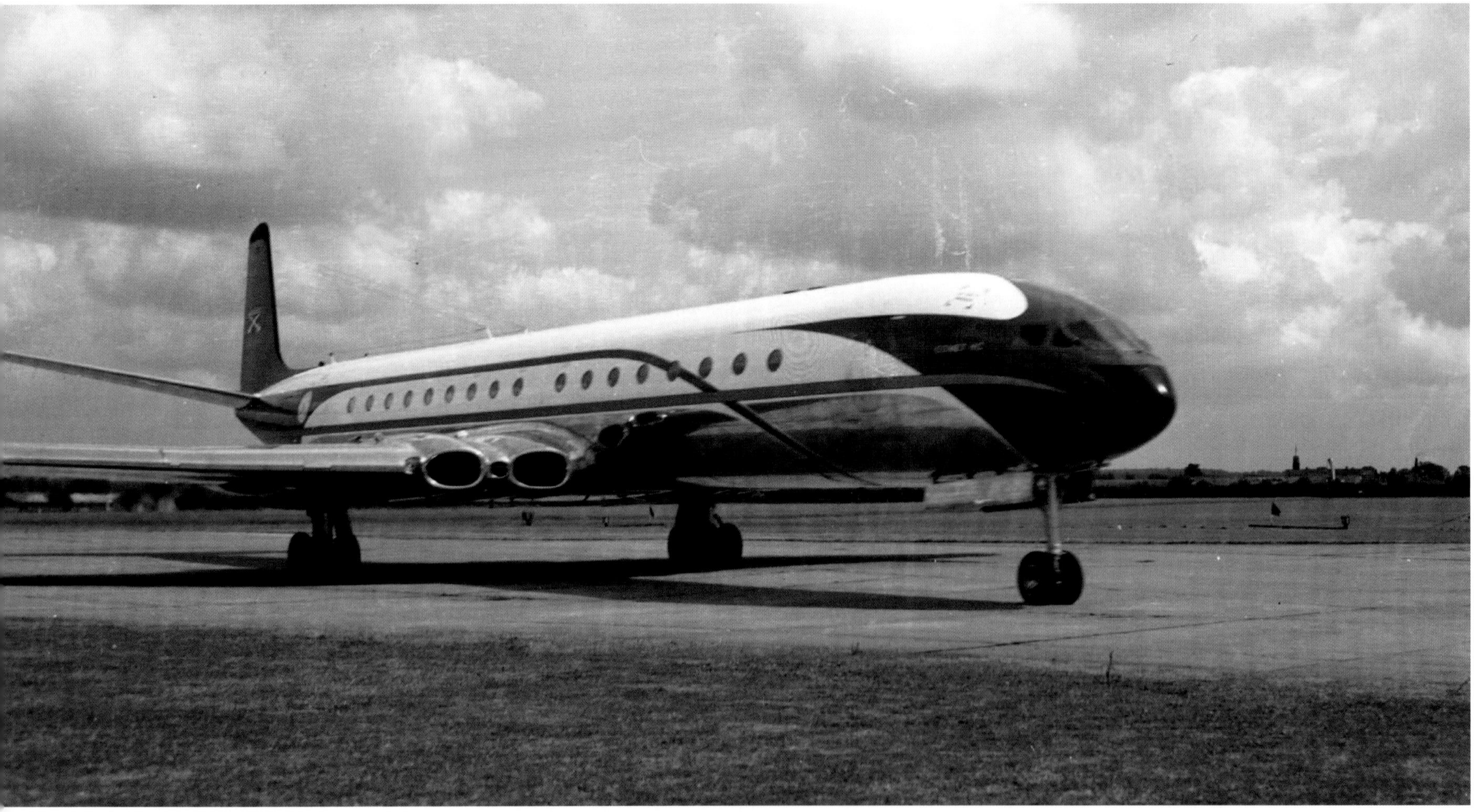

ABOVE: The unique VIP-configured Comet 4C, SA-R-7, was operated by the Saudi Royal Flight, mainly for the use of King Ibn Saud. He was not on board, however, when the aircraft hit a mountain ridge during a flight from Nice to Geneva in March 1963, killing all on board.
TOP LEFT: Part of the wreckage of Dan-Air's Comet 4 G-APDN, which crashed on a hillside south of Barcelona in July 1970 while on charter to the tour operator Clarksons. All 112 on board were killed.

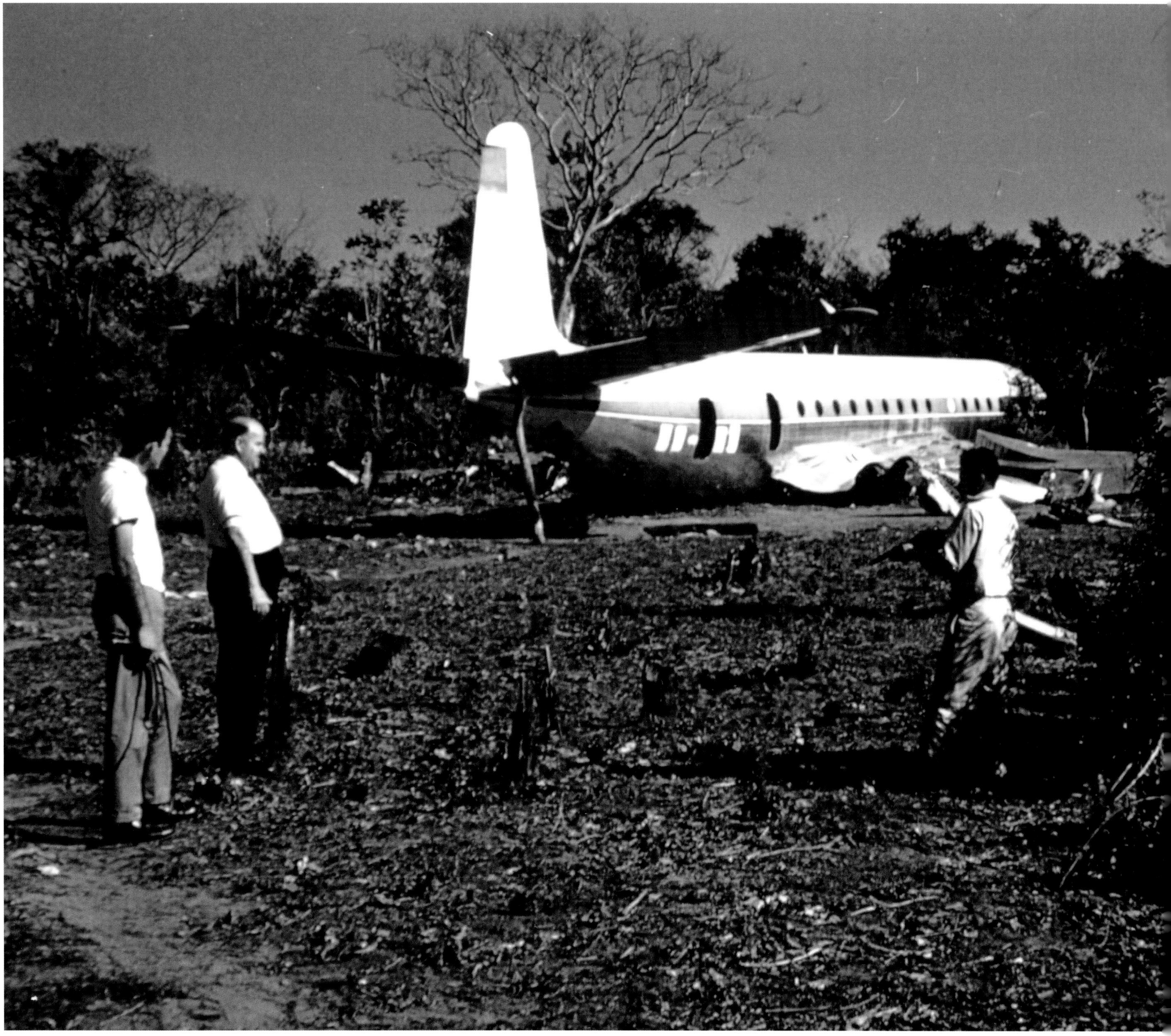

ABOVE: Aerolineas Argentinas lost three of its Comet 4s in accidents. LV-AHR, Arco Iris, crashed in November 1961 shortly after take-off from Campinas Airport, São Paulo, Brazil, killing all 40 passengers and 12 crew members. The aircraft was operating a scheduled service from Buenos Aires to New York. It reached an altitude of about 300ft but lost height and crashed after hitting eucalyptus trees.

aircraft had broken up in flight and consequently suspected its wreckage would be scattered over a 35sq mile area of the sea bed at up to 10,000ft (3,077m) below the surface.

When an aircraft drop tank was recovered from the sea it seemed possible that the Comet might have collided with a military aircraft. But then a seat cushion found floating in the sea changed the investigators' minds because it was found to have traces of a military plastic explosive. This clearly indicated that the aircraft had been the victim of a mid-air explosion.

The cushion and other objects recovered from the sea were analysed by the Forensic Explosive Section of the Royal Armament and Development Establishment at Fort Halstead, Kent. From this detective work, which involved plotting the trajectory of metal fragments passing through the cushion - by threading wires through the perforations - it was possible to determine that the bomb had been detonated under seat 4A or 5A.

In its issue of 5 September Flight published a picture of the seat cushion complete with the wires passing through it. It reported that investigators built a mock-up of the Comet's cabin and the floor with seat assembly. *"An explosive charge was placed in the position indicated,"* the journal noted. *"The effects produced by its explosion exactly matched the effects observed in the cushion from the aircraft. The trials showed that such an explosion would produce a hole in the adjacent side of the aircraft of about 3 – 6sq ft in area with outward petalling of the metal. Petalling would lead to ripping back in the slipstream."*

The cause was determined to have been in-flight break-up of the aircraft following the detonation of a high-explosive device within the cabin while the aircraft was cruising at 29,000ft (8,900m).

The investigation meant that both the AIB and the RADE were able to accumulate further knowledge about the tell-tale signs of explosives on fragments of aircraft even after immersion of sea water. It was to enable them assist in future investigations.

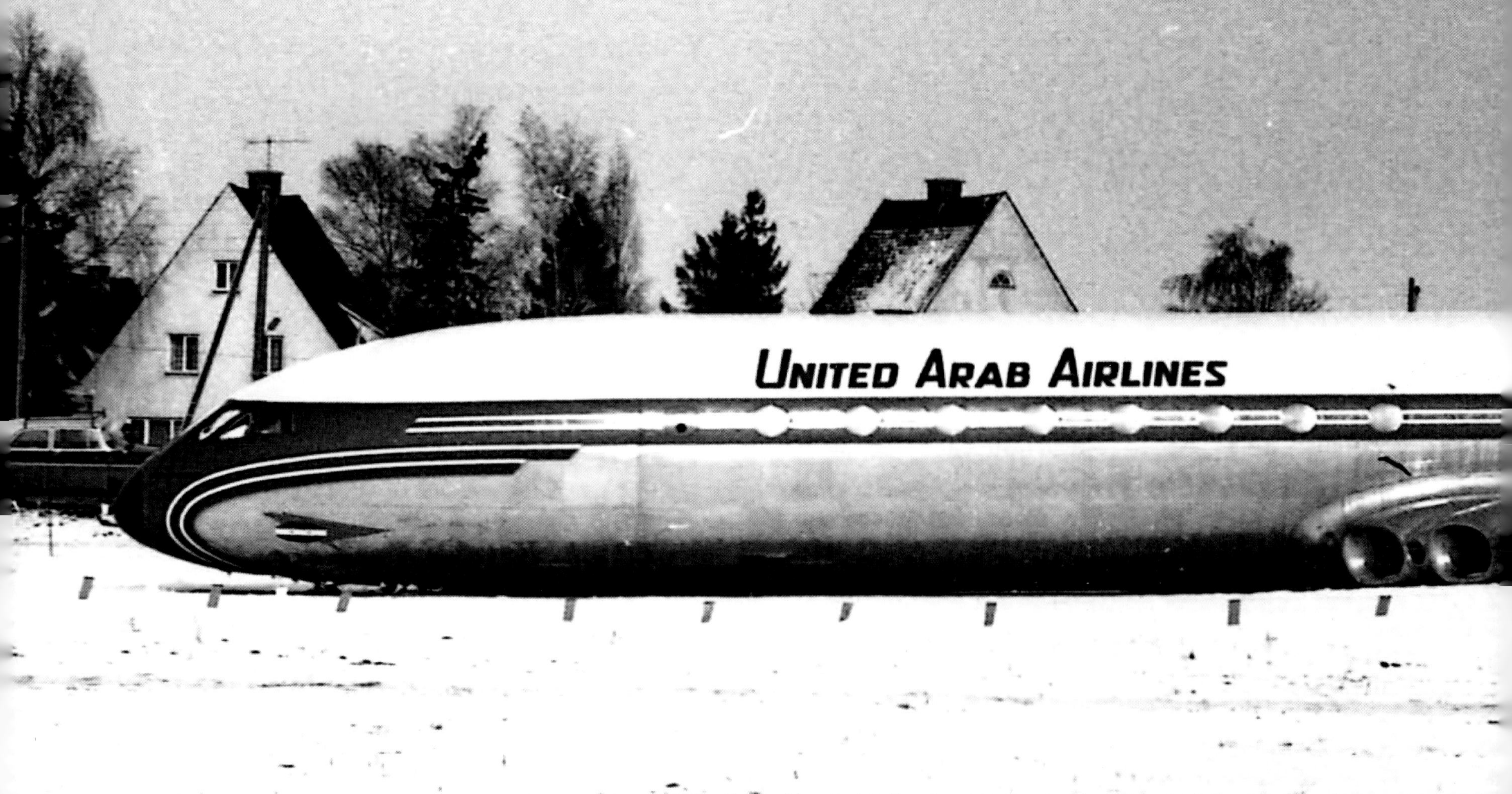
UNITED ARAB AIRLINES

ABOVE: United Arab Airlines' SU-ALE pictured resting on its belly at Munich in February 1970. Due to buffeting, the take-off from Munich's Riem airport had to be rejected at a height of 30ft. The pilot attempted to touch down but the aircraft overran the runway and hit a fence, tearing off the undercarriage and starting a fire. The cause of the buffeting was attributed to ice on the wings and the flight crew over-rotating.

In-Service Comet Hull Losses

DATE	TYPE	REGISTRATION	S/N	OPERATOR	FATALITIES	LOCATION
26 Oct 52	Comet 1	G-ALYZ	6012	**BOAC**	-	**Rome**
03 Mar 53	Comet 1A	CF-CUN	6014	**Canadian Pacific**	**11**	**Karachi**
02 May 53	Comet 1	G-ALYV	6008	**BOAC**	**43**	**Calcutta**
25 Jun 53	Comet 1A	F-BGSC	6019	**UTA**	-	**Dakar**
25 Jul 53	Comet 1	G-ALYR	6004	**BOAC**	-	**Caluctta**
10 Jan 54	Comet 1	G-ALYP	6003	**BOAC**	**35**	**Elba**
08 Apl 54	Comet 1	G-ALYY	6011	**South African Airways**	**21**	**Stromboli**
13 Sep 57	Comet 2R	XK663	6027	**92 Sqn RAF**	-	**RAF Wyton**
27 Aug 59	Comet 4	LV-AHP	6411	**Aerolineas Argentinas**	**2**	**Asuncion**
20 Feb 60	Comet 4	LV-AHO	6410	**Aerolineas Argentinas**	-	**Buenos Aires**
23 Nov 61	Comet 4	LV-AHR	6430	**Aerolineas Argentinas**	**52**	**Sao Paulo**
21 Dec 61	Comet 4B	G-ARJM	6456	**BEA**	**27**	**Ankara**
19 Jul 62	Comet 4C	SU-AMW	6464	**United Arab Airlines**	**26**	**Thailand**
20 Mar 63	Comet 4C	SA-R-7	6461	**Saudi Arabian Government**	**18**	**Italy**
27 Jul 63	Comet 4C	SU-ALD	6441	**United Arab Airlines**	**63**	**India**
22 Mar 64	Comet 4	G-APDH	6409	**Malaysian Airlines System**	-	**Singapore**
12 Oct 67	Comet 4B	G-ARCO	6449	**BEA**	**66**	**Nicosia**
28 Dec 68	Comet 4C	OD-ADR	6445	**Middle East Airlines**	-	**Beirut**
28 Dec 68	Comet 4C	OD-ADS	6448	**Middle East Airlines**	-	**Beirut**
28 Dec 68	Comet 4C	OD-ADQ	6446	**Middle East Airlines**	-	**Beirut**
14 Jan 70	Comet 4C	SU-ANI	6475	**United Arab Airlines**	-	**Addis Ababa**
09 Feb 70	Comet 4C	SU-ALE	6444	**United Arab Airlines**	-	**Munich**
03 Jul 70	Comet 4	G-APDN	6415	**Dan-Air**	**112**	**Spain**
07 Oct 70	Comet 4	G-APDL	6413	**Dan-Air**	-	**Newcastle**
02 Jan 71	Comet 4C	SU-ALC	6439	**United Arab Airlines**	**16**	**Tripoli**

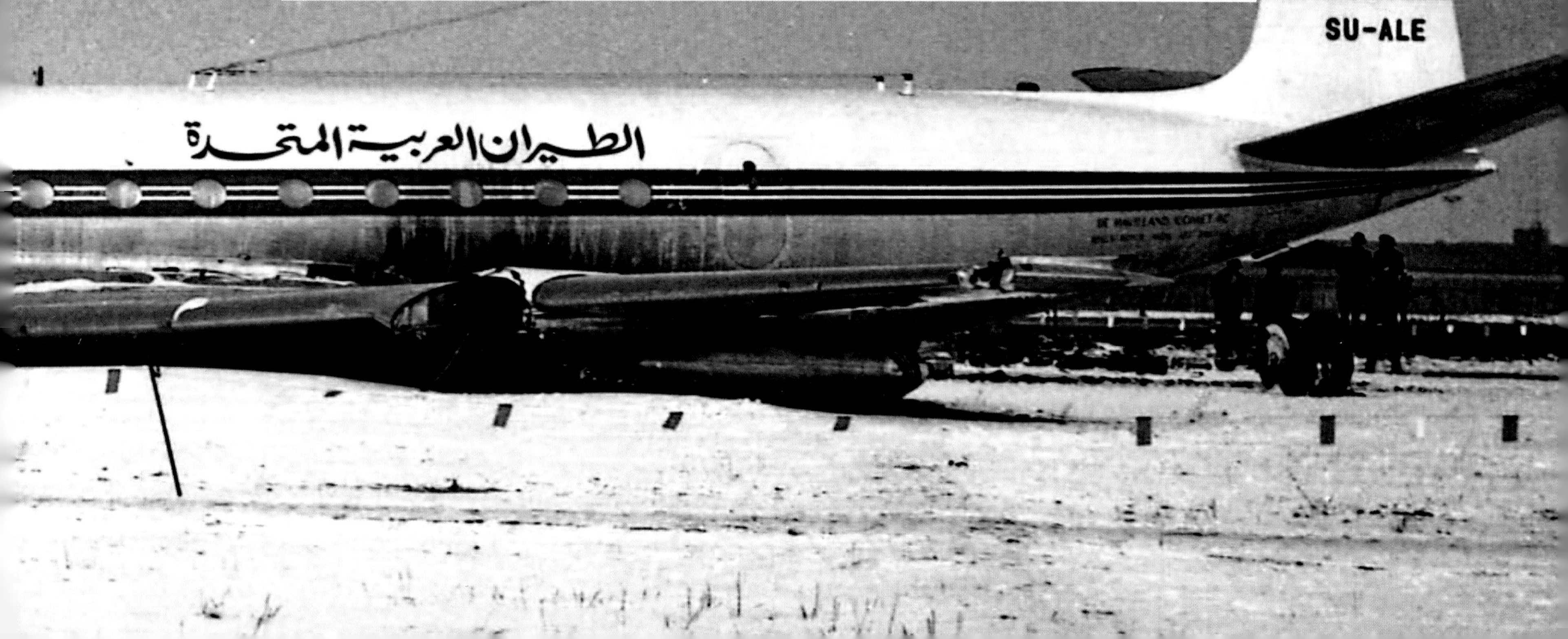
SU-ALE
الطيران العربية المتحدة

THE COMET'S LEGACY

AIR FRANCE — DE HAVILLAND — D.H. 106 "COMET"

1 Pilot and co-pilot	10 Hostess' table
2 Radio operator	11 Hostess' seat
3 Navigator	12 Cloakroom
4 Crew entry door	13 Cloakroom
5 Baggage hold	14 Bar store
6 Steward's seat	15 Men's toilet
7 Galley	16 Ladies' toilet
8 Emergency exits	17 W. C.
9 Passenger entrance.	18 44 passengers

A talented team of visionaries starts work under a highly respected but autocratic boss on a brand new concept which will revolutionise travel and put their country years ahead. They are having to do this in the middle of a war which threatens their very existence but they receive help and encouragement from a former minister who was sacked for talking out of turn. Eventually they get government support and win orders from the major customer but their ideas are so radical that virtually every step of the way they have to meet and overcome unprecedented technical challenges. The climax comes when the revolutionary new airliner goes into passenger service and is widely acclaimed as a huge success.

Cue the stirring music and fade to black. But wait: that is just part one. In part two, things take a darker turn with mysterious crashes but in part three a new version of the aircraft goes on to a glorious finale with more success.

You could hardly make it up. Indeed, you might think a story so rich in triumph and tragedy, so full of twists and turns that sound almost like cinematic clichés and populated with characters out of central casting is rich enough not to require further embellishment.

The Comet has always been a controversial aircraft and the subject of continuing debate. But attempts to advance the frontiers of knowledge often attract negative comment especially if innocent lives are lost in the process.

In his Empire of the Clouds, published in 2010, James Hamilton-Paterson quoted a de Havilland test pilot as saying that during the Comet's display at the 1949 Farnborough show the floor at the entrance to the flight deck was "*bulging up.*" There was also a loud bang from the nose where the skin flexed. Wilson said: "*In later years we realised these were indications of how flimsy the structure really was.*"

In 2002 a Channel Four Secret History TV documentary alleged that de Havilland had ignored warnings that the Comet's fuselage would fail from fatigue and had refused to fatigue test it. Mike Ramsden, former de Havilland technical apprentice turned respected aviation journalist, denounced the suggestion as "*wilfully untrue.*"

This also shows that there are times when the margin between success and failure, triumph and tragedy can be very thin indeed. In the Comet's case the need to produce a structure light enough to cope with the modest thrust available from the Comet's Ghost engines meant the de Havilland engineers working to very fine margins. But it would be a gross distortion of the truth to imply they had done so

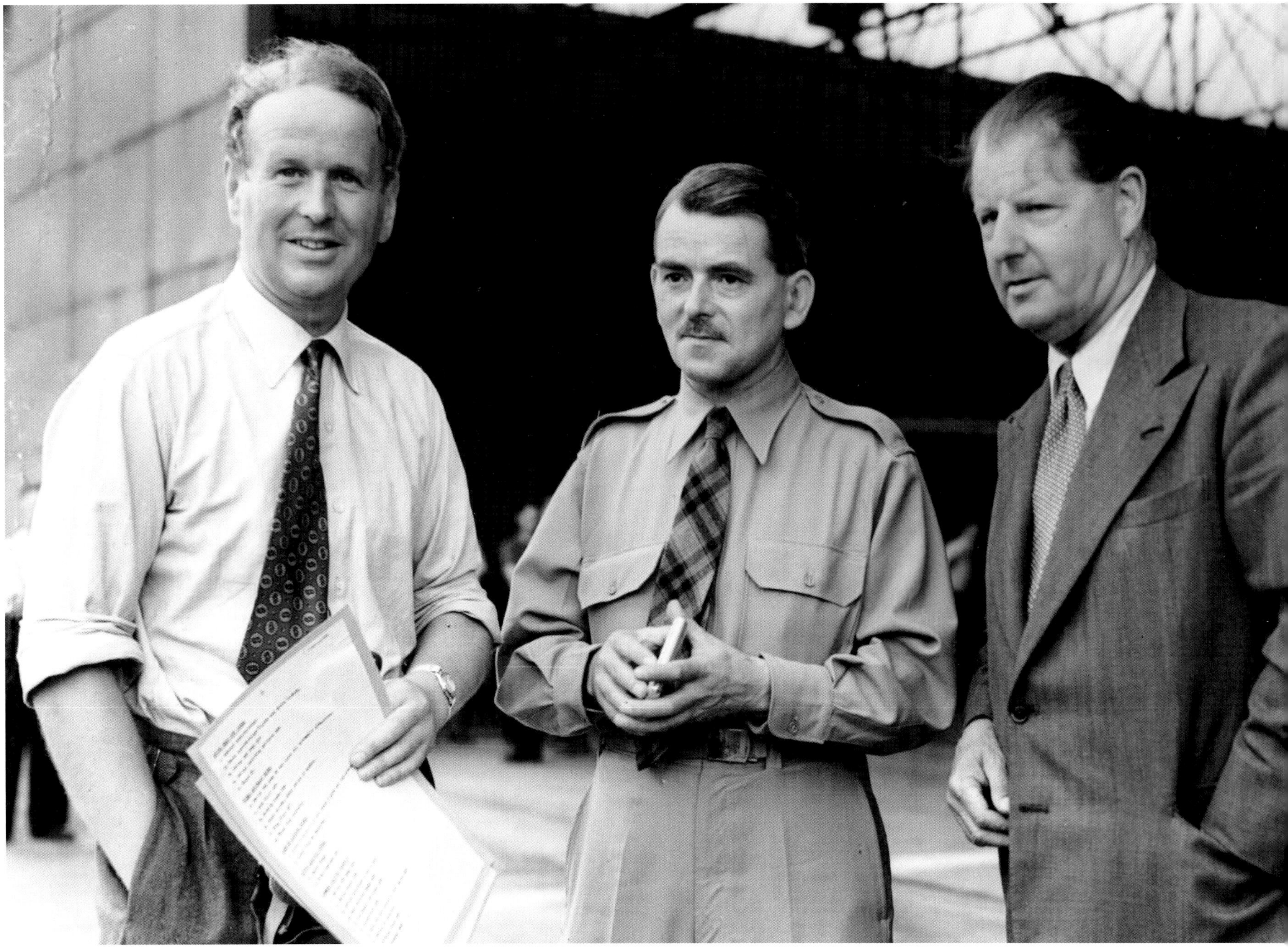

without much research and an unprecedented amount of testing.

One of the weight saving methods they employed was the use of adhesives to bond components rather than conventional rivets with all they entail. The result was a combination of light weight and strength as well as an aerodynamically clean outer skin.

Today "autoclaves", huge cylindrical ovens in which composite parts for advanced vehicles ranging from space craft to formula one race cars are produced, are at the cutting edge of technology. But back in the early 1950s de Havilland had to devise tools for simultaneously pressing together and heat-curing the bonds.

Many years later this accumulation of expertise was recognised by Airbus when it was seeking a partner to develop and manufacture wings. These wings continue to form an essential element of the success enjoyed by the multi-national airliner manufacturer's products. Indeed, de Havilland's Chester plant has been progressively developed to become what it is today: the world's most advanced

ABOVE: Men of the jet age: three of the key figures behind the world's first jet airliner pose for the camera on 27 July 1949, the day of the Comet's first flight. They are, left to right, John Cunningham, the test pilot, Sir Frank Whittle, whose ideas provided the initial motivation, and Maj Frank Halford, whose Ghost engines powered the first Comets.

THE FIRST COMMERCIAL JET AIRLINER IN THE WORLD

Pursued with the great enthusiasm worthy of such and enterprise, the first "Comet" was developed in a remarkably short time. Long before the first flight took place on 27 July 1949, the various sections of the aircraft, built at full scale, had been tested in special installations under conditions many times harsher than those likely to be found in flight. These tests were so accurately carried out that, from the moment it took the air, the "Comet" was found to be perfect in almost every detail. After 33 months of trials, certification and training, it took off on 2 May 1952, to make its first regular commercial flight.

The "Comet" is a low wing monoplane, with a wing sweep-back of 20°. Its span is 115 feet, length 93 feet and height 28 feet. The maximum take-off weight is 105,000 lbs. and the maximum landing weight 76,000 lbs. Equipped with four De Havilland Ghost turbojets, each giving 5,000 lbs. of thrust, the Comet is the world's first commercial jet airliner; in other words, it is propelled not by airscrews, but by the ejection of gases compressed and ignited in its engines.

The essential characteristic of the "Comet" is its speed, which, in cruising, reaches nearly 500 mph; nevertheless, when landing or taking-off, its speed is only slightly greater than that of conventional airliners of the same weight. The tricycle undercarriage consists of steerable twin nosewheels, and two main bogies, each with two pairs of two wheels. The brakes and shock-absorbers are particularly powerful. The fuel tanks contained in the wings and the central part of the fuselage, will hold 7000 gallons of kerosene, which is much less volatile than petrol. Fuel consumption varies considerably during the course of the journey. Very high when climbing, and when speed is low, it is reduced at the cruising speed to between 6000 and 7000 lbs an hour.

The cruising altitude, which varies in flight according to the air temperature and the trim of the aircraft, lies between 30,000 and 45,000 feet. But the excellent pressurisation equipment shields passengers from any effect of air rarification, keeping the air pressure within the cabin similar to that experienced in an ordinary aircraft at 8,000 feet. The cabin air, humidified and conditioned, is completely replaced every two minutes by the powerful ventilation system, while every passenger has an individual ventilator.

The "Comet" is an admirable medium stage-length airliner. Over these distances, its great speed cuts flying time very considerably.

Ref. 747.P.6 - 53 Printed in France PERCEVAL-PARIS

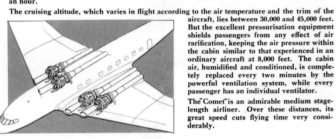

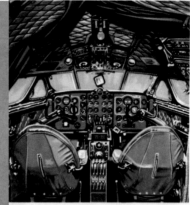

The cockpit

The galley

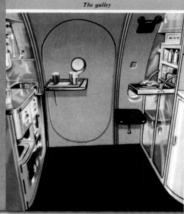

CLASSIC...

The De Havilland "Comet", which opens a new era in aviation, retains the classic lines of aircraft which have long proved their worth on the air routes of the world. Yet it seems racier, more elegant than its predecessors, with its tapered, swept-back swallow wings, thickening at the roots for the oval air intakes of its four jets, its slim, sleek fuselage, tall fin and butterfly tailplane. The clever blend of modern techniques with time-proved methods has been crowned with resounding success. Slashing flying time by half, and radically changing the conditions of air travel, the Comet has risen magnificently to the confidence placed in its design.

SIMPLE...

In industry, most mechanical progress leads inevitably to increased complexity. The Comet's engines, however, mark a return to extreme simplicity. There are no pistons or valves, no connecting rods or crankshafts; the only moving parts are the compressor and turbine, rotating on the same shaft. The output of power is smooth, without jerk or surge. Even by placing the hand on the cowling of one of the jets, it is impossible to say whether it is working or switched off!
It is evident that this simplification eases maintenance to a singular degree, and is a certain guarantee of reliability.

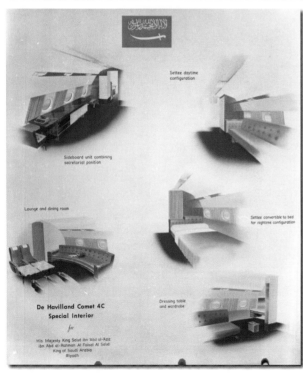

Settee daytime configuration
Sideboard unit combining secretarial position
Lounge and dining room
Settee convertible to bed for nightime configuration
Dressing table and wardrobe
De Havilland Comet 4C
Special Interior
for
His Majesty King Saud ibn Abd al-Aziz ibn Abd al-Rahman Al Faisal Al Saud
King of Saudi Arabia
Riyadh

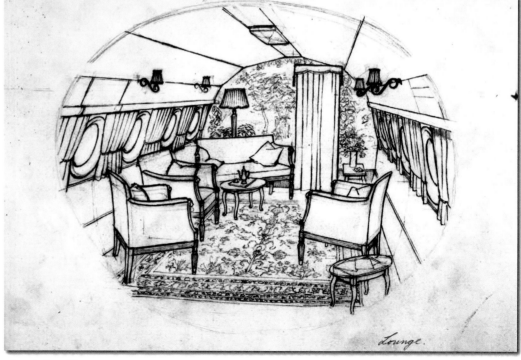

Lounge.

These de Havilland archive drawings provide a fascinating insight into the company's projection of the Comet. Of particular interest are those at bottom left because they depict the luxurious interior of the Saudi Arabian Royal Flight's Comet 4C, which has been called the world's first executive jet.

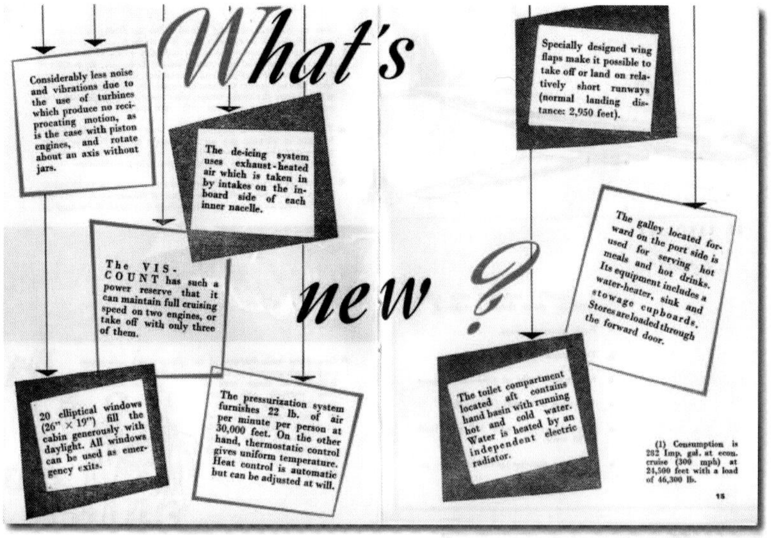

What's new?

Considerably less noise and vibrations due to the use of turbines which produce no reciprocating motion, as is the case with piston engines, and rotate about an axis without jars.

The de-icing system uses exhaust-heated air which is taken in by intakes on the inboard side of each inner nacelle.

The VISCOUNT has such a power reserve that it can maintain full cruising speed on two engines, or take off with only three of them.

20 elliptical windows (26" × 19") fill the cabin generously with daylight. All windows can be used as emergency exits.

The pressurization system furnishes 22 lb. of air per minute per person at 30,000 feet. On the other hand, thermostatic control gives uniform temperature. Heat control is automatic but can be adjusted at will.

Specially designed wing flaps make it possible to take off or land on relatively short runways (normal landing distance: 2,950 feet).

The galley located forward on the port side is used for serving hot meals and hot drinks. Its equipment includes a water-heater, sink and stowage cupboards. Stores are loaded through the forward door.

The toilet compartment located aft contains hand basin with running hot and cold water. Water is heated by an independent electric radiator.

(1) Consumption is 282 Imp. gal. at econ. cruise (300 mph) at 24,500 feet with a load of 46,300 lb.

15

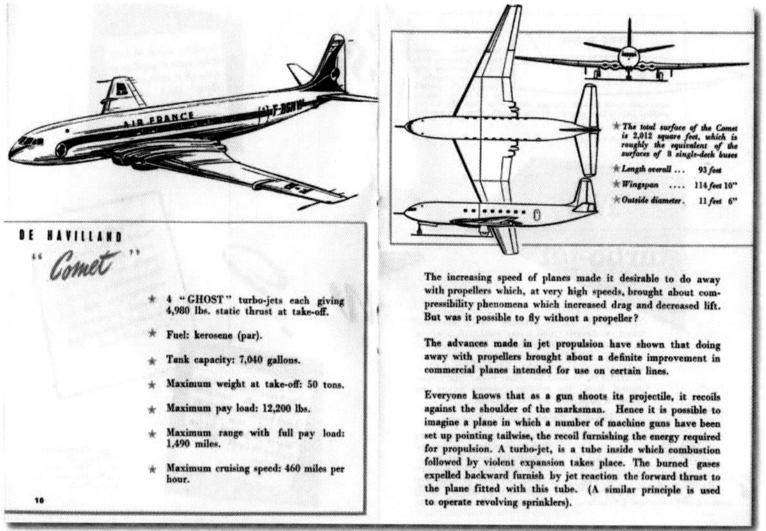

DE HAVILLAND
"Comet"

- ★ 4 "GHOST" turbo-jets each giving 4,980 lbs. static thrust at take-off.
- ★ Fuel: kerosene (par).
- ★ Tank capacity: 7,040 gallons.
- ★ Maximum weight at take-off: 50 tons.
- ★ Maximum pay load: 12,200 lbs.
- ★ Maximum range with full pay load: 1,490 miles.
- ★ Maximum cruising speed: 460 miles per hour.

16

★ *The total surface of the Comet is 2,012 square feet, which is roughly the equivalent of the surfaces of 8 single-deck buses*

★ *Length overall* ... 93 *feet*

★ *Wingspan* .... 114 *feet* 10"

★ *Outside diameter*. 11 *feet* 6"

The increasing speed of planes made it desirable to do away with propellers which, at very high speeds, brought about compressibility phenomena which increased drag and decreased lift. But was it possible to fly without a propeller?

The advances made in jet propulsion have shown that doing away with propellers brought about a definite improvement in commercial planes intended for use on certain lines.

Everyone knows that as a gun shoots its projectile, it recoils against the shoulder of the marksman. Hence it is possible to imagine a plane in which a number of machine guns have been set up pointing tailwise, the recoil furnishing the energy required for propulsion. A turbo-jet, is a tube inside which combustion followed by violent expansion takes place. The burned gases expelled backward furnish by jet reaction the forward thrust to the plane fitted with this tube. (A similar principle is used to operate revolving sprinklers).

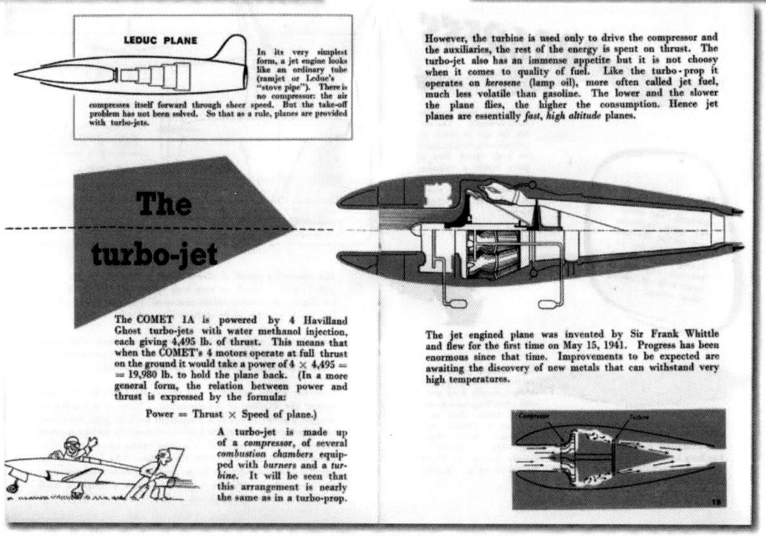

LEDUC PLANE

In its very simplest form, a jet engine looks like an ordinary tube (ramjet or Leduc's "stove pipe"). There is no compressor: the air compresses itself forward through sheer speed. But the take-off problem has not been solved. So that as a rule, planes are provided with turbo-jets.

The turbo-jet

The COMET 1A is powered by 4 Havilland Ghost turbo-jets with water methanol injection, each giving 4,495 lb. of thrust. This means that when the COMET's 4 motors operate at full thrust on the ground it would take a power of 4 × 4,495 = = 19,980 lb. to hold the plane back. (In a more general form, the relation between power and thrust is expressed by the formula:

Power = Thrust × Speed of plane.)

A turbo-jet is made up of a *compressor*, of several *combustion chambers* equipped with *burners* and a *turbine*. It will be seen that this arrangement is nearly the same as in a turbo-prop.

However, the turbine is used only to drive the compressor and the auxiliaries, the rest of the energy is spent on thrust. The turbo-jet also has an immense appetite but it is not choosy when it comes to quality of fuel. Like the turbo-prop it operates on *kerosene* (lamp oil), more often called jet fuel, much less volatile than gasoline. The lower and the slower the plane flies, the higher the consumption. Hence jet planes are essentially *fast, high altitude* planes.

The jet engined plane was invented by Sir Frank Whittle and flew for the first time on May 15, 1941. Progress has been enormous since that time. Improvements to be expected are awaiting the discovery of new metals that can withstand very high temperatures.

19

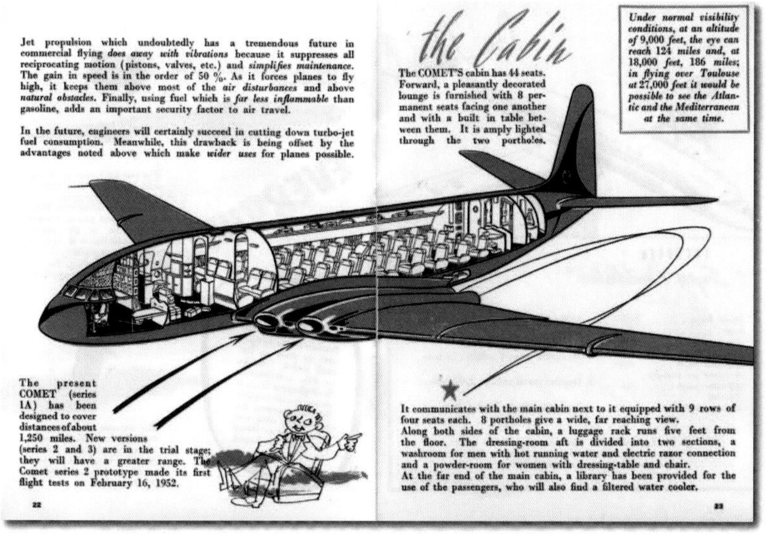

Jet propulsion which undoubtedly has a tremendous future in commercial flying *does away with vibrations* because it suppresses all reciprocating motion (pistons, valves, etc.) and *simplifies maintenance*. The gain in speed is in the order of 50 %. As it forces planes to fly high, it keeps them above most of the *air disturbances* and above *natural obstacles*. Finally, using fuel which is *far less inflammable* than gasoline, adds an important security factor to air travel.

In the future, engineers will certainly succeed in cutting down turbo-jet fuel consumption. Meanwhile, this drawback is being offset by the advantages noted above which make *wider uses* for planes possible.

The present COMET (series 1A) has been designed to cover distances of about 1,250 miles. New versions (series 2 and 3) are in the trial stage; they will have a greater range. The Comet series 2 prototype made its first flight tests on February 16, 1952.

22

the Cabin

The COMET'S cabin has 44 seats. Forward, a pleasantly decorated lounge is furnished with 8 permanent seats facing one another and with a built in table between them. It is amply lighted through the two portholes.

Under normal visibility conditions, at an altitude of 9,000 feet, the eye can reach 124 miles and, at 18,000 feet, 186 miles; in flying over Toulouse at 27,000 feet it would be possible to see the Atlantic and the Mediterranean at the same time.

It communicates with the main cabin next to it equipped with 9 rows of four seats each. 8 portholes give a wide, far reaching view.
Along both sides of the cabin, a luggage rack runs five feet from the floor. The dressing-room aft is divided into two sections, a washroom for men with hot running water and electric razor connection and a powder-room for women with dressing-table and chair.
At the far end of the main cabin, a library has been provided for the use of the passengers, who will also find a filtered water cooler.

23

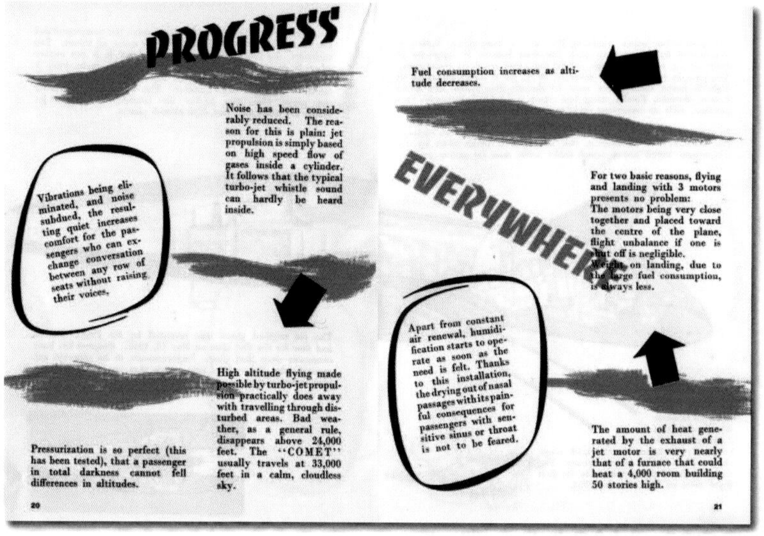

PROGRESS

Noise has been considerably reduced. The reason for this is plain: jet propulsion is simply based on high speed flow of gases inside a cylinder. It follows that the typical turbo-jet whistle sound can hardly be heard inside.

Vibrations being eliminated, and noise subdued, the resulting quiet increases comfort for the passengers who can exchange conversation between any row of seats without raising their voices.

High altitude flying made possible by turbo-jet propulsion practically does away with travelling through disturbed areas. Bad weather, as a general rule, disappears above 24,000 feet. The "COMET" usually travels at 33,000 feet in a calm, cloudless sky.

Pressurization is so perfect (this has been tested), that a passenger in total darkness cannot fell differences in altitudes.

20

EVERYWHERE

Fuel consumption increases as altitude decreases.

For two basic reasons, flying and landing with 3 motors presents no problem:
The motors being very close together and placed toward the centre of the plane, flight unbalance if one is shut off is negligible.
Weight, on landing, due to the large fuel consumption, is always less.

Apart from constant air renewal, humidification starts to operate as soon as the need is felt. Thanks to this installation, the drying out of nasal passages with its painful consequences for passengers with sensitive sinus or throat is not to be feared.

The amount of heat generated by the exhaust of a jet motor is very nearly that of a furnace that could heat a 4,000 room building 50 stories high.

21

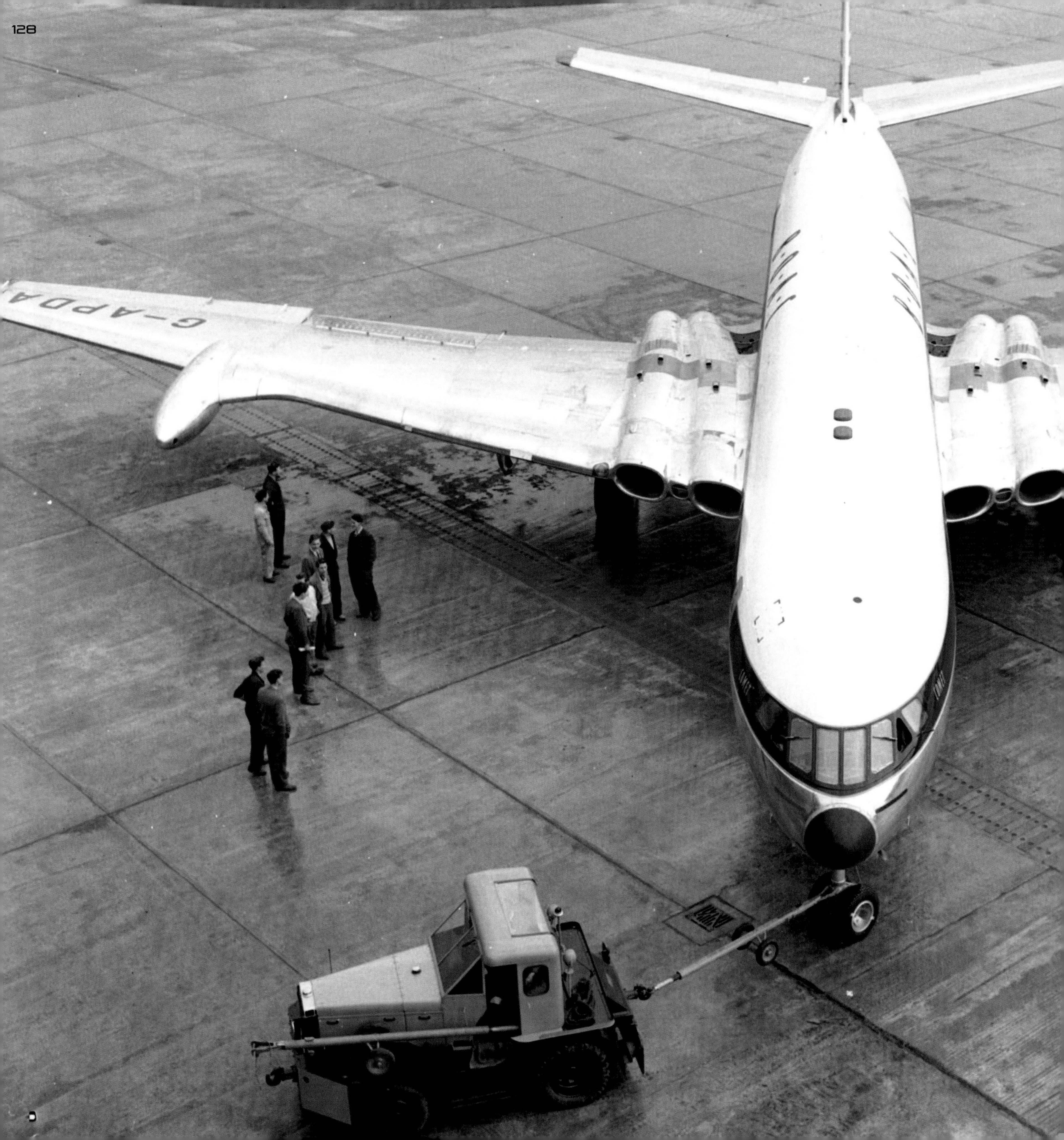
G-APDA

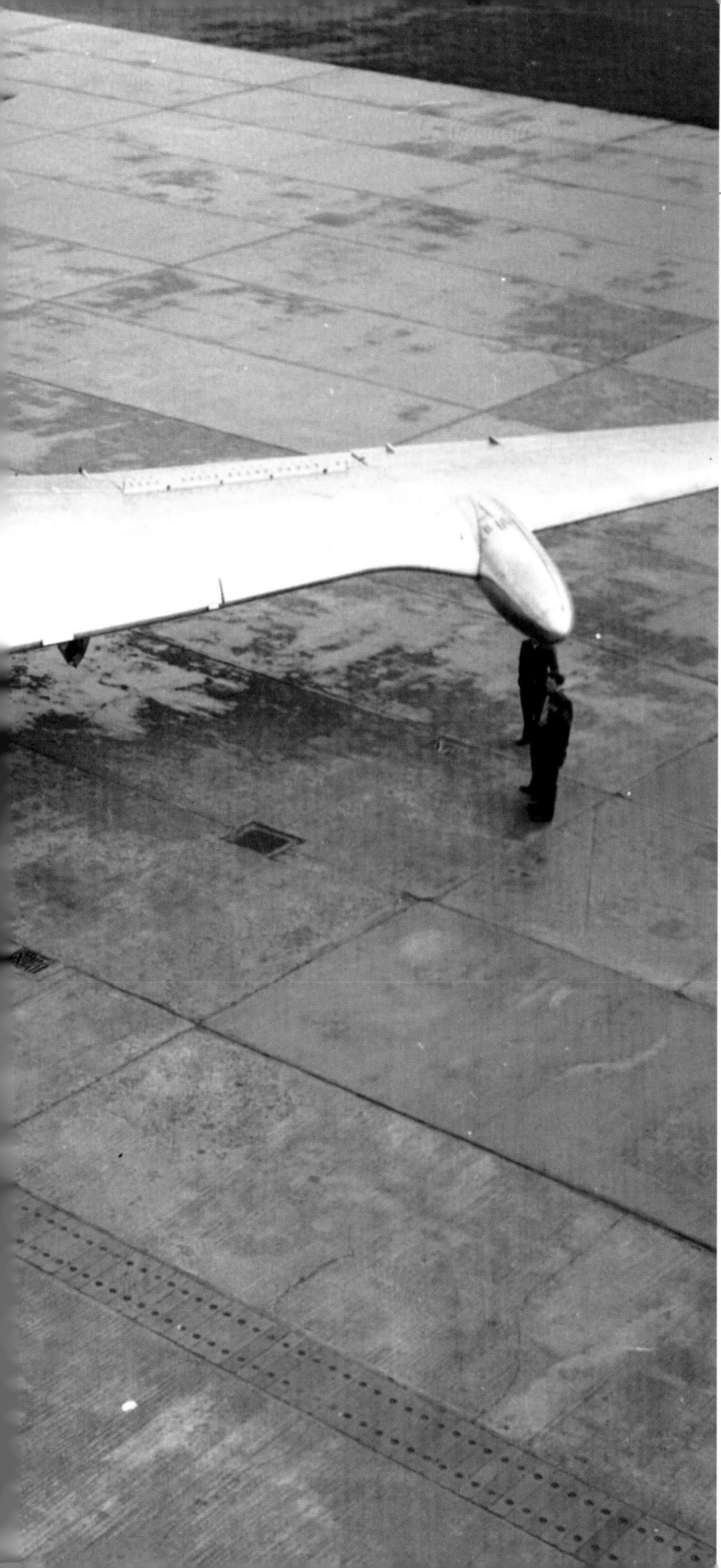

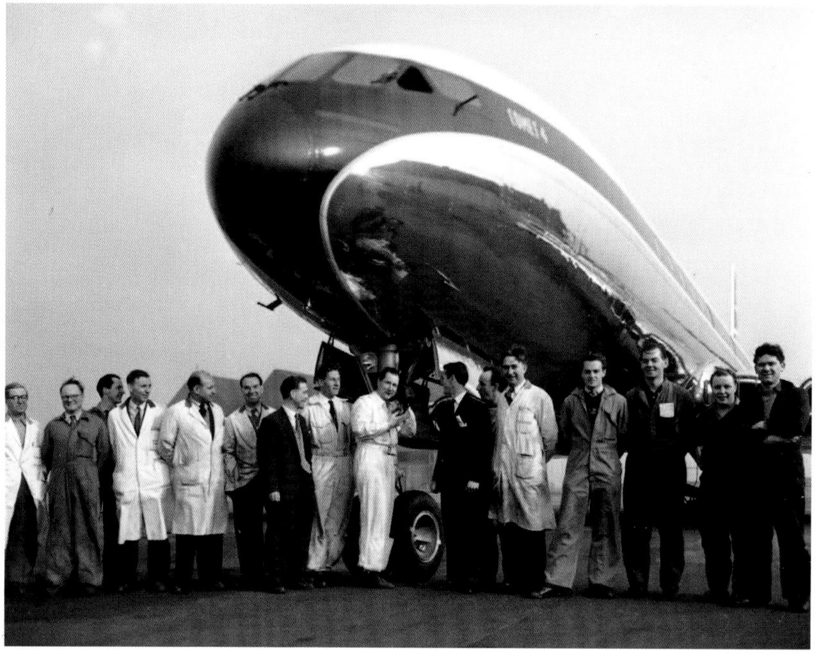

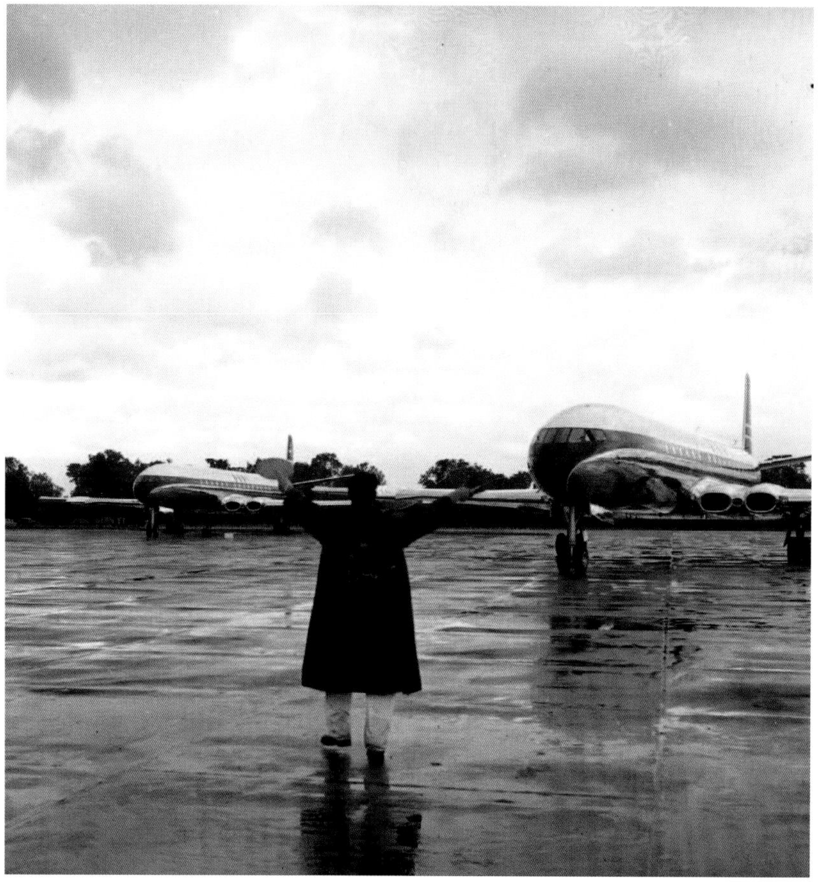

LEFT: G-APDA was the first Comet 4 to fly, taking to the sky, with John Cunningham in command, on 27 April 1958. In this picture, taken on 9 April, clearly shows the way the jet pipes of the inboard Avons were angled outwards.
TOP: On 4 October 1958 Comet 4 G-APDC flew the first Transatlantic jet airliner flight from London's Heathrow to New York. BOAC and de Havilland beat Pan Am and Boeing to that honour by almost a month.
ABOVE: `DC alongside `DB on 30 September 1958.

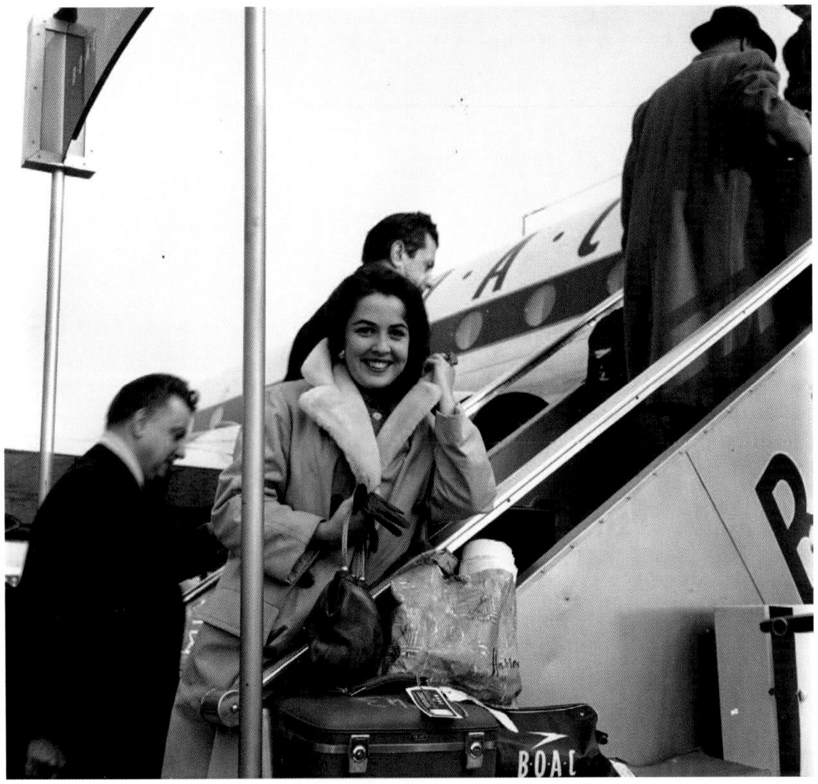
B·O·A·C

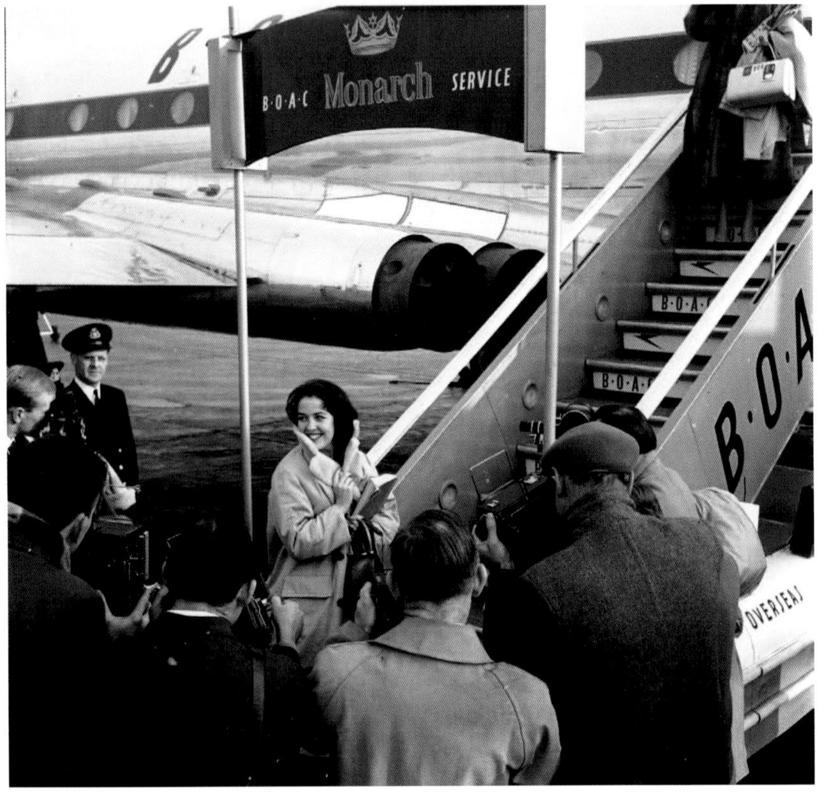
B·O·A·C Monarch SERVICE
B·O·A
OVERSEAS

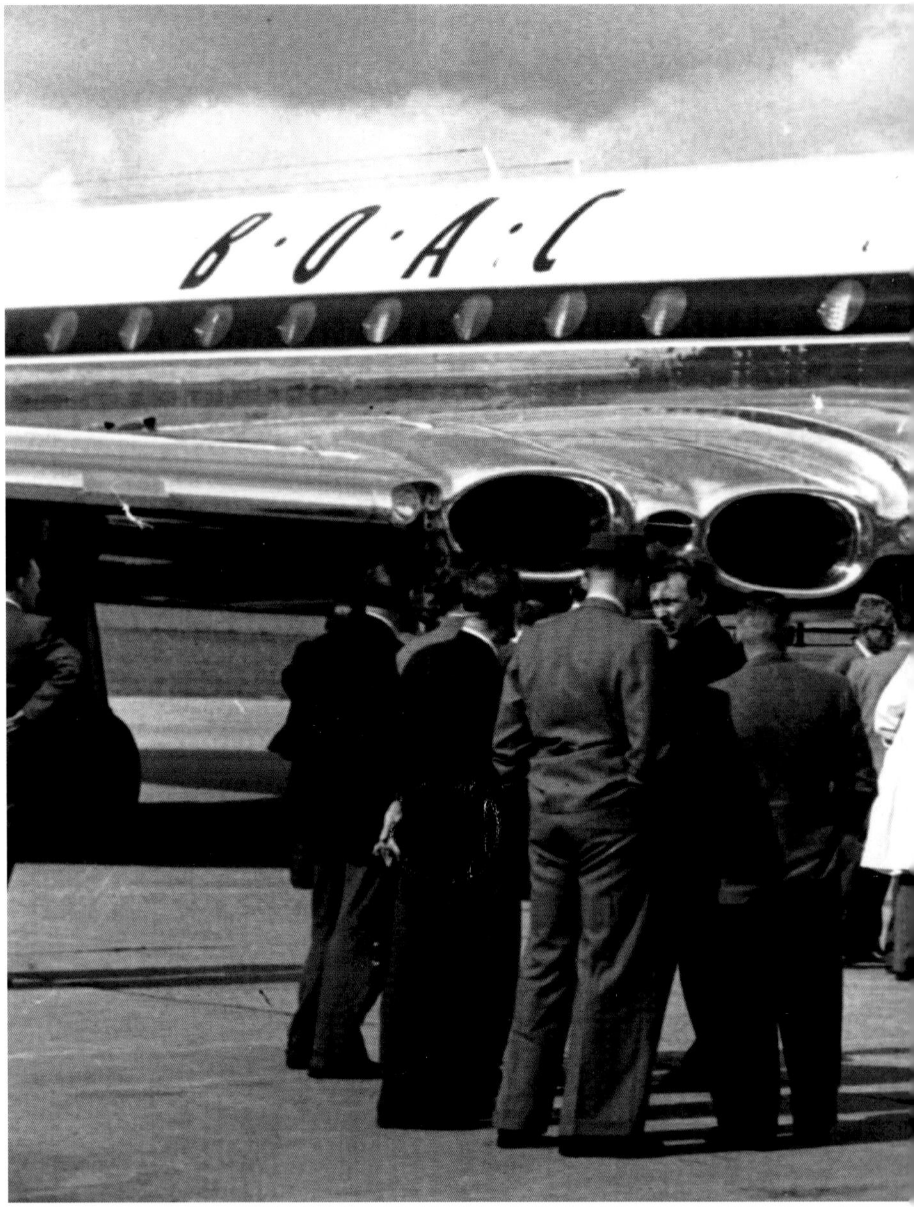
B·O·A·C

Departures and arrivals in the days when air travel was glamourous:
LEFT, TOP AND BOTTOM: BOAC's Transatlantic Monarch service was, for a while, the way to cross the pond. Chester-built G-APDE is pictured on 14 November 1958.
TOP, RIGHT: passengers disembark from `DE's forward door.

wing manufacturing facility.

In 1989, to mark the 40th anniversary of the Comet prototype's first flight Mike Ramsden penned an appreciation of the world's first jet airliner for the journal Flight which he now edited.

The Comet, he wrote, was quite simply, the *"mother"* of the many thousands of jet transport aircraft that came after it.

Tony Fairbrother, flight test observer on that 1949 maiden flight, put it another way. He recalled: *"The world changed as our wheels left the ground."*

Both were, of course, correct. But the Comet's legacy is more even than that of the world's first jet airliner.

For years historians have been debating the extent to which the 1954 Comet

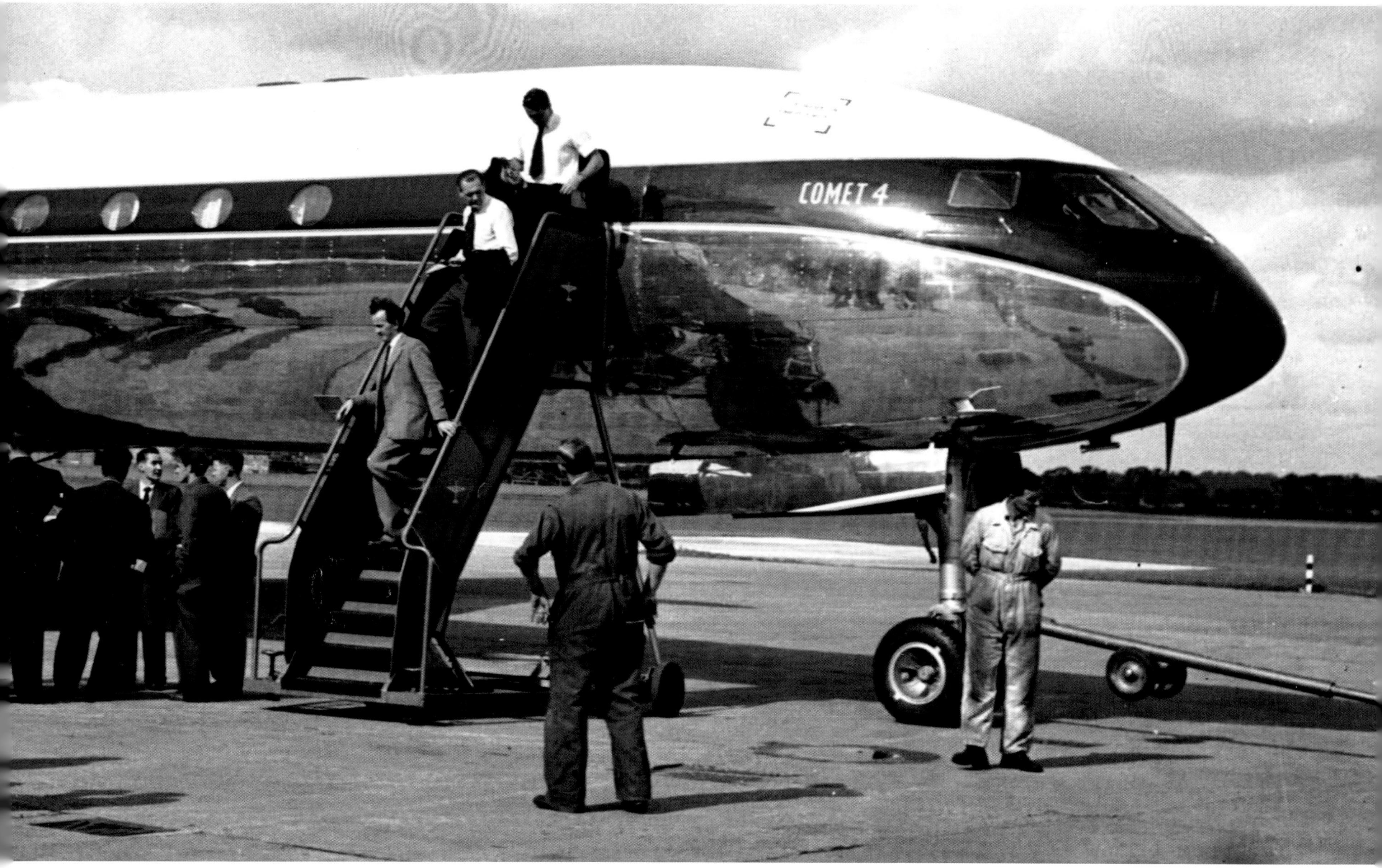
COMET 4

losses damaged the reputation of Britain's aircraft industry. But it seems unlikely that Airbus would have turned to Hawker Siddeley, successor to de Havilland, for advanced wing design and construction if there had been such damage.

On the other hand it is just as unrealistic to suggest that without the accidents the Comet would have enjoyed stunning export success and provided a springboard for British manufacturers to offer a more credible challenge to their US competitors.

Prof Keith Hayward, research director of the Royal Aeronautical Society, has pointed out that of the aircraft types identified by the wartime Brabazon Committee only the Vickers Viscount and the de Havilland Dove can be judged as successful in pure sales terms.

"The Viscount was a success towards the late 1950s," he said, *"but it was the Comet which had been seen as the way for the aircraft industry to make its way in the world,"* he said.

The loss of the two Comets changed that profoundly. Hayward said: *"The government stepped in with an emergency bail-out for de Havilland by taking on and reinforcing the order for Comets for Transport Command, effectively keeping the company and the design alive. Even though de Havilland was pushing hard to take on the Americans the government was insisting on the Transport Command order being fulfilled first."*

Another intriguing question is whether or not the Comet's problems had an impact on projects like the promising Vickers V.1000 which was cancelled in

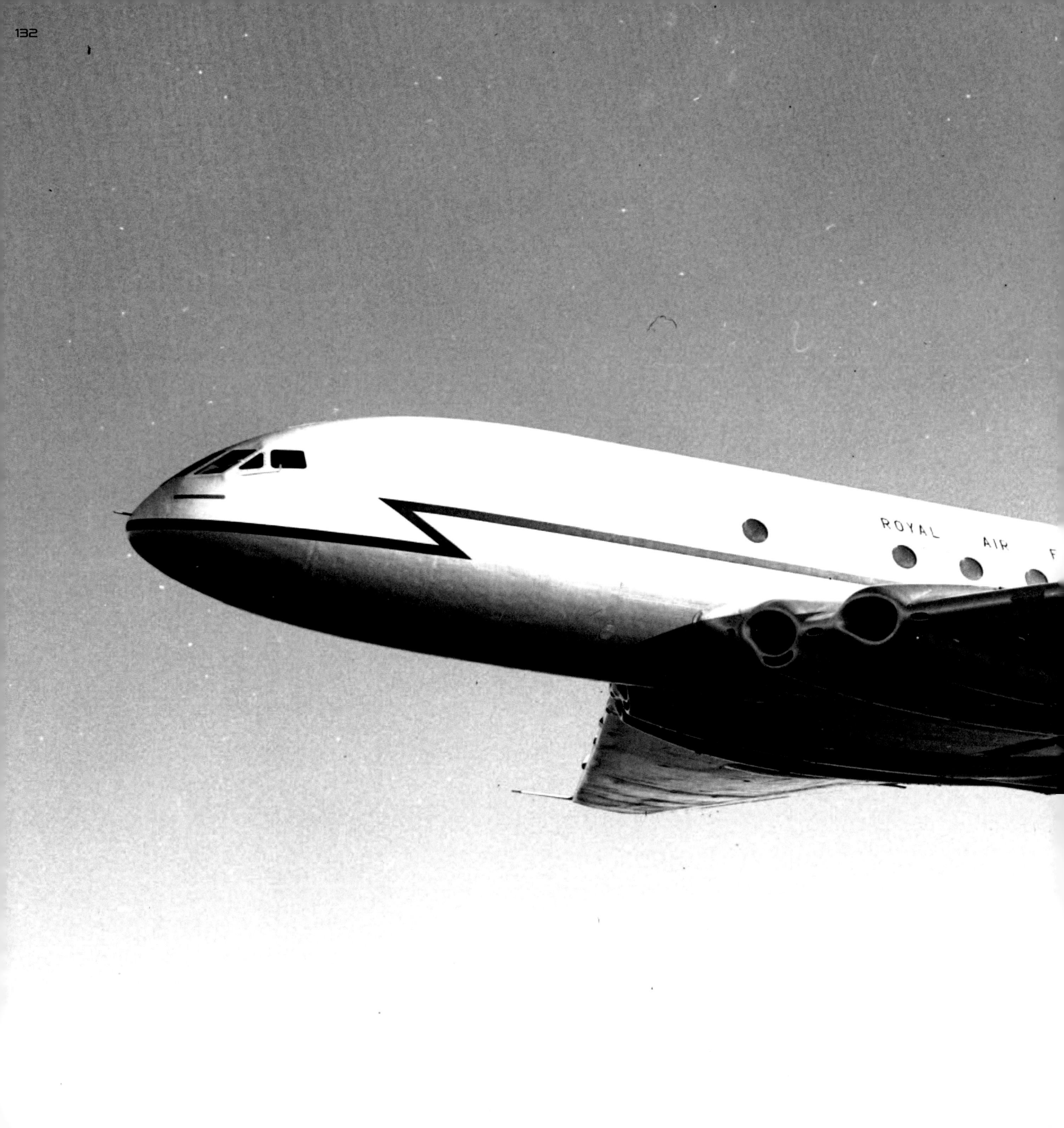
ROYAL AIR F

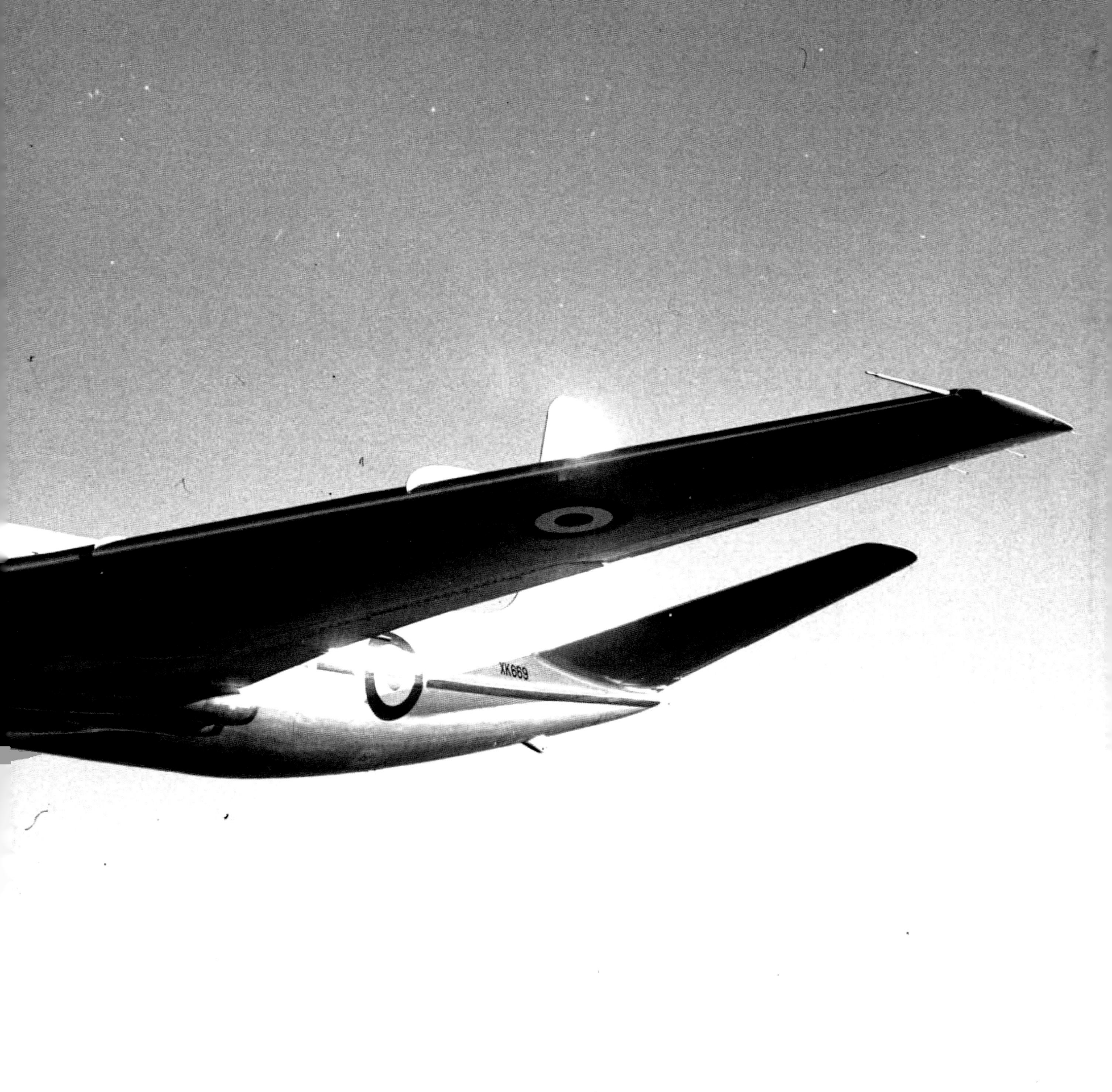
XK669

RAF T2 XK669, taken in December 1955, accentuates the Comet's grace and elegance. Originally ordered by BOAC and registered G-AMXB, the aircraft was delivered to 216 Sqn's Lyneham, Wiltshire base in June 1956 for crew training.

1955. On one level the Comet losses may have supplied BOAC with a ready-made argument for buying American and become the starting point for what was to become a very strong preference by Britain's nationalised airlines.

The V.1000's cancellation has been seen as a major blunder in the history of discarded British airliner projects. Yet it might have been a flawed design. Prof Hayward told the author: *"The buried engines would have been a nightmare to service. The Comet 4 was a very fine platform, serving the inclusive tour industry well - and look how long the basic airframe survived in Nimrod. But how good an aircraft was it to maintain with those buried engines compared with the 707?"*

Certainly, without the Comet losses BOAC would probably have found it more difficult to resist pressure to buy the V.1000. And the government would possibly have had the encouragement it needed to support the Vickers programme.

It is, though, true that while the Comet 1 was not generally an economic proposition the Comet 3 might well have attracted substantial orders. Whether they would have been sufficient to cause sleeplessness in Seattle (or Santa Monica) is another matter. Was Pan Am's canny Juan Trippe serious about wanting Comet 3s or was he simply trying to goad Boeing and Douglas into building something more suited to Pan Am's needs?

Whatever the answer to that question, the US aircraft manufacturing industry's true capability was graphically illustrated when Boeing delivered the first 707 to Pan Am within less than a year of the model's first flight. This demonstrated an unmatched production and technical capability.

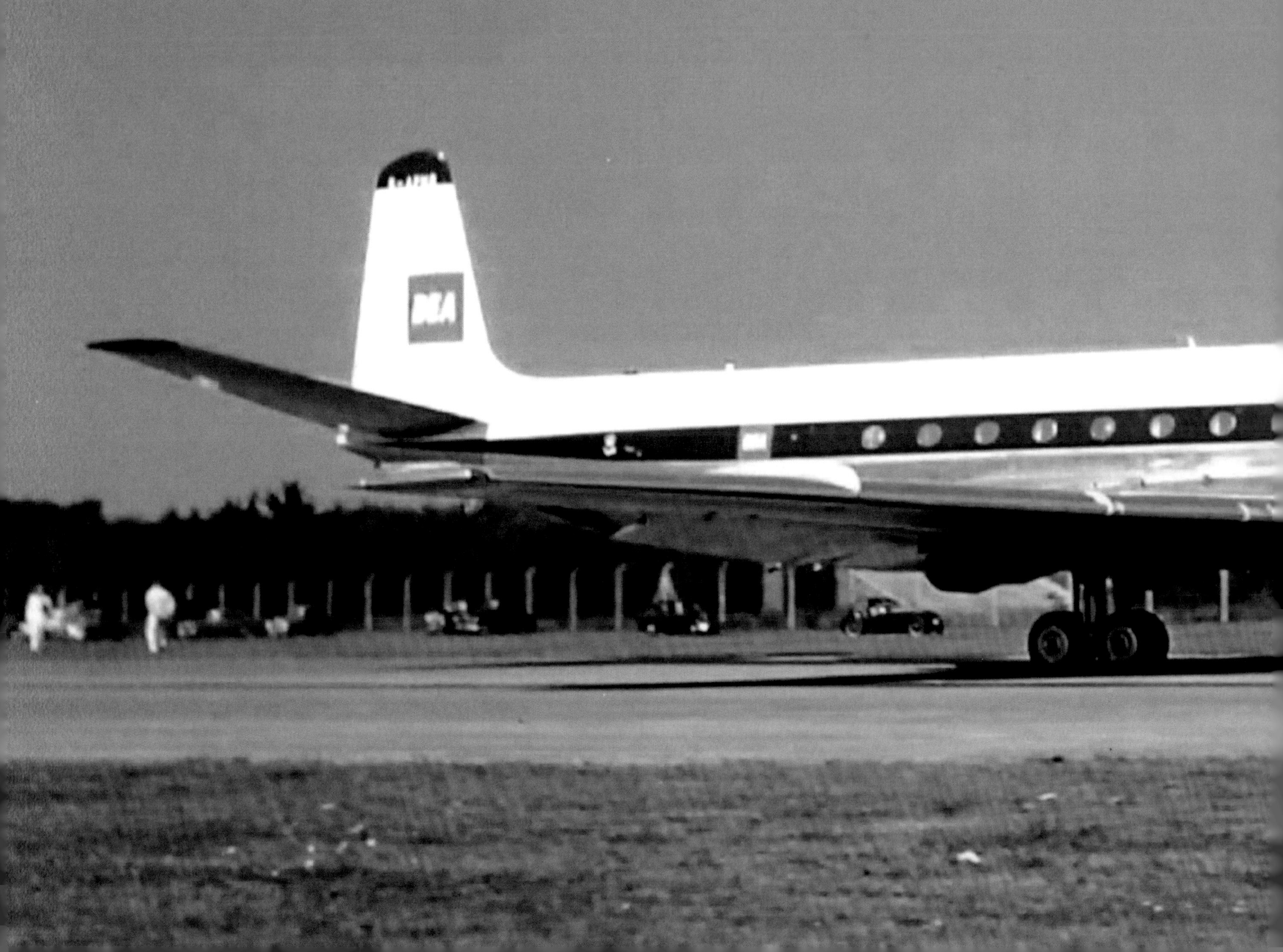
BEA

By 1960 161 707-320s had been built together with 208 DC-8s of all types. By comparison, a total of 75 Comet 4s, by far the bulk of production, had been turned out. So the Comet story which started with the Brits trying to leap-frog the Americans ended with the reverse happening.

So to what extent had the Comet's troubles and the well-publicised accident investigation findings contributed to this success? Sir Geoffrey de Havilland was never in any doubt. In 1960, five years before his death, he was reflecting wryly on what had happened when he said he was proud of the part his company had played in the development of the American airliner industry. *"I got the impression he was playing the irony-card,"* Arthur Ord-Hume, aircraft engineer and writer recalled in conversation with the author.

"Boeing, Douglas and Lockheed all benefited from Hatfield's pioneering work," Ord-Hume said. *"The characteristic British attitude of generously wanting to share information around the world meant that everything about the Comet and its design was already in the hands of its potential competitors around the world."*

But perhaps the Comet's real legacy to the aviation industry and, indeed, the world at large was that it showed not only that jet airliners were feasible but also that they represented the only way to travel.

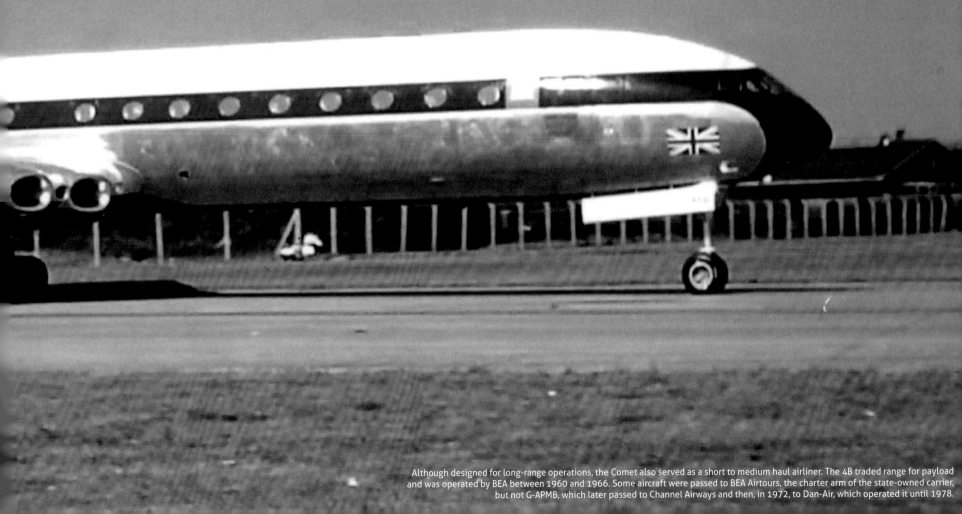

Although designed for long-range operations, the Comet also served as a short to medium haul airliner. The 4B traded range for payload and was operated by BEA between 1960 and 1966. Some aircraft were passed to BEA Airtours, the charter arm of the state-owned carrier, but not G-APMB, which later passed to Channel Airways and then, in 1972, to Dan-Air, which operated it until 1978.

WHERE TO SEE THEM

Several complete Comet airframes have survived and are preserved in museums together with nose sections of others. The majority of complete aircraft are Comet 4s and, perhaps not surprisingly, most survivors are in the UK.

The only complete Comet 1 (c/n 06022) is displayed at the RAF Museum, Cosford. Although in BOAC colours and bearing the registration G-APAS, the aircraft was originally delivered to Air France and registered F-BGNZ. It was withdrawn with the grounding of Comet 1s in 1954, subsequently acquired by the Ministry of Supply and converted to Comet 1XB standard at de Havilland's Chester plant. As XM823 the aircraft was used on infra-red missile research, initially for Red Top and Firestreak. It was later operated at Edwards Air Force base for USAF trials.

The sole surviving Comet fuselage with the original square-shaped windows is part of a Comet 1A registered F-BGNX (c/n 06020). It is currently on display at the de Havilland Aircraft Museum in Hertfordshire. The collection also includes the nose section of 2R XK695 (c/n 06030), and part of a Comet 2 simulator.

Comet C2 XK699 Sagittarius (c/n 06035), which subsequently received the maintenance serial 7971M, was on display as a gate guardian at RAF Lyneham, Wiltshire from 1987 having been unveiled there by Princess Anne. In 2012 the closure of the base meant a move to Cosford was scheduled but extensive airframe corrosion meant a change of plan. Accordingly, 32ft (10m) of the aircraft's forward fuselage was removed in an operation funded by the scrap value of the rest of the airframe. What remains of the only surviving C2 is now on display at the Boscombe Down Aviation Collection at Old Sarum airfield, Wiltshire.

The nose section of Comet C2/R2 XK659 (c/n 06023) is on display at the Al Mahatta aviation museum, Sharjah, United Arab Emirates, having been previously exhibited in the public viewing area at London's Gatwick airport. As G-AMXA it was the first C2, making its maiden flight in 1953. The RAF's first C2, it was later modified by Marshall's of Cambridge as an R2 for the gathering of electronic intelligence with 51 Sqn RAF. After retirement from flying it was acquired by the Strathallan Collection in Scotland before being scrapped in 1990. All that remains is the nose section which is displayed in BOAC colours.

The Imperial War Museum collection at Duxford, Cambridgeshire has Comet 4 G-APDB (c/n 6403) in its AirSpace building. This historic aircraft was delivered to BOAC in September 1958 and operated the first jet service from New York to London the following month. The aircraft was later acquired by Dan-Air but is now displayed in BOAC colours. Comet 4B G-APYD (c/n 6438) is stored at the Science Museum's Wroughton, Wiltshire facility. This aircraft was delivered to Olympic Airways of Greece in May 1960 and named Queen Olga. It was returned to BEA in

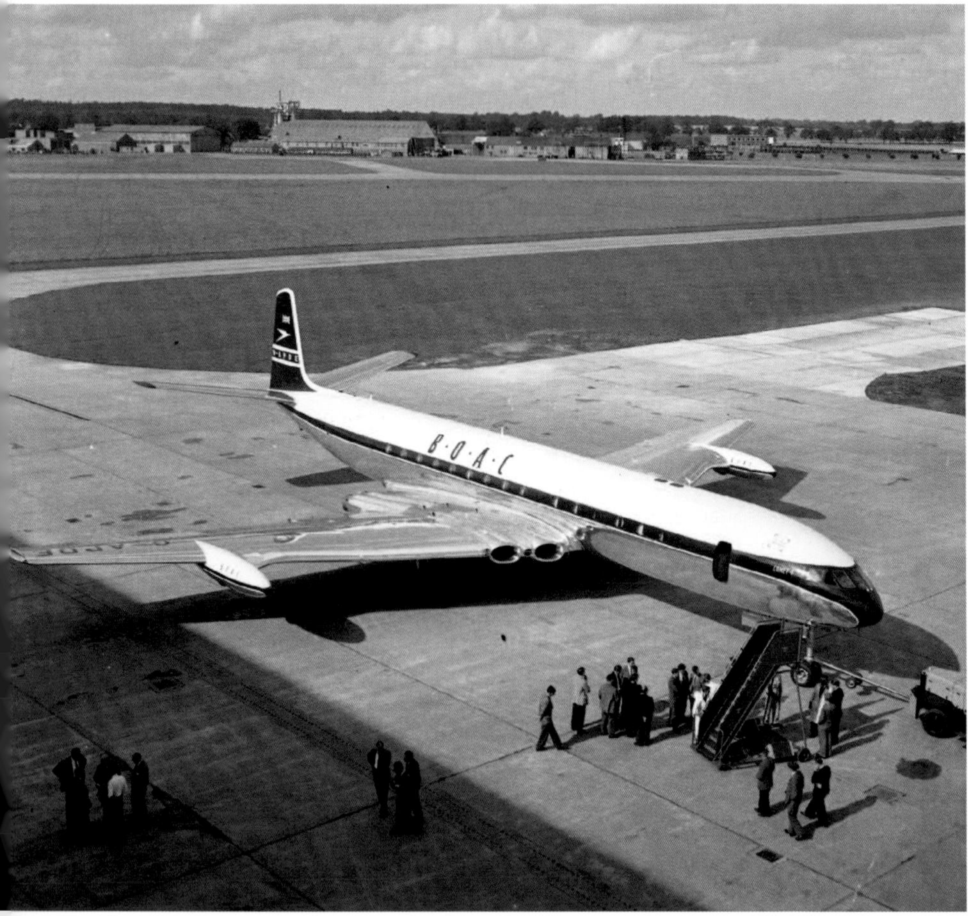
B.O.A.C

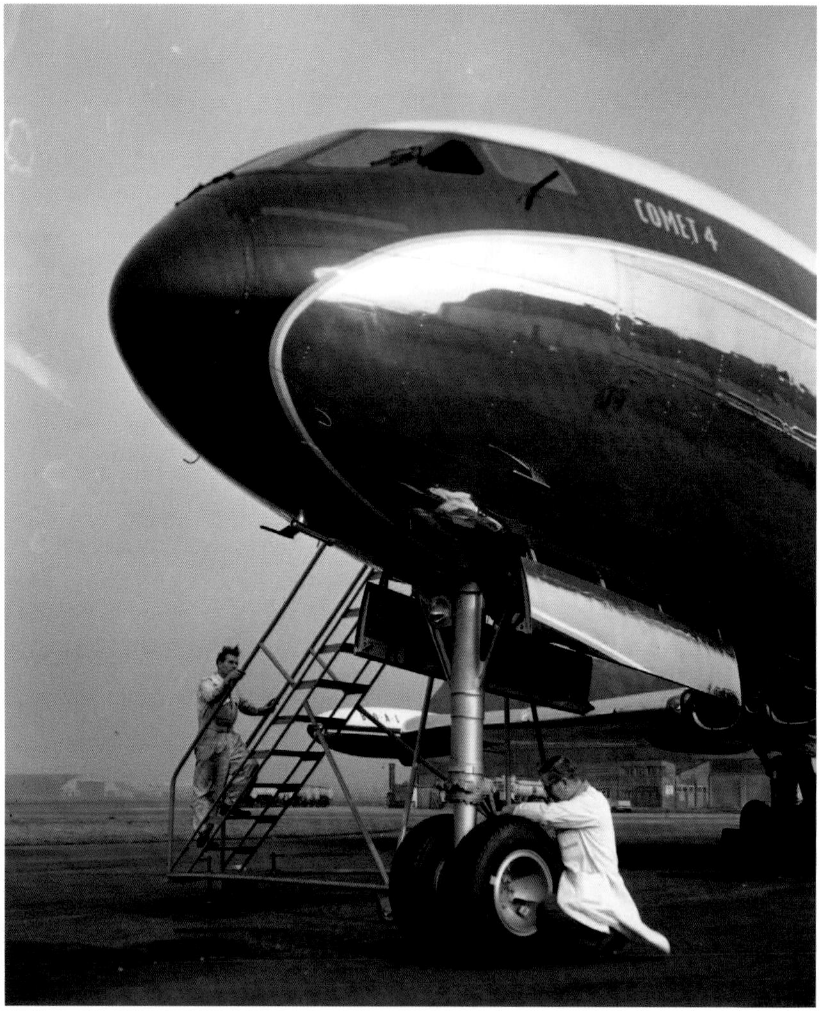
COMET 4

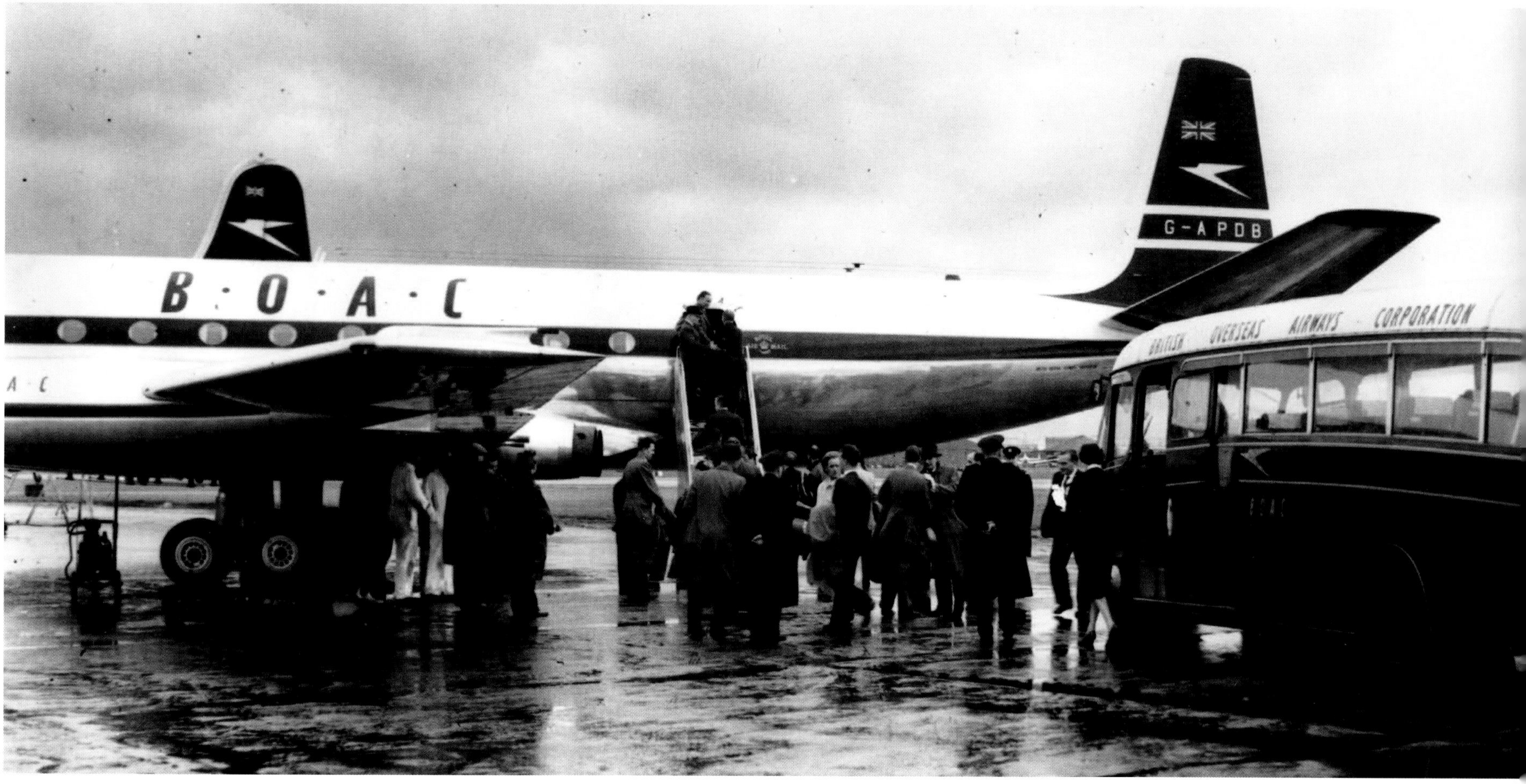
B·O·A·C
G-APDB
BRITISH OVERSEAS AIRWAYS CORPORATION

1969, acquired by Dan-Air in 1972 and retired to Wroughton for preservation. It is still in Dan-Air colours.

On display at Scotland's National Museum of Flight at East Fortune Airfield near Edinburgh is Comet 4C G-BDIX (c/n 6471). The aircraft is painted in the colours of Dan-Air with which it served from September 1975 until September 1981 when it was flown to East Fortune for preservation. It had previously served with the RAF as XR399.

The last Comet to fly, Comet 4C XS235 (c/n 6473) is now part of the Cold War Jet Collection at Bruntingthorpe Aerodrome, Leicestershire. The collection also includes examples of such RAF types as Victor, Hunter, Canberra, Lightning and Buccaneer. Fast taxi runs are regularly conducted with the Comet and over the last decade the idea of restoring Canopus, to flying condition has been proposed by the volunteers who maintain the aircraft. Also at Bruntingthorpe is a Hawker Siddeley Nimrod MR2.

The nose section of Comet 4C G-BEEX (c/n 6458) is on display at the North East Aircraft Museum near Washington, Tyne and Wear. The aircraft, previously operated by Egyptair as SU-ALM, was bought by Dan-Air for spares and scrapped in the mid-1970s with the nose section retained for display.

Not all the surviving Comets are in the UK. Comet C4/4C G-BDIW (c/n 06470) made the last Comet commercial flight with Dan-Air in November 1980. It had been acquired from the RAF (by whom it was known as XR398) and was retired to Dusseldorf in February 1981 for preservation. It is now exhibited at Flugausstellung Leo Junior, a private aviation museum in the town of Hermeskeil in the German state of Rhineland-Palatinate.

In the USA Comet 4C (c/n 6424) is undergoing long-term restoration at the Museum of Flight, near Seattle, Washington. The aircraft was the first 4C to be built and in October 1959 was delivered to the Mexican airline Mexicana with which it inaugurated the Golden Aztec service between Mexico City and Los Angeles in July 1960. In 1972 the aircraft was acquired by Westernair of Albuquerque, New Mexico which registered it in the US as N888WA. With the end of its operational career it was painted in BOAC colours and acquired by the Seattle Museum of Flight in 1994.

Another ex-Mexicana Comet 4C is c/n 6443, which is located at the Parque Zoológico Irapuato, Guanajuato, Mexico. The aircraft was originally delivered to Mexicana in November 1960 and after a crash landing at Mexico City in 1970 it too was sold to Westernair and registered N777WA.

PRODUCTION LIST

CONSTRUCTION NO.	SRS	REGISTRATION	CUSTOMER	FIRST FLIGHT	DELIVERY
06001	1	G-ALVG	Min of Supply	27 Jul 49	01 Sep 49
06002	1	G-ALZK	MoS	27 Jul 50	02 Apl 51
06003	1	G-ALYP	BOAC	09 Jan 51	08 Apl 52
06004	1	G-ALYR	BOAC	28 Jul 51	17 May 52
06005	1	G-ALYS	BOAC	08 Sep 51	04 May 52
06006	1	G-ALYT	MoS	16 Feb 52	01 Mar 52
06007	1	G-ALYU	BOAC	13 Dec 51	06 Mar 52
06008	1	G-ALYV	BOAC	09 Apl 52	23 Apl 52
06009	1	G-ALYW	BOAC	25 May 52	14 Jun 52
06010	1	G-ALYX	BOAC	09 Jul 52	25 Jul 52
06011	1	G-ALYY	BOAC	10 Sep 52	23 Sep 52
06012	1	G-ALYZ	BOAC	23 Sep 52	30 Sep 52
06013	1A	G-ANAV	(Canadian Pacific) BOAC	11 Aug 52	12 Aug 53
06014	1A	CF-CUN	Canadian Pacific	24 Dec 52	02 Mar 52
06015	1A	F-BGSA	UTA	13 Nov 52	11 Dec 52
06016	1A	F-BGSB	UTA	21 Jan 53	19 Feb 53
06017	1A	VC5301	RCAF	21 Feb 53	18 Mar 53
06018	1A	VC5302	RCAF	25 Mar 53	13 Apl 53
06019	1A	F-BGSC	UTA	15 Apl 53	30 Apl 53
06020	1A	F-BGNX	Air France	13 Nov 52	11 Dec 52
06021	1A	F-BGNY	Air France	22 May 53	07 Jul 53
06022	1A	F-BGNZ	Air France	16 Mar 53	22 Jul 53
06023	2R	(G-AMXA) XK655	(BOAC) RAF	29 Aug 53	17 Feb 56
06024	2T	(G-AMXB)XK669	(BOAC) RAF	03Nov 53	08 Jun 56
06025	2R	(G-AMXC) XK659	(BOAC) RAF	25 Nov 53	12 Jul 57
06026	2E	(G-AMXD) XN453	(BOAC) RAF	20 Aug 54	29 Aug 57
06027	2R	(G-AMXE) XK663	(BOAC) RAF	18 Jul 55	19 Apl 57
06028	T2	(G-AMXF) XK670	(BOAC) RAF	12 Mar 56	07 Jun 56
06029	C2	(G-AMXG) XK671	RAF	16 Jul 56	22 Aug 56
06030	C2	(G-AMXH) XK695	RAF	21 Aug 56	14 Sep 56
06031	C2	(G-AMHI) XK696 `	RAF	29 Sep 56	14 Nov 56
06032	C2	(G-AMHJ) XK697	RAF	17 Nov 56	12 Dec 56
06033	2E	(G-AMXK) XV144	MoS	10 Jul 57	26 Aug 57
06034	C2	XK698	RAF	13 Dec 56	09 Jan 57
06035	C2	XK699	RAF	02 Feb 57	20 Feb 57
06036	2	test airframe	MoS		
06037	C2	XK715	RAF	26 Apl 57	22 May 57
06038	Not completed				
06039 – 06044	Not built				
06045	C2	XK716	RAF	06 May 57	07 May 57
06401	4	G-APDA	BOAC	27 Apl 58	24 Feb 59
06402	4	test airframe			
06403	4	G-APDB	BOAC	27 Jul 58	30 Sep 58
06404	4	G-APDC	BOAC	23 Sep 58	30 Sep 58
06405	4	G-APDD	BOAC	05 Nov 58	18 Nov 58
06406	4	G-APDE	BOAC	20 Sep 58	02 Oct 58
06407	4	G-APDF	BOAC	11 Dec 58	31 Dec 58
06408	4	LV-PLM	Aerolineas Argentinas	11 Dec 58	02 Mar 59
06409	4	G-APDH	BOAC	21 Nov 58	06 Dec 58
6410	4	LV-PLO	Aerolineas Argentinas	25 Feb 59	18 Mar 59
6411	4	LV-PLP	Aerolineas Argentinas	24 Mar 59	02 May 59
6412	4	G-APDK	BOAC	02 Jan 59	12 Feb 59
6413	4	G-APDL	BOAC	27 Apl 59	06 May 59
6414	4	G-APDM	BOAC	21 Mar 59	16 Apl 59
6415	4	G-APDN	BOAC	29 May 59	19 Jun 59
6416	4	G-APDO	BOAC	29 Apl 59	14 May 59

CONSTRUCTION NO.	SRS	REGISTRATION	CUSTOMER	FIRST FLIGHT	DELIVERY
6417	4	G-APDP	BOAC	29 May 59	11 Jun 59
6418	4	G-APDR	BOAC	09 Jul 59	20 Jul 59
6419	4	G-APDS	BOAC	06 Aug 59	16 Aug 59
6420	4	G-APDT	BOAC	02 Oct 59	19 Oct 59
6421	4B	G-APMA	BEA	27 Jun 59	20 Dec 59
6422	4B	G-APMB	BEA	17 Aug 59	09 Nov 59
6423	4B	G-APMC	BEA	01 Oct 59	16 Nov 59
6424	4C	XA-NAR	Mexicana	31 Oct 59	08 Jun 60
6425	4C	XA-NAS	Mexicana	03 Dec 59	
6426	4B	G-APMF	BEA	05 Jan 60	27 Jan 60
6427	4	G-APDG	BOAC	12 Nov 59	28 Nov 59
6428	4	G-APDI	BOAC	07 Dec 59	18 Dec 59
6429	4	G-APDJ	BOAC	23 Dec 59	11 Jan 60
6430	4	LV-POY	Aerolineas Argentinas	15 Feb 60	08 Mar 60
6431	4	VP-KPJ	East African Airways	14 Jul 60	25 Jul 60
6432	4	LV-POZ	Aerolineas Argentinas	18 Feb 60	19 Mar 60
6433	4	VP-KPK	East African Airways	28 Jul 60	06 Sep 60
6434	4	LV-PPA	Aerolineas Argentinas	02 Jul 60	26 Jul 60
6435	4B	G-APMD	BEA	17 Mar 60	29 Mar 60
6436	4B	G-APME	BEA	26 Apl 60	10 May 60
6437	4B	SX-DAK	Olympic Airways	07 Apl 60	26 Apl 60
6438	4B	SX-DAL	Olympic Airways	03 May 60	14 May 60
6439	4C	SU-ALC	Misrair/United Arab Airways	21 May 60	10 Jun 60
6440	4B	G-APZM	BEA/Olympic	30 Jun 60	14 Jul 60
6441	4C	SU-ALD	Misrair/United Arab Airways	15 Jun 60	26 Jun 60
6442	4B	G-APMG	BEA	25 Jul 60	31 Jul 60
6443	4C	XA-NAT	Mexicana	07 Oct 60	29 Nov 60
6444	4C	SU-ALE	United Arab Airways	22 Nov 60	23 Dec 60
6445	4C	OD-ADR	Middle East Airlines	03 Dec 60	19 Dec 60
6446	4C	OD-ADQ	Middle East Airlines	04 Feb 61	15 Feb 61
6447	4B	G-ARDI	BEA/Olympic	18 Mar 61	25 Mar 61
6448	4C	OD-ADS	Middle East Airlines	05 Mar 61	14 Mar 61
6449	4B	G-ARCO	BEA	05 Apl 61	13 Apl 61
6450	4C	OD-ADT	Middle East Airlines	09 Mar 61	18 Mar 61
6451	4B	G-ARCP	BEA	11 Apl 61	19 Apl 61
6452	4B	G-ARJE	BEA	04 May 61	15 May 61
6453	4B	G-ARGM	BEA	27 Apl 61	06 May 61
6454	4C	SU-ALL	United Arab Airlines	30 May 61	12 Jun 61
6455	4B	G-ARJL	BEA	19 May 61	31 May 61
6456	4B	G-ARJM	BEA	08 Jun 61	26 Jun 61
6457	4C	ST-AAW	Sudan Airways	05 Nov 61	14 Nov 62
6458	4C	SU-ALM	United Arab Airlines	30 Jun 61	15 Jul 61
6459	4B	G-ARJN	BEA	21 Jul 61	04 Aug 61
6460	4C	LV-PTS	Aerolineas Argentinas	21 Aug 61	27 Apl 62
6461	4C	SA-R-7	Govt of Saudi Arabia	29 Mar 62	
6462	4C	SU-AMV	United Arab Airlines	25 Mar 62	06 Apl 62
6463	4C	ST-AAX	Sudan Airways	08 Dec 62	21 Dec 62
6464	4C	SU-AMW	United Arab Airlines	03 Apl 62	16 Apl 62
6465	4C	9K-ACA	Kuwait Airways	14 Dec 62	18 Jan 63
6466	4C	SU-ANC	United Arab Airlines	08 Dec 62	22 Dec 62
6467	C4	XR395	RAF	15 Nov 61	01 Jun 62
6468	C4	XR396	RAF	28 Dec 61	12 Mar 62
6469	C4	XR397	RAF	17 Jan 62	15 Feb 62
6470	C4	XR398	RAF	13 Feb 62	13 Mar 62
6471	C4	XR399	RAF	20 Mar 62	26 Apl 62
6472	4C	VP-KRL	East African Airways	12 Mar 62	10 Apl 62
6473	4C	XS235	A&AEE	26 Sep 63	21 Dec 63
6474	4C	9K-ACE	Kuwait Airways	17 Dec 63	02 Feb 64
6475	4C	SU-ANI	United Arab Airlines	04 Feb 64	26 Feb 64

* Note that 6476 and 6477, designated 801 and coded XV147 and XV148 respectively, were Nimrod prototypes for the Ministry of Defence. They first flew in 1965 and 1967 respectively.

THE COMETS

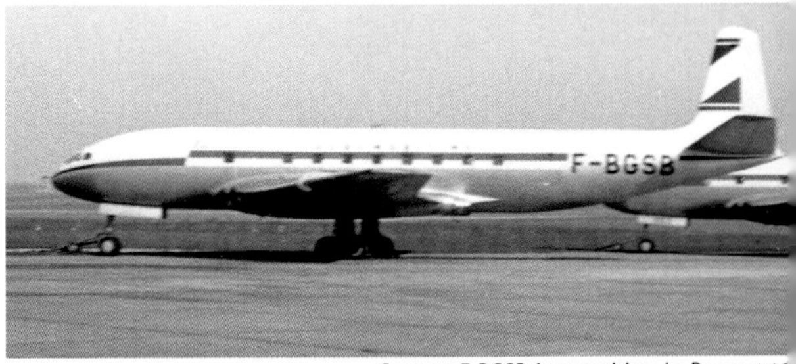
F-BGSB
Comet 1 F-BGSB Aeromaritime Le Bourget 19

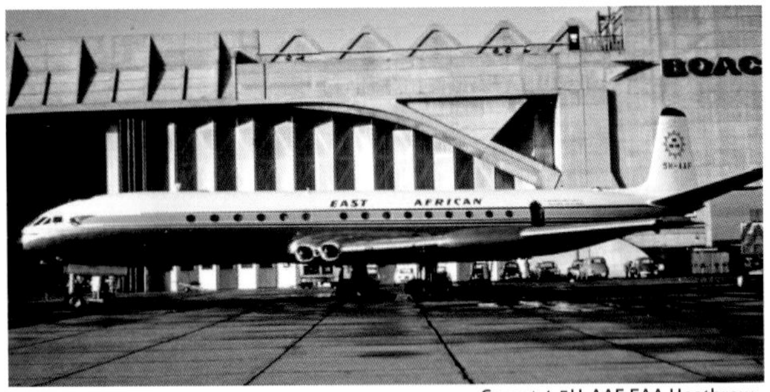
BOAC
EAST AFRICAN
Comet 4 5H-AAF EAA Heathrow

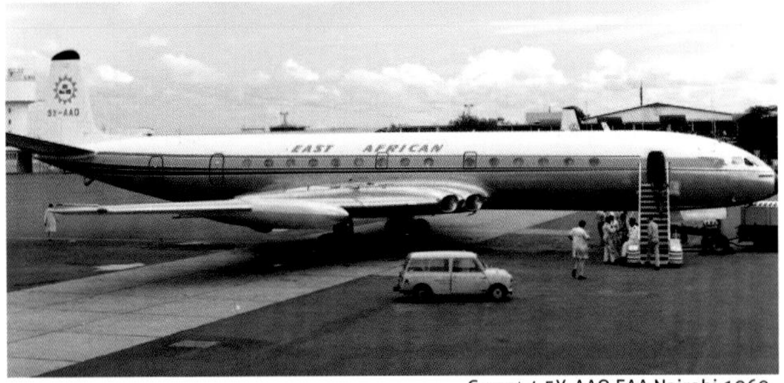
EAST AFRICAN
Comet 4 5X-AAO EAA Nairobi 1969

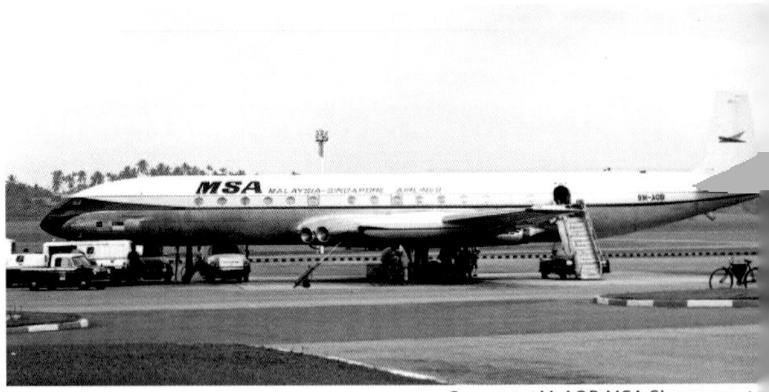
MSA
Comet 4 9M-AOB MSA Singapore 1

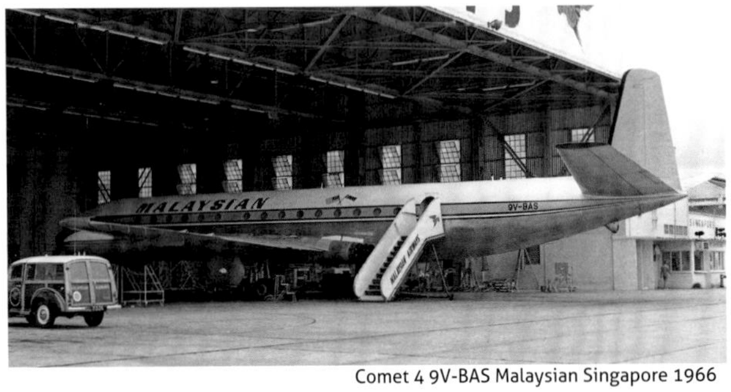
MALAYSIAN
Comet 4 9V-BAS Malaysian Singapore 1966

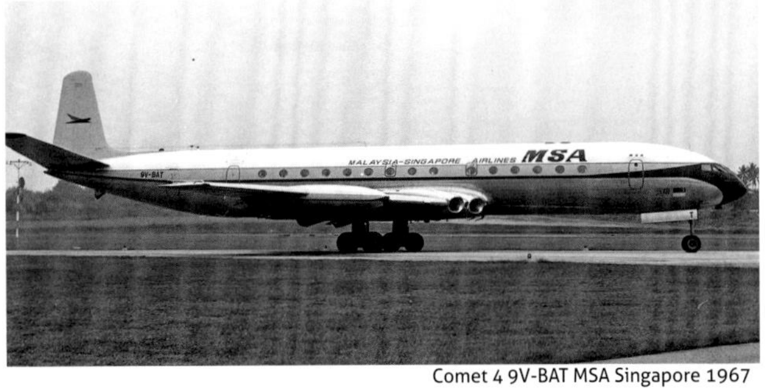
MSA
Comet 4 9V-BAT MSA Singapore 1967

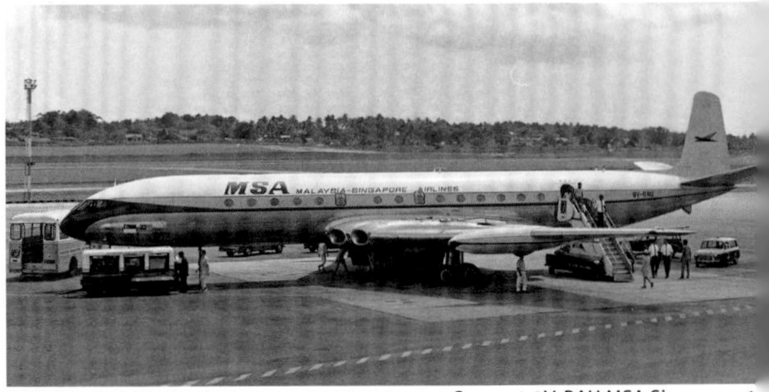
MSA
Comet 4 9V-BAU MSA Singapore 1

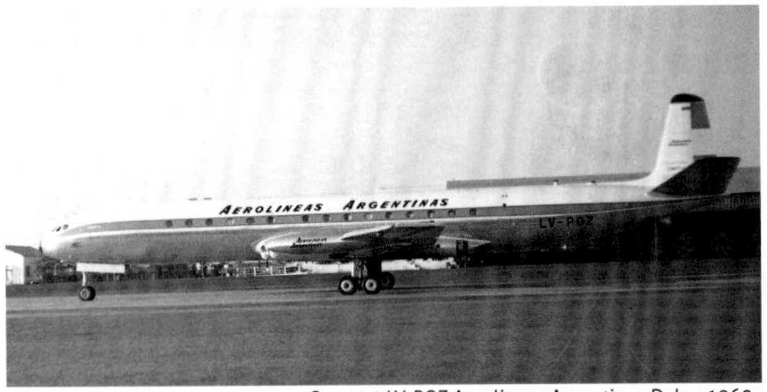
AEROLINEAS ARGENTINAS
LV-POZ
Comet 4 LV-POZ Aerolineas Argentinas Dakar 1960

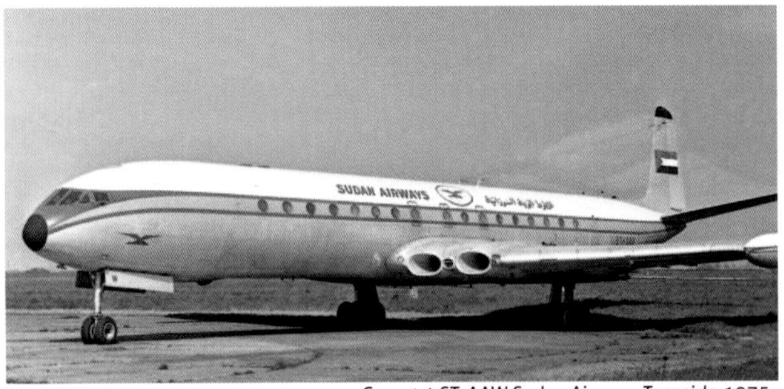
SUDAN AIRWAYS
Comet 4 ST-AAW Sudan Airways Teesside 1975

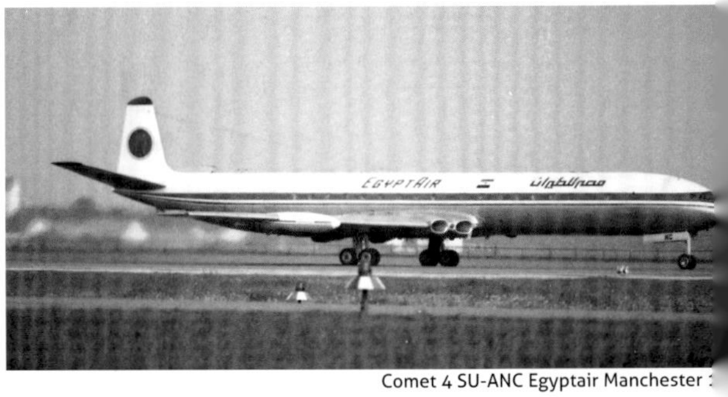
EGYPTAIR
Comet 4 SU-ANC Egyptair Manchester

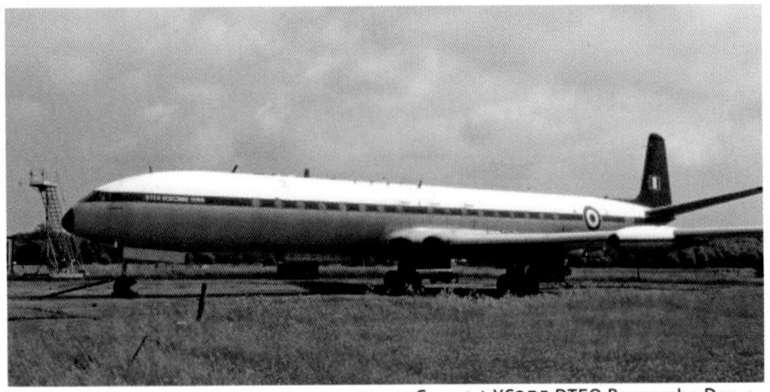
Comet 4 XS235 DTEO Boscombe Down

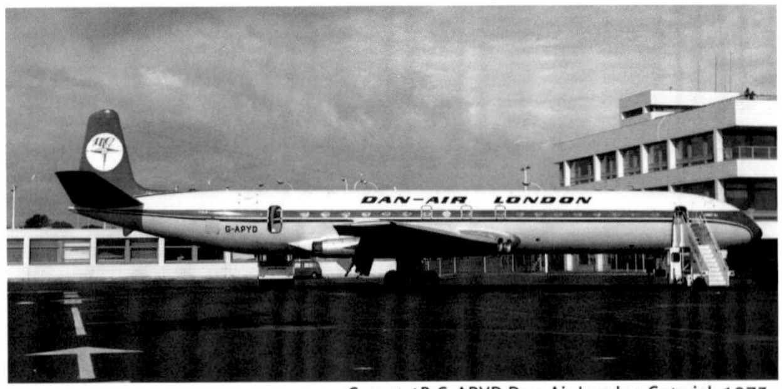
DAN-AIR LONDON
Comet 4B G-APYD Dan-Air London Gatwick 1973

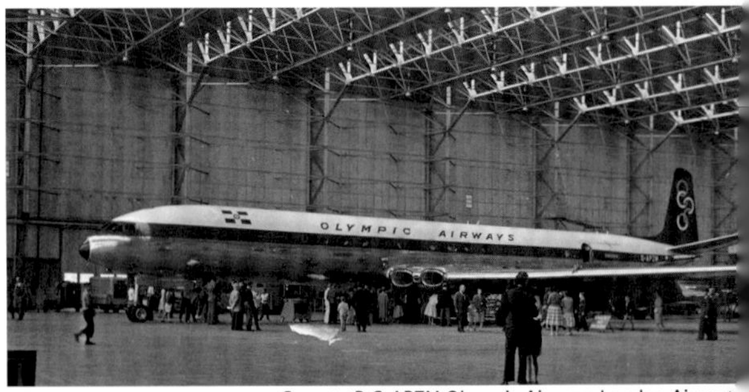
OLYMPIC AIRWAYS
Comet 4B G-APZM Olympic Airways London Airport

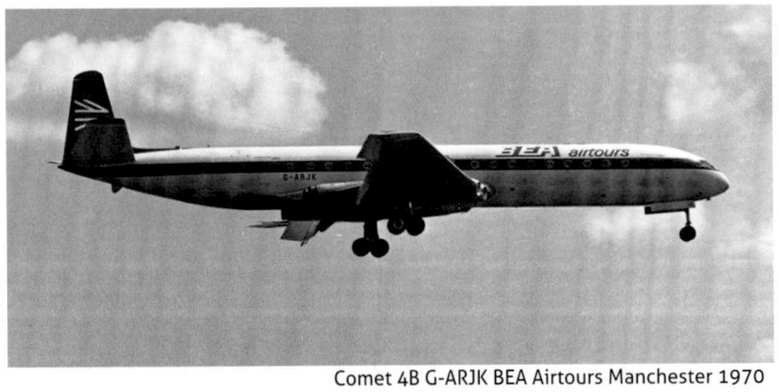
BEA airtours
Comet 4B G-ARJK BEA Airtours Manchester 1970

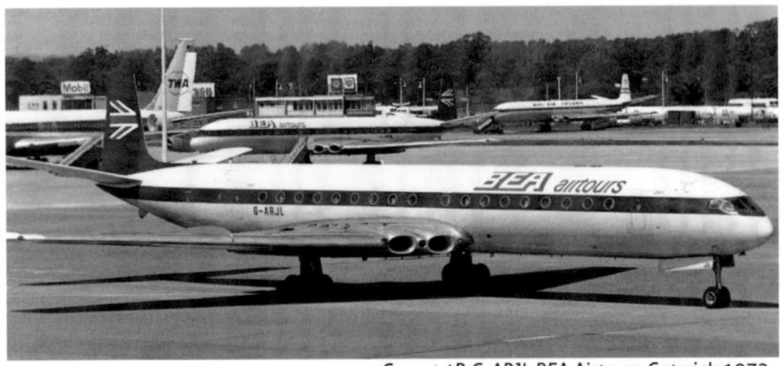
BEA airtours
Comet 4B G-ARJL BEA Airtours Gatwick 1972

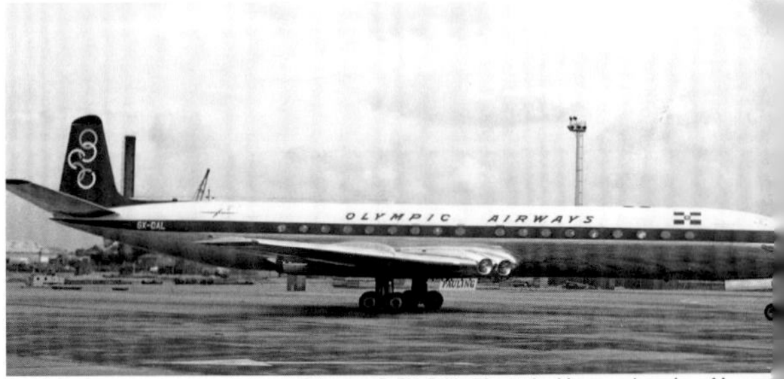
OLYMPIC AIRWAYS
Comet 4B SX-DAL Olympic Airways London Airport

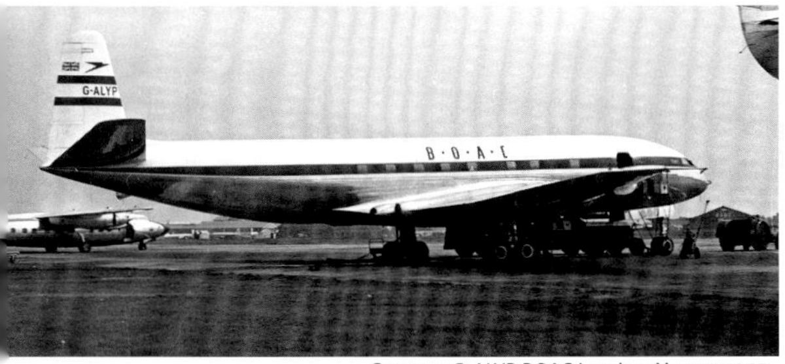
G-ALYP
B·O·A·C
Comet 1 G-ALYP BOAC London Airport 1953

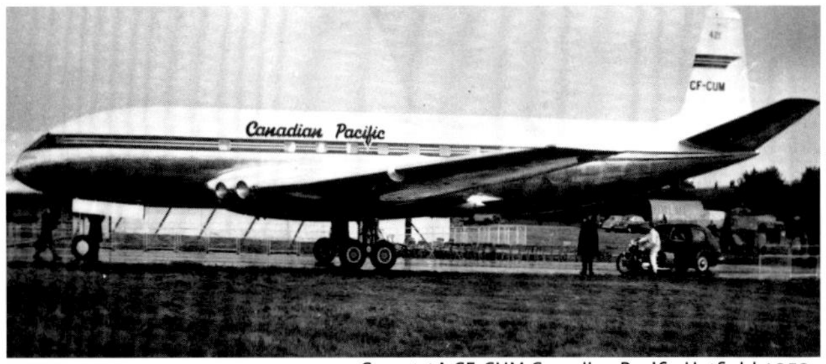
CF-CUM
Canadian Pacific
Comet 1A CF-CUM Canadian Pacific Hatfield 1952

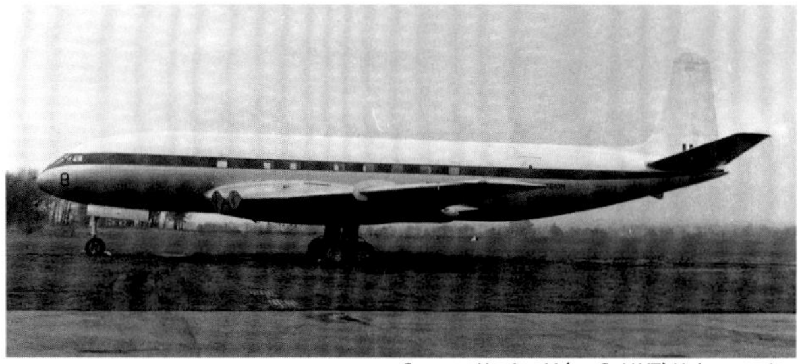
Comet 2X 7610M (ex G-ALYT) Halton 1962

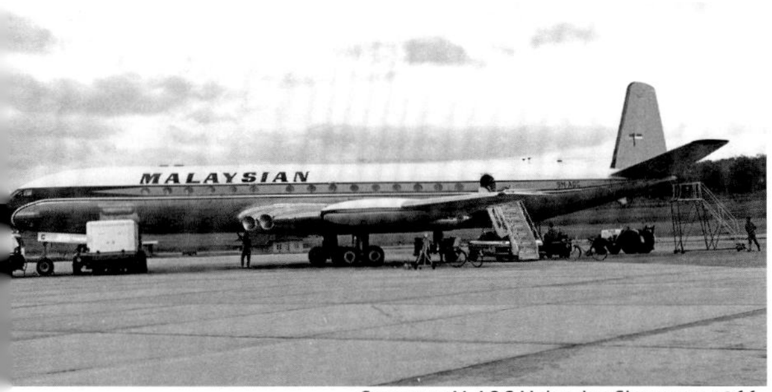
MALAYSIAN
Comet 4 9M-AOC Malaysian Singapore 1966

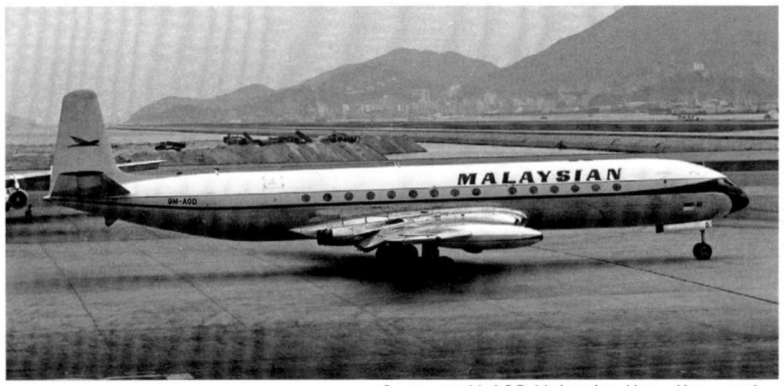
MALAYSIAN
Comet 4 9M-AOD Malaysian Hong Kong 1967

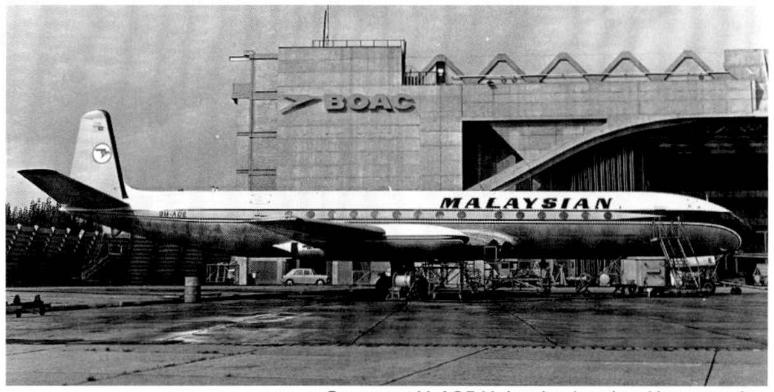
BOAC
MALAYSIAN
Comet 4 9M-AOE Malaysian London Airport 1965

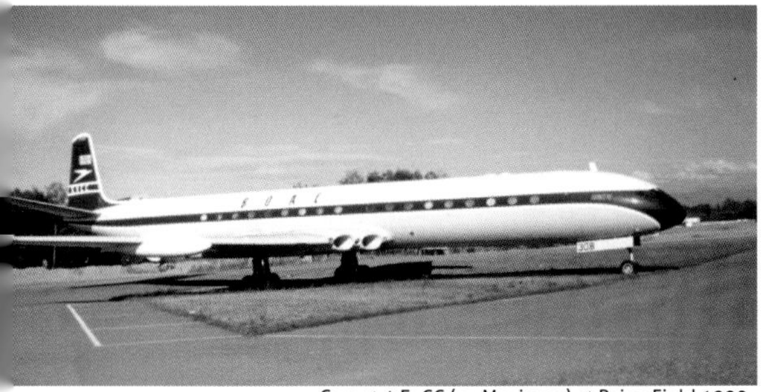
Comet 4 EvCC (ex Mexicana) at Paine Field 1990

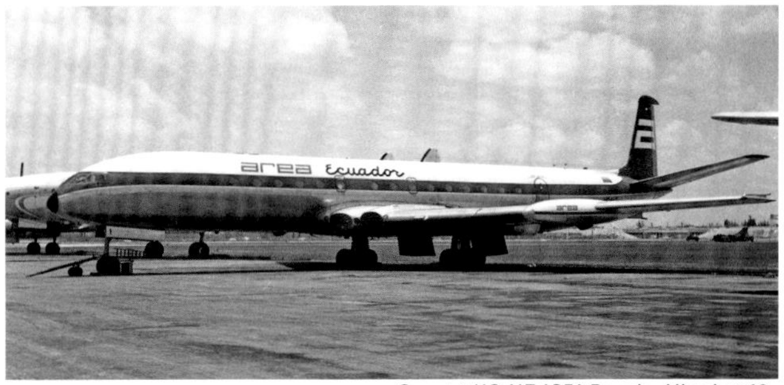
area Ecuador
Comet 4 HC-ALT AREA Ecuador Miami 1968

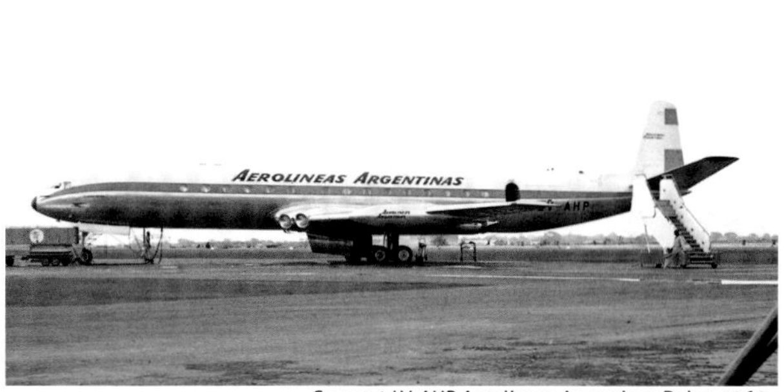
AEROLINEAS ARGENTINAS
Comet 4 LV-AHP Aerolineas Argentinas Dakar 1960

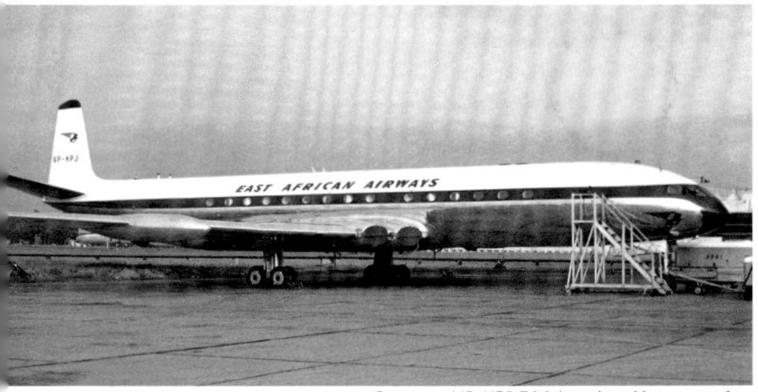
EAST AFRICAN AIRWAYS
Comet 4 VP-KPJ EAA London Airport 1960

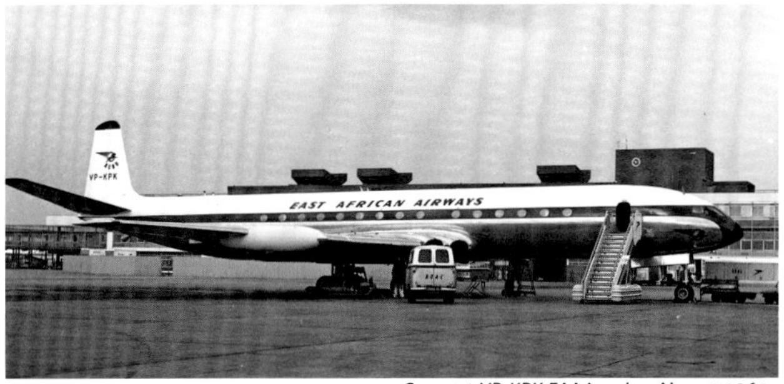
VP-KPK
EAST AFRICAN AIRWAYS
Comet 4 VP-KPK EAA London Airport 1961

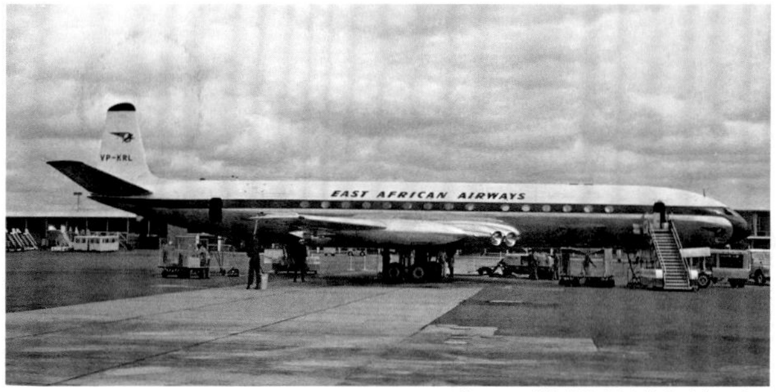
VP-KRL
EAST AFRICAN AIRWAYS
Comet 4 VP-KRL EAA Nairobi 1962

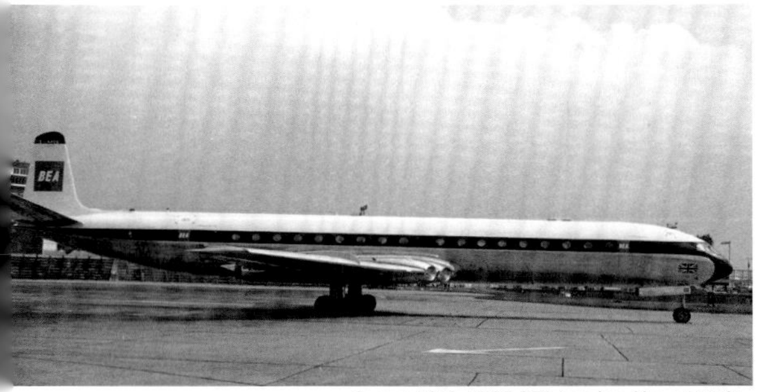
BEA
Comet 4B G-ARCO BEA London Airport 1961

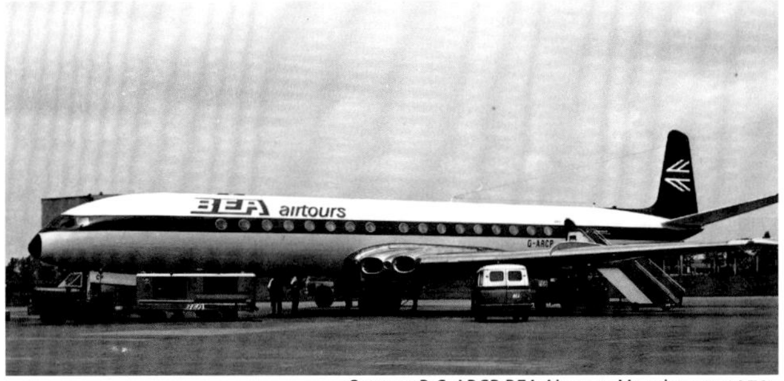
BEA airtours
G-ARCP
Comet 4B G-ARCP BEA Airtours Manchester 1970

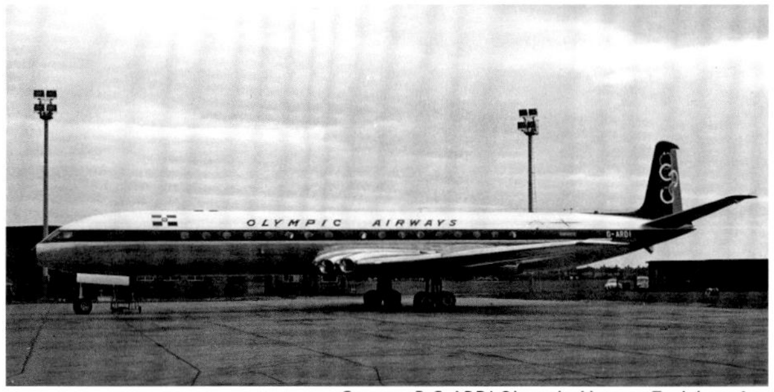
OLYMPIC AIRWAYS
Comet 4B G-ARDI Olympic Airways Zurich 1961

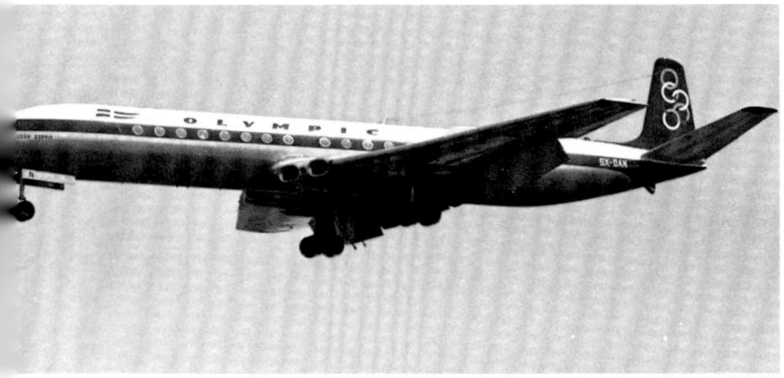
OLYMPIC
SX-DAN
Comet 4B SX-DAN Olympic Airways London Airport 1968

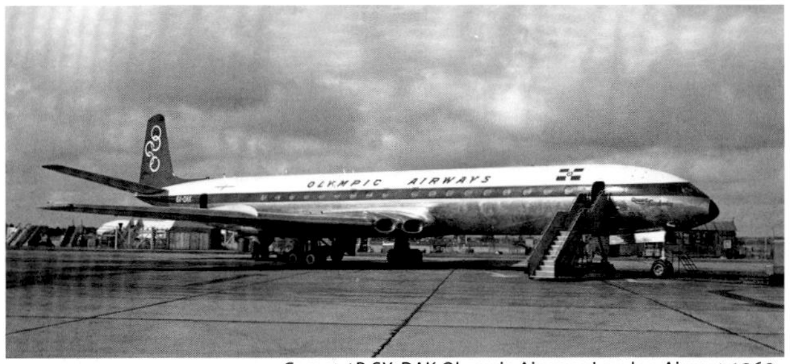
OLYMPIC AIRWAYS
Comet 4B SX-DAK Olympic Airways London Airport 1960

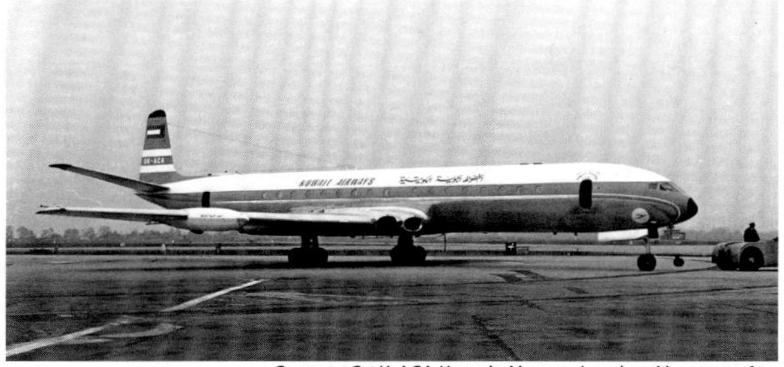
KUWAIT AIRWAYS
Comet 4C 9K-ACA Kuwait Airways London Airport 1964

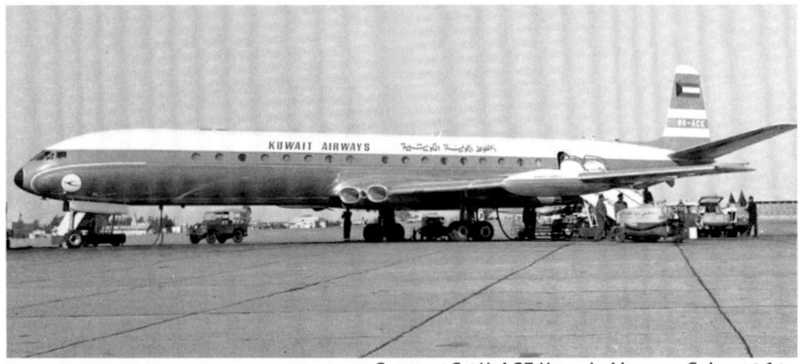
KUWAIT AIRWAYS
Comet 4C 9K-ACE Kuwait Airways Cairo 1964

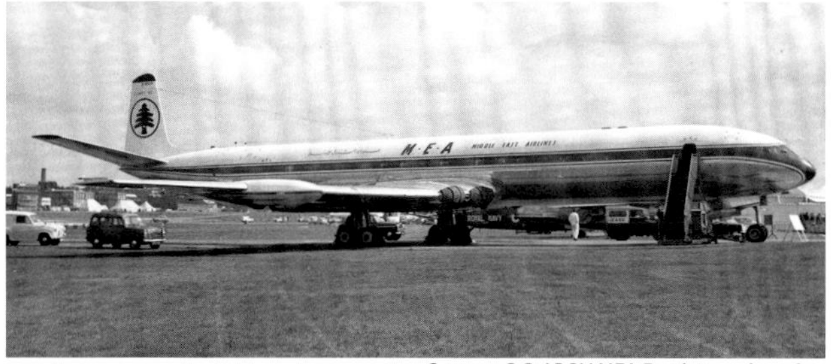
M E A
Comet 4C G-AROV MEA Farnborough 1961

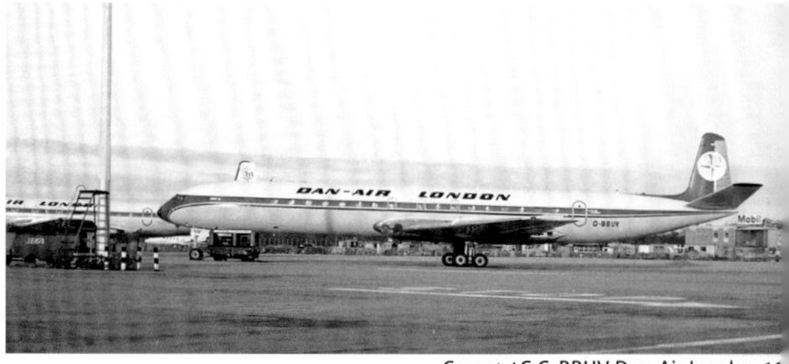
DAN-AIR LONDON
Comet 4C G-BBUV Dan-Air London 1

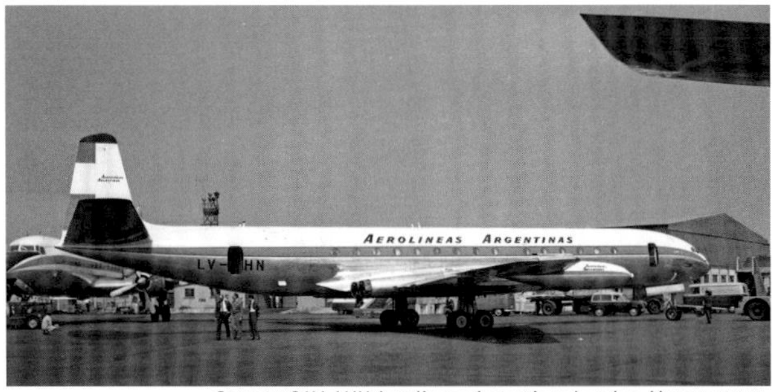
AEROLINEAS ARGENTINAS
Comet 4C LV-AHN Aerolineas Argentinas London Airport 1959

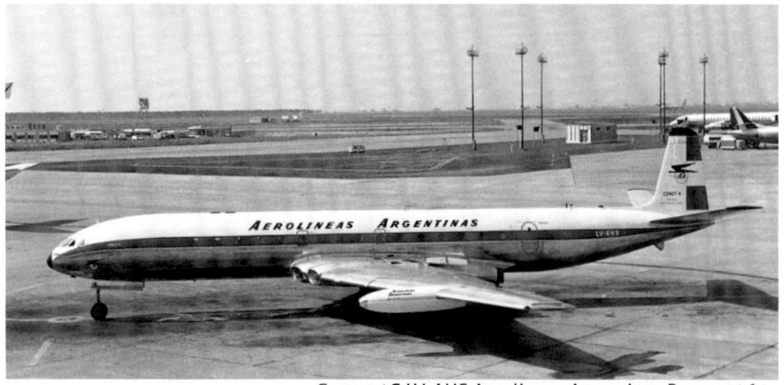
AEROLINEAS ARGENTINAS
Comet 4C LV-AHS Aerolineas Argentinas Rome 1964

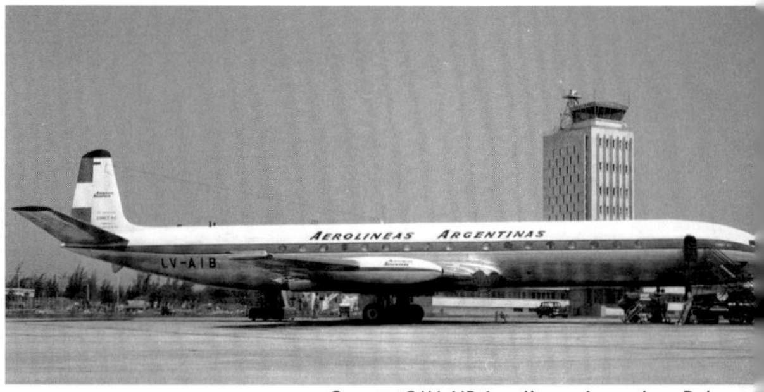
AEROLINEAS ARGENTINAS
LV-AIB
Comet 4C LV-AIB Aerolineas Argentinas Dakar 1

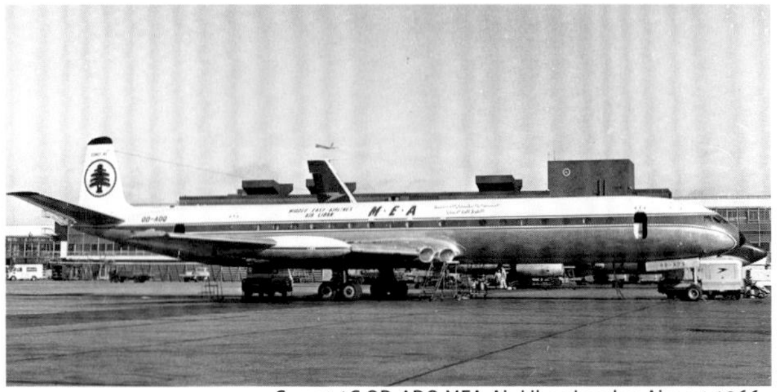
M E A
Comet 4C OD-ADQ MEA-Air LIban London Airport 1966

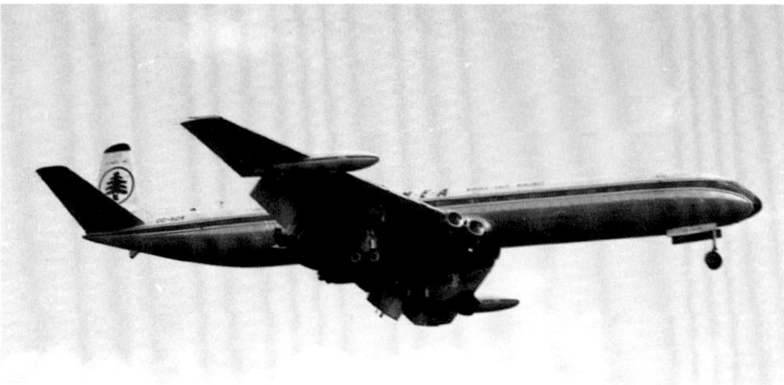
Comet 4C OD-ADR MEA London Airport 1961

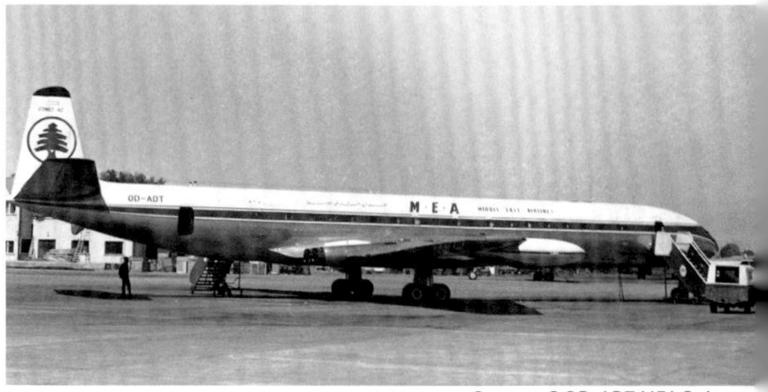
OD-ADT
M E A
Comet 4C OD-ADT MEA Beirut 1

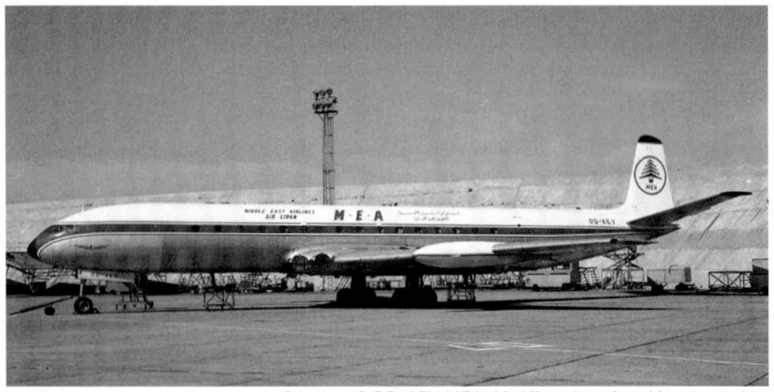
M E A
Comet 4C OD-AEV MEA-Air Liban London Airport 1967

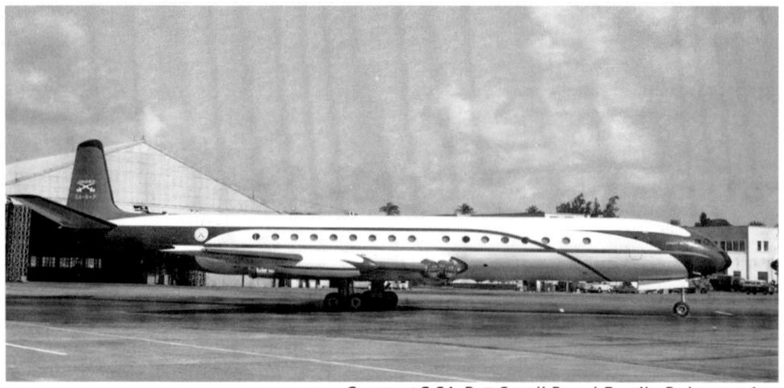
Comet 4C SA-R-7 Saudi Royal Family Beirut 1962

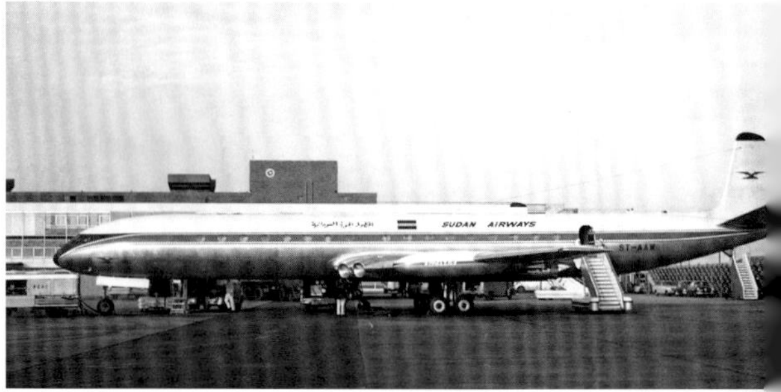
SUDAN AIRWAYS
Comet 4C ST-AAW Sudan Airways London Airport 1

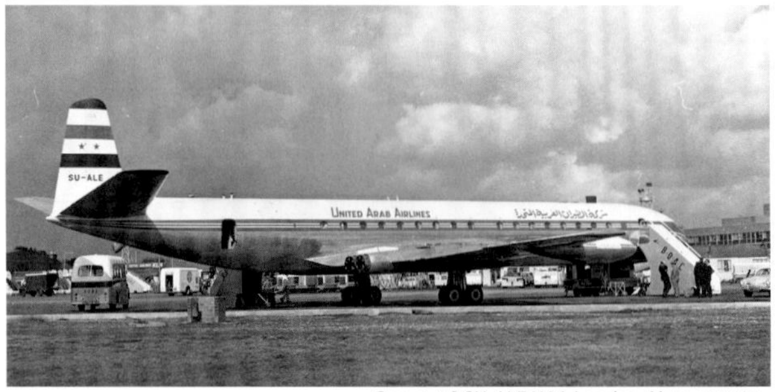
SU-ALE
United Arab Airlines
Comet 4C SU-ALE UAA London Airport 1961

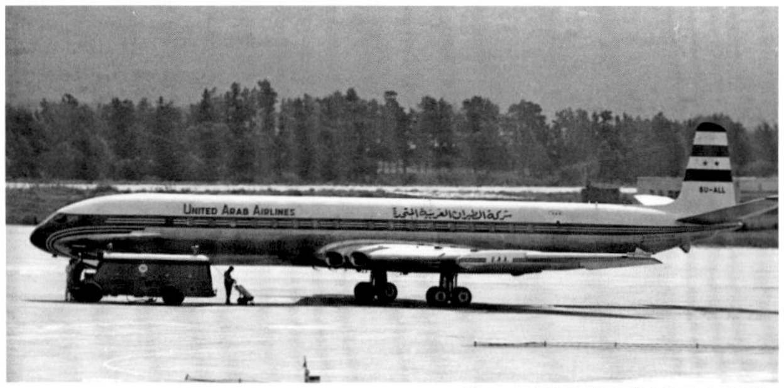
United Arab Airlines
SU-ALL
Comet 4C SU-ALL UAA Beirut 1966

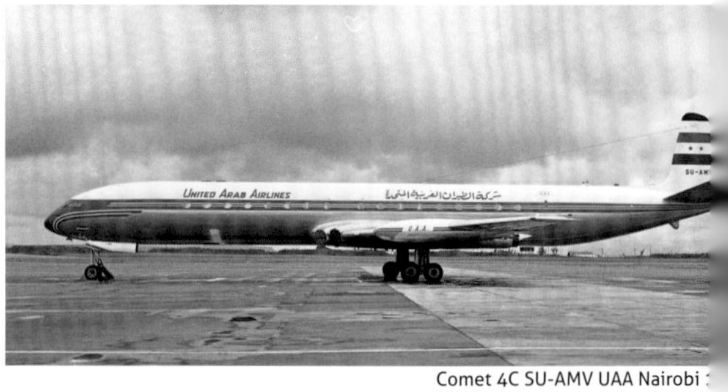
United Arab Airlines
Comet 4C SU-AMV UAA Nairobi

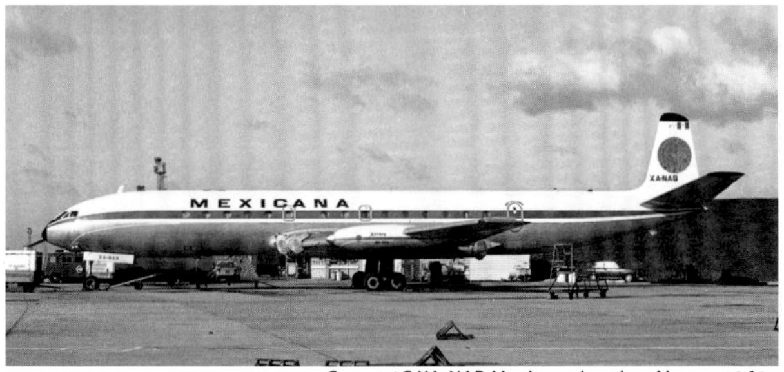
MEXICANA
XA-NAB
Comet 4C XA-NAB Mexicana London Airport 1969

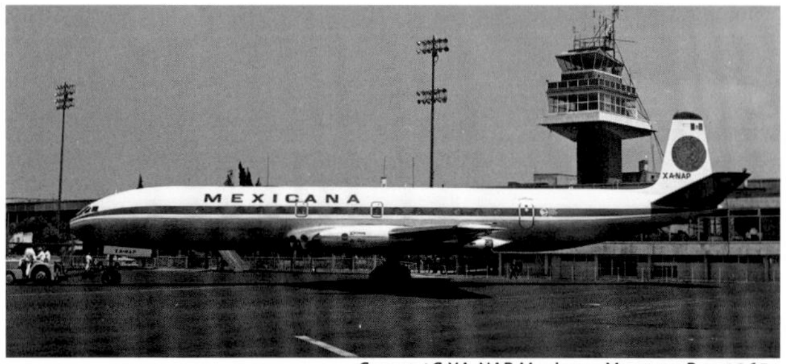
MEXICANA
XA-NAP
Comet 4C XA-NAP Mexicana Montego Bay 1965

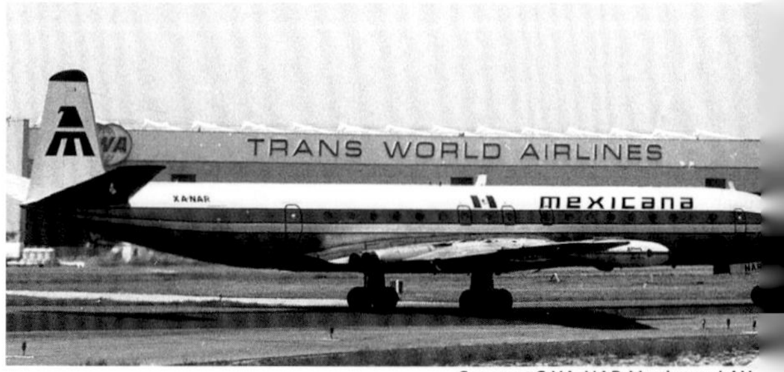
TRANS WORLD AIRLINES
mexicana
Comet 4C XA-NAR Mexicana LAX

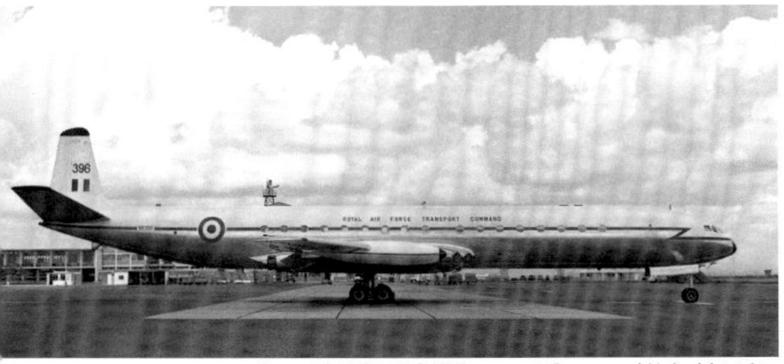
Comet C4 XR396 RAF Transport Command Nairobi 1963

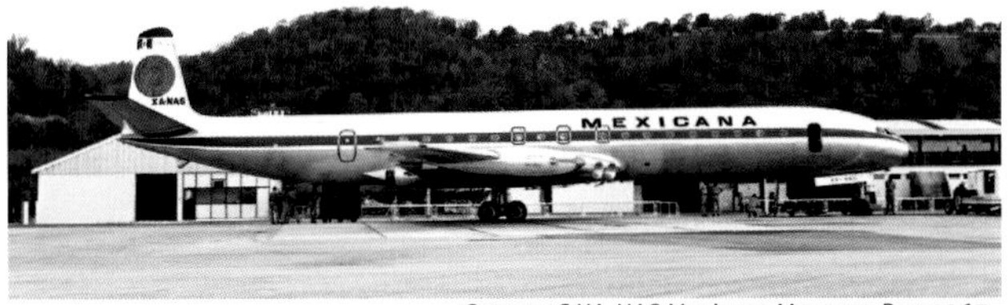
MEXICANA
Comet 4C XA-NAS Mexicana Montego Bay 1967

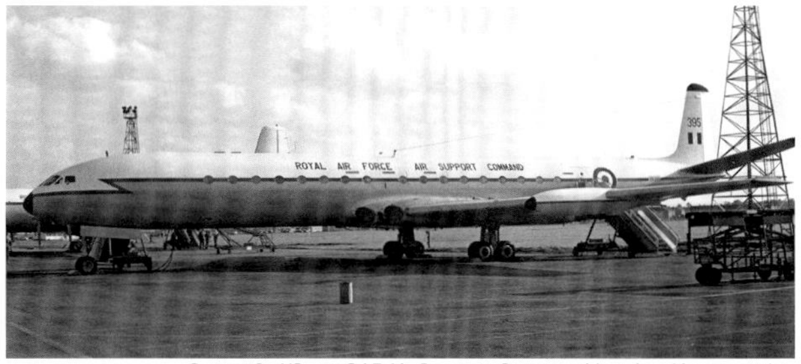
Comet C4 XR395 RAF Air Support Command London Airport 1967

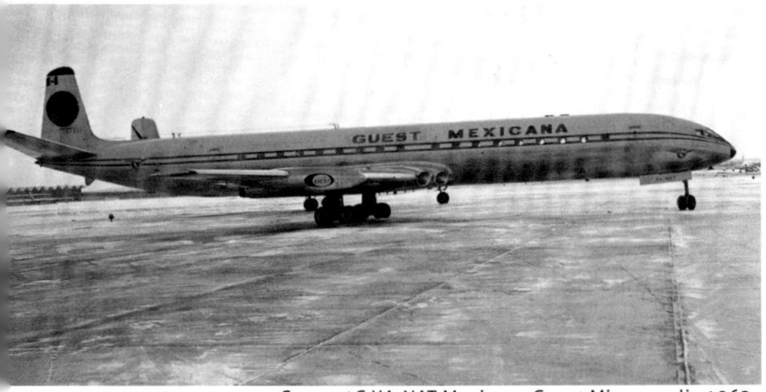
GUEST MEXICANA
Comet 4C XA-NAT Mexicana Guest Minneapolis 1962

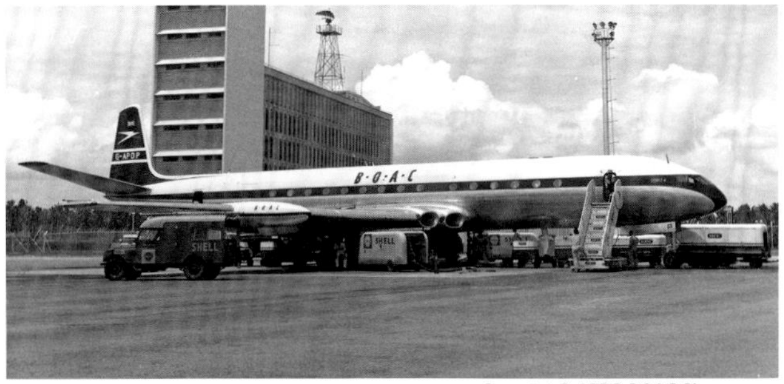
B·O·A·C
Comet 4 G-APDP BOAC Singapore

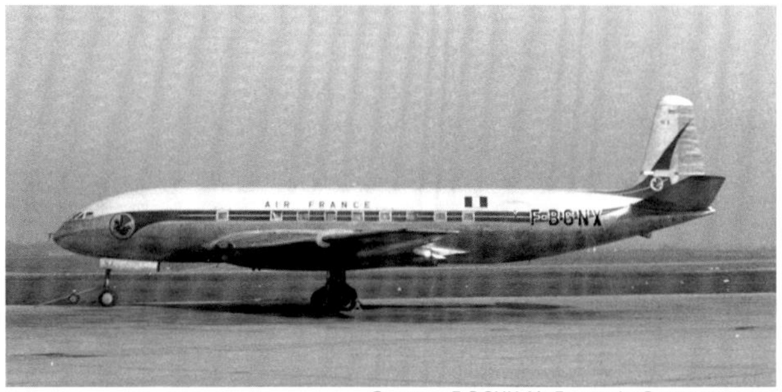
AIR FRANCE
F-BGNX
Comet 1 F-BGNX Air France Le Bourget 1955

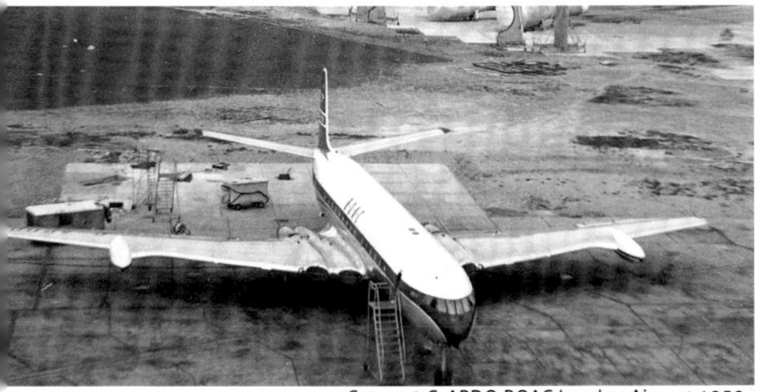
Comet 4 G-APDO BOAC London Airport 1959

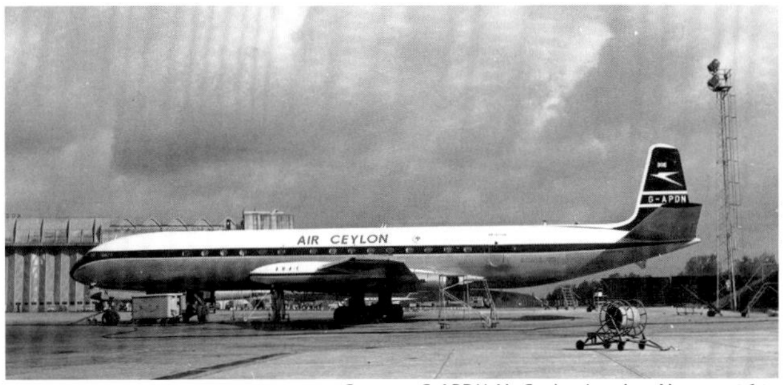
AIR CEYLON
G-APDN
Comet 4 G-APDN Air Ceylon London Airport 1964

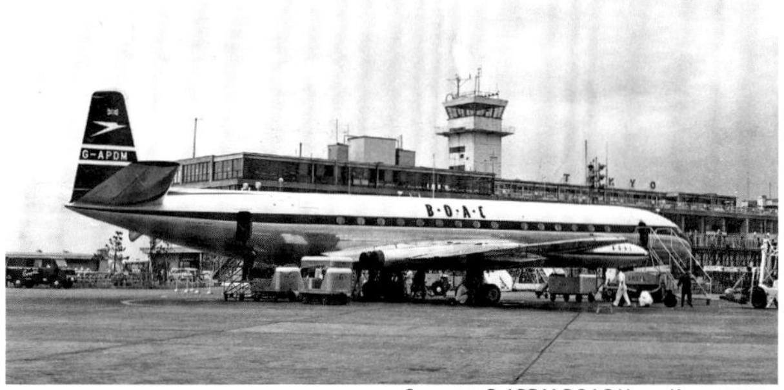
G-APDM
B·O·A·C
Comet 4 G-APDM BOAC Hong Kong 1959

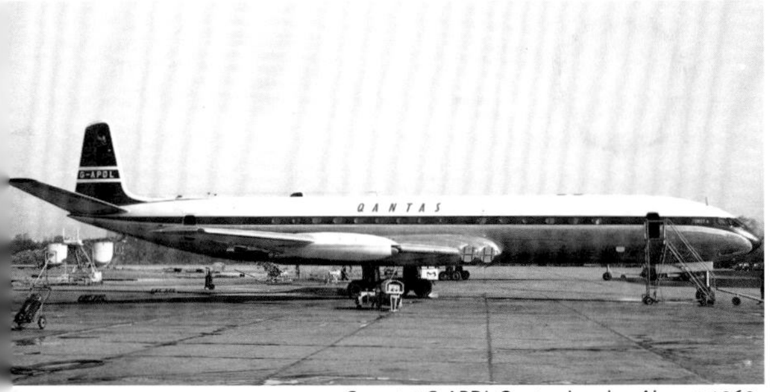
G-APDL
QANTAS
Comet 4 G-APDL Qantas London Airport 1960

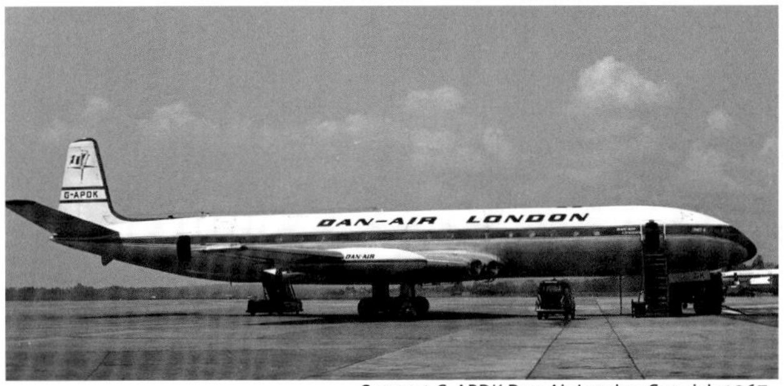
G-APDK
DAN-AIR LONDON
Comet 4 G-APDK Dan-Air London Gatwick 1967

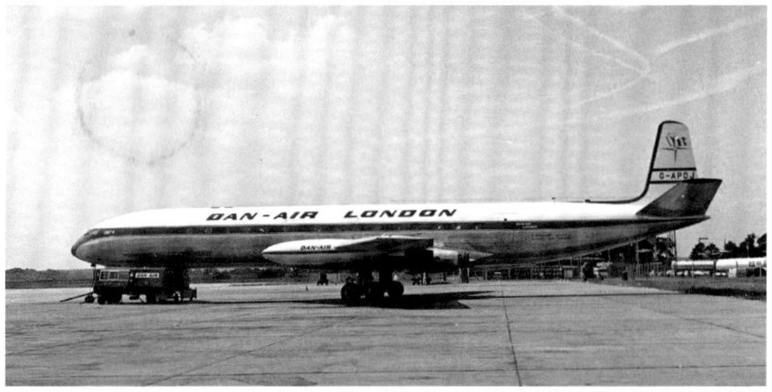
DAN-AIR LONDON
Comet 4 G-APDJ Dan-Air London Gatwick 1967

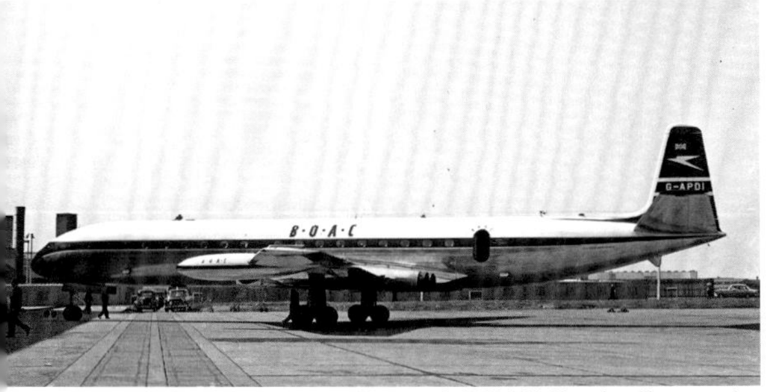
G-APDI
B·O·A·C
Comet 4 G-APDI BOAC London Airport 1960

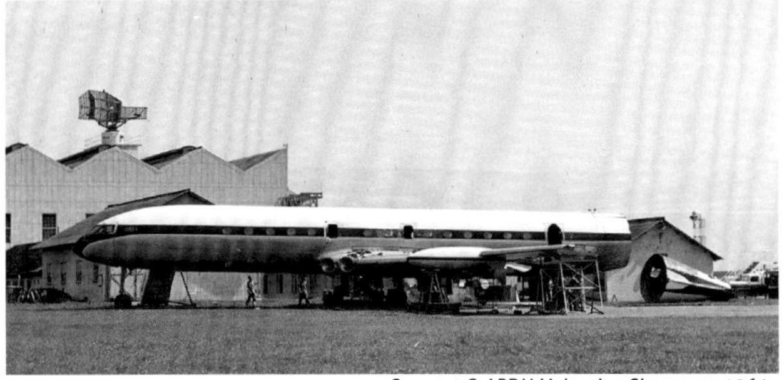
Comet 4 G-APDH Malaysian Singapore 1964

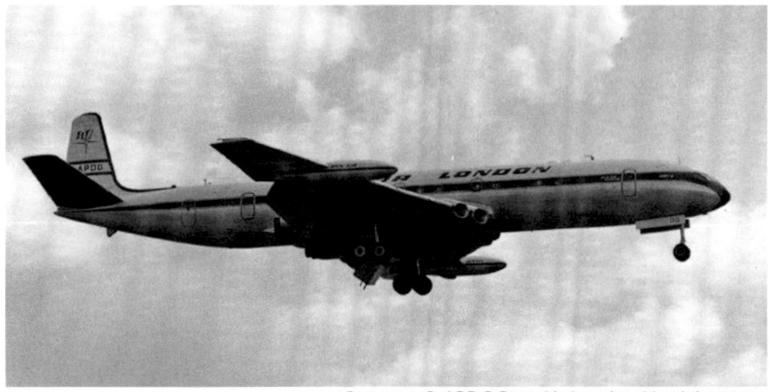
LONDON
Comet 4 G-APDG Dan-Air London Munich 1972

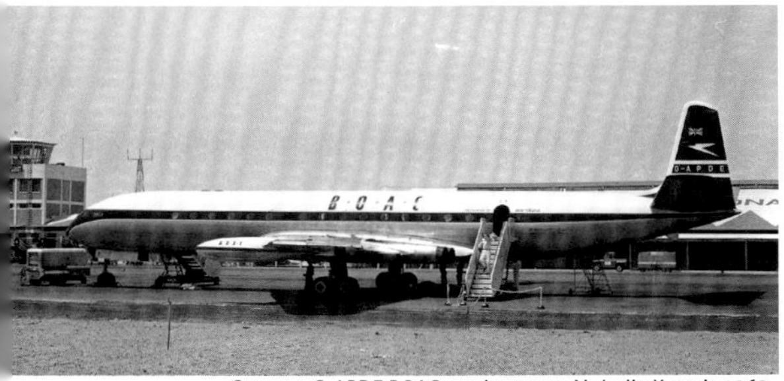
B·O·A·C
Comet 4 G-APDE BOAC on charter to Air India Kuwait 1962

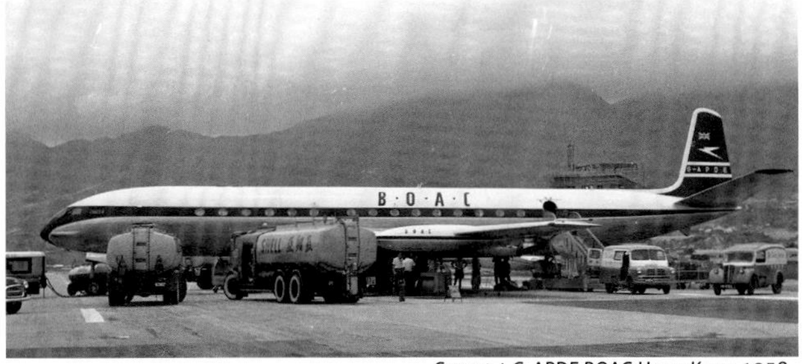
B·O·A·C
Comet 4 G-APDE BOAC Hong Kong 1958

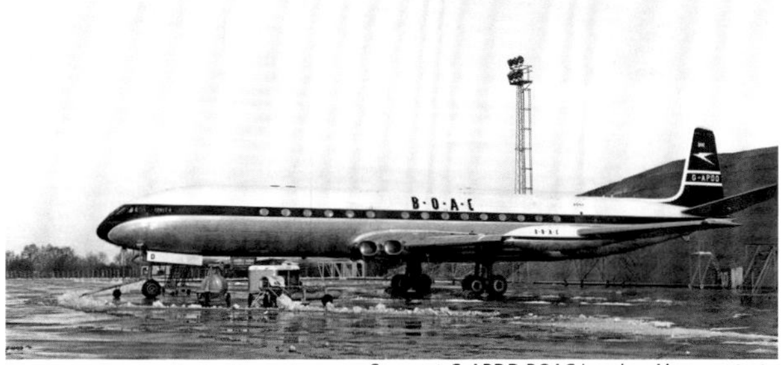
B·O·A·C
Comet 4 G-APDD BOAC London Airport 1959

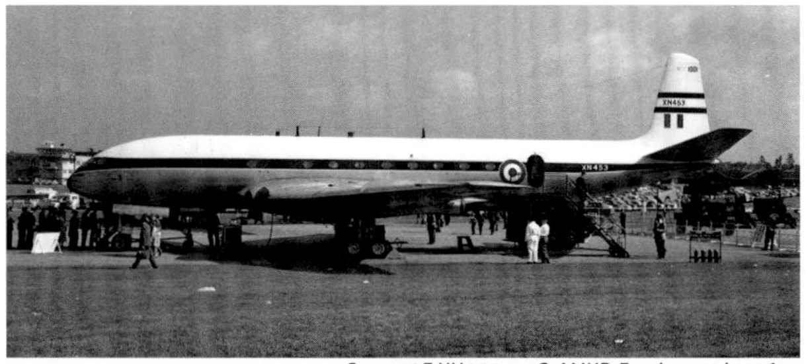
Comet 2E XN453 ex-G-AMXD Farnborough 1960

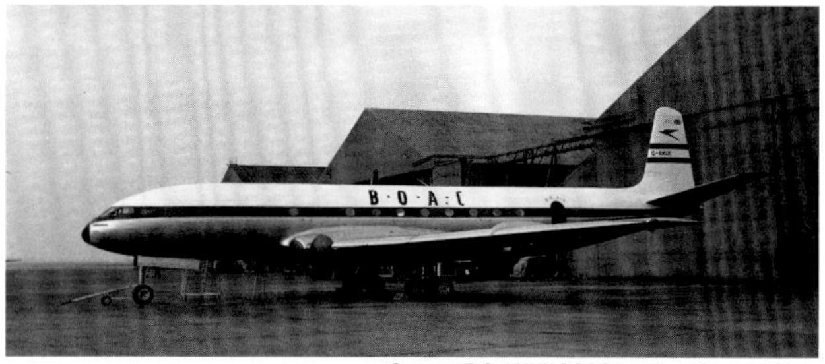
Comet 2E G-AMXK BOAC London Airport 1957

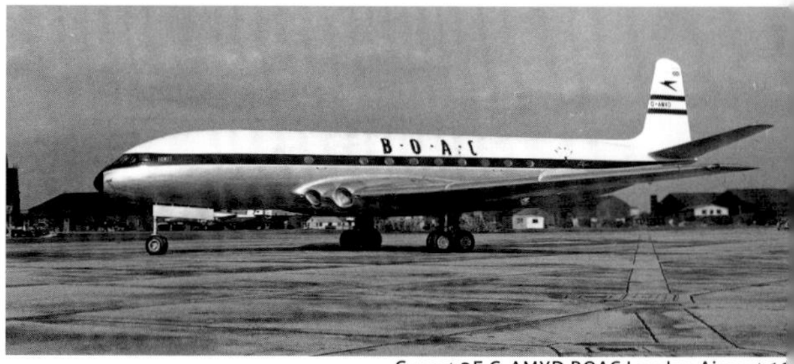
Comet 2E G-AMXD BOAC London Airport 19

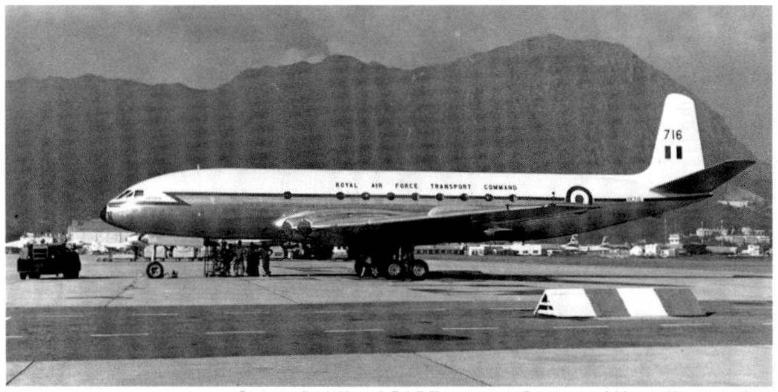
Comet C2 XK716 RAF Transport Command Hong Kong 1961

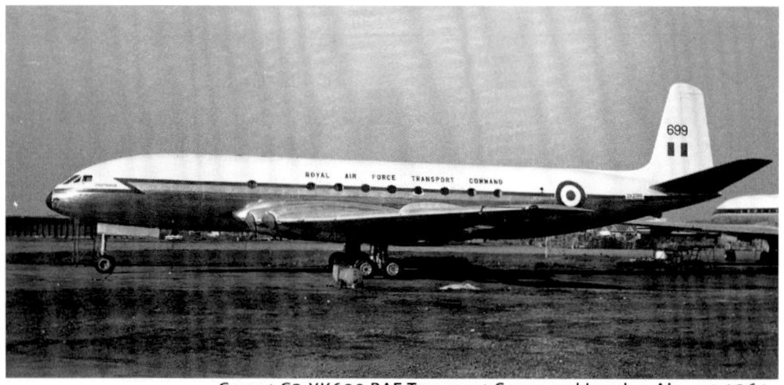
Comet C2 XK699 RAF Transport Command London Airport 1961

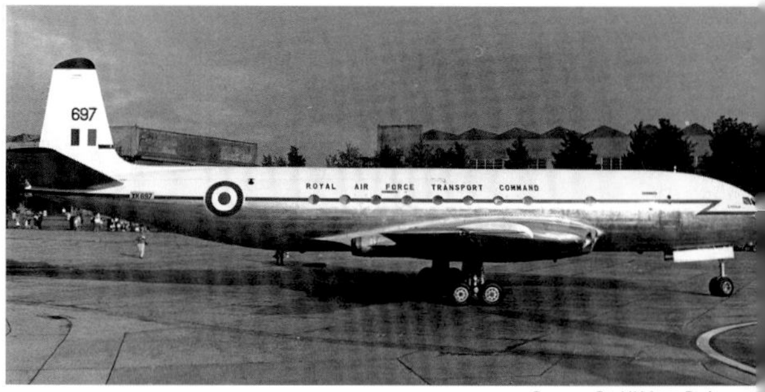
Comet C2 XK697 Dakar 1

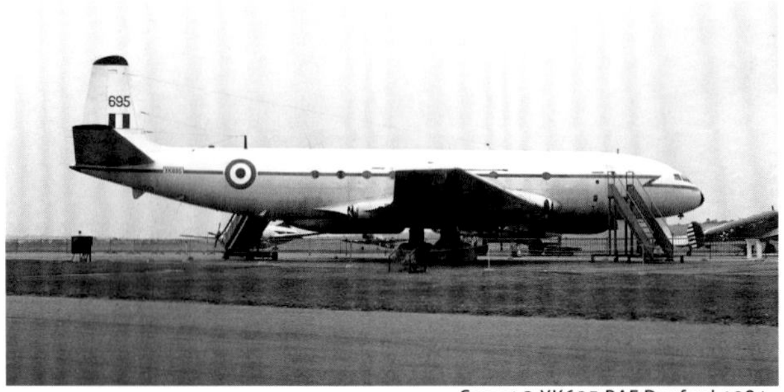
Comet 2 XK695 RAF Duxford 1984

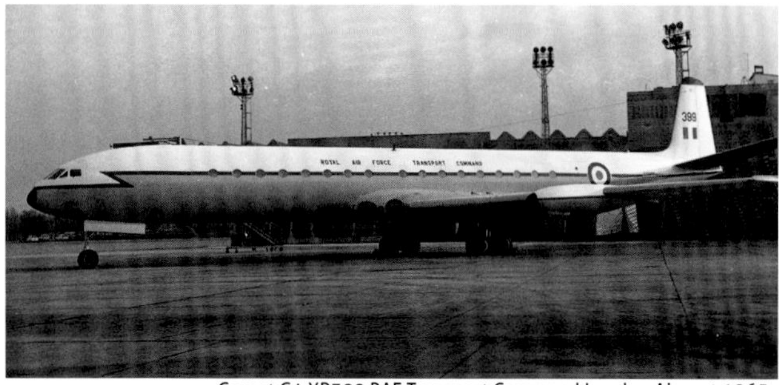
Comet C4 XR399 RAF Transport Command London Airport 1965

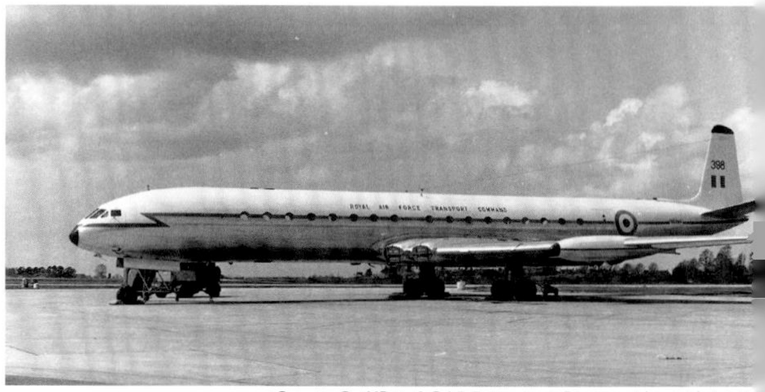
Comet C4 XR398 RAF Transport Command Lyneham 1

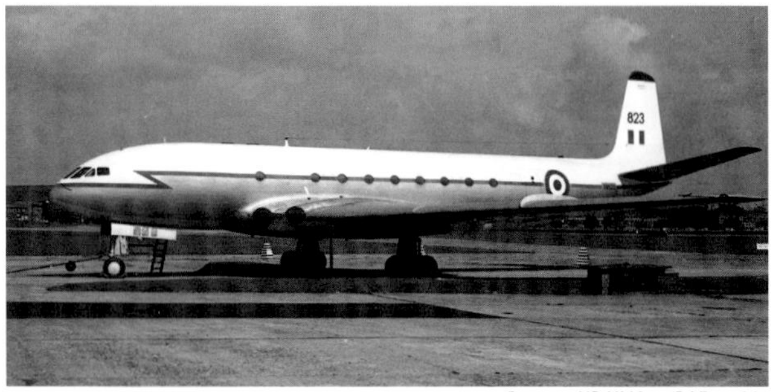
Comet 1XB XM823 RAF 1966

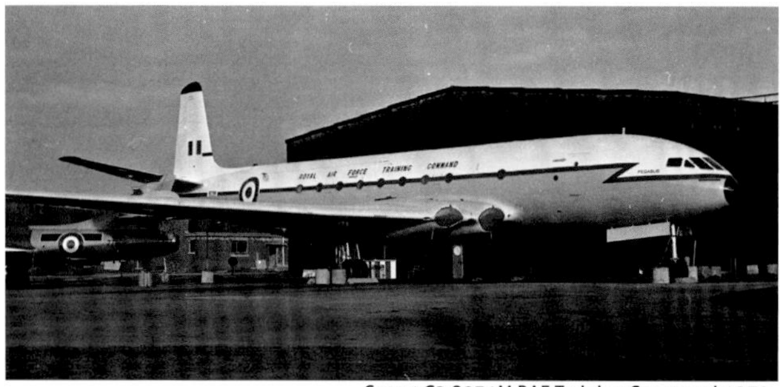
Comet C2 8031M RAF Training Command 1970

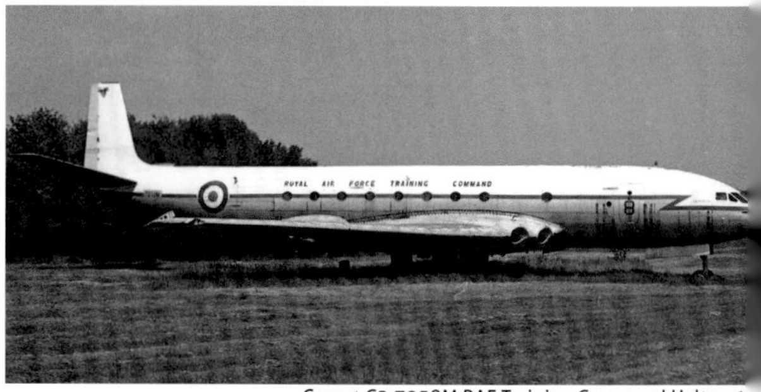
Comet C2 7958M RAF Training Command Halton 1

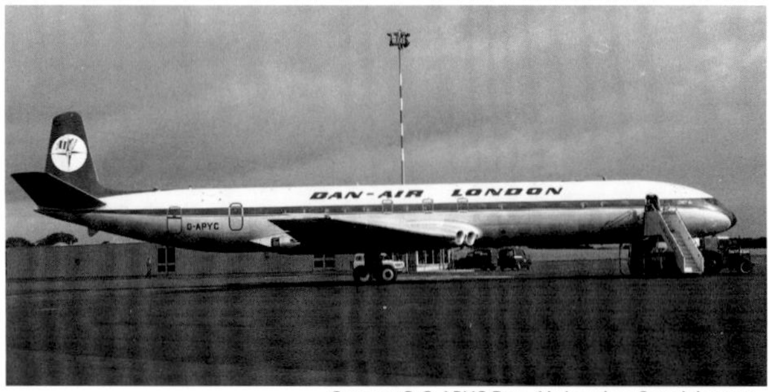
Comet 4B G-APYC Dan-Air London Gatwick 1972

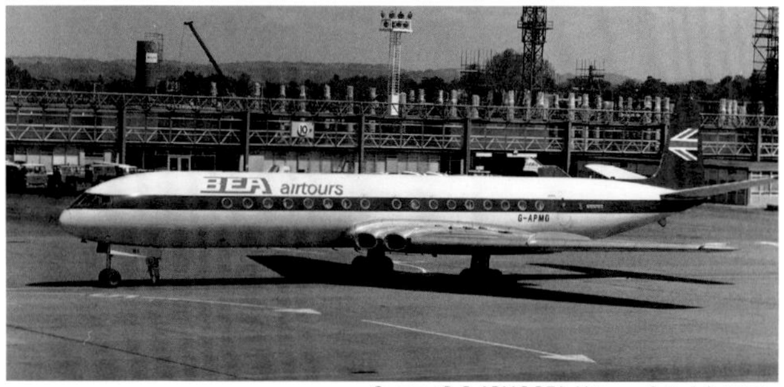
Comet 4B G-APMG BEA Airtours Gatwick 1974

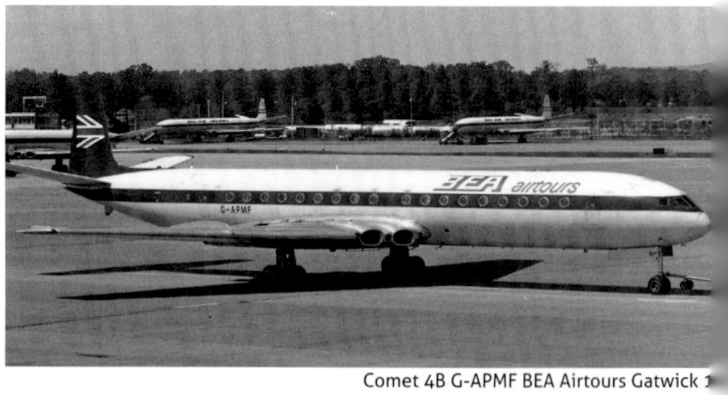
Comet 4B G-APMF BEA Airtours Gatwick 1

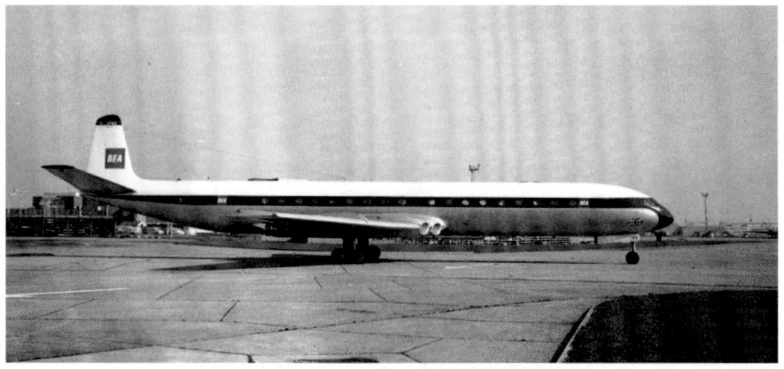
Comet 4B G-APME BEA London Airport 1960

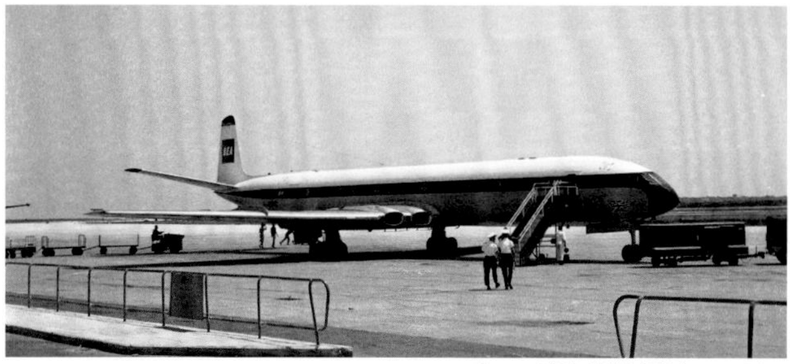
Comet 4B G-APMD BEA Luqa 1965

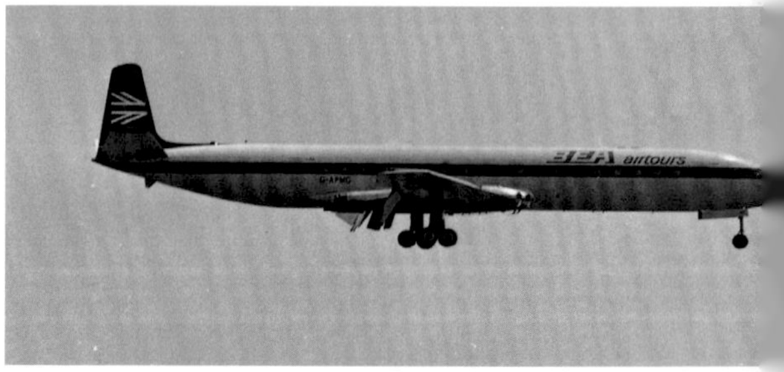
Comet 4B G-APMC BEA Airtours Gatwick

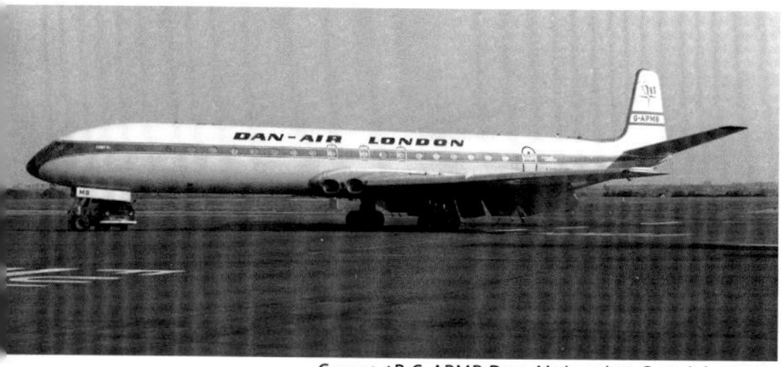
DAN-AIR LONDON
Comet 4B G-APMB Dan-Air London Gatwick 1973

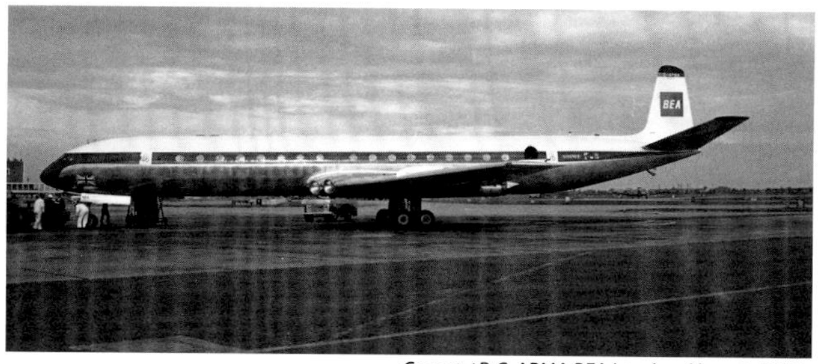
BEA
Comet 4B G-APMA BEA London Airport 1960

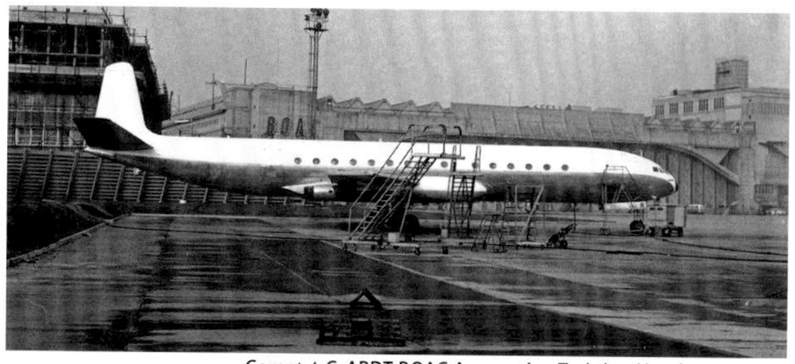
Comet 4 G-APDT BOAC Apprentice Training Heathrow 1971

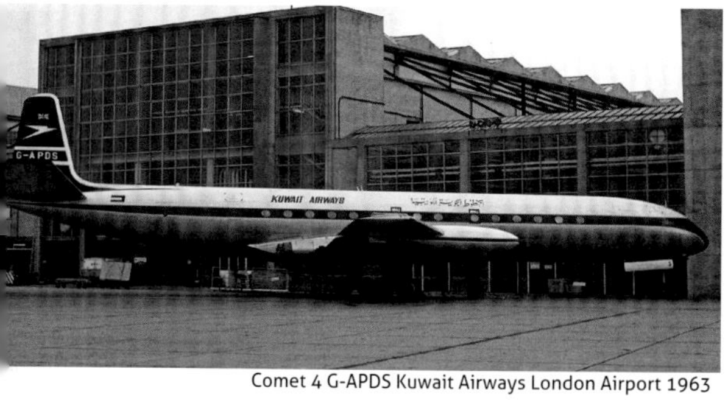
G-APDS
KUWAIT AIRWAYS
Comet 4 G-APDS Kuwait Airways London Airport 1963

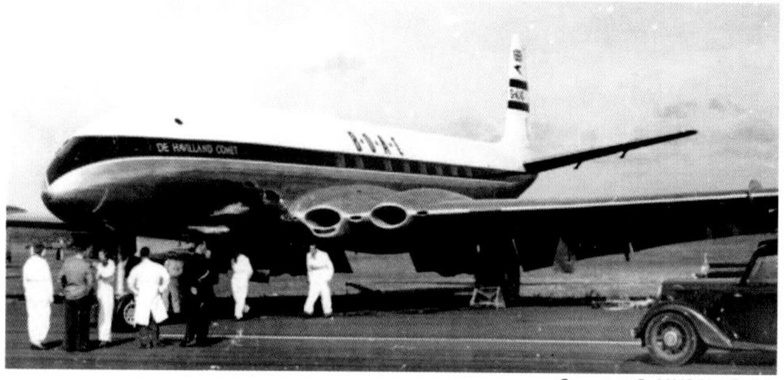
DE HAVILLAND COMET
Comet 1 G-ALYS Hatfield

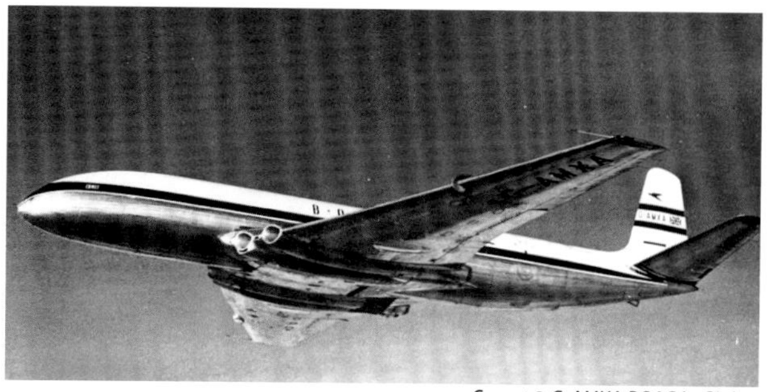
Comet 2 G-AMXA BOAC in flight

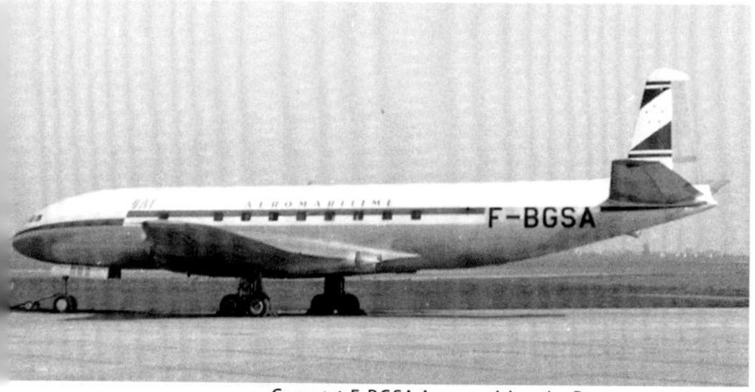
F-BGSA
Comet 1 F-BGSA Aeromaritime Le Bourget 1955

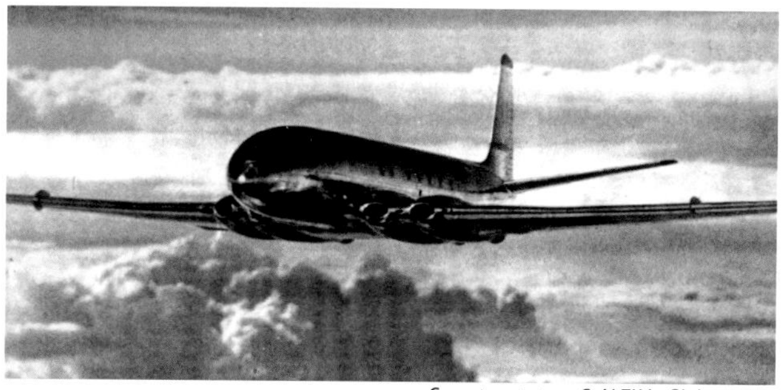
Comet prototype G-ALZK in flight 1950

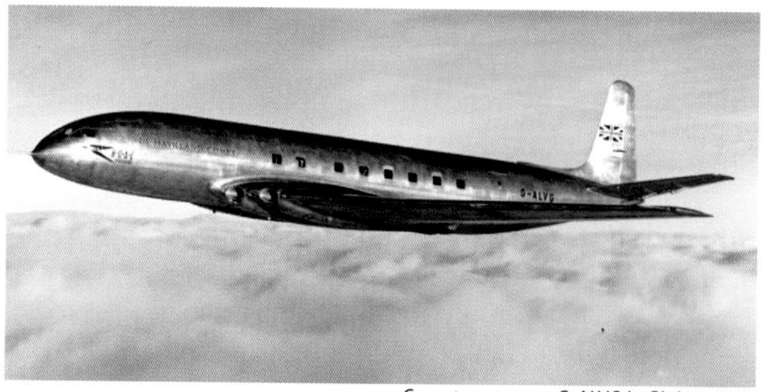
Comet prototype G-ALVG in flight 1950

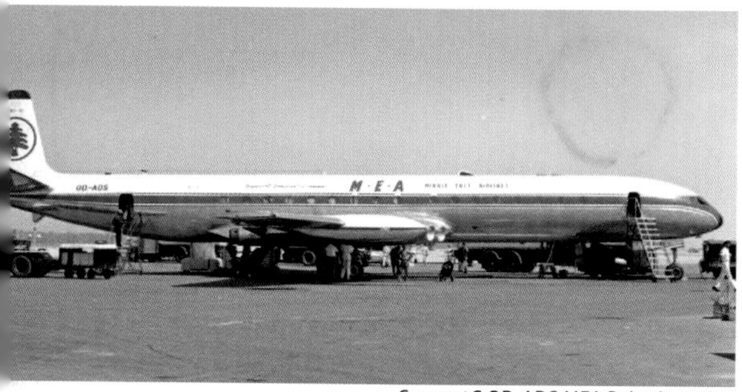
M·E·A
Comet 4C OD-ADS MEA Bahrain 1961

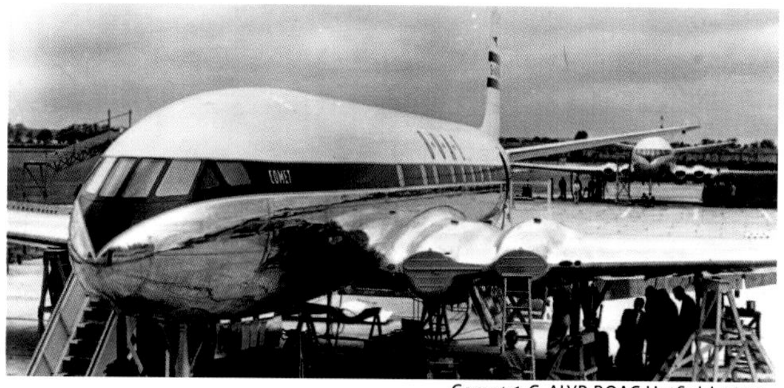
Comet 1 G-ALYR BOAC Hatfield 1951

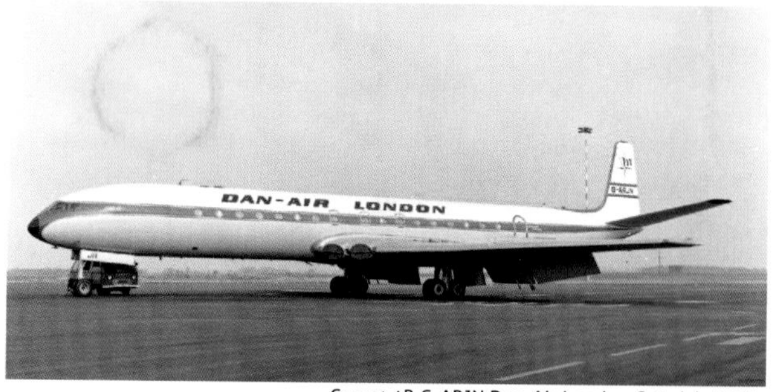
DAN-AIR LONDON
Comet 4B G-ARJN Dan-Air London Gatwick 1974

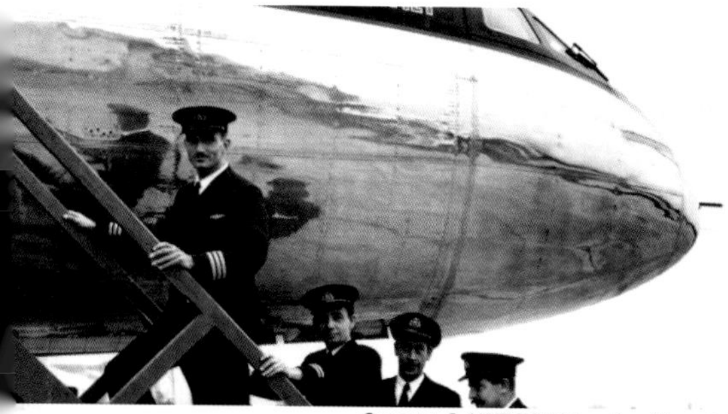
Comet 1 G-ALYZ BOAC London Airport 1952

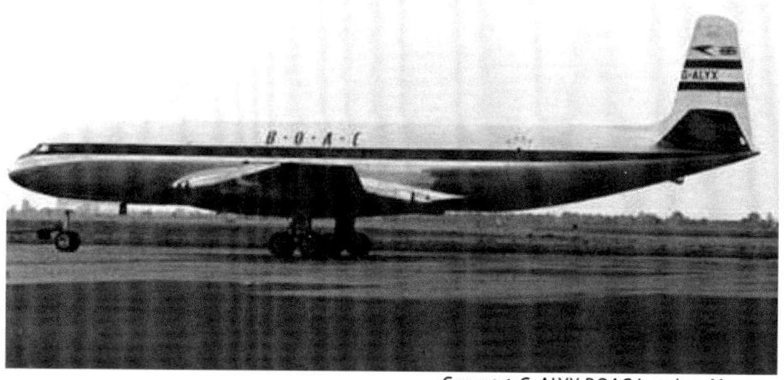
B·O·A·C
G-ALYX
Comet 1 G-ALYX BOAC London Airport

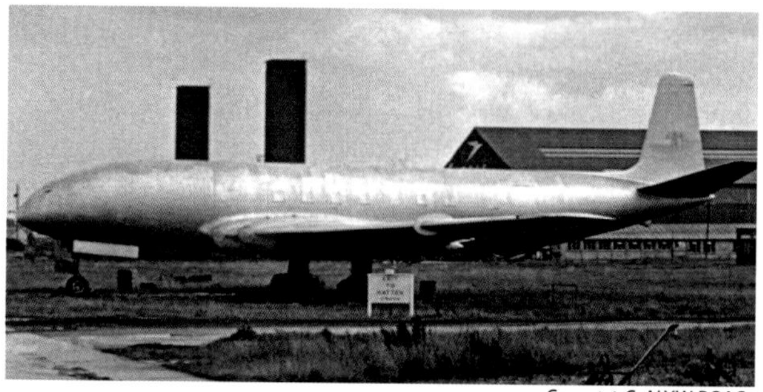
Comet 1 G-ALYW BOAC

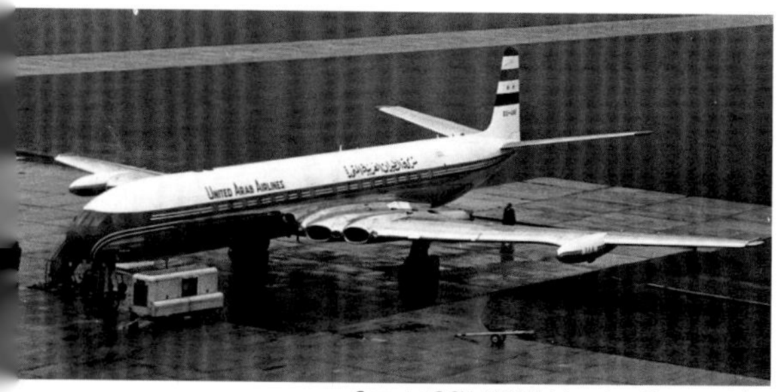
UNITED ARAB AIRLINES
Comet 4C SU-ANI UAA London Airport 1964

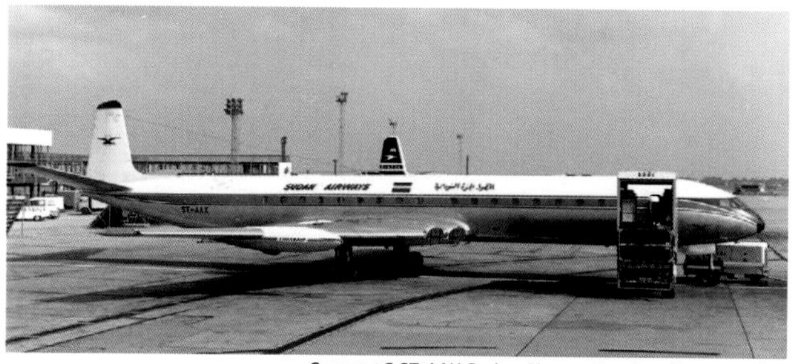
SUDAN AIRWAYS
Comet 4C ST-AAX Sudan Airways London Airport 1963

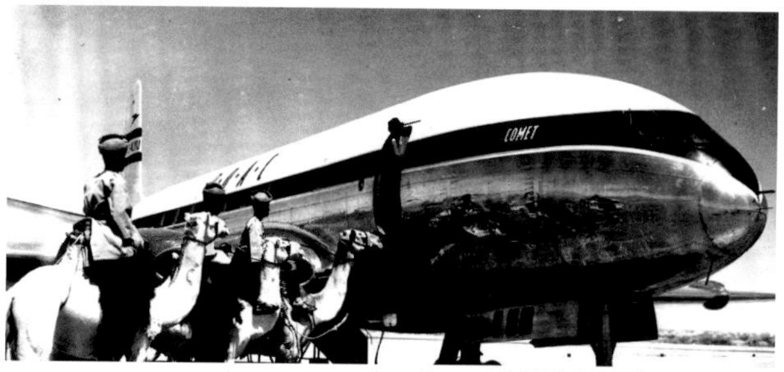
COMET
Comet 1 G-ALYU BOAC Khartoum 1952

COMET VARIANTS

PROTOTYPES

G-5-1, later G-ALVG, and G-5-2, later G-ALZK. Four wheel bogie main undercarriage installed on `VG December 1950; other tests included drooped wing leading edge, wing pinion tanks used on Comet 3 and 4 and rocket motors to improve take-off performance. Broken up 1953 and 1957.

COMET 1

Four wheel bogie main undercarriage, additional windows and altered emergency exit configuration. `YP operated first commercial jet passenger service from London to Johannesburg 2 May 1952; grounded April 1954 following Stromboli crash.

COMET 1A

Featured reinforced structure, additional fuel carried in centre tank, Ghost 50 Mk 2s. First customer Canadian Pacific Airlines.

COMET 1XB

Converted 1A with reinforced structure and oval windows, Ghost 50 Mk 4s. Four 1As upgraded to 1XB standard.

COMET 2X

Sixth Comet 1 airframe used to test the Rolls-Royce Avon engines intended for Comet 2 for which it acted as prototype. `YT first flew 16 February 1952 powered by Avon RA.9 Mk 501/502s.

COMET 2

Stretched fuselage; fuel capacity identical to 1A. Not used for commercial operations as production ceased after Elba and Stromboli accidents. Of 22 Comet 2s five were scrapped, three were stored and remaining airframes converted to other standards.

COMET C2

Military transport eight of which operated by 216 Sqn RAF with reinforced fuselage and cabin floor, oval windows and Avon Mk 117/118s. Airframes permitted to operate 8,000 cycles only.

COMET T2

Identical to C2 but without reinforced floor; both T2s later upgraded to C2 standard.

COMET 2R

Original Comet airframe with square windows, unpressurised fuselage and Avon Mk 117s used by RAF for electronic intelligence gathering. One C2 upgraded to 2R standard.

COMET 2E

C2 with Avon RA.29 Mk 524s – as used by Comet 4 - in outer positions and Avon RA.25 Mk 504s in inner.

COMET 3

First real evolution of basic design with stretched fuselage, oval windows, pinion fuel tanks, Avon RA.26 Mk 522s. Engine outlets angled outwards to reduce noise and corrosion. Programme abandoned after 1954 accidents; 10 airframes scrapped with one retained for Comet 4 development.

COMET 3B

G-ANLO converted to 4B standard 1958 to produce sole 3B with removal of pinion tanks.

COMET 4

Based on considerably modified Comet 3 with revised fuselage construction and higher differential pressure. Truncated certification process made possible by work already undertaken by Comet 2E and 3. Used by BOAC to operate first non-stop London-New York jet service October 1958.

COMET 4A

Short-range Comet 4 with stretched fuselage. Announced June 1956 but not built as launch customer Capital Airlines cancelled order.

COMET 4B

Further short-range variant with 4A wing but no pinion tanks, further stretched fuselage and Avon RA29 Mk 525s. Outer engines equipped with thrust reversers.

COMET 4C

Combined 4B fuselage and engines with Comet 4 wings.

COMET C4

Military transport 4C operated by 216 Sqn RAF.

COMET 5

Projected development to compete with Boeing 707 and Douglas DC-8; not built.

COMET SPECIFICATIONS

	1	1A	C2	3
Wingspan ft/m	115 / 35	115 / 35	115 / 35	114.8 / 35
Length ft/m	93.1 / 28.35	93.1 / 28.35	96.1 / 29.3	111.5 / 33.99
Height ft/m	25.8 / 8.65	25.8 / 8.65	25.8 / 8.65	25.8 / 8.65
Wing area sq ft/m	2,105 / 187.2	2,105 / 187.2	2,027 / 188.3	2,121 / 197
All-up weight lb/kg	105,000 / 45,540	115,000 / 49,877	120,000 / 52,046	145,000 / 62,889
Cruising speed mph/kph	490 / 790	490 / 790	490 / 790	500 / 805
Cruising height ft/m	35,000 / 10,667	40,000 / 12,190	40,000 / 12,190	40,000 / 12,190
Max range miles/km	1,500 / 2,400	1,750 / 2,800	2,535 / 4,000	2,700 / 4,320
Passengers	36	44	44	78
Engines	Ghost 50 Mk 1	Ghost 50 Mk 1	Avon 117	Avon 502
Thrust lb/kN	4,450 / 19.8	5,000 / 22.25	7,300 / 32.47	10,000 / 44.48
Fuel capacity gal/lt	6,000 / 27,585	6,906 / 31,750	6,906 / 31,750	8,360 / 38,435
Number built	11	10	17	1

	4	4B	4C
Wingspan ft/m	114.8 / 35	107.8 / 32.88	114.8 / 35
Length ft/m	111.5 / 33.9	118 / 35.97	118 / 35.97
Height ft/m	29.5 / 8.99	29.5 / 8.99	29.5 / 8.99
Wing area Sq ft/m	2,121 / 197	2,059 / 191.3	2,121 / 197
All-up weight lb/kg	162,000 / 73,483	158,000 / 71,670	162,000 / 73,483
Cruising speed mph/kph	503 / 810	532 / 856	503 / 810
Cruising height ft/m	42,000 / 12,800	23,500 / 7,162	39,000 / 11,886
Max range miles/km	3,225 / 5,190	1,840 / 2,961	2,590 / 4,168
Passengers	81	101	101
Engines	Avon 524	Avon 524	Avon 525B
Thrust lb/kN	10,500 / 46.7	10,500 / 46.7	10,500 / 46.7
Fuel capacity gal/lt	8,900 / 40,450	7,800 / 35,459	8,900 / 40,450
Number built	29	18	28.

ABOUT THE AUTHOR

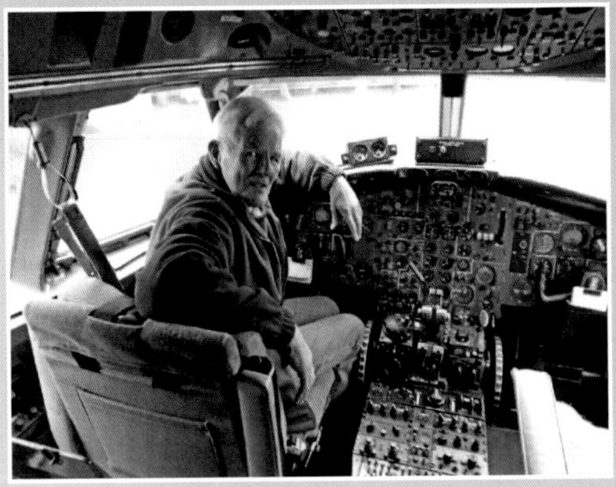

Bruce Hales-Dutton's professional involvement in aviation goes back a long way. Having started as a newspaper journalist in the 1960s he became a senior press officer at the Department of Trade and Industry, a role which involved him in the development of major news stories such as the start of Concorde services to North America and the debate about London's third airport.

Later he moved to the British Airports Authority as a media relations specialist and then to the Civil Aviation Authority. He was the CAA's head of public relations when he retired in 2000. Today Bruce combines his journalistic skills with a life-long interest in aviation as a regular contributor to aviation magazines on current aviation industry topics and historical subjects. He is the author of a publication on the BAC One-Eleven and a volunteer steward at the Brooklands Museum.

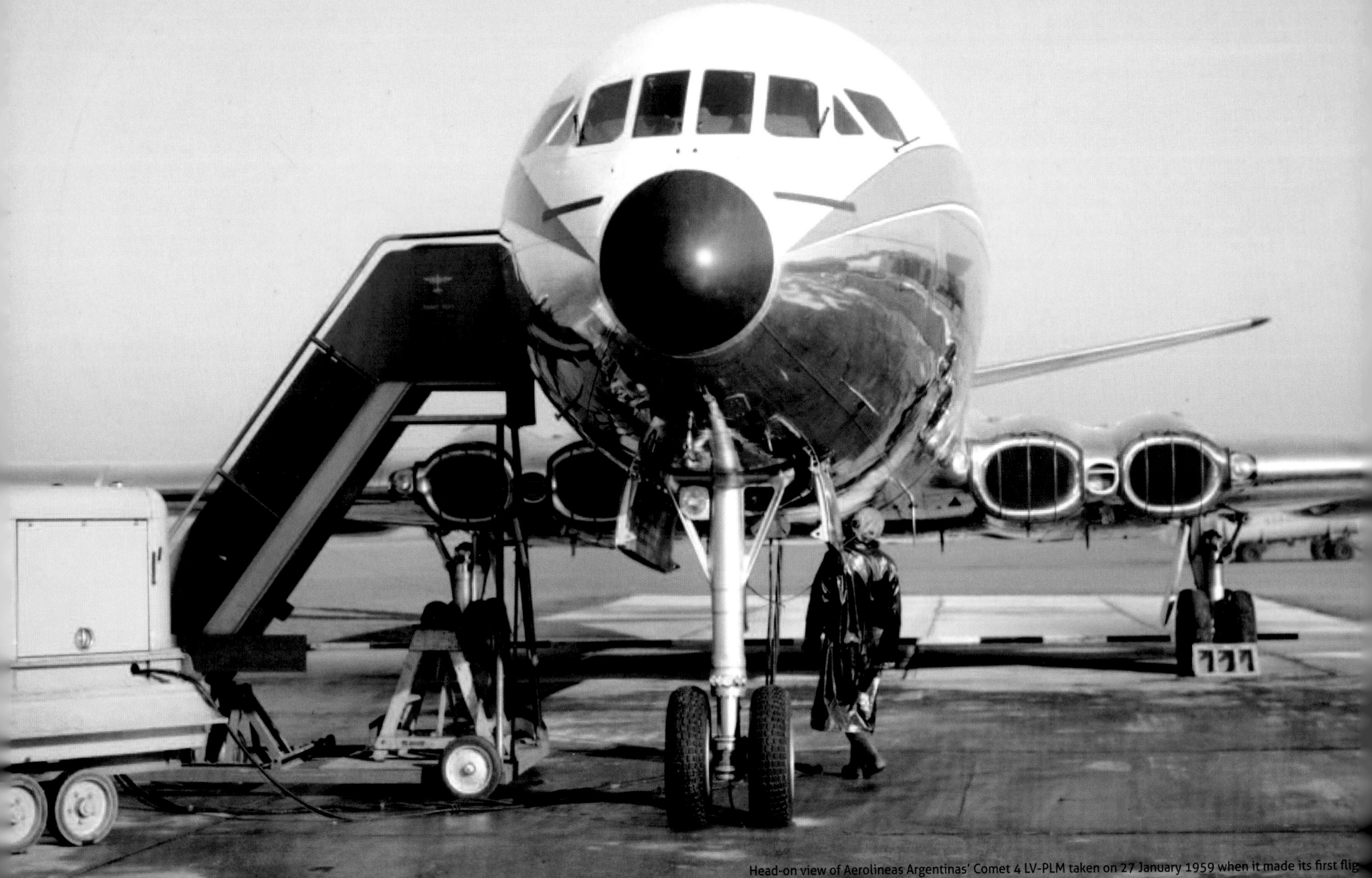

Head-on view of Aerolineas Argentinas' Comet 4 LV-PLM taken on 27 January 1959 when it made its first flig

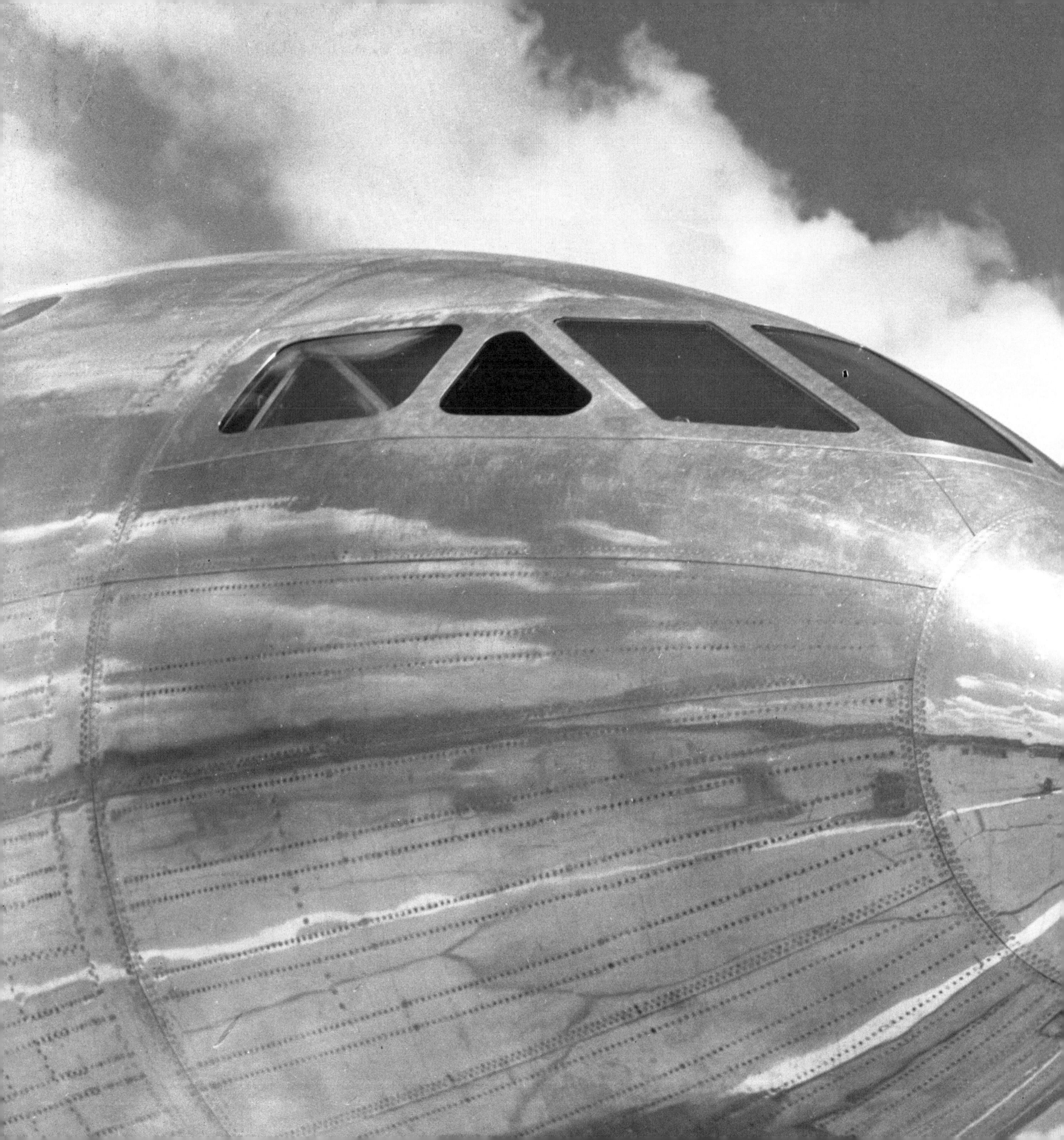